BOOTED AND SUITED

THE REAL STORY OF THE 1970S –
IT AIN'T NO BOOGIE WONDERLAND.

BOOTED AND SUITED

CHRIS BROWN

JB

JOHN BLAKE

Published by John Blake Publishing Ltd,
3 Bramber Court, 2 Bramber Road,
London W14 9PB, England

www.johnblakepublishing.co.uk

Parts of this book were previously published as *Bovver*
This edition published in paperback in 2009

ISBN: 978-1-84454-746-3

All rights reserved. No part of this publication may be reproduced, stored in a retrieval system, or in any form or by any means, without the prior permission in writing of the publisher, nor be otherwise circulated in any form of binding or cover other than that in which it is published and without a similar condition including this condition being imposed on the subsequent publisher.

British Library Cataloguing-in-Publication Data:

A catalogue record for this book is available from the British Library.

Design by www.envydesign.co.uk

Printed in Great Britain by CPI Bookmarque, Croydon CR0 4TD

3 5 7 9 10 8 6 4 2

© Text copyright Chris Brown

Papers used by John Blake Publishing are natural, recyclable products made from wood grown in sustainable forests. The manufacturing processes conform to the environmental regulations of the country of origin.

Dedicated to Gary Mallett, Lyndon 'Lil', Matthew 'Maff' and Ian 'Tommo' Thomson top lads, what a waste. Sadly there are more names to be added to this illustrious list: Chrissie Woodland, Mike 'Butch' Richards, Kelvin 'Frank the Blad' Hare, Dave 'Doctor Teeth' Pearce and the legendary Pete Creber have all passed away over the last few years – as has my dad. Thanks dad for all the advice and wisdom you endeavoured to give me, it's a shame that at times I chose to ignore it.

Acknowledgements

On consecutive Friday nights for more years than I like to remember, a certain individual who shall remain nameless turned back the clock and reminded us all of what 'eventful' times we experienced in the 1970s. I eventually tired of hearing, 'If someone wrote a book about what we got up to, no one would believe it.'

This is that book, believe it. Without the likes of that 'certain individual' and another unnamed person in particular, I could still have written *Booted and Suited* but, unfortunately, it would not have been worth reading. To both of you, thanks for making my life more 'eventful' and for making this book possible.

Although the terrible two supplied my inspiration, many others supplied the memories, anecdotes, evidence and newspaper cuttings: Straff, Rich, Bob, Brian and 'big' Andy fall into this category, as do many others too numerous to mention.

For the memories, thoughts and recollections of the 'Never on Sunday' cafe and the embryonic skinhead movement, a massive thank you to Lloyd Sutherland. Without him, Part One of this book simply would not have existed. Others who helped me write about this era and to whom I owe a huge debt are (in no particular order) my brother Mike, his long-time mate Dave Baker, my old workmate Phil Peacock, Eugene, Pat, Chris, Andy, Jimmy Dee and Bob Feltham. My old Rovers' cohorts Dobbsy and Adge who likewise has had a book published, documenting the history of the now defunct Lockleaze school in Bristol, also contributed some invaluable information and anecdotes relating to this period.

The even earlier mod scene was fondly remembered by Jim Burnham, Chris Powell, Steve Holloway and Colin Birch, all members of the thriving Bristol Mod Scooter Club. Others who helped in some shape or form were Pete Webb of the Electric Pavilion project and Mike Darby of Sugar Shack Records.

Tim Williams especially needs a huge thanks as well as a few pints of Gem ale. I promise I'll never bad mouth Northern Soul again. They say that there's a book inside everyone, well in Tim's case there's got to be an encyclopaedia, this man's forgotten more about music than I've ever learnt.

Paul Alexander, John Stallard, Steve and Adryan Ashby of Soultrain helped me to fill in the gaps on the music front while Seymour Baugh and his mate Anthony contributed some great tales relating to the early Bristol funk scene. I'm not sure if any of these guys realised at the time just how influential they were to become.

Neil Emery, like Tim Williams, one of Brislington's as well as Wigan's chosen few, supplied an invaluable view from across both the fashion and football divide. At one time I was hopeful that I was going to receive further contributions from south of the river from a couple of old adversaries but unfortunately it wasn't to be, come on Angus, pull your finger out and get that book published.

ACKNOWLEDGEMENTS

To George Marshall of ST Publishing, both thanks and apologies.

To Martin Knight and Dougie Brimson, I know the two of you would not like to be mentioned in the same sentence but, even so, thanks for the words of encouragement and advice. To William Avery, thanks for proofreading the original manuscript.

I owe a debt of gratitude to Keith M: thanks for the memories and for the legal advice, talk about poacher turned gamekeeper.

To John Sellers, John Blake, Adam Parfitt and Michelle Signore, a big thank you for doing the business, and a mention must go to Gary 'Groovy' Davies for his part in what was to become an incredible twist of fate.

I would also like to say a big thank you to Steven Wells of *4-4-2* Magazine, Dave Higgitt of Venue Magazine, John Malyckyj of Bristol Rovers Supporters Club and Hazel Potter of the *Second of May* football fanzine for their various reviews and articles, plus Alex Roest of the Uppers Organization website for stating that the original book was 'by far the best book on the subject' [terrace culture].

Thanks must also go to John King of *Football Factory* fame for his biting one-liner which acknowledges and confirms what I personally always thought was the book's correct and proper description: a social history.

On reading *Booted and Suited*, you will become aware that I may have upset and harmed certain people. No malice was ever intended, only to those who endeavoured to do exactly the same to me. To the only people I really hurt in the 70s, my mum and dad, I say sorry, perhaps for my dad it's too late.

One of the great things that came out of the original book was that a lot of my old mates who I hadn't seen for a number of years made contact with me (mostly to congratulate me), one in particular, Dave Ward, contacted me after a 35 year absence, so to Dave, thanks for making contact and thanks for the memories.

BOOTED AND SUITED

This edition not only includes brand new copy but also some amended copy relating to certain events which have come to light since the writing of the first draft – events which, though not incorrectly reported in the first place, nevertheless needed clarification and amplification regarding dates, locations and the like. Similarly, some of the music references have also been amended following further research again, these were merely oversights and not done with any intention of misleading or misrepresentation whatsoever.

My genuine thanks go to all of you who bought the original book, *Bovver*, over the last few years, and especially to those of you who have taken the time to post, in the main, complimentary reviews on the various websites. To get praise from, among others, fans of Bristol City and Cardiff City, is indeed both surprising and welcome, as in the past it could be said that we didn't exactly see eye-to-eye.

A special message must go to Tom Henry and Cris Warren, hopefully by the time the next edition comes out the play will be in the West End, keep the faith boys, it will be worth it in the end.

Finally, the biggest thanks of all go to my wife Carole and my children Dan and Chloe for both believing in me and putting up with me (not once, but twice). Hopefully, it will all be worth it. To Dan, a very special message: do as I say, not as I do.

Contents

Introduction – Never Mind the Bollocks   xiv

Part I
The Late Sixties – Birth of the Boot Boy   1
1. In Search of 'Wally'   2
2. 'This is a Scene, There's Some Kind of Code'   9
3. The Service Engineer and the Fruit Wagon   17
4. Warriors in Boots   44
5. Dancin', Sounds and the Dear Old 'Loccy'   57
6. The Never-ending Story   71

Part II
The Seventies – A Decade of Disturbance   79
7. A History Lesson   82
8. Out to Impress   91

9	A Welcome in the Hillsides	103
10	Front-page News	116
11	Strides and Shooters	130
12	New Faces	137
13	The Divide Widens	149
14	A Bit of Psychology, A Bit of Humour and Who the F**k are Man United Anyway?	161
15	Celebrity Status	172
16	Like Clockwork	178
17	All Mouth an' no Trousers	194
18	We're on the Telly!	204
19	When the Lights Went Out	216
20	One Team in Bristol	222
21	From Miami to Philly, Via Sheffield	228
22	A Momentary Respite and a Musical Interlude	241
23	Back in the Old Routine	253
24	Changin' Times	264
25	The Temperature Rises and the Bomb Drops	281
26	Dark Days, Darker Deeds and a Savaging by Sheep	291
27	Doing Something Outrageous	300
28	Do Anything You Wanna Do	309
29	No Fun	326

30	A Day to Remember	335
31	No Let-Up	348
32	Saints and Sinners	367
33	A Battering at the Bell	378
34	Notes from a Big Country	391
35	Working-class Heroes	397
36	Bridewell Blues	407
37	The Melting Pot Boils Over	414
38	The End of an Era	430

INTRODUCTION
Never Mind the Bollocks

It looks like the bookshops of Britain had a bit of a problem with the classification of *Bovver* – should it sit alongside the plethora of 'hoolie lit' that has adorned the shelves over the last few years, next to the impressive eponymous *Cass*; the classic, granddaddy of them all, *Steaming In*, by Colin Ward; the scary *Scally* by Andy Nicholls; or the frankly embarrassing *Inside the Forest* by Gary 'Boatsy' Clarke? Or maybe it should be classed as an autobiography, right next to Beckham's, as I have seen in Waterstones? Then again, I've also seen it under 'Real Crimes', nestling cosily between *Happy Like Murderers: The True Story of Fred and Rose West* by Gordon Burns and *Real Hard Cases: True Crime from the Streets* by Les Brown. David Beckham and Fred West – not quite exalted company, but interesting dinner-party guests nonetheless. Well, one of them at least.

Of course, many Bristol City fans have said that it should be found under 'Fiction' – they're entitled to their opinion. Mind you, so is the bloke I see wandering around the city centre in his

INTRODUCTION

underpants holding a flagon of White Lightning who claims the world is flat.

An anonymous Sunderland fan wrote: 'If you love the wannabe hoolie fantasy life then don't buy it. If you want a bit of reality then have a read,' while John King of *Football Factory* fame called it 'Social history with steel toe-caps...', which, to me, not only encapsulated what *my book* was all about but also conveniently classified it better than I – or Britain's bookshops, for that matter – ever could. It will be interesting to see where Waterstones place *Booted and Suited*. I can promise one thing though – it won't be under 'Fairy Stories'.

When I wrote the original book some ten years ago, the 'hoolie lit' genre was in its infancy. I never envisaged that, in later years, Britain's academia would not only be studying books such as mine but actually making a career out of it (and being paid to do so in part with Government grants), all supposedly to determine just what makes football hooligans tick. Steve Redhead, Professor of Sport and Media Cultures at the University of Brighton, who also dubbed the books 'hit and tell' stories, offers up the following in his article 'Terrace Terrors? Post-Subcultural Criminology and the Rise and Fall of Football Hooligan Subcultures', which may not explain why hoolies act as they do but certainly explains why the academics are fascinated by the subject: 'The methodological work which is being undertaken is a study of the simulacrum of hooliganism, which includes the strange "pulp faction" of football hooligan literature. The study of football hooligan literature, it is argued, might eventually lead us to better, more informed ethnographies of football hooligan subcultures.'

Confused? Me too. Didn't understand a bloody word of it. Which brings me back to the fairy stories. Professor Redhead even delves into the world of homo-eroticism that is allegedly apparent in the genre: 'The football hooligan memoir authors' interest in the male violence and male bonding of what were once labelled in pulp fiction "terrace terrors" is wrapped up in an almost "camp" fascination with hardness in male youth culture... the link between gay and skinhead subcultures is certainly worth reconsidering.'

Really? Not with the skinheads I know it isn't, but then again I'm not a scholar — and I don't live in Brighton. I'm just wondering who's getting the hard-on over these books — the lads who read and write them or the academics who study them. For less of the psychobabble and a more concise reason as to why British males indulge in hooligan activities, I'll offer some of my own thoughts later in the book.

In the Introduction to the original book, I mentioned something about regret. Like the late, great Frank, I had one or two — regrets about actions from my formative years, that sort of thing, but it's often been said that you should only have regrets about what you haven't done, not about what you have done. So, yes, there are a few regrets, like not delving deeper into the Bristol music scene and not giving Northern Soul the recognition it deserves, which I've endeavoured to put right in this new edition, but the biggest regret I've got is that I wasn't born just a couple of years earlier — 'I was 14 in January 1970, a perfect age for a perfect era...' Well, not quite, maybe 16 would have done it; 18, and it would have been a totally different story.

I had touched upon the late Sixties in the first edition, but because *Bovver* was autobiographical I only wanted to write about my first-hand experiences, my memories, my recollections, my thoughts on the world around me in 1970s Britain. 'Welcome to the real 1970s — it ain't no boogie wonderland...' proclaimed the cover. To write about this earlier period, I would need to draw upon the experiences of my elders, my betters, those more knowledgeable than me — after all, I was still into Chopper bikes, climbing trees and

INTRODUCTION

Jubblies in 1968 – and so this new edition now also includes a prequel which attempts to throw more light on Britain just before the 1970s, an intense few years that witnessed man walking on the moon, student riots, Enoch Powell's infamous 'Rivers of Blood' speech and the metamorphosis of the quintessential and very acceptable British youth cult of the mod (clean living under difficult circumstances) to the birth of the most misunderstood and vilified – the skinheads (no one likes us and we don't care).

As well as exploring this earlier period, I've also expanded on other areas which I think I sadly neglected in the original – the contribution of black DJs to the Bristol funk scene and how the shift from funk to punk was not such a quantum leap as it at first seems. It was a shift which was to have far-reaching consequences in future years, something which I guess at the time I was completely oblivious to, so there's as much Seymour and the Pop Group as The Specials and Paul Weller – a good trade-up, I think.

In the summer of 2004, I was approached by Radio 2 to take part in a documentary called *Way Out West: The Bristol Underground*, to be produced by Simon Poole and presented by David Quantick, the freelance journalist with a penchant for acidic wit, one-liners and a rather annoying habit of pronouncing 'Avon' as if he's flogging overpriced women's cosmetics on the doorstep. As well as myself and other corpulent, middle-aged members of the Avon (rhymes with 'raven', Mr Quantick) Soul Army, the documentary featured such luminaries from the Bristol music scene as Mark Stewart, Nellee Hooper and Grant Marshall from the Wild Bunch, and an enthusiastic and educated Brislington (Briz) kiddie by the name of Tim Williams. Tim shone through with his vast knowledge of not just the provincial Bristol music scene, but the national scene as well. Back in the late Seventies/early

BOOTED AND SUITED

Eighties, he produced Bristol's equivalent of the infamous *Sniffin' Glue* fanzine, *Loaded*; his other claim to fame was that his brother Leigh was mentioned in Briz's very own born-and-bred harpie Julie Burchill's autobiography *I Knew I Was Right*, so that's two famous people to come out of the south Bristol suburb. I knew of Tim; he was a mate of Neil Emery who I knew back in the Seventies and who helped me write the first edition of this book. Listening to the finished *Way Out West* which went out in the July of 2004, it became evident that Tim was a 'top kiddie' – I needed to speak to him.

I caught up with Tim in the Wellington pub on Gloucester Road in north Bristol, a regular watering-hole for Rovers' fans and which, as is very much the style these days, features stripped floorboards as well as stuffed olives and bruschetta on the menu, not to mention, bizarrely, morris dancers performing in the garden. It was all a bit surreal. We were debating whether 'Change' by Donald Byrd or 'Commando' by The Ramones best represented Seventies music, while, in the background, all we could hear was a fucking accordion and Noddy bells. Tim regaled me with tales of visits to the Wigan Casino where he learned precisely when to clap during 'Cochise' by Paul Humphrey like the locals, and how walking in front of the speakers was an alternative, and painful, way to get your ears syringed.

If that's not enough, his recollections of the early punk scene and how, of all places, Newport in South Wales had a fair shout in rivalling the King's Road as a main player in the world of spit and bondage are revealing to say the least. But there's much more to Tim than an encyclopaedic knowledge of the Seventies music scene and a predilection for Vivienne Westwood shirts (yes, an original still adorns his wardrobe), so I've handed a couple of chapters over to Tim for his recollections in his own words. You'll really think you were there – you can almost smell the Hai

INTRODUCTION

Karate in your nostrils and taste the Billy buzzing in the back of your throat.

I'm not trying to rewrite history. There is no specific aim or agenda about this book, but I am trying to correct a few misconceptions of not only the late Sixties and the Seventies but also the present day. If nothing else, I hope after reading *Booted and Suited* some people may have a less prejudiced view of certain things.

One of the biggest misconceptions of those days revolves around the much maligned aforementioned skinhead. Their propensity for violence can't be denied, but their perceived racist views and supposed links to extreme political groups certainly can be. To a certain extent, this may have been true for many of the second generation of skinheads from the late Seventies and early Eighties who found themselves hijacked by various right-wing movements, but the original summer of '69 boot boys cannot be tarred with that same brush. Their beginnings were apolitical, humble and basic – a basic need to belong and a basic need to look smart and tough. Perhaps many of them didn't realise it at the time but they had more links with the Fifties and Sixties immigrants to Britain than they did with their own peers and parents.

The second misconception is linked but much more contemporary – if the original bad boys of Britain were having a hard time with the media, it was nothing compared with today's chavved-up hoodies. Again, it would be foolish to deny their misdeeds – those *Daily Mail* headlines can't all be wrong, can they? No, they can't, there *are* some real bad lads out there who wear their ASBOs as a badge of honour, but to suggest that they are 'feral' and to think that many of today's youth are members of knife-toting gangs is not only delusional but also insulting.

Having said that, this fear in adults of youngsters – this 'pedophobia' – is very real and a sad reflection of today's troubled times but, if I've learned anything through my research, it's that many of today's youth are no better, or no worse, than their predecessors of 40 years back. Indeed, the incidents, both recorded and anecdotal, of youths carrying (or wearing) offensive weapons were as high then as they are now and, in some cities, I would suggest it was even higher back then. As Barbara Ellen wrote in the *Observer* in response to the UNICEF report on our troubled youth, 'However frightening as it sometimes gets, maybe we should accept British adolescence for what it is, *has always been* – a whirling out-of-control carousel. You can only watch and hope that your particular (stroppy, nihilistic, establishment-hating, maddening, indispensable) Brit teenager manages to cling on for the ride.'

The third and final wrong that I want to put right is perhaps the most far-fetched and the most controversial, but in part it's my *raison d'être* behind the book – I know it may sound like sacrilege now but not everyone back then thought music started and finished with Abba. Hopefully, this book will prove an antidote to *I Love the Seventies*, the TV series where the decade has been sanitised, repackaged and rewritten to fit in with cosy Saturday-evening viewing.

There's been a whole industry built around the Abba myth; of course they were big, they sold shedloads of records, but so has Jive Bunny over the years – did anyone who was really into their music in the Seventies buy their records? No. Did your mum and your little sister buy their records? Yes. In the words of Public Enemy, 'Don't believe the hype.'

'Mamma Mia… my my… how can I resist you?' Well, in my case and for many thousands of others back then, quite easily, as it happens.

Part I
The Late Sixties – Birth of the Boot Boy

1

In Search of 'Wally'

Can you remember those illustrated kids' books from a few years back called *Where's Wally?* where you had to find a gormless, bespectacled bloke in a red striped jumper among a myriad of similarly dressed characters? Trying to find when the first skinhead appeared in Bristol, let alone Britain, is a bit like that. It goes without saying the first sightings would have been in London. 'Course it was, me old china – you wouldn't expect anything else, would you? Those Cockney geezers have always been one step ahead of the rest of the country, haven't they?

Dick Hebdige, the British media theorist and sociologist, claims that some mods were spotted with boots and braces during the notorious riots with rockers at Margate and Brighton as early as 1964 – which also ties in with Micky Smith's observations in his book *Want Some Aggro?* – whereas the spring of 1968 seems to be the more commonly accepted date for their historic debut. As for the exact location of where he first saw the light of day, Bermondsey, Willesden and Plaistow can all lay claim to be the birthplace of the forerunner of the modern-day hoodie.

One of the first recorded instances of this new teenage

IN SEARCH OF 'WALLY'

phenomenon appearing in public came during the Great Vietnam Solidarity March in London on 17 March 1968 – 30,000 anti-war demonstrators were heckled and abused by 200 'closely cropped local youths dressed in Millwall Football Club's team colours'. Not that these lads were making a political statement; their venom was aimed at the massed-ranked hippies as opposed to the USA's involvement in south-east Asia – political animals they were not.

John Waters, an original Sixties mod from Upper Holloway, London, remembers vividly two very different sorts of mods: the easy-on-the-eye West End dandies and those with a tougher outlook, the so-called 'hard mods' who were just a step away from being bona fide East End boot boys. Writing on the *Modculture* website, he recalls, 'There were two distinct types of mod within the London area. The first was the familiar scooter boys which has become the generally accepted face of Sixties Modernism. However, there was another type of mod back in those days. These were the members of the many mod "firms"... members of these gangs would not be seen dead on a scooter, their preferred mode of transport being a car.'

These gang members not only had a different outlook but also dressed differently, their style being more uniform – 'They were meticulous in their dress, the order of the day being the mohair suit, velvet-collar overcoats and, as often as not, a "Blue Beat" hat.' Dick Hebdige even puts forward the idea that these hard mods 'started sporting close-cropped hair which artificially reproduces the texture and appearance of the short Negro hairstyles'. There's even claims that these first skinheads were, in fact, 'aspiring white Negroes' – the very first 'wiggers' even. How odd then that, in years to come, skinheads would always be associated with being far-right racists.

It's hard to dispute therefore that the early crophead evolved from the dying embers of the mod movement which had acrimoniously split and gone its separate ways once LSD replaced dexidrine and Meher Baba influenced Pete Townshend more than John Lee Hooker. What is harder to determine is what the original boot boys were called – 'peanuts', 'lemonheads', 'cropheads' and the previously mentioned 'hard mods' were all used by the rabid red-tops, desperate to find a tag for the delinquents on to whom they could then heap all of Britain's ills. Certainly in those early days, 'skin' heads would have been way off the mark. Witness the 1969 film *Bronco Bullfrog*, in which Bronco's hair is a rather scruffy, and very common, short-back-and-sides, while the amateur 'star' of the docu-film, Dale, is constantly flicking the hair from out of his eyes. Take away his size-ten boots and you're back searching for Wally.

Contrary to popular belief, the haircut itself was not a direct descendant of the American crew-cut, which left virtually no hair at the back and sides but a longer length on the top. Despite this, rather amusingly in the late Sixties, US military personnel based in this country were advised to wear hairpieces to avoid being mistaken for native, booted hooligans. More often than not, a request at the local barbers for a 'square cut' resulted in the desired effect. It was not until a year or so later that the term 'skinhead' entered the argot of the English language and became the tag that would stay for ever with any future hooligan possessing a short hairstyle, with or without the boots. Even the Prime Minister of the time, Harold Wilson, speaking in Parliament in 1969, used the terminology, in describing certain Tory rivals as 'the skinheads of Surbiton'.

Surprisingly, though, as the embryonic skinhead took centre stage it was not the hairstyle but the footwear that defined the cult. However, the greatly revered Doc Martens were hardly worn at all – it was their surly, ugly older brothers in the guise of calf-high paratroopers, steel-toe-capped workboots, army hobnails or (my own personal favourites) the infinitely more comfortable Monkey boots that were the preferred choice.

IN SEARCH OF 'WALLY'

In April 1970, Bristol's *Evening Post* even saw fit to send their fashion reporter Barbara Buchanan out to hunt down the 'bovver boot'. Full of curiosity about the boots, she made a trip to GB Brittons in Kingswood, who, at the time, were the largest manufacturer in the world for 'safety footwear' – an oxymoron if ever there was one when the boots were in the hands, or rather on the feet, of the young skinheads.

Jim Burriss, a director of the company, was naturally delighted with the latest teen fashion. Brittons had seen an increase of 29% in sales of steel-toe-capped protective footwear in the previous year but, not wishing to align himself with the bovver boys, he disputed that the sales were down to them entirely. 'It's a greater awareness of factory safety plus our first-class bunch of salesmen,' he stated. Of course it was, Jim, and just to give more credence to the fact he added that he thought ex-army stores were a more likely source for the favoured footwear. 'The old army boot could be pretty lethal... there are plenty of them available in surplus stores.'

The intrepid reporter then tried her luck at an unnamed army surplus store where the proprietor stated that more and more teenage boys were buying a certain type of boot that 'have a very heavy sole and lightweight upper, they're marvellously comfortable to walk in but the boys are buying them as a fashion'. I can only guess that they are describing Monkey boots as Doctor Martens certainly didn't fit this description. When asked if the boys bought the lethal-looking hobnails, the answer was that they did, and at 52s 6d (less than three quid) they were a lot cheaper than the others but it seems that it was the former unnamed boot that they wanted.

Ironically, Doc Martens came to be the boot synonymous with skinheads by a strange quirk of fate. Later on in 1970, the police across the country decided that the steel-toe-capped boot should be classed as an offensive weapon and that anyone wearing them could have them confiscated, or the wearer could even face arrest. That ban saw the shift to Doc Martens and, within a few months, they virtually became standard issue, with their simple utilitarian design becoming as much an anti-fashion statement as a very noticeable nod in recognition to their working-class roots.

Of course, you could answer 'so what?' Does it really matter why and where it all started? Click on Wikipedia, search for mods and you'll find prosaic and flowery expressions such as 'existentialist philosophy', 'middle-class teenage boys' and references to French new wave films and 'penchants for jazz' – nice. Click on 'skinheads' and the hackles start to rise and the vitriol cranks up: 'entrenched class system' and 'working-class subculture' jump out at you and – surprise, surprise – once the brief history gets dispensed with, there's a whole chapter on racism, anti-racism and politics – not so nice. It's all a bit clinical and prescriptive, too, with the accurate but obvious references to the influence of home-grown West Indian rude boys and the skinheads' love affair with ska and reggae – but that's it. Nothing that actually gets under the skin, as it were.

In some respects, the early skinheads had a great affinity with the counter-culture of the punks who were to burst on to the scene spitting and screaming less than a decade later. A young East End skinhead quoted in the Penguin Educational paperback *The Paint House* states, 'Everywhere there are fucking bosses… they're always trying to tell us what to do… don't matter what you do, where you go, they're always there. People in authority, the people who tell you what to do and make sure you do it. It's the system we live in, it's the governor system.'

Like the late-Seventies anarchists, skinheads grew out of disillusionment with not just those in authority but with pop and its excessive trappings. The über-coolness of the 'swinging Sixties' when London music and fashion had ruled the world was on the wane. The summer of love of 1967 was the last straw; the

IN SEARCH OF 'WALLY'

music had lost its way, fashion had lost its head, and the hair, well, that was just asking for trouble. The working-class youth needed their adrenalin rush as much as the more cultured middle classes, but, whereas the grammar-school types from the leafy suburbs escaped from their tedious life by immersing themselves in the flamboyant, expressive, drug-infused hippy culture, the comprehensive-school kids from the post-war concrete council estates tried to revisit an earlier period. They craved for a time when life was simpler and they tried desperately to recover a sense of tradition in a fast-changing Britain, a tradition which, to them, the hippy movement was trying its hardest to destroy. The social dynamic behind the skinhead cult is obvious, unequivocal and cannot be over-emphasised.

Thankfully, these were the days when the working class were still looked upon with some affection. Forty years on and the working class have been replaced by the Indian-inked, hooded underclass – for the salt of the earth, now read the scum of the earth.

It's often been said that the modern-day sportswear-clad chavs have no respect for anyone or anything around them; they deliberately cover their faces and hide their eyes beneath hoods and ubiquitous checked caps. It's not respect for others the hoodies don't have, it's respect for themselves, something the first generation of skinheads had by the bucketload. Ask any skinhead from that era and they'll constantly remind you of how much they respected older people, embraced the traditional British work ethic, loved their country, loved themselves and, most importantly, loved their mums.

While the cult of the hippy and flower power had weak roots, all things skin had strong ones based on traditional values. Skinheads viewed hippies with their mantra of individualism, drug taking, free love and doing their own thing as the enemy within. As one 16-year-old 'peanut' bluntly stated in an interview

BOOTED AND SUITED

in 1968 when asked about what he was against, 'Long hair, pop, hippy sit-ins, live-ins and the long-haired cult of non-violence'.

The reaction to the hippy movement and its music featuring sitars, cowbells and those obligatory ten-minute guitar solos was as extreme as it was rapid. The skinheads chose to grossly exaggerate their working-class background and deliberately accentuated its hard image: the braces, overtly exposed working boots, close-cropped hair, collarless shirts – all stereotypical working-class imagery. It could even be argued they were making a political statement but, back then, politics was the last thing on a young skinhead's mind, they didn't really care much for Vietnam, Tariq Ali or CND; their thoughts were elsewhere. It's those thoughts that I now hope to reveal and retell in the next few chapters – thoughts, memories and recollections of those first-generation skinheads, those boys and girls who were around when the mods drew their final breath, cast off their parkas and laced up their boots. Welcome to *Booted and Suited*.

2
'This Is a Scene, There's Some Kind of Code'

I read somewhere that Bristol could have been as glorious as Rome, except the locals couldn't be bothered, or that it could be Britain's equivalent of San Francisco. Certainly, the geography resembles the Californian city and Bristol's got an amazing bridge – and a prison – but that's where the similarities end. San Francisco was the birthplace of the free-loving hippies, Bristol the birthplace of Methodism; somehow, I can't see the connection.

Since the 1950s, coffee bars have played an important part in the life of the British teenager. From 'Coffee An' off Wardour Street in London to the 'Cona Coffee Bar' in Tib Street, Manchester, teenagers flocked to them in their droves – it's amazing what a jukebox, pinball machines and a Gaggia can do. Warm, inviting, slightly racy, with a hint of the Continent, British youth is easily pleased.

In Bristol, we had the 'Never on Sunday' in Fairfax Street, just around the corner from Woolworth's and the Co-op and just a stone's throw from the Central Police Station in Bridewell. Good thinking, lads.

BOOTED AND SUITED

Iain McKell, the well-known fashion photographer who learned his trade back in the Seventies and Eighties through shooting skinheads and new romantics, and who photographed Madonna for her first magazine cover, recalls, 'I remember skinheads the first time round, in 1969, when it was really hardcore. I must have been 12, 13 and I was in a café in Bristol when this bloke walked in, hair cropped, wearing a Ben Sherman shirt, braces, Levi's and DM boots. Then another one... and another one. And I thought, Hang on a minute, there's something going on here, this is a scene, there's some kind of code. And in those days, it was shocking to see something like that.'

A public schoolboy with working-class parents from Weymouth, McKell was awestruck by the skinheads' defiance and aggression, and it wasn't long before he wanted to be part of this 'scene'. 'This big firm of lairy skinheads would stand behind the goal at Bristol City's ground [no accounting for taste], so one day I joined them, just to experience this feeling, this roar. They'd bang their boots against the corrugated tin wall behind them, then they'd surge forward in this big wave.'

'Defiance and aggression...' It's easy to see how the movement roared through Britain in the summer of 1969, a bit like Concorde had done in April that year on its maiden flight... from Filton, Bristol, for the record.

This 'scene' was being repeated up and down the country. Chris Welch, the esteemed rock journalist, writing in *Melody Maker* in 1969 made a similar observation: 'it's a curious thing that whenever... a pillar of our bewildered society wants to cast stones, they instantly start talking about long-haired louts/yobs/hippies/students etc... Yet anybody who has ventured on the streets will instinctively know that they have nothing to fear from the long-haired youth who merely wants to turn on in peace to his favourite band and chick. The sight of cropped heads and the sound of heavy boots entering the

'THIS IS A SCENE, THERE'S SOME KIND OF CODE'

midnight Wimpy bar or dancehall is the real cause for sinking feelings in the pit of the stomach.'

Strangely for someone who supposedly had his finger on the pulse of Britain's street culture, Welch identified the new breed as 'mods'. It's probably easy now to look back and be critical but, as the modernists first kick-started their Lambrettas some six or seven years earlier, it's difficult to see how he arrived at this tag, but then again 'post-modern mods with big boots' just doesn't put the fear of God into anyone.

Welch wasn't the only one who was unsure what to call this new breed of cropped-haired adolescents roaming the streets of Britain. As mentioned previously, the media of the day, although aware of the new youth phenomenon, were also unsure what to call them. During the period of unrest that erupted during the summer of 1969 on the streets of Bristol, the *Evening Post* constantly referred to them as 'the Cropheads' with their enemy of choice being 'the Rockers', as if they were two distinct street gangs in the mode of 'the Jets' and 'the Sharks' in *West Side Story*, not that Bristol's city centre resembled Manhattan's Hell's Kitchen and it certainly didn't feature Natalie Wood singing 'I Feel Pretty'.

Although there had been sporadic clashes between these two groups throughout the year, it appears that the catalyst for all this mayhem was an assault on Saturday, 19 July 1969 inside the Never on Sunday itself. A 19-year old ballsy greaser (the more common reference of the day for the rockers, or 'greebo' if you really wanted to chance your arm) from Knowle West entered the café and assaulted one of the Never boys. In court on the Monday, he admitted that he 'butted the youth in the face, threw him to the ground and kicked him', claiming that the youth had 'kept interfering with him and he just lost his head'. He had six previous convictions and was fined £30 plus £2 costs.

BOOTED AND SUITED

This assault quickly resulted in a revenge attack by the enraged cropheads on the 63 Club,* the motorcycle gang's café in Old Market less than a mile away, but this was just a prelude to the mass battle which took place on the following Tuesday when up to 300 youths fought in the city centre. Under the headline GANGS AT WAR, the *Evening Post* reported with as much relish as the modern-day *Daily Mail* gleefully informs its outraged readers of yet another attack on a frail pensioner by a hooded thug: 'About 300 youths from rival gangs were involved in a series of running fights near the centre of Bristol... a number of "nasty implements" were later found to have been discarded, including iron bars, sticks, broken bottles, knives and a scalpel. A number of youths faced charges including assaulting a policeman, malicious wounding, threatening behaviour and carrying offensive weapons.'

Detective Sergeant Peter Webster, who opposed an application for bail by one youth, stated, 'There is concern by the prosecution that they haven't heard the last of these incidents...' – an understatement if there ever was one. Most arrested that night were teenagers; in fact, nearly all were just 17. Most ended up with £25 fines while others were put on remand. The most serious offence by a 23-year-old greaser of an assault on a police officer resulted in a two-month prison sentence – or 'gaol' as it was commonly called back then.

In an entirely separate incident, the *Evening Post* also reported a 21-year old man being shot and two other people suffering stab wounds at a party in woods in nearby Stroud in Gloucestershire. Of course, this was the period of 'peace and love' – the Rolling

---

* My research threw up several names for this café, many seemed to think it was called the '63 Club' but others offered up the '69 Café', while one of the few bikers who I managed to talk to from that era thought there were two cafés, the '66 café' and the '99 café' while someone else suggested it was the 'Route 66 Club'. There was certainly a motorcycle gang called the '63 Club' so it seems logical that they were named after the café they frequented.

'THIS IS A SCENE, THERE'S SOME KIND OF CODE'

Stones were performing for free in Hyde Park in the name of love in a concert which got hijacked by London skinheads, while John Lennon and Yoko Ono were singing 'Give Peace a Chance' from their hotel bed. It sounds like it was falling on deaf ears. Well, in the West Country at any rate.

The following Thursday, the ante was well and truly upped. Barry Cowan, an 18-year-old greaser from Stoke Gifford, was killed when his 650cc Norton motorcycle was in a collision with another motorcycle and a Triumph Herald car in Temple Way. His distraught mother denied that Barry had ever been part of a gang, saying, 'He wore a flying jacket and jeans when riding his motorcycle but never dressed way out, and behaved well at home... and as for the German helmets and swastikas [common regalia for the bikers of the day] he never wore anything like that and knew his father and I would not allow him in the house like that.'

Undoubtedly, the incident was related to the troubles of that week and perhaps this was a step too far. The next day, the cropheads and the greasers met on College Green in front of Bristol Cathedral for a 'truce'. Under a photo of the two warring tribes shaking hands, the *Evening Post*'s headline proclaimed: GANGS RELAXING BUT POLICE STAY ALERT. The report went on to say that a crowd of 120 gathered and the truce was signed with a handshake, and the two gang leaders collected £3 from their own members for a wreath for Barry. The *Evening Post* continued, 'Many members of the motorcycle gang seem to think his accident was an indirect result of their war with the cropheads. Police said it was being treated the same way as any fatal accident and that witnesses were still being interviewed.'

What you can't fail to notice about the photo is the difference in both age and physique of the two gangs' members – the fresh-faced cropheads barely reach the shoulders of the greasers and while the bikers proudly display moustaches and sideburns

BOOTED AND SUITED

the short-haired cropheads haven't got as much as a bit of bum-fluff between them. One other curious thing about the photo is that, if you look very closely, you can make out a couple of black guys among the cropheads. More of them later.

After a week of reflection on the events, the *Evening Post* took its eye off the Apollo 11 moon mission which was enthralling the nation and ran a half-page interview with the Bristol Police. The headline read: THIS UGLY RASH WILL BE STAMPED OUT. The report by the esteemed reporter Roger Bennett went on to say, 'First there were the Teddy Boys. Then came the Mods and Rockers. Now, in Bristol, it's Hells Angels v Cropheads. The names change. So do the uniforms – from drape jackets and crêpe-soled shoes to crash helmets and swastika-emblazoned jackets. But the disease is the same – an ugly rash of teenage terrorism. The battleground has moved from the dancehalls to the streets over the years. And this makes police all the more determined to stamp out the new wave of juvenile belligerence.'

Chief Superintendent George Fisher, commander of the Bristol Police 'A' division, discounted the suggestion that the teenage gangs should be put in a field and left to fight out whatever they are fighting about, 'whereas in the Teddy Boy era, most of the trouble was among young people in places frequented by young people. Over recent years, it seems to have moved into the streets. The general public, in particular elderly people and the very young, can be badly frightened by this kind of behaviour, and we cannot allow it to continue. I must make it clear that, if these young people continue with their course of conduct in the centre of Bristol or elsewhere, they will be dealt with firmly by the police.'

Another senior police officer, the aptly named DS Frederick Clash, commented, 'The increasing use of weapons like sticks,

'THIS IS A SCENE, THERE'S SOME KIND OF CODE'

knives, chains and stones also increases the danger that someone will be seriously hurt. But it is unlikely to spiral into the use of firearms.' Then, in a sentence that could be lifted from any of today's tabloids, he states, 'The teenage gangs are composed of youths with juvenile minds influenced by films and TV.' However, he then tries to lighten the picture somewhat, by saying, 'This isn't gang warfare. It's two little groups of silly kids.'

The night before this report, in a scene reminiscent of the film *The Wild One*, over 60 of one group of these 'silly kids' – with names such as Danny the Pervert, Doc Puffer, Maverick, Big Jim, Ruby and Tank, all members of either the Bristol Nomads or West Coast Chapter of the Hells Angels – rode into Keynsham on their Triumphs and Nortons where they stayed for an hour before leaving without causing any trouble. However, the following evening, 30 of them rode into Chipping Sodbury where they fought with local youths. 'Beer glasses were thrown and there was fighting and swearing under the clock tower.'

Contrary to the police's optimistic message, this 'teenage terrorism' was not about to fade away – the tension of that blisteringly hot summer continued into the flame-red autumn. On Friday, 5 September, the violence erupted again, youths fighting toe-to-toe on the streets culminating in a near riot. When 200 youths clashed in the Centre, one lad was seriously injured when he was thrown through a plate-glass window; a police officer also received a broken arm in the disorders which lasted for over an hour and also saw the overstretched Bristol Police having to call for reinforcements from across the region – the truce was well and truly forgotten.

The aggro wasn't confined to Bristol, though, as the same weekend saw 13 'soccer hooligans' from London arrested and fined after trouble flared at the Aston Villa v Millwall match in Birmingham. The cult of bovver was well and truly on the march.

3

The Service Engineer and the Fruit Wagon

It was time to take off my anorak and stop leafing through the archives of the local press. I needed to talk to the instigators of all of this chaos – the faces behind this wave of juvenile belligerence. What made the young Turks of Bristol flock to the Greek-Cypriot-owned café Never on Sunday, named after the Nana Mouskouri record, on the fringe of the grim, post-war Broadmead shopping centre in the first place?

I put the question to Jimmy Demitriou – aka Jimmy Dee – who was born in 1953 in Bristol and whose Cypriot-born father (also known as Jim) opened up the café in 1966. I had first met Jim at a reunion for the 'Never' boys at his smart café club, Bar Celona, in Bristol's tough, uncompromising Kingswood district in April 2008.

'The Never on Sunday was first one unit... he [Jim's dad] opened it as a restaurant, serving mixed grills, omelettes, that sort of thing, but the kids would come in just for drinks – milkshakes, Cokes – then the shop next to him came up and he bought that and put in juke boxes and pinball machines. He encouraged the mods to come in – the whole wall was just pinball machines, the other side was seating and the jukebox. We were the first café in Bristol catering for the kids.

'It was up to me and my brother [George] to buy the music – we used to get the records from Picton Street. It was Blue Beat and Motown – we had quite a few [black guys] around us like Carlton and Seymour who introduced us to Picton Street and, from there on, they knew we were from the Never and put the records aside for us. My own favourite was "Wet Dream" by Max Romeo.'

This was a nice little earner for the tiny but famous RCA record store in Montpelier run by ex-Teddy Boy Roy Pugh and his dad. These were the days when press coverage of black music was almost non-existent and there was certainly very little airplay on national radio. Even when it was played, tinny transistors didn't do the heavily bassed-up Jamaican sounds justice. Black music charts were unheard of – word of mouth was how these records sold. Get the Never to put the records on their jukebox and the teenagers would flock to Roy's little emporium the following week to spend their hard-earned cash on classics by Jimmy Ruffin, the Four Tops, Derrick Morgan and Prince Buster.

There was, of course, the record which the Never made its own – 'Whisky and Soda' – by the amusingly named Mopeds. In gratitude for boosting their profits, Roy gave Jimmy a signed copy of Millie Small's 'My Boy Lollipop' (given to RCA when she once visited the shop herself) which he framed and proudly displayed in the café.

Jim had a good memory. He remembered fine details about his clothing and where he got it all from. 'Millets,' he said, without a hint of irony, 'for the basics,' he added quickly, 'but a cousin to my father used to make our three-piece suits.' He also had a mate, Paul, who was a mechanic who souped up his Lambretta. 'It had copper-sprayed side panels,' he said, beaming.

THE SERVICE ENGINEER AND THE FRUIT WAGON

He also recalled wearing a gold chain in his waistcoat. 'No watch on it, mind, just the chain,' he said with a smile. He was out to impress the girls.

'How about the clientele in the Never, Jim... can you remember the change from mods to skinheads?' I asked.

Jim was hazy about the actual year but he could quite vividly recall the cold wind of change that blew down from the east. 'Of course, the first skinheads were in London, but I remember lads being in the café one day dressed as mods, then literally the next day the hair was shorter and the jeans were up here and within two weeks they were all like it.'

Jim went on to regale me with tales of how the lads would nick money from the pinball machines but how his dad turned a blind eye to it. They obviously had a lot of respect for Jim Sr. Well, enough to nick his livelihood from under his nose, that is.

It turned out that the Never not only had a reputation with the local constabulary for the aggro but also for the shoplifting. 'If you wanted something, you could get it in the Never... there was one guy, he could get you anything. If you wanted a fridge, he would get it for you, anything you want. Someone once said, "I saw a lovely TV in Fairfax House..." [the large nearby Co-op departmental store] and this bloke would ask, "What make was it?" Then he would go along to Fairfax House, suss out the make, take a note of the serial number on the back, then go out and get changed into a pair of white overalls he owned – it even had "Service Engineer" on the back! He would then go back in with his overalls on and his clipboard – he even had a trolley. He would just load it up and walk out with it. If anyone stopped him, he would quote the serial number and show it on his pad, saying it had to go back to the factory for repair. Worked every time.'

The Never eventually shut down for good in 1974; the café which the skinheads used to frequent closed a couple of years earlier, due in no small part to the criminal activities of the lads and the fact the kids had moved on to pastures new. The restaurant continued for a while but, without the boys' patronage, the takings started to dwindle.

On top of that, Jim's old man was heavily into gambling, which didn't help. 'He went out one night with a top-of-the-range Merc and came back with an old banger – lost it playing cards.'

Jim himself obviously wasn't one of the 'top boys', and neither did he profess to be, but his clientele and his closeness with the lads in the Never ensured that Jim and his dad always commanded a certain amount of respect on the streets of Bristol. If ever they found themselves in need of a bit of 'muscle', the boys would not let them down. 'If someone threatened us, we knew we had huge back-up.'

Jim remembered an incident in the Silver Blades ice rink one Saturday afternoon. 'I remember once I got whacked in the ice-skating rink. I got nutted, there was blood all over the ice, and that was because I was chatting to some girl. Angelo [Pascoe – he and his brother Willie were notorious characters on the Bristol scene] spotted me, and said, "Jim, Jim… who did this?" Angelo wasn't skating, he walked on the fucking ice and – bang, bang – this bloke went down. It took five guys to get Angelo off him.

'Our ties with the Pascoes go further back than the Never – they worked in the fruit market and my dad had his first café there. I used to take them their coffees and egg and bacon sandwiches. It was a real, real buzzing place… by four in the morning it was packed.'

It turned out there were quite of few of these Never lads who worked in the nearby fruit market, including a certain individual whose name would crop up time and time again, who, as it turned out, would 'borrow' his parents' lorry to transport the skinheads around, often hidden behind the crates of fruit. More of him later.

THE SERVICE ENGINEER AND THE FRUIT WAGON

I could have spoken to Jim for hours; he was an engaging character and he looked back on those days with a great deal of affection, his eyes misting over with many of the recollections. He was clearly not a big-time player, though, and, whether through a fading memory or just a reluctance to name names, I wasn't really getting into the zeitgeist of the day. I knew the Never was not up there in the league of the Soho coffee bars that spawned the mods at the start of the decade, where Jack Kerouac and Colin McInnes were debated with gusto over their espressos, while Miles Davis played effortlessly in the background, but I had expected a bit more than 'Viennese steaks were popular with the lads'.

So I decided to go for the $64,000 question with Jim: 'Can you remember the very first skinhead in Bristol, Jim?'

I waited with bated breath. Would my search for 'Wally' be resolved right at the start of my investigation?

Jim cast his eyes over his restaurant, scratched his head, looked at the ceiling and took in a breath. 'No,' he answered.

Thanks, Jim. My search was to continue, then.

Prior to the Never reunion at Jim's club, the *Evening Post* ran a feature on the infamous café. Perhaps not surprisingly, there was no reference to 'skinheads' or of the bovver that was associated with it. Even the photo that was reproduced, which clearly showed a group of mischievous, cropped-haired and booted youths was accompanied by the caption: MODS OUTSIDE THE CAFÉ IN THE LATE '60S. Forty years on and the *Post* was still struggling with the taboo terminology.

A week or so after the article in the *Post*, letters started appearing listing name after name of bygone boys who had at one time stomped with pride through the streets of Bristol. One such letter appeared from Bob Feltham of Whitchurch, who wrote, 'I got to know the café through a guy called Gary Briar who

BOOTED AND SUITED

I worked with at the old Robertson's jam factory in Brislington in the late Sixties, and after that through the Number 9 scooter boys from Broomhill. These included friends Johnny Love and Gerry Hodgson (who were neighbours) and the Broomhill and St Anne's crowd. This included Lawrence Hobden, Craig Britton, Martin "Jinx" Jenkins, John "Fitz" Fitzgerald, Martin "Tap" Walters, Martin "Taz" Taylor, Eggy, Tinker, Joe, Andy Gunton, Martin Webster, Danny, Johnny Calabrese, Brian Strange and Charlie Travis, among others. The names that I remember from the Never crew were Brian Balson, Johnny Cowley, Chris Summers, Martin and Paddy Walsh, Andy and Paul Stone, Stevie Elvins, John Onuyfrick, Vernon, Snowy, Keith Langdon, Tony Horton, "Daddy" Stevens, Mike Thorne, Dave Mealing, Carl and, of course, Angelo Pascoe… The Never crowd were either in or outside the Locarno or at the Horse and Groom or the Way Inn on College Green. I also recall the trips to Burnham on a Sunday and to the Devon coast on bank holidays.'

I managed to make contact with Bob and, after several conversations via email, he went into a bit more detail about those days. Bob was born in 1952 and started frequenting the Never in his teens in the late Sixties. Like many of the guys from back then he's a family man (married for over 30 years to Caroline) and a successful businessman who runs his own international shipping business. Perhaps those 'bad old, good old days' taught these kids a thing or two. Many of them were ruthless risk-takers on the streets back then and maybe that 'savvyness' and sense of loyalty that they shared with their mates stayed with them in later years.

'I lived in Edward Road, Brislington, in those days and travelled into town either on the back of a scooter or in Johnny Love's Triumph Herald. At the same time, I introduced some other friends such as Dave Bonomi, Eamonn Kelly and Steve Pawlak to the "town" scene, although Steve already knew two of

THE SERVICE ENGINEER AND THE FRUIT WAGON

the existing members [of the scooter club], John Onuyfrick and Bob Knight who both hailed from Shirehampton. The Number 9s were mostly all already acquainted with the café...

'I had an old Mark 1 Lambretta when I moved to London to work at Heathrow in late 1969, but returned in 1970 back to the area. I remember that the Number 9s had a variety of souped-up Lambrettas and Vespas with all the "bells and whistles". In those days, I used to wear a pair of "Royal" brogues [bought from Hounslow], Ben Sherman shirts with or without braces, Sta-Prest trousers or jeans. I also had a Crombie coat, pair of Doc Martens and, of course, we were all spotless and smelled of Brut aftershave. If we wore a suit, the trousers were, of course, flared and the jackets had about a dozen buttons on the sleeves. I guess that I was a true skinhead in those days.

'We used to hang around either inside or outside the Locarno, in the Top Rank, in the Gaumont picture house, in the "Groom" or in the café. I can remember the running battles in Weston-super-Mare during the bank holidays, the mass fight and subsequent peace "charter" with the greasers in the city centre.

'Also at that time I played rugby with Bishopston Colts with Gerry Hodgson [rugby seems to be a common theme with a lot of the Never boys]. Other members of the side were Seymour Baugh, Tennis Russell and Caron Downer, who were later to become famous for their DJ activities in town. The music at this time was soul, Blue Beat and reggae, with *Tighten Up Volume 2* the top reggae album. I was a Rovers' fan in those days and used to travel away to watch matches, invariably ending up in some sort of "rumble" with the away supporters – something that I am not proud of now that I think back, but it seemed the thing to do at the time.

'As usually happens I became friendly with certain members of the Never crowd such as Brian Coombes, Daddy Stevens (you didn't tangle with these guys), Austin Hardwick (Ossie) and

BOOTED AND SUITED

Les English. I also met Steve McManus, who is a friend to this day, and Dave Mealing, who I still see from time to time. There were so many guys that I knew from that era that I could not possibly name them all. Having said that, how could I not mention Roy and Mike Thorne (Thorny), Martin and Paddy Walsh and Chris Summers?'

In later years, Bob and his mates spread their wings and started going further afield. Maybe the lure of the Never itself was on the wane. Bob added, 'As time went on, Johnny Love and I became friendly with Les Gortat and the inimitable Willy Pascoe. We used to collect them from Willy's flat in Clifton (Willy would not sit down in case he creased his Sta-Prest trousers) and drive to the Star at the top of the "Roddy" in Congresbury where they had a disco. The Broomhill guys and a fair few of the Never crowd used to meet up and chaperone the local "country" girls. Good days! Other places that we frequented with the boys were the Mexican Bar and the Hawthorns and, as mentioned earlier, "The Rank" where Jason was the DJ. The pre-club drinks were usually downed at the Way Inn on College Green, part of the old Royal Hotel.'

Some of the names that Bob mentioned I recognised, and one or two sent a chill down my spine. These guys were the stuff of myth and legend.

Someone else who was making a name for himself back then was Phil Peacock, who then lived in Sea Mills but who now resides in the USA. I worked with Phil in the early 1970s, and I had a lot of respect for him (as well as an irrational fear — he was built like the proverbial brick out-house) and I knew that he had some stories to tell.

Phil, if not remembering who or where he saw the first skinheads, recalled the momentous day when he decided to have all his hair shaved off, which wasn't as common as you might

THE SERVICE ENGINEER AND THE FRUIT WAGON

think in the late Sixties. 'As for the first [skinhead] in Bristol – I remember the mods with their stylish hair and the primping. I think the scooter riders were some of the first to start chopping the hair ever shorter as it wouldn't get in their eyes while riding, since helmets were not required. They were carried more as a weapon than to protect your noggin. That would have to be in 1967, early '68.

'I got my head shaved for the first time in Lewis's department store in 1968. I remember there was a young kid probably getting his first haircut and he was throwing a fit. The barber called me up to the chair, I sat down and he asked what I wanted. I said, "Shave it off." He did a double-take and asked again. I replied, "Shave it off," and he then took the clippers and went right down the middle saying, "You can't change your mind now." Meanwhile, the little kid's eyes were as big as saucers and he stopped screaming. His dad took him by the hand and they left the shop. Mind you, when I got home my mum had a fit! I believe I was the first in Sea Mills to do that voluntarily, other than the kids who had their hair cut every Saturday morning by their fathers who only knew one way to cut hair!'

Once you'd taken that giant leap in getting your hair cut, there was no going back; the next stage was to get kitted out. Phil recalled how the ex-Army stores saw an opportunity for a quick profit in the burgeoning market. 'The army surplus stores were quick to catch on and cash in on the trends. They would bring in American "Bomber" jackets in nylon and leather, and the boots – you could get a pair of hobnails [authentic British Army] for ten shillings [50p]. However, when the demand increased, the prices went up exponentially. I think a shop was selling them for £2 a pair for well-used ones and a fiver for the good ones at the height of the movement. The police also started cracking down on the shops that sold them, too, in an effort to thwart the violence on the streets.'

BOOTED AND SUITED

No matter what your choice of clothing – your strutting gear or your fighting gear – you had to be prepared for the aggro that, not surprisingly, was never too far away. 'I remember a black Fred Perry with black braces, black brogues with double soles, black socks and black Tonics. Man, that was sharp dressing in those days. Everyone wanted to see and be seen in those days. Everyone wanted to look their very best when they went out for the night, not like the wankers these days with their hoodies and their underwear showing. These guys would be beaten to a pulp on a regular basis 40 years ago. Even when going to a fight, we dressed well. Nothing stopped you from looking good. I got the biggest beating of my life from someone who also ran with the Never boys. I was drunk on my ass and he sucker-punched me as I came through a door, breaking my nose. He then proceeded to beat the crap out of me, but, hey, I looked good!'

Phil then went on to elaborate on those trips to Weston-super-Mare that Bob Feltham had mentioned. 'It was customary to ride down to Portishead on the scooters and meet up with the locals there, Skippy being one. And then, after several laps of the town, we'd head on down to Clevedon via the back roads. Once there, the same thing would happen – ride around for a while gathering up anyone else who wanted to ride. Then on towards Weston-super-Mare.

'At this point, we normally would meet up with others from Bristol also heading towards Weston. Many of these would be just blokes and their girls out for a Sunday ride. However, on those occasions when the Never boys were out, there was chaos in the air. One of their clan drove a lorry from the fruit market. They would put all of these empty crates up around the edges and the boys would be inside, hidden from view. However, once they came upon some unsuspecting greaser on his bike – and there were a few as many from Fishponds and the other more popular motorcycle neighbourhoods would also ride down to

THE SERVICE ENGINEER AND THE FRUIT WAGON

Weston on a Sunday, usually for the same purpose – there was always a bit of fun and perhaps a fight or two. Anyway, once alongside the bloke and his bike, the lads on the lorry would begin to hurl crates at the unsuspecting biker. Needless to say, there was many a biker run off the road, knocked of his bike by flying crates or lost a passenger. There was quite a lot of carnage to be had between Bristol and Weston in those days.

'As for myself... one Sunday I had a friend on the back of my Lambretta headed from Portishead to Clevedon and then on to Weston. There were quite possibly 20–25 scooters. About 15 miles out of Weston, I blew a spark plug. So I pulled over to the side of the road to effect repairs. Paul, my buddy, was crouched down watching me; he was to my right. The next thing I see is Paul rolling over on to the grass with his mouth all busted open and blood all over his face. Looking back, I see a procession of greasers riding by. I then looked up the road and there is one riding with his left foot trailing. Paul later recalled that he heard the noise of the bikes and turned towards the sound and the next thing he knew there was a boot kicking him in the face.

'My scooter took a few kicks from passing greasers as did most of the others who had stopped to wait for me. That was one thing – you never left someone on the road by themselves for this very reason. Once back under way, our group caught up with some of the back markers and took revenge. I smacked one biker's right hand with a big spanner, used for the rear suspension on my scooter. The police would stop you and want to see if you had any weapons, so anything that could be explained away as a tool for repairing the scooter was not seen as a weapon per se. Anyway, I'm sure I broke his hand and then a couple of kicks and he was in a ditch, bike and all. The others began to harass the greaser and they finally took off towards Weston.

'The greasers would hang out in a café across from the pier. It was down a few steps and located in a basement of sorts. The name escapes me. I recall an ornamental garden across the street from it and I think it was the Winter Garden at the end of the road. Ken Dodd was playing there, or was coming.

'Anyway, upon arriving in Weston, most if not all of the mods, skinheads and Never boys would park their rides across from the beach front. Word soon spread of the incident and I would estimate a hundred of us began a march on this little café. Funny really, the beat cops began to scurry away and call for help, as did most of the locals. Businesses would lock their doors. Vandalism reigned.

'Upon arriving at the café, a steady stream of us began to enter through the front door. Once the place was jammed tight, with all of the greasers confined to the back of the café, with no avenue of escape, all hell broke loose. I cut one bloke's face open with a razor knife. He may well have lost the use of that eye, but he has a spare. That was the feeling then, anyway; today, it would be different (I hope)!

'Blood covered everything. You didn't dare go to the floor for fear of being made part of it. Chairs and table legs were being used as clubs. Some of the lads went over the counter and began throwing crockery and others helped themselves to the cash register.

'The scrap went on for maybe five minutes and then the call went out that several Panda cars were seen coming our way. Exit stage left! The stream of bodies that exited that café was something to behold, lads were running this way and that so as not to get caught. Those that couldn't get into the café knocked over bikes and smashed them as best they could, and slashed the tyres. I later heard from a friend travelling in a Morris Minor with three others from the Never that they were pulled over by a single cop in a Panda as they tried to head out of Weston towards Brean Down. He said that a certain individual wanted to get out and do the cop in, but he was talked down by the other

THE SERVICE ENGINEER AND THE FRUIT WAGON

three! They were able to bullshit the cop and get on their way, although several were caught and arrested. I was able to get out of Weston with my buddy Paul, Skippy and a few others. We went out past the old pier and high-tailed it through the country roads back to Clevedon and Portishead.'

I had unearthed stories in the *Evening Post* which confirmed Phil's recollections. The Bank Holiday weekends of 1970 in particular saw large-scale outbreaks of violence, with the Easter weekend signifying the start of the aggro season. After a long, dark winter, it would be inevitable that the youngsters from the cities would want to stretch their legs, grab some rays and breathe in the sea air... and cause mayhem. The *Evening Post* reported that an estimated 200 youths were involved in disturbances in Weston over the Easter weekend of 1970 and that nine were arrested and charged 'after clashes between skinheads and rockers' broke out on the town's seafront. At least the *Post* was beginning to get the hang of the terminology, even if they were still confused over what they should call the bikers. 'Extra police had to be called in when steel-helmeted and crop-headed youths were seen converging in packs on the Promenade. Officers posted near the pier went into action immediately fighting broke out near the pier entrance... a running fight ensued and spread on to the nearby sands – several youths were arrested on the sands and frogmarched across the Promenade before being bundled into police cars.'

Superintendent Gerald Lockyer of the local police believed that their decision to break up the gangs of youths had in the main been successful. 'If it had not been for our prompt action, I believe a very nasty situation could have developed.'

Not that the bovver was confined to the beleaguered Somerset town. There were outbreaks of violence at many seaside resorts around the country; any beach town with the misfortune to be within a motorcycle or train ride from a large city was likely to be targeted by the greasers or the boot boys. That same Easter weekend also saw trouble break out in Rhyl, North Wales, between a 200-strong gang of bikers and a much smaller gang of only 30 skinheads. This in itself was unusual as, in the main, the bikers were usually heavily outnumbered, but what made this attack even more bizarre was that, among the standard terror fare of weapons used to inflict damage – wooden posts, metal rods, studded leather belts and motorcycle kick-starters – an 'animal bone of unknown origin' was also used. Six 'long-haired youths' subsequently appeared in court where a Nazi steel helmet was confiscated and fines totalling £165 were handed out.

The Whitsun Bank Holiday in May saw a repeat of the trouble at Weston when up to 500 teenagers caused a 'frightening scene', according to the police, and, in Brighton on the south coast, skinheads wrecked the train they had been travelling on from London and knocked over people as they strolled along the Promenade.

By the time the Bank Holiday season drew to an end, the boot boys were in the mood for a last huge hurrah. The police estimated at the time that around 2,000 skinheads from Bristol invaded Weston on the August Bank Holiday Monday of 1970 and around 200 were involved in an afternoon of running battles, assaults and general mayhem. Under the headline SKINHEAD BATTLE – TOWN COUNTS COST, the *Post* went on to report that, 'at one stage, a bunch of bovver boys and girls, complete with reinforced bovver boots, were parading down the seafront clapping and chanting, "We are from Bristol." The police were less than impressed. Nevertheless, vicious fights still broke out all over town but those tended to be between various gang members. More frightening were mass charges by packs of howling teenagers which bowled over any unfortunates who happened to get in the way.

THE SERVICE ENGINEER AND THE FRUIT WAGON

'Skinheads hurled bottles, stones, dustbin lids and clods of earth at the police who were trying to confine the gangs on the beach. One policeman was cut on the face and others badly bruised by the missiles as the battles moved into Oxford Street and the roads leading from the seafront. A gang of 50 rampaged through an outfitters in the High Street grabbing anything they could before police arrived.'

Another incident occurred in the famous Forte ice-cream parlour on the seafront where one youth went into the toilet and stole the pipework, presumably to use as a weapon. Miss Olga Forte, owner of the parlour, told the *Post*, 'This youth came out of the toilet. He didn't buy anything. He just said "Thank you" and left. Five minutes later we had a flooded toilet and we have to get new pipes fitted.'

At least he had the manners to say thanks. More disturbing was the group who 'enjoyed frightening the ponies and donkeys on the sands'... I mean, you wouldn't want 'animal worrying' on your police record, would you? People might think you were Welsh!

The *Evening Post* continued, 'Twenty youths were arrested and twelve detained. At a special court the following day, one was sent to a detention centre for assaulting a policeman and seven were fined for obstructing police, blocking the highway and threatening behaviour.'

No doubt, many of those involved in the disturbances that day frequented the Never. Like the outraged *Evening Post*, I sensed with Phil Peacock that, although he was very much part of this 'scene', he wasn't particularly enamoured with the Never boys. 'Quite a few out there saw them as nothing but a bunch of yobs who stole everything in sight and beat the crap out of everyone that either crossed them or had something they wanted. I walked up on one lad and a few of his cronies mugging a bloke just off the Centre one night. Not a pretty sight... the poor bastard looked like raw meat in a suit. This geezer saw me and told his buds to split; he then told me that I'd better not say a word to anyone, stuffed a fiver in my hand then high-tailed it towards the fruit market. I picked the bloke up, took him into the Unicorn [a hotel on the waterfront] and cleaned him up. Then I gave him his fiver back and got him a cab.'

After my meeting with Jimmy Dee, I knew that to get a sense of what drove these lads on, I needed to talk to the real 'movers and shakers' of the day. I wanted to know what attracted them to the Never but, more importantly, what attracted them to the skinhead movement in the first place.

Lloyd Sutherland was one of the black 'kiddies' that Jim had mentioned and whose young fresh face can be seen in that famous photo of the 'truce'. Lloyd was astute, meticulous on detail and, at 58, a few years older than Jim. His memory was unfailing and, best of all, he had an impressive, if faded, collection of photos circa 1969–71 featuring the Never gang, one of which he permanently kept in his wallet. Those days obviously meant a lot to Lloyd; he loved that sense of camaraderie and loyalty with his mates, many of whom he still counts as friends to this day.

He was now employed by the prison service, working with young offenders; you could tell he had a real sense of responsibility about him, so was he trying to give society something back? Not that I was suggesting that he took anything out in the first place.

Lloyd brought along one of his good mates from those days, Eugene. We met in the Shakespeare Tavern in Prince Street, one of the few remaining pubs in the city centre and one that probably hadn't changed much since the heyday of the skinheads. I let them put their sides of the story. These guys remembered the good times, but their memories

THE SERVICE ENGINEER AND THE FRUIT WAGON

faded somewhat when I probed them on the bad times. One question I asked related to the supposed drug scene that undoubtedly featured strongly in the mod era but seemed less important to the emerging skinheads, and how about the 'hard Cokes' that I had read about that could be bought in the Soho cafés with a nod and a wink, the ones that had the 'extra' ingredients?

'Phensic,' said Lloyd, 'we used to add Phensics to our Coke.' The two giggled like naughty schoolboys – London had Drinamyl, Bristol had Phensic (which contained aspirin and caffeine). Yeah, baby.

Although it's been well documented that the early skinheads evolved from their older cousins, the mods, it appears that many of them didn't really have much time for their close relations – perhaps it was the arrogance, the peacock-strutting of the mods they objected to. There was even a hint of the effete about many of the mods and their choice of clothing, hairstyles and mannerisms; their Italian palaces on wheels that they lovingly cared for and coveted were not for the skins. If the young cropheads did manage to get their hands on a scooter, it was not looked upon as a fashion statement in the way that the mods viewed them. The skinheads would routinely strip them of their fripperies and crank up the engines; gone were the banks of mirrors with which the mods adorned their Lambrettas (in order to check themselves out more often than not). Also binned were the fox tails and the myriad fog lamps, to be replaced with the pared-to-the-bone, engine-exposed, down-to-earth embodiment of the skinhead itself, the 'skelly'.

Eugene, however, put forward a more simplistic explanation as to why the skinheads weren't so taken with Milan's finest. 'We were skint! We would scrounge lifts... we had limited amounts of money. If you were spending it all on scooters, you had nothing for going out or buying clothes.'

BOOTED AND SUITED

As an apprentice engineer on less than £6 a week, Eugene found the choice was simple – what was the point of being able to afford a flash mode of transport if you couldn't afford to go out on it, and 'going down town' was, without a doubt, what mattered to the lads more than anything else. It's an interesting observation – virtually all of the skinheads from that period were young lads, mostly in the 16–18 age group, barely out of school. Booted and suited but without a pot to piss in.

There's a certain amount of 'rose-tinted glasses' going on when it comes to looking at the past, especially when it comes to Britain's teen cults. Nostalgia certainly isn't what it used to be. We now look back on mods with a great degree of affection, even fondness, at that 'clean living under very difficult circumstances' as The Who's manager Peter Meaden observed of the self-obsessed, working-class dandies, while we conveniently overlook the gratuitous violence, the drug taking and petty criminality. An admission now that you were an original mod back in the 1960s will earn you admiring glances, a slap on the back and furtive questions about what scooter you owned. Admit to the fact you were a skinhead and you're in big trouble; you might as well confess to being a kiddy-fiddling Islamic fundamentalist.

Yet perhaps skinheads should also be looked upon in the same favourable light – certainly in the fashion stakes they were up there with the mods. They, too, had a penchant for sharp clothes and sharp looks. Ben Shermans, Doctor Martens, Crombies, sheepskin coats... all cost big money and were all worn at some stage by the sartorial street warriors but, truth be told, for a lot of lads back then, you made the most of what you could get, so with money being tight the boys sought out ways of 'looking good' without breaking the bank. As well as the army surplus stores, another cheap way of obtaining your boots was remembered by Eugene who recalled buying his first pair of

THE SERVICE ENGINEER AND THE FRUIT WAGON

steel-toe-caps from works catalogues where you could purchase them by paying in instalments of five bob (25p) a week. Once he had moved on to Doc Martens, it was KBK on Cheltenham Road where the legendary eight-eyelet 1460s DMs became standard issue. As for heading into the metropolis to buy his threads and footwear, he says that was the stuff of dreams. 'I could never afford to go to London, let alone shop there.' But the Never lads were resourceful if nothing else, especially when it came to getting around.

As I was to discover through many interviews, there was one mode of transport that was as unusual as it was practical for the boys from the Never – the fruit and veg wagon that both Jim Dee and Phil Peacock had mentioned which was owned by a character called 'Barney'. Eugene recalled a time when all the lads piled in to Barney's ex-army wagon (it wasn't just boots the skinheads got from the MoD) and headed towards the coast. On the way, they inevitably got stopped by the law. The young copper looked into the back at the gathered boot boys all eagerly looking forward to their outing to the seaside. The copper, who clearly had a sense of humour, eyed them all up and stated the obvious: 'You lot must be bananas.'

Being a Bristol Rovers' fan, I got on to the topic of football allegiances within the clientele of the Never, something I had already brought up with Jim Dee; like him, Lloyd and Eugene both confirmed that football didn't feature highly on the list of their pastimes. This surprised me. Skinheads and their proclivity for violence, together with football's tribal history and the lure of the terrace for a rumble, seemed to me an obvious attraction, but, although many of the Never boys had a passing interest in the beautiful game (mainly, it seemed, with Bristol City – perhaps because of the amount of greasers who followed Rovers), it didn't seem to be the obsession it was with me. They had other priorities and, perhaps, better ways to spend their money. I suppose, if you analyse it, there is an absurdity about getting up at four in the morning, as I often did, to travel halfway across the country just to roll around in the dirt of a gravel car park of some grubby northern town and, more often than not, get a split lip in the process.

Of course, you could turn this on its head and say it dispels the myth that all football hooligans aren't interested in the game itself, just the violence. While I enjoyed the football as much as the aggro, the Never boys, with their fearsome reputation, would have been naturals for the terraces. Some were and, indeed, many of them forged their notoriety on the terraces of City's East End or Rovers' Tote End, but it clearly didn't form part of the cachet of the café or indeed divide it — reds and blues rubbed shoulders with each other in there. Sometimes it may have been uneasy but it rarely, if ever, spilled over in the café itself, as Lloyd observed, 'The crowd down there was never into football, or, if they were, it wasn't mentioned.'

Eugene recalled his first excursion into the world of the terrace terrors which perhaps goes some way to explaining why the Never boys weren't so enamoured with football. 'I went into the Never one Saturday morning, and these kids said they were going to a game, so we jumped on the train and went up to Birmingham. As soon as we got off the train, there was all these local kiddies waiting for us — the kids I had gone with weren't regulars at the Never and we wouldn't have run, but they all legged it. I was lucky there was a couple of coppers there and they chucked me in a shop doorway, stopped all these other kiddies doing me in like. I was thinking this gang of kids I went up with, if they was going to have something, they would stay and fight.'

The fact that they didn't 'stay and fight' had a long lasting impact on the young Eugene, and to this day he has little interest in football.

THE SERVICE ENGINEER AND THE FRUIT WAGON

It became quite evident during my research and talking to some of the older lads that the divide in Bristol football in the late Sixties and early Seventies didn't manifest itself on the streets or in the pubs and clubs of Bristol as it did in later years. The aggro was more or less restricted to the terraces and the surrounding area when the two teams played each other – as in the Gloucester Cup Final in 1969 at Eastville when City fans invaded the pitch after a lucky 5–0 win and not only broke the crossbar and painted the goalposts red and white but also trampled the famous flower beds behind the goal.

The following year really made the headlines when a ferocious battle erupted in the exotically named Maritas greasy-spoon café on Winterstoke Road before the game, which saw not only rival skinheads fighting each other but greasers thrown into the mix as well. Something else that was thrown was the lit workman's lamp which went through the window. Thankfully, it failed to ignite, unlike the flare that was let off during the game itself. There were over 50 ejections from the ground and 43 arrests, some of whom were fully paid-up members of the Never who weren't particularly interested in the football. Most bizarrely of all, one of those arrested was a Rovers-supporting Never boy who really found his loyalties tested when he came face-to-face with his arch-rival greasers decked in the blue and white of Rovers – a rock and a hard place if there ever was one. The subsequent court case resulted in hefty prison and Borstal sentences being handed out to those involved, including one or two well-known Never boys.

At the time, Rovers' General Manager, Bert Tann, commented in the local press, 'I can only repeat what I have said many times before – we will only stop these things [the violence] happening when we start smacking their bottoms hard.' The comment is as laughable now as it was back then.

These divided loyalties were causing quite a headache for

many of the skinheads, although it was not unknown for both Rovers and City skinheads to join up and take on visiting supporters if it seemed necessary. One old mate of mine, whom I had always assumed was a dyed-in-the-wool Rovers fan, got arrested at Ashton Gate in 1969 for fighting with visiting Watford fans. He was fined £50, but to his eternal shame he was referred to in the local press as a Bristol City hooligan, something that, to this day, still haunts him.

As well as the Never, Lloyd and Eugene recalled other venues the skinheads would gather in – the Top Rank, which was actually part of the same building complex that the Never was in; the Locarno, with its famed Bali Hai bar, resplendent with plastic palm trees; and two small but significant pubs, The Horse and Groom and The Horse and Jockey (now the Queen's Shilling, a well-known gay establishment).

The Horse and Groom in St George's Road behind the Bristol Council House in particular had been a favourite with 'town kiddies' for a number of years. My brother Mike and his mates Dave Baker and Rodney Manns were regulars in there, showing off their bespoke mohair suits in the post-mod, pre-skinhead era. The 'Groom' was a honeypot for lads around town. It was here you could serve your apprenticeship in town and sample the favoured drinks of the day – the famed light or brown splits, lager and lime, rum and Coke, vodka and orange, rum and black and the fearsome barley wine. Strange, then, that following on from the wave of violence that erupted on the streets of Bristol in the summer of 1969, the landlord of the Horse and Groom, Peter Jacobs, speaking in the *Evening Post*, stated, 'I've had to turn away scores of them... but the main gathering point seems to be outside, in the car park opposite. I'm afraid to leave my car there. I'm leaving soon to take over a pub at Stapleton and I shan't be sorry to go.'

Another popular pub was the nearby Pineapple. Speaking in

THE SERVICE ENGINEER AND THE FRUIT WAGON

the same article, landlord Roger Baker-Gill stated that he 'planned to give up his pub and emigrate if teenage mob rule continued in central Bristol'. In just three nights, he had barred more than a hundred young people from his pub, and stated, 'These gangs of youths and girls are taking over the central part of the city and frightening away respectable people.' Nearly 40 years on and the same complaint is being reeled out about today's alcopop-swilling chavs – no change there then.

So determined were the lads to get in an extra bit of drinking time they would often jump into cars and head into nearby north Somerset where the pubs were open until 11pm (Bristol pubs shut at 10.30pm in those days). As Bob Feltham had recalled, The Star near Congresbury on the Weston Road was a particular favourite. He had mentioned that the local girls were particularly taken with the boys from the big city, although the local lads weren't so keen on the booted and suited interlopers. The inevitable conflict was brewing – 'They took umbrage,' as Eugene put it.

I had heard rumours of one notorious incident which occurred one weekend when 20 or so Never boys entered the pub and a ferocious brawl broke out almost straight away. Various weapons, including an axe, were allegedly used, but neither Lloyd or Eugene could recall this incident.

The two of them were honest enough to admit that they had a few run-ins with the law or 'bogies' as they were known back then. Eugene, who was obviously up for a laugh at any opportunity, recalled one incident with a distinct amount of glee. 'I remember coming out of the Locarno one night and a Panda car was parked outside – the coppers had gone up the stairs [to the Locarno] to sort out some trouble. This was a two-door car, a Morris 1000, and we thought we'd take it to get home.

'I was just getting in the back and the fucking copper seen us and shouted, "Oi!" and the others legged it. I was getting out of the car and I seen a helmet on the back parcel shelf so I thought I'd have that... I was running down the road with this copper's helmet on and I just got under the bridge on Park Street when they caught up with me... I chucked the helmet up in the air. I got a beating for that, I got a £10 fine, but they got a bigger bollocking for leaving their car unlocked.'

You sometimes have to question the mentality of some of these lads. I mean, who in their right mind would think of getting away with nicking a police car? (See Part 2, Chapter 16.)

Eugene continued, 'Then down Weston, I got done for obstructing the pavement just outside the pier. They told me to move on, I said, "No," I was waiting for someone. They pulled me in, took me to the police station and put my arms up behind me back. Made us miss the last train home... got a £10 fine.'

Eugene continued with his perception of the much reported disorder on the streets of Britain today. 'When you look in the papers now and you read about the problems and violence and that, bloody hell, if you wanted to get into violence [then] you didn't have to look very hard, there was always someone willing to accommodate you.' Lloyd added, 'We used to walk through Broadmead and you could see people terrified, they would get out of the way. We didn't have mobile phones – if you wanted it, it just happened.'

Neither of them could recall that momentous day when the first skinhead appeared on the streets of Bristol. 'The clothing just evolved,' observed Eugene, who recalled many mods in previous years wearing boots of one form or another, but they did offer up some names of guys who seemed to have had all the skinhead accoutrements at an early stage – Des Lewis, Keith Langdon, Alan 'Beaky' Hope and the legendary Pascoe brothers were certainly among the first cropheads viewed on the streets of Bristol. Eugene himself became a full-on skinhead with boots and an attitude to go with them. Lloyd never owned a pair – he

THE SERVICE ENGINEER AND THE FRUIT WAGON

had a cheap pair of Sta-Prest, managed to get a Ben Sherman, never wore the braces, 'kept the hair short otherwise it would have been an afro'. They both remembered buying their clothes in Austin's, Mr Zeus 'used to be a moddy shop called Carnaby One,' said Eugene, or Stuckeys and Millets.

Like many young males from that era, the boys would have at least one quality, hand-made suit adorning their wardrobe, usually purchased from Burtons, Jacksons or John Collier – 'the window to watch' – and, occasionally, from bespoke tailors such as David Ferrari on the Gloucester Road. Material, the length of the vent, stitching, the amount of buttons on the sleeve and the width of lapels were all exact and precise in their detail. Mostly, they got it right, ensuring admiring glances from both males and females as they paraded their latest threads. Occasionally, they got it wrong, very wrong, as did one lad known as 'Dosser' who turned up one evening in the Never in a bright-orange suit.

Saturday night couldn't come round quick enough for them to show off their finery and strut their stuff on the dancefloor of the Top Rank, and, if the latest sounds from Jamaica or Detroit didn't give them their instant hit of gratification, their almost weekly punch-ups with the visiting hordes from the Welsh valleys surely would.

Although the Never boys' obvious nemesis were local greasers and their ilk, it was not unknown for them to have a row with fellow boot boys from across the country, whether they were the visiting Celts from across the Bristol Channel on a Saturday night or, more often than not, 'mouthy Cockneys' who would cross their paths when they visited coastal resorts on bank holidays. Eugene recalled trips to Weston and Bournemouth, 'but Torquay was the main one – you would go round the Never and no one would be around, they would all have gone away. It was more territorial when we went to Torquay, fighting with Londoners in the Yacht if they were bouncing over, but the Never were the biggest mob.'

BOOTED AND SUITED

Racism rarely reared its ugly head in those days; in fact, there was a great deal of racial harmony on the streets between the skinhead and West Indian community, perhaps surprisingly when you think Enoch Powell was trying his hardest to stir up trouble between the two ethnic groups. Lloyd never had any trouble with black and white issues – 'There might be comments but that would be it.' He even recalled one incident when 'a young black girl got slapped by a greaser – she used to go in the Never so we went around the Top Rank and got the black guys [who used to gather around their own bar at the back] and we all went around Old Market to sort them out.'

Eugene added, 'The West Indians were working-class people like us – all the music was Motown or reggae – there was more harmony then between white and black kids. I can remember me, Carl [another black member of the Never boys] and one or two others would go to the Bamboo Club* for the reggae. You'd be taking your life in your hands if you tried that a few years later. We just went for the music.'

The last words of the evening came from Eugene when I queried him about regrets and how he had managed to leave it all behind. 'There was a lot of violent behaviour back then. Regrets about it? Yes, but it was part of my life, I enjoyed it. Things could have gone seriously wrong. People got locked up but you weren't aware of it, unless you were a close friend. Not many people would know. You would say, "Haven't seen so and so for a while..." An easy decision was to not go down town again. You got a girlfriend, your circumstances changed.'

Although Lloyd and Eugene remembered Barney's fruit wagon with fondness and affection, for others, not associated with the Never, the sight of the wagon coming into view wasn't

---

* The famous, and notorious, West Indian club in St Pauls, owned by Tony Bullimore who went on to became a well-known, if somewhat accident-prone, round-the-world lone sailor.

THE SERVICE ENGINEER AND THE FRUIT WAGON

a laughing matter. For some, it caused genuine fear, 'that sinking feeling in the pit of the stomach', as Chris Welch noted. And this fear wasn't just felt by hippies and greasers; other lads around town weren't immune from the attention of the Never boys.

Jim Burnham, a streetwise mod (both then and now, he and other enthusiasts from that era are involved in the Bristol Mod Scooter Club: www.bristolmod.co.uk), remembered the Never and the fruit wagon well. 'The Never gang went around for a while in what was called "the fruit wagon"... I guess one of their guys maybe worked down the fruit market and I guess he would "borrow" it from work. They would cruise around, all piled in the back of this truck, on their way to "do" some other gang over, allegedly with a few tools (crowbars, bits of wood and even, again, allegedly a few scaffold poles!). Whether they actually used these, I don't know, but the thought of it at the time scared the living daylights out of everybody!

'I can remember being in Clifton village with a couple of mates one Saturday night, we were wearing suit jackets, Ben Shermans and Levi's (I guess it's what you might call smart/casual) and we saw the fruit wagon coming around the corner. I don't mind admitting that we were shit scared and ran like fuck! They were notorious for beating up anybody they didn't know or didn't like the look of – we weren't prepared to hang about!'

4

Warriors in Boots

My old workmate, Phil Peacock, was becoming even more lucid, whether through living thousands of miles away in the States or just due to the fact that he was a natural-born storyteller. Perhaps he saw it as cathartic. Either way, Phil's frank and honest recollections echoed Eugene's thoughts. 'Yes, it feels good to get it out of the system. I sure as hell know that it was a tough time to be living in England in those days... I did some pretty rotten things and can only hope that I'm forgiven in some way or another. There was never any real maliciousness to it all.'

Phil, however, did have his own very strong opinions about what was happening politically in Britain in the late Sixties and how it impacted on and influenced young, white, working-class kids like him, which may partially explain why, to many skinheads, the relationship with black kids was working but why some saw the need to delve into 'selective racism', which ultimately manifested itself as 'Paki bashing'.

'Personally, I blame Harold Wilson and the Labour Party for folding under pressure from the international community to help those immigrants in Uganda and Bangladesh... for opening up the flood gates to all of the immigrants who had ever been under British rule at one time or another, or had family that were to come on in. It was this, I believe, spurred on the skinhead movement. All of these frustrated kids with no prospect of getting anything other than a blue-collar job and then that was being taken away from them by immigrants who were getting a free ride with assistance, housing, medical... you name it. These kids saw their parents become second-class citizens in their own country. These were the parents that suffered through the trials and tribulations of World War II and now they were being fucked once more by their own government and country! Fuck that! We'll make it so fucking tough on these bastards that they'll go home from whence they came. And while were at it, we'll also fuck with the greasers – a dirty bloody bunch of bastards. We were working-class people. We didn't care if you were white or black – if you worked for a living, you were one of us.'

Phil was obviously on a roll. He then sent me a candid and honest email which gives a great snapshot of the day and confirms that the violence was not restricted to the city centre. Suburban cafés and youth clubs, in particular, were also the scene of some horrendous violence. 'In 1967, I started hanging out down town with a few of my friends from school – Nick, Paul, Andy and brothers Rich and Steve. We started going into town on a Saturday to hang out and do the shops and the record stores. There was one record store located on Union Street that was so easy to rip off it was pitiful. We would go in and listen to some of the latest records in these booths. After finding something we liked, it was only a matter of slipping it inside your Levi's jacket or Crombie coat and out the door you went.

'We also would hit the Coke and Clobber and, my favourite, Beau Brummel on the Centre – always had the best selection of Ben Shermans. Then it would be off to the chemist shop on Broad Street, I think, and lift a bottle or two of Brut. Now we're set for

BOOTED AND SUITED

a night out on the town. The Horse and Groom, The Hatchet, Horse and Jockey, The Pineapple, Three Tuns, Bunch of Grapes, The Mail Coach and The Crown were some of the pubs where you could drink under-age without too much of a problem down town. Of course, most of the market pubs were good, too. We would also go to the ice rink in the afternoon for a few hours of picking up the birds and some speed skating. This is where I had most of my run-ins with the Never boys.

'It's 1969 and a few friends of mine who lived in Fishponds wanted me to come to one of their clubs (a church one!) one Friday night. I was 16 then; I had a Lambretta LI150 with a lot of upgrades taken from here and there. Anyway, the purpose was for me to rough it up with this kid from the Concorde (a café on the Fishponds Road) who had been beating up some of the local kids at this club. I took Andy along with me and here we are waiting for the local thug – George someone – to show up... and in he walks.

'He whacks Andy (we used to call him Bert – why, I have no fucking idea to this day). Andy's mouth is bleeding like a stuck pig. George then focuses on me. I get a couple of haymakers in and break his nose. Meanwhile, Andy gets his senses together and pulls a badminton net off the wall and wraps it around this guy's neck and begins to choke the bastard. Long story short, George blacks out and is unceremoniously stomped by all the local kids.

'Then the fun begins in earnest. A friend of mine who invited me to the club, Richard, and some others from school – Bob and Steve – come running in saying that there is a whole bunch of Hells Angels coming down the road from Staple Hill and the Concorde. So Andy and myself with a few of the other locals pour out of the club.

'We meet these guys coming into the parking lot and Andy kicks one off of his bike which leads to others either running into the downed bike or the rider and others, while trying to avoid the mess, running into each other. I took my belt off and whacked a few in the head and face. It was a firemen's belt with a freaking huge brass belt buckle. I remember it being soaked in blood. After a few minutes, it was apparent that we were vastly outnumbered, especially since many of the local kids had run back into the club and locked the door. Andy and I took the better part of valour and took off running. We climbed a fence at the back of the church and took off across a field and hid in the back gardens of some of the homes behind the church. Must have hid there for what seemed like hours before coming out and heading home. I was later told that George wanted to have my head on a pike for breaking his nose.'

As an afterthought, Phil mentioned another scooter gang that was not connected with the Never but who were known to enjoy a ruck as much as the boys from Fairfax Street. 'They were out of Bedminster and led by a kid named Bridges I think. They were always up for a scrap and were involved in some big fights in Queen Square and on the Centre. They ran by themselves but would help out the Never boys.'

Phil then confirmed what both Eugene and Lloyd had mentioned regarding football allegiances on the streets of Bristol back then. 'I was never a soccer fan, although I'd root for the Rovers as my Dad was a City fan, just to piss him off.'

Perhaps as a way of curbing his aggression, Phil took up rugby and, for many years, played for Bristol Harlequins before emigrating to the States in 1975 where he worked at one stage for the US Coast Guard. He's revisited Bristol a few times over the years and isn't sure he likes what he sees. 'Bristol has changed so much... not always for the better I'm sure.' I could add that it's a lot quieter since the Sea Mills warrior left.

Phil's recollection of aggro at youth clubs was not in isolation — I had heard and read of other incidents at clubs in and around Bristol. One club on Briscoes Avenue in Hartcliffe was frequented by, among others, a fearsome duo of greaser brothers. The story goes that the Never boys made a trip to the youth club with the sole intention of attacking the greasers and cutting off the prized frills from the sleeves of their leather jackets. The urban myth circulated for years that, indeed, they had been successful in capturing the trophies of war. However, on further investigation, I found out that, although the lads did attack the club, they were repelled by a volley of chairs from inside it, which dented the pride of the Never boys as much as it did their car panels.

There were other such rumours, including attempts by some of the lads to tie wires across roads in order to decapitate passing greasers but, not surprisingly, this story was not corroborated by any of the interviewees.

One brawl at another youth club, though, definitely took place on a Saturday evening in April 1970. A dance at the Catholic Church Hall in Keynsham was the scene of a pitched battle between two separate gangs; up to a hundred skinheads fought in the street outside the hall throwing punches, kicking each other and using weapons that ranged from sticks studded with nails to the all-too-common knives and sharpened combs. More worryingly, according to the *Evening Post*, 'a rifle had been spotted'. The local Canon (Reidy) went on to say that 'There will not be a recurrence next weekend. We will have a Saturday-night whist drive – it will be a very sedate affair.'

The Never café itself, not surprisingly, was not immune from the violence. On Friday, 13 March 1970, a greaser from Marshfield was stabbed and kicked as he left the café with his mates, and you've got to question what they were doing in there in the first place. He stated in the subsequent court case that he left the café 'after receiving hostile looks'. Up to 30 youths then rushed out and attacked the greaser gang. One of the Never lads was sent to Borstal while others were fined up to £100.

WARRIORS IN BOOTS

Another stabbing occurred in nearby Dursley in June of the same year when a skinhead gang from Southmead, not associated with the Never café, invaded the small Gloucestershire town with the sole intention of attacking greasers. A 21-year-old skinhead was jailed for four years for the attack on a 'local, long-haired passer-by'. In court, the assailant made the following astonishing, frank admission: 'I stuck the knife in, it went into his ribs somewhere... I twisted it while it was in him... and the blade snapped off.'

Later on that summer, some of the Never boys made another one of their excursions out of town, this time to Bournemouth on the south coast, which over the years has often witnessed outbreaks of trouble between Bristol, Birmingham and London lads, not to mention the local residents. Lloyd Sutherland had recalled that often the locals would weigh up the situation to see whose mob was the most impressive – and then join forces with them against the others. It's not clear where the greasers who the Bristol boys battled with that day were from, but what is clear is that it was a pretty vicious altercation.

A group of 50 skinheads, all from the Bristol area, attacked a smaller number of greasers. 'Fists and boots were used as well as missiles such as bricks and bottles, and at least one knife was used to inflict a very serious wound.' So intense was the attack that one scared greaser escaped by jumping off the pier into the sea and, when the greasers tried to make their exit in a van, the skinheads attacked and tried to overturn it.

In the ensuing court case, three Bristolians were imprisoned, one for three years, while another four were sent to Borstal. The judge, Mr Justice Wills, commented, 'I don't pretend to know what skinheads are or why you become skinheads, but I have been told by the police what people like you do.'

'Tony', one of the Never lads who was imprisoned for this incident, recalled that when he was banged up word got around

BOOTED AND SUITED

that Jimi Hendrix, who had been performing at the nearby Isle of Wight rock festival, sent out a message from the stage to the jailed skinheads and greasers asking for peace between the two warring groups. It appears that, yet again, the calls for calm, whether from outraged provincial newspapers or bona fide guitar legends, were falling on deaf ears.

The events of the previous few months once again made the front page of the *Evening Post*: IT'S ALL-OUT WAR ON THE HOOLIGANS, the paper declared, but you get the impression the authorities and the police in particular were fighting a losing battle. A joint statement by councillors and police pledged an 'all-out fight against hooligans and violence in Bristol caused by a rash of disturbances', but it was all hyperbolic rhetoric, and, just when they thought it couldn't get any worse, the new football season kicked off.

On 1 August, 250 youths of 'the skinhead type' from the Midlands descended upon Eastville for a pre-season 'friendly' between Rovers and Birmingham City. It was a ferocious battle, one which I could only watch with both fear and wonderment from the sidelines. The Brummies comprehensively took the Rovers' Tote End and it wasn't until half-time when reinforcements arrived from around the city that Rovers' fans managed to claim some of their terraces back. The main recipients of the Midlanders' violence was the small gathering of Rovers' greasers. One in particular got a severe beating at the back of the Tote End. I can recall seeing him prostrate on the ground, barely moving; it was a sickening and disturbing sight, but, like a rubber-necker at the scene of a car crash, I found it difficult to look away.

One of the Brummies appeared in court on the Monday and was giving a derisory fine after stating, 'Two Rovers kids who were Hells Angels started following us. We got in first, I kicked this kid once, it was either him or us, we thought they were going to work us over. I was wearing working boots... I tripped over him, someone put the boot in but it wasn't me.' Putting the boot in was becoming a way of life for many... and it was a way of life I was soon to take up myself.

If that Saturday's events weren't bad enough for Rovers fans, the following Monday's friendly game at Newport County proved just as eventful. In a crowd of under 2,000, over 200 youths from both sides battled it out on the terraces. One Rovers fan ended up in hospital with serious head injuries after a group of Newport youths charged through the crowd waving metal chains.

Two weeks later, the new season kicked off with, once again, the *Evening Post* reporting that authorities were determined to stamp out the trouble. 'SOCCER BOVVER SQUAD IN ACTION', they declared, more in hope than anything else, but the opening weeks of the new season brought more violence than ever before with serious crowd disturbances across the country. From Plymouth to Aberdeen, the boot boys were stamping their authority and throwing down the gauntlet to the police and the use of weapons in particular was causing alarm. This was no more true than at Highbury where, among the many who were arrested for fighting, was a youth from Swindon who was fined for being in possession of a tin opener at the Arsenal v Manchester United game – I can only assume it was not an electric one.

I'm not trying to make light of events that happened nearly four decades ago or even romanticise the skinhead movement. Many of them were bad lads who enjoyed nothing better than a ruck and whose only rationale for kicking the living shit out of someone they didn't like was just that – they didn't like them. But, like me and my mates who I hung around with a few years after the Never boys were causing mayhem, these lads thought, rightly or wrongly, that a lot of their escapades were just 'high spirits' that often would get out of hand, inevitably leading to violence and, at times, serious injury and incarceration.

This violence is not something that can be denied; it was a violent time and something that should be remembered by today's tub-thumpers who regularly berate modern youth on how 'it was safer to walk the streets 40 years ago'. The plain truth is: it wasn't. The papers from those days are full of reports of stabbings, robberies and vicious assaults; there were even reports of 'a gang of knife-wielding coloured youths' or 'the shadow gang' as the local press dubbed them, who were based in Stokes Croft and who would jump out from shop doorways and demand money with menaces from passing pedestrians. The word 'mugging' had not entered the language of the day.

This little island of ours has long been a violent place. Today's much-maligned youth are no better or no worse than their parents, grandparents and, in some cases, great-grandparents. 'Victorian values' is a figment of Tory politicians' imagination. Where do they think the original 'hooligans' came from? If you want a real eye-opener, read *Hooligan – A History of Respectable Fears* by Geoffrey Pearson for an amazing insight into the history of the British hooligan. What must be remembered, however, is that becoming a skinhead is not about making a fashion statement. If you were prepared to wear the boot, then you were prepared to use – and receive it – as General George 'old blood and guts' Patton once said, 'A soldier in shoes is only a soldier, but in boots he becomes a warrior.'

The Bar Celona reunion brought a lot of the old 'warriors' out from the comfort of their armchairs and their slippers. I was a tad disappointed that few, if any, wore any of their old clothing from back in the day, although judging by the waistlines on show even if they did still own any it was unlikely it would still fit. At least Angelo Pascoe made an effort – his brogues looked as polished and pristine as the day he must have first bought them.

WARRIORS IN BOOTS

Of course, at the time, although you were aware that you were part of a 'scene', you didn't really appreciate just how significant it all was. Your threads were just that – threads – that would be updated and replaced as quickly as the 'scene' itself was updated.

One of the lads who turned up that night and who was an original Never boy was Chris, still looking as fit and trim as he was nearly 40 years previously. In fact, he had more hair now than he did then and a moustache to rival those of his old enemies, the greasers. After several phone calls, I arranged to meet him in the centre of Bristol.

'Where do you fancy meeting?' I asked.

'How about the Way Inn?' replied Chris.

'Sorry, mate, been shut about 30 years,' I replied.

Fortunately, when we did meet, in the aforementioned Horse and Groom, Chris's memory had been restored and we spent an enjoyable evening reliving those distant days, only this time he didn't have to keep on eye on the door for the law who regularly visited the hostelry searching for under-age drinkers.

Chris, like Lloyd, who also joined us for the evening, was born in 1950 and started frequenting the Never at the age of 16. At the time, he lived in Knowle West and recalled buying his first boots at an army surplus store in Bedminster. Like Eugene, he remembered being skint most of the time so couldn't afford a scooter. 'Couldn't even afford to buy any records,' he recalled. He brought along one of the younger members of the 'crew', Pat 'Paddy' Walsh, who, along with his brother Martin, were up there with the Pascoes, the Stones (Andy and Paul) and the legendary Roy and Mike Thorne as 'top boys' on the town circuit.

Chris and Paddy both remembered the fracas at The Star pub where, allegedly, 'that axe' was used, but again the memory became selective. They both admitted to being involved in the clashes in and around the city centre with the greasers, recalling how a mob of them would go to the greasers' café but how they would only send four or five to gather outside to goad the greasers into coming out, where they would then face the full force of the gathered Never boys. Again, the devilment inside them was the main cause of the mayhem. Paddy recalled his brother Martin 'taking a pair of scissors out with him, not as a weapon but to go around the Locarno cutting the ties in half of other lads'. You can only guess at the reaction from the 'victims' – the consequences likewise can only be imagined.

Fights in the dancehalls were a common occurrence. I read of one in the Locarno in the *Evening Post* from late 1969 that resulted in one poor lad receiving 200 stitches in a face wound after being attacked with a glass. The boots may have been outlawed on the dancefloors but the result of a 'glassing' were just as serious, if not more so. The fighting in the Locarno or the Top Rank, whether over a girl, a spilled drink or, more often than not, just a look ('You dogging I up?' would often be the precursor to a smack in the mouth) led to police being stationed in the clubs themselves. The Bali Hai became a battleground, the pint mug became a weapon of mass destruction and the acrid smell of Brut filled your nostrils – all to a blistering backing track featuring Jamaica's finest. Desmond Dekker, Jimmy Cliff and The Maytals sung of freedom, wonderful worlds and pomp and pride while blood flowed and stained the polished maple sprung dancefloor.

Chris recalled another weapon being used with devastating effect one Christmas when the BBC's Radio One Club visited the Top Rank for a live broadcast – as it turns out, the only one in history that was ever cancelled live on air due to the disorder. 'We heard that the Radio One Club was in the Top Rank that night so one of the boys paid to get in then let the rest of us in by opening the side door. The bouncers (who truly lived up to their name in those days) knew we had done this so they were looking for us.

WARRIORS IN BOOTS

'Once we got in, we mingled with the crowd. We saw a handbell on stage so we nicked it and would ring it to annoy the bouncers, because they could not see who had it. Later, we went upstairs where I bumped into one bouncer who I had frequent encounters with. I had the bell and he asked me for it so I said, "Are you sure you want it?" He said yes, so I gave it to him right on the head.'

In a way, the bouncer got off lightly; the weapon could have been a lot worse. On a trip to London, a group of the Never lads visited the Imperial War Museum in Lambeth where one of the boys tried to purloin a World War II machine-gun from a display – thankfully, he didn't succeed.

It was inevitable that Barney's trusty fruit and veg wagon would come up again. Paddy remembered how his brother Martin would 'hold on to bars on the back as Barney drove around the Pithay, then lift his legs off as he careered around the corners... thought he was Superman!' It seemed many of the lads thought at some stage they were super heroes, from moonwalking around the Top Rank in homage to Neil Armstrong, to their choice of stylised, sometimes even uniform clothing. The language, the swagger, but mostly the attitude set them apart from the rest of the proletariat.

At the time, Chris was a kitchen porter, Pat was still at school and Lloyd, like Eugene, was an apprentice engineer. But, unlike their predecessors, the aspirational and elitist mods who proclaimed 'mods didn't do sweat', the skinheads 'did do sweat' and were fiercely proud of their working-class roots, even their 'Britishness', despite coming from backgrounds as diverse as Ireland, Jamaica and, as with the Pascoe brothers, Italy.

True mods with their narcissistic splendour strove to leave their working-class backgrounds behind them – it could be argued they were the first yuppies. They looked to French art-house films, Italian Soho coffee bars and American jazz musicians for their inspiration. Skinheads looked to the military, American astronauts and Jamaican rude boys for theirs. Mod was a way of life; skinheads, on their own admission, were more one-dimensional and lived for the weekends and the immediate satisfaction that went with it. They set their sights slightly lower.

Paolo Hewitt, the mod historian and author of such books as *The Soul Stylists — 40 Years of Modernism* and *My Favourite Shirt: A History of Ben Sherman Style*, when asked to write an essay in school about 'what you most want out of life' chose to write a two-page treatise on the attributes of a blue window-pane-check trim-fit Brutus Gold shirt. His classmates no doubt wrote of train drivers, nurses and the astronaut heroes of that era.

Personally at the age of 13, I longed to emulate the young skinhead who worked on the paper-sack wagon that came down our street. I thought Mervyn from Lawrence Weston had the best job in the world, standing atop the caged lorry, stomping down the sacks that were chucked up to him by his colleagues, stripped to the waist with his braces hanging down, his oversized bovver boots doing the business with extreme efficiency. If Richard Allen's Joe Hawkins had lived in Bristol and not the East End of London, he would have been called Mervyn and instead of being a coalman he would have worked on the paper-sack lorry. Mervyn was my hero.

Apart from setting my sights on those paper sacks, I also longed for a pair of Monkey boots, as did Pat Walsh, who recalled travelling to Camden in North London with his mum to get his as they couldn't be found on the streets of Bristol. Brutus Gold shirts and Monkey boots…we were easily pleased in those days.

5

Dancin', Sounds and the Dear Old 'Loccy'

Brothers often seem to be at the heart of trouble, whether on the mean streets of Bristol or the meaner ones of the Krays' East London manor. Sibling rivalry, as well as a deep bonding, meant that it was inevitable, if you had a row with one, you invariably had a row with two. The previously mentioned Thornes, Walshes, Pascoes and Stones were notorious back then. One of these brothers, Andy Stone, lived in my neck of the woods, Brentry, the smaller, rougher council estate next to Henbury (or Henburberry as it's now known). He sent me his recollections of a typical weekend in 1969. In his own inimitable style, he remembers those days like they were yesterday:

'Friday night. Travelled over to The Bell pub in Stapleton to meet up with the Pickerings (Lee and the twins John and Dave), Ginger Evans, Twiggy and others. Had a few beers and made our way to The Horse and Groom. Met up with the rest of the lads, my brother Paul, Brian Coombs, Mike Thorne, Martin and Pat Walsh, Lloyd, Herbie and others (too many names to mention). After a few more beers decided we would go to The Way Inn. A few guys outside The

BOOTED AND SUITED

Pineapple started shouting abuse at us... some of our group walked over to them and asked them to be quiet. SORTED. Arrived at The Way Inn, barman gave us six-for-one before two-for-one was invented. Soon it was closing time so walked to the Centre and met up with my girlfriend (now my wife Debbie) who had been out with her mates.

'The Centre was packed when a few of our friends from across the Bristol Channel started scrapping with a few of the lads. I think their coach had to stop at the B.R.I [Bristol Royal Infirmary]. for a few running repairs before they got home. Arrived at the Never and ordered Viennese steak, chips and peas for Deb and me (did I know how to treat a girl!!). Saw Tony Simms, asked him if I could borrow his minibus to take Deb and her mates home. On the way back to town saw Colin Moore — somebody had attacked him with a metal comb. Drove around for a while but could not find people who did it. Got back home about 2am.

'Saturday night. The BIG night out — been waiting for this all week. Pick up Debbie from her house, borrow her dad's car and drove to The Bell, meet up with the Pickerings and the rest of the lads from that side of town and their girlfriends. Travelled to The Horse and Groom and met up with the rest of the lads. Ended up in the Top Rank, most did not pay to get in as somebody had opened the emergency door by the Never café. Most of the night was spent drinking and dancing. Most of us blokes thought we were great dancers but I don't think the girls did.

"At the end of the night somebody said there was a party at a house on the outskirts of Whitchurch so we all got in cars, scooters and fruit lorry. When we got there we were greeted by a guy giving out free cigs and cigars. There was a table about ten feet long filled with booze situated by the swimming pool. We thought we were dreaming, somebody said the guy's parents had won the football pools. We were having a great time when somebody (we did not

DANCIN', SOUNDS AND THE DEAR OLD 'LOCCY'

know) threw one of our girlfriends in the pool. All hell broke loose — we were hitting blokes all over the place. End of what could have been a great party. Got back home about 6am.

'Sunday. Arranged to meet Debbie and her mates in Weston-super-Mare in the afternoon. My brother Paul and me were picked up at our house by Brian Coombs in his Consul Convertible (pre-MOTs). We thought we were the bollocks with the roof down. Halfway up Falcondale Road the clutch was slipping so Paul, Ossie Hardwick and myself ended up pushing the car to the top of the hill. How we got to WSM I do not know.

"Got to Weston at last, found out a few of the lads had a bit a trouble in a bar could The Doll's House, so we met up with the Pickerings, Walshes, Thorney etc. and walked around to the club. The Weston lads did not realise only two of them could get out of the club door at one time, so we waited outside and baited them. As they came out, they were dealt with. Meanwhile, Debbie had managed to get thrown in the boating pool and Lloyd, forever the gentleman, let her have his jumper. I do not know to this day if he ever got it back. Because of the trouble in Weston that day the police closed all roads out of Weston, but we found a way out! The toll road — what a cheap price two bob. Ended up back in Bristol in the Horse and Groom. Back to work on Monday. Roll on next Friday.'

As an afterthought, Andy added, 'I know we have all moved on since those days, but they were brilliant. As the man said, "Long gone, but not forgotten."'

Another lad who frequented the Never back in the day was 'Dobbsy' Sellwood who, at the time, lived in Knowle. As in Pat Walsh's recollections, he also travelled to London, not just for his footwear but also for the clothing. As well as being a terror on the terraces, Dobbsy was known for his sartorial style and, unlike some of the others I was to interview, he quite clearly

BOOTED AND SUITED

remembered the first time he spotted the boot boys: '1968 in the Croydon area of South London.'

Dobbsy had relatives there and, as well as following Bristol Rovers (as did Paddy Walsh), he also had an allegiance to Crystal Palace. He continued, 'They would have been Palace and Millwall fans. I was 15 years old and fell for the clothes, the reggae, the gorgeous skinhead girls and the excitement of the whole scene. I became one of the Tote End Boot Boys.'

In common with all the other lads that I had spoken to, Dobbsy confirmed that their enemy of choice was the greaser, but conversely on the Rovers' terraces, unlike at Ashton Gate, their differences were put aside for the honour of the club, something which was quite evident in the incident at the Maritas café. 'We hated greasers, although, funnily enough, a lot of our fans were greasers. We fought with other skins at football – they used to chant "soap and water" at the greasers because they were so filthy, but it still caused offence to us, so we stuck together with the greasers for the cause.'.

Dobbsy was an archetypal, stereotypical skinhead, but, whereas most of the Never boys wouldn't be seen dead fraternising with the greasers, he didn't seem to have a problem with it. He also frequented Cora's café on Colston Avenue and the well-known Rovers' café and haunt of the greasers, the Monte Carlo on Stapleton Road. 'Full of 'em but they were Tote Enders,' he recalls.

As well as remembering where he first laid eyes on the early skinheads, he quite clearly recalled where he bought his clothing and footwear. He even reckoned he was one of the first Bristolians to wear Doc Martens. 'I bought them in Jacobs in Old Market for about £2 15s (£2.75) in 1969.' He also recalled buying his first Ben Sherman, a yellow one, on the King's Road in London for about £2 10s (£2.50) and shrink-to-fit Levi's for £3. 'You had to sit in the bath for hours to get them to fit,' Dobbsy added.

DANCIN', SOUNDS AND THE DEAR OLD 'LOCCY'

I asked him if he still had any items of clothing from back then. 'No, but I still wear similar clothing, like button-down shirts, Levi's – but full-length now, not short. A smart pair of "Weejun" loafers [hand-made, all-leather slip-on shoes] – classic look, still instantly recognisable to anyone from that era.'

Although Dobbsy clearly retained a great deal of affection with the original skinhead era, he wasn't so enamoured with the second wave that emerged later. 'Skins and suedeheads naturally progressed to smoothies. The second generation of skins in the late Seventies lost the edge in clothing, music and politics,' he declared wistfully.

'Have you got any regrets about being a skinhead?' I asked.

'No regrets. Had a great time. Still see a lot of people from that era who are like-minded. Could have done without the criminal record though!' he answered with a wink.

Ian 'Adge' Haddrell, back then a young skinhead from Horfield, was a contemporary of Dobbsy and likewise followed Rovers and a London club, in this instance Chelsea, but, while Dobbsy recalled his first glimpse of skinheads, Adge was unsure of exactly when it may have been. He recalled seeing pockets of them in Bristol in late 1968 but his first mass sighting was in March 1969 at a Chelsea v Manchester United match at Stamford Bridge, where he was amazed not only at the size of the crowd (63,000) but also at 'the number of skinheads walking along the Fulham Road to the ground'. He also remembered the media's obsession with them.

'There was a considerable amount of media coverage about the emergent youth culture and the violence that accompanied it. I do remember that some of the articles dealt with the fashion of the skinheads – both male and female. This would have been around 1969–70. As I regularly attended football, I was drawn to being a skinhead together with my mates as that was what many working-class young males were doing. It also served that basic human need to belong to an identifiable group.'

Adge, like Dobbsy, also remembered his first Doc Martens if not his first pair of boots. 'Doc Martens identified you as a skinhead. They became associated with the culture of bovver more than anything else – and they were very comfortable to walk in. I think that's why I kept them for so long after I ceased being a skinhead. I bought them for £4 19s 6d (£4.97)'.

Like a lot of skinheads, though, Adge wasn't as 'hard' in front of his parents as he was in front of his mates. He smiled as he added, 'For a long time, I kept them in the garage, not telling my parents, and put them on once I'd left the house in my "sensible" shoes!'

Once changed into his more streetwise Docs, Adge would often head to the RCA record shop in Montpelier. 'Saturday mornings became somewhat of a ritual visiting Roy's record shop in Picton Street, prior to going into town shopping, watching Rovers or playing football. It was in Roy's shop that I spent a good proportion of my hard-earned cash, paid to me as an apprentice with a local engineering company, on "sounds". At school, I was very much into Motown and popular reggae, such as that offered on *Trojan Chartbusters* albums. I already had the basis of a collection of Tamla Motown singles, supplemented by some American imports on the "Soul" and "Gordy" record labels.

'However, it was following these regular visits to Picton Street that my interest in soul music burgeoned and my singles collection grew rapidly. The format of a visit to Roy's shop was always the same. I would take along the latest copy of *Blues and Soul* magazine, which provided British and American R&B singles and albums charts, features on soul singers and groups and, most importantly for me, reviews of the latest releases, both 45s and LPs. Selecting from the chart list or review in the *B&S*, Roy would be asked to play the particular record on the turntable

DANCIN', SOUNDS AND THE DEAR OLD 'LOCCY'

located behind the counter – invariably he had it, no matter how obscure. In most cases, this would be the first time that I heard the song and, depending on whether I liked it or not, made the decision to purchase or send it back to its place on the closely packed shelves. Sometimes, a few bars from the record were sufficient to indicate whether it was going to join my collection or not, but often the whole record was played in an attempt to make a decision. Throughout this oft-repeated ritual, Roy remained impassive, playing record after record without comment. I never knew what music he really liked.*

'The shop was tiny and six customers would practically fill the small interior. As well as white youths buying soul records, the shop was regularly frequented by older West Indians buying ska, reggae and Blue Beat records. They, too, went through the same procedure as me, requesting Roy to play their selected "sound". Very often, once a record started playing the requestor and his mate – there always seemed to be two of them – would begin laughing out loud at the lyrics being sung. As my comprehension of West Indian patois was fairly limited at the time, I didn't have a clue what these songs that were causing such amusement were about, although I suspect that due to the nature of many reggae songs ("Wet Dream" – Max Romeo, "Wreck a Pum Pum" – Prince Buster) there was a sexual connotation to them. The tunes were always good, though!

'Not only did I buy the latest releases at Roy's but I also started to build up my collection of older classic soul records that pre-dated my interest in R&B music. Some notable sounds purchased from Picton Street were Sonny Charles and The Checkmates' "Black Pearl", Eddie

---

* I also recall Roy's indifference to the very music he sold. You would assume that such a specialist shop as his would be run by an enthusiastic collector, just like his customers no doubt were, but I found out in later years that, in fact, Roy couldn't abide the music, reggae in particular, simply seeing it as a market to exploit.

BOOTED AND SUITED

Floyd's "Bring It on Home to Me", American Poets' "She Blew a Good Thing", Contours' "Just a Little Misunderstanding", J J Barnes's "Please Let Me In", and Doris Troy's "I'll Do Anything".'

Like Dobbsy, Adge remembered the obsession with clothing and the detail of the hand-made suits in particular. 'We used to have our trousers and jackets made to measure by a tailor in Broadmead called Jacksons. You went in one week to be measured up and pay your deposit, then returned the following week to pick up the finished garment and pay the balance. It was important to have your trousers exactly in fashion, being prescriptive about the width of the trouser legs, width of the turn-ups, and having a ticket pocket. Similarly, jackets had to have a certain length for the centre vent, a specific style and width of lapels, and also a specified number of buttons on the sleeves.'

Once you had picked up your treasured suit, there was only one thing to do – pose. Adge continued, 'Many of the dancehalls and discos within pubs were playing Motown and reggae, so it attracted us. I used to go to the Locarno on a Monday night with mates, where we'd meet other skinheads. It was an opportunity to wear *de rigueur* black brogues with extra leather soles and my favourite brown suit and light-green Ben Sherman, together with a tie pin through a silk handkerchief in the top pocket, which was an absolute must.'

During my interviews and research, the loveable old 'Loccy' ballroom was getting as many mentions as the Never café. It was a place I also frequented in the early Seventies as well as the late Seventies when it changed its name to The Studio and bands such as The Jam, The Clash and U2 appeared there. One can only imagine what effect it had on the youngsters of Bristol when it opened as part of the New Entertainments Centre in 1966; up until then, the Corn Exchange and The Glen, later Tiffany's, on

DANCIN', SOUNDS AND THE DEAR OLD 'LOCCY'

the Downs had been the main ports of call for the lads and lasses about town.

This place wasn't just big, it was huge – at the time, it was the largest entertainment centre of its kind in Europe, boasting not only the legendary Locarno but also an ice rink, a cinema, more than a dozen licensed bars, a casino and the Heartbeat (later Raquels) disco, where (allegedly) Jimi Hendrix relaxed after appearing at the Loccy, although the rumours of him enjoying a brown split can't be confirmed. At its height, this leviathan concrete complex built by Mecca for a cost of £2 million pulled in 5,000 punters a night, 2,000 of whom could fit in the Locarno alone.

The *Evening Post* reported of its opening night on 19 May 1966, 'There were girls in grass skirts who brought on the pineapple confection for the buffet supper. There was a glitter and glow of myriad lights... an atmosphere of rich opulent intimacy warming the place in a way not to be expected. Guests were served in the South Seas climate of the Bali Hai bar, in the swish Le Club bar and by check-waistcoated, bowler-hatted barmen in the Victorian bar.' No mention of the Neanderthal Teddy-Boy bouncers waiting to punch your lights out and chuck you down those concrete stairs, though.

It had been a pivotal year; not only had the Locarno opened but England were the 1966 World Cup winners, the cult of the mod had gone mainstream and the scooter boys were in the ascendancy. It seems an appropriate juncture, therefore, to include some memories from those pre-skinhead 'Sawdust Caesars'. Steve Holloway, a young mod who then lived in Southmead, recalled a defining moment. For many like him, it was a rite of passage, a battle of wills between cunning youth and animalistic brawn. Once you had passed this milestone, there was no going back, it marked the transition from a boy to a man – getting past the gorilla in a suit at the door of the Bali Hai bar.

BOOTED AND SUITED

'I well remember my elation, aged about 16, at getting my first "brown split" in a mug with a handle, not a sleever, in the Bali Hai bar in the Locarno, after getting past the bouncer. If I remember rightly, the bouncer used to stand at the entrance to the bar by the totem pole.'

Another mod from back then, Chris Powell, was so enamoured with the Locarno that when it was demolished in 1997 he managed to salvage the famed totem pole as well as many of the signs from the ballroom, including a bright-red one that will be remembered by many. 'The bouncers' warning sign... this was positioned opposite the DJ. If there was any "trouble" within the Locarno, a panic button would be hit and the area in which the trouble was located would be illuminated. The DJ would then broadcast a coded message to the bouncers and the trouble would be "politely" dealt with.'

Chris lovingly restored the totem pole and it now adorns his garage. 'We used to put out our Embassy dog-ends up the nostril on the pole. When I painted it, I found one still in place!'

Chris recalled a famous night in Bristol in 1967 when the doyens of the mod movement paid a visit to the Locarno. '1967 was a very special year for me. London had begun swinging the previous year, England were the World Cup Champions and I turned 15. While London had its trendy discos and clubs, Bristol had always lagged behind, with gigs taking place at the Corn Exchange and occasionally The Top Rank opposite Bridewell nick. However, this was all to change with the opening of the New Bristol Centre and particularly the Locarno towards the end of 1966.

'At last, Bristol had an entertainment centre to be proud of and a decent venue for bands to play. I was introduced to the Locarno by a school friend by the name of Chris Reeves, who had already sussed out the location and the fact that Monday nights were for 14–18-year-olds, and that it was *the* place for

DANCIN', SOUNDS AND THE DEAR OLD 'LOCCY'

chatting up the local Bristol talent. This was heaven to two 15-year-old single-sex schoolboys. If you were really lucky, you might even get served a half of Woodpecker in the Bali Hai bar.

'The Locarno became our Monday-night haunt. Smooth wasn't the word, what with our blue mohair suits (£15 from John Collier in Broadmead) with slant pockets, ticket pocket and rear centre vent (the longer the better), the obligatory Ben Sherman shirt and the thin tie, we were the business – or so we thought. However, real mods rode on Lambrettas, not the number 8 bus from Kingswood. Word came about that *the* mod band of the moment, The Who, would be playing the Locarno in May 1967, and Chris and myself decided to attend. The first obstacle was the entrance price of 8s 6d (yes, 42p in today's money). However, a plea to my parents raised the readies and I was off.

'The queue stretched all the way down the steps and halfway up Frogmore Street, and attracted the main "faces" on the Bristol scene. After about an hour, I reached the front of the queue, deposited my 8s 6d and met Chris inside, slap-bang in the centre of the balcony. Class seats for a class band.

'The Who were scheduled to start at around 8.30pm. Eight-thirty came and went, as did nine. Eventually, at just gone ten, they appeared – Roger, John, Pete and Keith. They may have been there in body, although I have grave doubts whether they were really there in spirit, as they all seemed to be on another level – I never had that problem with my illicit half of Woodpecker. The level of sound that reached what remained of the crowd's eardrums was deafening with the boys going straight into "I Can't Explain", swiftly followed by "Anyway, Anyhow, Anywhere" and the mod's favourite, "My Generation". This was class. This was history in the making.

'Around that time, The Who had a reputation for smashing their equipment and this evening was to be no different. Pete made short work of the loudspeakers with his guitar, and Keith demolished his very impressive drum set with a 'small' charge of explosive. After a quick repair/replacement job, they proceeded on to "I'm a Boy", "Happy Jack" and their latest hit "Pictures of Lily" and then they were gone. Forty-five minutes of sheer quality and I was travelling home on the number 8 bus. Within two years, The Who were playing gigantic stadia, with even higher plains to reach.'

Chris then explained how he came about owning the various mementos, including that totem pole. 'During 1997, I learned that most of the New Bristol Centre was to be demolished to make way for student accommodation, and I found myself again in Frogmore Street for one final look. I took the escalators (now sadly broken) up to the old Locarno and was amazed to find the entrance ajar. The site foreman very kindly allowed me to take a walk round the old haunt before the bulldozers moved in and also agreed that I could have the old gents "Stag Room" sign that now adorns my bathroom!

'I spent about an hour in the Locarno before it was finally sealed, taking photos and reminiscing about the Sixties. I stood on the stage where so many class acts had performed and excited Bristol's youth – none more so than The Who – and wondered if demolition was the only way forward for the building. But then again, The Who would probably have wanted it that way!'

Once the lads finished posing under the illuminated ceiling of the ballroom, it was time to pose on the streets of Bristol. Jim Burnham – the mod who had a close encounter with the Never boys' fruit wagon one night and who's still very much part of the latter-day mod scene, recalled, like Adge and Chris, that Monday was one of the main nights of the week. 'Coming out of the Locarno on Monday nights, and seeing all the scoots parked outside the Hatchet pub – maybe 30 of 'em – magnificent! Then we'd start 'em up – the noise and smell of two-stroke engines echoing around the buildings, then we'd just ride up and down,

DANCIN', SOUNDS AND THE DEAR OLD 'LOCCY'

past the Entertainment Centre, maybe three or four times, just showing off and trying to impress the birds. No crash helmets in them days either, maybe a bobble hat if it was a bit cold! To me, as a 16-year-old, it was pure joy – scooter heaven!'

Sixteen seemed to be when these lads came of age; it was then you were able to buy your beloved 'scoot'. Chris Powell remembered the significance of reaching that momentous age. 'Once you'd reached the magical age of 16, you needed to get yourself a scoot, and you could either do this from the motorbike section in the *Evening Post* on Friday, or visit one of the dealers. The two main dealers in Bristol were King's and Grey's which were situated in Stokes Croft. Both had vast stocks of Lambrettas and Vespas and one shop always priced theirs in "guineas" which was an old term and related to 21 shillings (£1.05 in new money). This made the bike look cheaper than it was!'

Chris, like the younger lads I had interviewed, recalled the clothing. Much of it was similar to the skinhead/suedehead gear of a few years later. 'Suits were generally made to measure at places such as Burton's, Hepworth's and John Collier. Cost around £15–£20 all in, mainly two-piece, three-button (covered) with slant pockets, and a ticket pocket. Rear vent – as long as possible. These started around six inches and progressed higher and higher, as Jackie Wilson sang, up your back with some ending between your shoulder blades! Fourteen-inch bottoms with no turn-ups. Colour: dark with a nice herring-bone weave; sleeve buttons: anywhere between three and six on each side.'

My brother Mike also recalled the long, long vents in the jackets which sometimes gathered unwanted attention from certain lads in the dancehalls. 'You want a long vent, do you? Well, fucking 'ave this!' as they proceeded to rip the jacket in half. Not surprisingly, it was at that point that the bouncers' red light would often be illuminated and the gorillas in the mist would earn their pay.

BOOTED AND SUITED

It's incredible to think that the clothing from four decades ago can be remembered in such fine detail. I might be wrong but somehow I can't see today's 'yoof' getting all dewy-eyed remembering their present-day attire in 40 years' time – Ecko trackie bottoms made out of a nice nylon/polyester mix purchased from JD Sports for a tenner... not quite the same as one of Burton's finest, but then again I'm biased. And I've got half a brain.

In the mid- to late Sixties, Bristol became the centre for entertainment for youngsters from all across the West Country. Colin Birch was a young mod who lived in Yeovil at the time and, as well as the Locarno, remembered other cool hang-outs. 'Bristol was the Holy Grail of entertainment and scootering outside of London for our immaculately turned-out gang. Thursday nights straight after work we headed for Bristol to the Corn Exchange where Thursdays was the Rhythm, Blues & Soul night... just about anybody famous did a gig there. We saw Clapton, Geno Washington and the Ram Jam Band, John Lee Hooker, The Faces. Saturday nights was either ten-pin bowling, followed by egg and chips and a coffee at Aust Services or, if there was enough of us not to get yer head kicked in, we would head for the Bamboo Club.'

6
The Never-ending Story

Many of those who managed to avoid getting their heads kicked in no doubt moved on to become the hard mods, the cropheads and the skinheads as the years progressed. As the Sixties ended and the Seventies began, the skinhead style, once firmly identified, tagged and analysed by the British media as Adge had recalled, lost its harshness somewhat and, in the absence of style guides and fashion bibles (*The Face* was a decade away), the young doe-eyed wannabe skinheads had to rely on the good old *Daily* and *Sunday Mirror* for updates on what the bad boys of London were wearing. Under headlines such as AGGRO: THE CULT OF THE BOVVER BOYS, BOOT-IN DOWN WATER LANE and the insightful 'DOWN AMONG THE BOVVER BOYS' the tabloids ranted, raved but finally admitted that 'away from trouble, they are so normal'.

Harry 'the Spider' Carrock, an 18-year-old ex-Hells Angel and carpet-layer who claimed his nickname was given to him because when he put the boot in it looked like he had eight legs, got a full-page exposé complete with moody photo, while a grim-looking skinhead complete with sheepskin coat, braces and

BOOTED AND SUITED

Sta-Prest got the artist's impression look alongside the meaningless subhead 'LEVI'S, CLIP-ON BRACES AND BOOTS'. The military hardware of the previous years was disappearing rapidly – this newer, more stylish look was seized upon by the fashion industry with high-street stores up and down the country rushing to fill their shelves and racks with ever more colourful Sta-Prests, Fair Isle sweaters and gingham button-down check shirts. The aforementioned Brutus Gold in particular, successfully competed with the more expensive Ben Shermans in bringing out ever more colourful patterns and designs. The cult was now becoming a fashion, reaching back to its mod origins to cherry-pick its favourite stock. Crombie overcoats as favoured by the rude boys, Loake loafers, Baracutta 'Harrington' golfing jackets and the cool constant of street style, the Fred Perry polo shirt, were to become compulsory wear over the next year or so. But, while the look was changing, the attitude was not. While the rest of the world knew nothing of this ever-so-secret British street club with its penchant for city-gent attire and American college-boy class, its membership grew by the week to become the epitome of working-class pride and fury. Short hair, short tempers and a love of one's country – it was to become a deadly combination.

As the Seventies progressed, Britain lurched from crisis to crisis. Unemployment and class, as well as race-conflict, came to the fore. The dregs of the skinhead movement descended into a bitter pit of bigotry and hatred, forever to be remembered, rather harshly, as the 'Oi'-loving tattooed racists of a decade later. As George Marshall, the skinhead historian, put it in the excellent *Spirit of '69 – A Skinhead Bible*, 'In the national horror league, skinheads weigh in somewhere between serial killers and devil dogs. It's as if shaving your head and lacing up a pair of DMs turns you into some sort of dangerous alien life form.'

These Never boys may have been tough but 'alien life forms'

THE NEVER-ENDING STORY

they weren't. These were the lads who skanked and sang along to 'Young, Gifted and Black', the lads who raised Desmond Dekker to number 1 in the charts and the same lads who lined up alongside the West Indian youths to fight the swastika-clad Hells Angels on the streets of Bristol during that red-hot summer of 1969.

So what brought about the demise of the Never? Not surprisingly, the Never's decline mirrored that of the skinheads themselves — any street cult worth its salt has a life-span of just three to four years and so, by the end of 1971, the cult of the skinhead was on the wane. The skinhead movement was no different to that of the mod and, in later years, the punk. By the time the cult went mainstream and the media and the schoolkids had discovered it, the instigators of it all were hanging up their boots, growing their hair and the cult was dying an ignominious death, only to be resurrected a few years later as a crude parody of its former glorious life.

On top of that, the law were at last getting organised and managing to keep a lid on the trouble, at the seaside resorts at any rate. When the bovver boys invaded Weston yet again on the Easter Monday of 1971, the law were waiting and 'Operation Skinhead' went into operation. The plan was simple: stop and search every youth on their arrival at the station, relieve them of their weaponry — boots, knives, studded belts, plastic hoses filled with lead, steel combs and knuckle-dusters — and break them up into small manageable groups and move them on their way. Throughout the day, only ten arrests were made.

The operation was deemed a great success as many of the skinheads left early and headed back to Bristol minus their weapons. 'The police made things very tough for us,' one 18-year-old beltless, combless skinhead from Bristol claimed.

He got off lightly. Seventy or so miles away, as the seagull flies, across the Bristol Channel I was getting my head stoved in by

BOOTED AND SUITED

Swansea skinheads. Perhaps I should have gone to Weston and strolled along the prom, prom, prom with my mates, with or without my boots.

One of the other reasons that the Easter weekend was relatively quiet in Weston, if not Swansea, may have been because the skinheads' old enemy, the Hells Angels, made a detour and headed for the small Somerset town of Axbridge where 70 of them, mainly from London, gatecrashed a dance at the village hall where they terrorised the locals, forcing them to flee as both male and female members of the gang began to strip naked. They obviously weren't used to that Somerset scrumpy and those Adge Cutler songs.

The last great invasion of Weston by the Bristol boot boys was the August Bank Holiday of 1971 when the same tactics were used as the previous Easter. For the first time in nearly three years, instead of reporting the violence, the *Evening Post* was able to smugly declare: PEACE AT SEASIDE AS YOUTHS ARE FRISKED. Only four youths were arrested and, as well as the usual array of weapons being confiscated, the first instance of 'umbrellas with sharpened tips' was reported. The skinheads were on their last legs. The smoothies were on the march, and waiting just around the corner were all those multicoloured tank tops and ludicrous platform shoes; the decade that fashion forgot was entering an even scarier stage.

Bob Feltham remembered the dying days of the skinhead movement. 'Towards the end of these days, I went into my "new" era, grew my hair and I started to frequent Tiffany's with some of my close friends and met new friends who were students and living in Clifton.' This in itself shows just how far the lads had moved on – hanging round with students? How low could they go?

Bob continued, 'Rick Markham became a close friend and Rick and I took over running the disco at the Fisherman's Wharf

THE NEVER-ENDING STORY

on the Triangle, later to become Shades. It was after this time that many of the old crew moved away from town and started frequenting the Clifton clubs, culminating in the best club ever to exist in Bristol, Platform One, where I have also DJ'd on the odd occasion. It was here that I met my wife-to-be, Caroline, and the rest, as they say, is now history.' Indeed, quite a history. As the song by the late Ernie K Doe goes, 'Here come the girls'.

The vast majority of the clientele of the Never were lads – at times, it resembled a high-octane boys club, oozing with testosterone with more alpha males on display than your average gladiator movie. Not surprisingly, this attracted the girls like moths to a flame – some of them embraced the skinhead cult themselves, if not in the violent behaviour then certainly in the fashion stakes, with many of them wearing Ben Shermans, Levi jeans and, in some cases, boots. They may not have resorted to the males' aggressive behaviour, but it was not unknown for the girls to conceal the lads' weapons in their handbags on their visits to the seaside.

'Flange', Mary, Jo, the twins – Mary and Sue – were all remembered with affection by some of the guys I interviewed. Some, like the unfortunately monikered 'Line-up Liz', more so than others. One of the interviewees recalled how often a couple would disappear out the back door of the café to appear a 'few minutes later with the knees on the lad's jeans all white' – you can only guess that they weren't out there to discuss the merits of *Motown Chartbusters Volume 3*, the first compilation album to get to number 1 in the charts in February 1970.

Of course, the fairer sex have always calmed the savage brow and the girls of the Never were no exception – not that the boys changed their behaviour overnight. The violence on Bristol's streets continued but the Never café itself lost its appeal. There's a rather obvious reason for this – most of the lads from the Never were just teenagers. The very reason for them using the café in the first place was because they couldn't get into pubs and, once they could, alcohol and the company of the fairer sex exerted a far stronger pull than a bottle of Coke, a pinball machine or one of Jim's Viennese steaks.

From the café, they moved on to the previously mentioned pubs and clubs, often meeting up with their newly acquired 'birds', by the map, the favoured meeting place for young Bristolians in the city centre outside the Victorian toilets. Of course, if you weren't so 'flushed', the lads would arrange to meet the girls inside a club. 'That way, you didn't have to pay to get them in,' chuckled Lloyd on remembering the days when he first started 'courting'.

As stated previously, the café closed down for good in 1974. Jim Jr moved to London where, among other things, he got into the clothing business. He lived there for a number of years but returned to his home town to work back in cafés and eventually to open up the Roma restaurant and Bar Celona club where the old Never boys held their reunion.

The boys themselves, in the main, have changed their ways. Most of them are happily married, many to girls they met in the Never; many are fathers; some are grandfathers; quite a few are successful businessmen and entrepreneurs; several run their own companies. One I interviewed drives a Rolls-Royce, and at least one is a millionaire. Very few, if any, turned out to be career criminals.

Not surprisingly, few of them have real regrets of those days. They hold their heads up; to them, there's no stigma about being labelled an original skinhead, far from it. 'The best days of their lives,' many of them stated.

Even before the reunion at Jim's club, many of them kept in touch; the camaraderie has continued over the years and they regularly meet up with their wives for meals, even taking family holidays together.

THE NEVER-ENDING STORY

A café of sorts still stands in Fairfax Street, a tired, sad little establishment called the Soup and Sandwich. No longer do the top boys of Bristol frequent it; no longer are Trojan and Motown classics blasted out from the jukebox; and no longer are Lambrettas and Vespas lined up outside earning admiring looks. Like the Top Rank, the Locarno and the adrenalin-filled trips to the coast in Barney's fruit wagon, the Never on Sunday café has gone but, as one of those proud boys said, 'The Never café – never beaten, never bettered, never forgotten'.

As the lads who frequented the Never moved on, skinny little suedeheads like me moved in. Personally, I never frequented the café – I was too young, too small and, truth be told, too scared. The football terrace was to be my stomping ground, for the next decade or so anyway.

It was now my time... and my story.

Part II
The Seventies – A Decade of Disturbance

BOOTED AND SUITED

People who say they have no regrets generally mean the complete opposite. I would be lying if I said I had no such regrets. I now regret many of my actions from my formative years, but at the time the word 'regret' was not even in my vocabulary, neither was remorse. It seems that a book of this sort has to be justified, rationalised and, for whatever reason, vindicated. I have no intention of justifying the actions of myself or my peers and certainly not those of people I barely knew. This book is merely an observation and record of actual events which, at the time, seemed nothing out of the ordinary; indeed, this book could be penned by hundreds, if not thousands, of others just like me. It's not a novel or a collection of dubious anecdotes collated by an ill-informed 'keyboard warrior' — it's a true story, or as true as my memory allows it, of true people. Make of it what you will, draw your own conclusions.

Hidden deep amongst the pages of *The Guinness Book of British Hit Singles*, gathering dust and tucked away somewhere between the Moody Blues and Mott the Hoople lies a solitary and somewhat pathetic entry: 'Derrick Morgan; Jamaica, male vocalist; entered chart 17 January 1970; title: 'Moon Hop'; Crab record label, 1 week at number 49'. The ultimate insult, one week at number 49.

To the uninitiated and ignorant devotees of all things seventies, busily thumbing their way through to 'Ride a White Swan', 'Waterloo' and 'Stayin' Alive' ad nauseum, the so-say 'classic' records of that decade, it would barely warrant a second glance. To those who were cut from an altogether different cloth, however, it may strike a chord, maybe raise a smile in appreciation and even evoke a warm memory of the plastic palm trees and light splits of the Bali Hai bar and of the music of the Locarno ballroom.

'Moon Hop' entered the record charts in the first month of that momentous decade and was as much an 'underground'

PART II

record as any of those by the likes of King Crimson and Yes who are more readily tagged with that same irksome label. What's more, 'Moon Hop' does not stand alone; 'Movin'' by Brass Construction, 'Shadow' by the Lurkers, 'Another Girl, Another Planet' by the Only Ones all only had a nodding acquaintance with the charts but, nevertheless, their impact and influence remains immeasurable. Scratch away the veneer, scrape off the dross and dismiss the detritus and you will find the music and the fashion from an altogether different world – my world, a world of Tonik suits, terraces and The Maytals, of race riots, safety pins and The Clash by way of P.Funk, platform shoes and discos. The true story of the most maligned decade in British youth history, through my eyes – my fashion, my music, my violence. Welcome to the real 1970s – it ain't no Boogie Wonderland.

7
A History Lesson

I must have been ten, maybe eleven. Either way my physique wasn't up to much. I came running in with a face full of hate and anger, demanding pity. Through the snot and the tears, I blubbed to my old man, 'That... that older kiddy just hit me!'

'Well, go and 'it 'im back,' my father replied matter-of-factly. I detected a wink and a grin and did as I was told. The scene had been set.

As the dreamy, idealistic, liberal 1960s drew to an end, dear old Britannia, who had hitched up her skirt, kicked off her sandals and danced barefoot in the park with the rest of Timothy Leary's peace-loving hippies suddenly received an abrupt dose of reality, and a reminder that she was not quite ready to lose her head and her customs to a bunch of junkies from across the pond.

The 'hard mods' or 'peanuts' had arrived as younger, more dysfunctional, hippy-hating cousins of the mods in early 1968 and by mid-summer the following year, the newly named 'skinheads' – after a short flirtation with the 'cropheads' moniker – had quickly taken over as the cult for the disenchanted, white

A HISTORY LESSON

working-class youths of Britain. It had been a long hot summer of mounting violence and thumping reggae. Desmond Dekker topped the charts and bovver boots stomped across the nation. The new decade was bracing itself.

January 1970. *That* Derrick Morgan record drifted unnoticed in the nether regions of the pop charts while Rolf Harris sung about his 'Two Little Boys'. Crushed-velvet loon pants, flowers in the hair and ten-minute guitar solos were not for me. I was 14, a perfect age for a perfect era. In all honesty I wished I was older. I had observed and learned from the sidelines, pored over every tabloid newspaper screaming out in 72-point headlines, full of the daring deeds of my heroes rampaging through Margate and Weston, causing mayhem on every terrace in the country.

I'd had the regulation haircut, nicked my old man's clip-on braces and sat in the bath wearing my Levi's in a forlorn attempt to shrink them, resulting only in blue-stained legs and a bollocking from my mum. I'd furnished the end product with a neat half-inch turn-up, and on a visit to the ex-army stores in Hotwells Road I had purchased my suede zip-up bomber jacket and bought the boots. And these weren't just any boots: 30 bob's worth of ex-army leather and hobnails that were so big and heavy I had to walk three paces before they moved.

No wonder we walked in that distinctive way – the arrogant, bow-legged swagger, the arms thrust deep into pockets of short zip-up jackets or sheepskin coats, poking out at right angles, ready to annoy, aggravate, bovver anyone who dared to cross our paths. This was the only way to recognise a true skin – surprisingly not by the hair length, which varied in length from an admittedly rare number one to a more common short-back-and-sides. Nor by the boots for that matter, which were a fearsome and varied mixed of either ex-army hobnails, calf-length NATO Paratroopers, Big T Tuf industrials or the ultimate, terrifying footwear, NCB steel-toe-capped real McCoys. The walk, that's what identified the skin, the walk – once I had mastered the all-important 'fuck-off-outta-my-way' walk, I knew I had arrived.

I had arrived all right, arrived just in time for everything to change. In less than 12 short months, the skins had evolved. It was more a case of them having to: the law had declared steel toe caps and hobnails as offensive weapons and anyone found wearing them was likely to have them, or their laces, removed, or worse still, be arrested on sight. The hair, which was never as short as to truly warrant the tag 'skinhead', was growing and the clothes were getting distinctly smarter. The look, which had been as much about expressing your pride in your working-class background if not your fictional East End of London hardness with its collarless union shirts, granddad vests and everything ex-army, was being replaced by something altogether more cosmopolitan and more pragmatic, which the high-street clothes stores of Britain were more than willing to cater for.

Black, bottle-green and even Prince of Wales check Harringtons competed with blue denim and beige, needle-cord Levi's and Wranglers in the jacket stakes, while brilliant-white Levi's Sta-Prest, which in 1969 had been worn by every self-respecting bovver boy on a Saturday evening or on a Bank Holiday trip to the seaside, were now available in a myriad of colours including my own preferred choice, olive green. For practical reasons the commonest colours by far were bottle green or jet black. Practical, because you could wear them to school matched with your shiniest pair of Royal brogues which, with half an inch extra leather sole and steel 'Blakeys' added on for good measure, more than made up for your absent bovver boots. Crombies, with the obligatory handkerchief in the top pocket had begun to replace sheepskins, which most young skins couldn't afford anyway, and the candy-stripe Ben Shermans were now available in a multitude of check patterns,

A HISTORY LESSON

as were the better-value and even more colourful Brutus or Jaytex versions, if your old lady thought £3 was too much to pay for the real thing.

Yeah, this was all right, I thought, I'll have some of this. But the boots, we still needed the boots, what about the fucking boots? The old hobnails might make you look tough, but the only time I used them in anger, against some young Barnsley greaser on the terrace at the tail end of 1969, I went a pisser and got a right hiding. They were all right for showing off in school, running and sliding across the playground, impressing the young sorts with the sparks flying, but practical, comfortable footwear? Forget it! No, get yourself a pair of the new smart, showy elevenhole Doc Marten Astronauts, or even the cutesy Monkey boot. For some unfathomable reason I decided on the Monkey boots. They looked great: shiny black, brown or Ox-blood with yellow laces. The only trouble with Monkey boots was that they came in small sizes so all the sorts could wear them, but I loved them, bought a pair in Ox-blood — what a name, even the polish sounded hard.

So this was it. Definitely arrived this time. Got my clothes, got my new haircut complete with a pencil-thin parting down the left-hand side, and got my mates. A decent crew really, headed up by Waddsy who just had to wear the cherry-red Astros, while Benny, Lil and me, Browner, sported the poor-relation Monkey boots. Sure there were plenty of other kiddies — Mogger, Harvey, Tommo, Smo — but we were the cream of the crop. Virtually all of our year in school were skinheads, at least the ones from the council estate. We had all read *the* book by Richard Allen and we could all recite the best bits verbatim from the book that bore *that* title.

Joe Hawkins was our hero. And did he, or even Richard Allen for that matter, really exist? Did they fuck! The day I found out that Richard Allen was in fact a 40-year-old Canadian by the name of James Moffatt and that Joe was a figment, albeit a very plausible one, of his overworked imagination was comparable to the day that I found out that the old fella dressed in red who came into my bedroom on Christmas Eve was not who he seemed. But who gave a fuck? Joe was the top man; anything Joe and his mates could do on the North Bank at Upton Park we could do on the Tote End at Eastville. We all looked the same, acted the same and followed the same rules; for Joe's West Ham, read Browner's Bristol Rovers; for Plaistow read Henbury. Not that we inhabited Joe's nightmarish and brutal world. Ours was the real world and the inner-city strife, poverty and racial conflict of the slums of Plaistow were not something we experienced on a daily basis in the relative comfort of a north Bristol council estate that bordered on the edge of open countryside and enjoyed views of the wooded Blaise Castle estate.

Henbury, like the majority of council estates built in post-war Britain, was still populated mostly by honest, hard-working families, largely free of the serious crime and drug problems that would dog them in later years. The rows of neat gardens fronting the tidy houses with their gates and doors uniformly painted in standard council-issue colours of blue and green had a consistency about them that ensured no resident felt he was better, or worse, than his neighbour. Moreover, the rent that was paid in cash each week was at a level that most people could afford; indeed, the success of council house estates was a testament to the Labour Government that had created this utopian dream back in the 1950s. It's a pity that, like Richard Allen's novels, this was all bullshit, although admittedly it was only in later years when Thatcher and her cronies set out to end socialism, and consequently abolish the working class as Britain knew it, that the dream turned into a nightmare and degenerated into the oblivion of drug abuse and street crime that is still prevalent today. Furthermore, the individuals who subscribed to Thatcher's beliefs

A HISTORY LESSON

convinced themselves they were no longer working class and rushed to buy their council houses, fit their Colonial doors and park their Sierras on their new driveways – in so doing depriving future generations of tidy, affordable housing – were as equally culpable as that scheming, misguided tyrant herself.

The drug use that was to become widespread on council estates in future years was virtually unheard of in the skinhead movement, and was regarded as the domain of the drop-out hippy and the loathsome greaser. The majority of skinheads abhorred drugs and, although their elder cousins, the mods, had imbibed performance-enhancing speed, purple hearts and the like, no self-respecting skin would partake of uppers, let alone the mind-expanding and hallucinatory drugs associated with the 'far out man' hippies.

If we weren't able to boast about our tough inner-city upbringing, then at least we could emulate Joe and his mates in other ways. Admittedly, our version of street crime and aggro was generally confined to nicking reggae LPs from Jones' department store, vandalising phone boxes and terrifying the local hippy population, which as it turned out was usually our fellow school pupils from leafy Westbury. We even dodged paying our bus fares, although our one and only incursion into racial abuse, when Waddsy abused the cheery West Indian conductor with a surly 'I ain't paying, wog', resulted in him getting a smack in the mouth and us being unceremoniously turfed off the bus. We even fashioned our own weapons and 'tooled ourselves up', with sharpened steel rat-tail combs and six-inch lengths of sand-filled bicycle inner tubes, though these only got an airing when you rapped your mates' knuckles round the back of the bike sheds while enjoying an illicit fag.

Life on the terraces, though, was an altogether different story. It was here that we came into our element and lived out our fantasy of being the hard men of the Tote End, Bristol

BOOTED AND SUITED

Rovers' (in)famous terrace. We rarely instigated the rucks, which kicked off with alarming regularity, but nonetheless we hovered like flies and mercilessly put the boot in with the best of them once an unfortunate visiting wretch found himself prostrate on the terrace. The Tote End was to become my stage where, hopefully, if I performed well and followed the script, I would become a star. But in 1970, participating only from the sidelines like the rest of my mates, I was nothing more than an extra, a bit-player. One, though, who was ever willing to learn from the real star turns and legends whom I studied, worshipped and longed to emulate.

I'd been a Rovers fan since 1968, in the days when 'Ziggar zagger! Zigger zagger! Oi! Oi! Oi!' bellowed out from the terraces. Unbelievably though, and to my eternal shame, my first ever football match was at Ashton Gate – Bristol fucking City versus Blackburn Rovers, 0–0, fucking crap. Was this really what they were eventually to call the beautiful game? I don't know why I went to Ashton – peer pressure seems such a lame excuse. At the time, all the rest of the kids in our street were City fans, England were holders of the World Cup and every snotty-nosed kid the length and breadth of England wanted to be the next Geoff Hurst, George Best or, in Bristol's case, the next John Atyeo or Alfie Biggs. Football, football, football, that's all I wanted out of life; instead, I got some ponces in red shirts making arses of themselves, and to top it all it was south of the river.

Now that football has become accepted, a compulsory topic for the chattering classes to discuss over dinner, celebrity supporters will regale one another and seek each other's approval for the reason they followed a particular club. 'It was in my blood, my father took me to Highbury when I was only two days old'; 'My great-uncle Ernie played for Liverpool'; 'I've followed Manchester United even when they were bottom of the

A HISTORY LESSON

league' (and just when was that exactly?). It was their destiny; bollocks was it mine! My old man was only concerned with putting food on the table and tending his fuchsias, while my older brother didn't know the difference between a flat back four and flatulence.

'Who do you support then, Dad?' I had asked my old man, thinking I could stir up some inspiration from him. 'City or Rovers?'

'Neither, son,' he said matter-of-factly, 'they're both crap.'

Couldn't argue with that, they were crap, with City languishing at the foot of the old Second Division and Rovers middle of the Third. Still, it had been worth a try. No, the reason I changed my allegiance and became a die-hard, true-blue Rovers fan wasn't destiny or fate or any other such claptrap that the latter-day middle-class supporters of the Premier League espouse. It was because, quite simply, Eastville Stadium, the home of Bristol Rovers, was on the bus route.

It was a rainy day in the middle of the winter of 1968. The opposition, some dreary northern-town cloggers. Our legendary beer-swilling, fag-smoking, grossly underrated centre-forward Alfie Biggs (now that's what I call a footballer's name) led the line for Rovers. And that's about it — as much as I can remember about my first game at Eastville. I've always thought it odd, I can remember the opposition at Ashton Gate and the score in that first ever game, but not my first furtive fumblings with what was to become the love of my life. What I do recall, however, was the stadium. What a place, what an atmosphere, what an ambience, but, above all else, what a smell — it was near a gasworks. The permanent rain from the cooling tower that fell at Eastville even on the sunniest of days, permeated your clothes, your hair, even your skin. It was like a drug. I needed that intake of gas every fortnight and I couldn't get enough of it. The place was nothing like Ashton Gate, which at that time was only covered on

BOOTED AND SUITED

two sides. Eastville had a long and somewhat decrepit old wooden South Stand, a large and more impressive North Stand, a huge open terrace and the pièce de résistance, the covered Tote End. To me Eastville Stadium was the Wembley of the West Country.

Violence at football started simmering in the mid-Sixties. It was natural – working-class kids, bit of money in their pocket for the first time and easy access to the rest of the country through the ever-expanding motorway network and rail system. But what it needed to really take off was a catalyst, something to bring it all together and to unleash its full potential to the unsuspecting world. That catalyst had arrived in 1969 in the form of the skinhead. At last, a cult that was actually based on, and more importantly thrived on, violence. Sure, the mods weren't opposed to the odd rumble at the seaside with the rockers, but the skinheads perfected the idea and found the obvious battleground to carry out their conquests every week, not just on Bank Holidays. But unlike all the other teenage cults that had troubled Britain over the previous 30 years, they had found their perfect and ever-ready enemy – each other.

8

Out to Impress

Waddsy – tall, good-looking, intelligent, a calculating bastard – was our Joe Hawkins. He was going through the throes of being expelled from school. The usual stuff really – drinking, thieving, fighting, same as all of us – but Dennis Wardell, well, he just did it a bit better than the rest of us. Naturally, we looked up to him.

'Look what I've nicked,' boasted Waddsy as he opened his haversack emblazoned with 'Trojan' and 'Tote End Skins' legends.

'Manky cheese sandwiches?' enquired Benny, ever the wag.

'No, these, you spotty-faced, ugly twat'.

Benny couldn't argue. He was, after all, indisputably all three. Waddsy took out a dozen silver disks. 'They're explosives, I've nicked them from that hut by the side of the railway line. They put 'em on the railway lines when it's foggy.'

'How do they get rid of fog?' asked Benny. We all ignored him.

'So what do we do with these then, Den?' I enquired, a simple enough question I thought.

'Blow some fucker's legs off,' he replied nonchalantly. 'Chuck 'em at the Villa fans, then when they start jumping up and down, you know, to "Bow-legged chicken" or something, they'll go off and, hey presto, one-legged Brummie twats!' Of course, I thought, why didn't I think of that?

'But first,' he continued, 'we need to try them out – Scully!'

Everybody at every school knew a Scully. The one who would do anything, try anything, eat anything, say anything... anything stupid. Scully still had hobnailed boots, perfect for jumping up and down on miniature anti-personnel mines, we thought. Scully duly obliged.

We were in detention for a week and on report for a month. Scully got a new pair of boots and Waddsy took a step closer to being expelled. But Waddsy's experiment had been a great success. Next stop, the Tote End.

Rovers had a tremendous run in the League Cup and had progressed to the fifth round against the 'old enemy', Aston Villa. Villa were our nemesis. Not in the same league as our hatred for Bristol fucking City of course – nothing could match that – but Villa were in the Third Division with us, whereas we only had the chance to hammer the City fans once a year at the Gloucester Cup Final and May was a long way off. A crowd of nearly 30,000 packed into Eastville on an unbelievably wet November night. There had already been skirmishes up and down Stapleton Road, but PC Rain had performed well and kept the aggro under control. Under the roof of the Tote End it was a different story: no segregation and as many rumbles as you wanted. Time for Waddsy to perform.

''E' 'are, Browner, chuck some of these.'

Waddsy handed me a couple of anti-personnel mines. 'Chuck 'em like this.' He jumped up and skimmed them across the cropped heads for maximum effect. I duly obliged, my heart beating with fear and excitement. We waited... nothing.

The game progressed. Stuart Taylor scored for Rovers. A goal

OUT TO IMPRESS

just before half-time was always a prelude to more violence. Off it went again, the boots and fists going in, thousands of damp, steaming teenagers beating the shit out of each other. 'Fertiliser, fertiliser, fertiliser, fertiliser,' the Brummies taunted us, mocking our accents.

'Birmingum, chewing gum', replied the Tote, rather pathetically.

'I don't believe it,' exclaimed Waddsy, 'No fuckin' stompin'!'

Skinheads loved to stomp; they were born to stomp.

'Jump up and down, you bastards,' he shouted at the top of his adolescent voice.

Still nothing. Waddsy started wishing the Tannoy would belt out Symarip's 'Skinhead Moonstomp', the skinhead's anthem, the clever and somewhat opportunistic reworking of Derrick Morgan's 'Moonhop'. That would get the bastards jumping.

'There's only one thing for it,' said Waddsy, 'I'm off. I'll get the cunts singing!'

'Where're you going, you daft bastard?' I asked, knowing full well where he was going.

Off he went, pushing and shoving his way through the mass, straight into the middle of the Villa fans.

'He's off his trolley,' said Lil. A bit out of his depth, was Lil. A five-foot-nothing middle-class son of an American businessman, now living in genteel Westbury-on-Trym, doing the right thing and sending his all-American kids to a comprehensive school in a north Bristol council estate. He was right though, Waddsy was off his trolley. We lost sight of him, I thought he was going to cop it. The Brum scum if they didn't notice his accent were sure to notice his Levi's jacket with 'TOTE' stencilled on the small leather patch above the breast pocket. We waited with bated breath.

'Oi'm a bow-legged chicken, Oi'm a knock-kneed hen, Oi ain't been so happy since Oi don't when. Oi walk with a wiggle and Oi wiggle when Oi walk, doin' the HOLTE END boot walk!' The Brummies roared, here it comes, we thought... 'La, la, la, la, la, la, la, la.' Up they jumped, as only football fans do, leaning on their mates, hands on the shoulders of complete strangers in front, riotous, joyous stompin'... but no fucking explosions.

We thought we had lost Waddsy for the night, either pummelled to death by some Quinton psychopath or nicked by the Old Bill, but unbelievably he found his way back to us, with a big grin on his face. So what if they didn't go off, what cunning, what bravado, what a nutter! He had pulled a stunt that was to gain him hero worship from the rest of us, that was what counted. As for the game, the Villa equalised, causing more mayhem and unleashing an attack of epic proportions from the disgruntled Tote Enders: 'A-G, A-G-R, A-G-R-O, AGRO!' If only, if only... we would have made the front page of the *Daily Mirror*.

There was only one thing we enjoyed more than a bit of bovver at a home game and that was a bit of bovver at an away game. I had been to away games before – my first journey into the unknown had been to Reading in 1969 when as well as a stunning victory on the pitch (Rovers won 5–1), the fledgling Tote End skinheads had run the Berkshire biscuitmen ragged. But that day I had journeyed on the irksome supporters' club coaches and now, several months on, I couldn't stand the thought of sitting next to some prat wearing a bobble hat and clutching a rattle and a flask of tea. There was only one way to travel – the football special, courtesy of a threepenny platform ticket – and did we have a cracking trip to the seaside lined up courtesy of British Rail: Torquay.

This time we were really going mob-handed. It seemed the whole of Henbury School was going and we were well tooled up for it. Not that many of us were prepared to actually use

OUT TO IMPRESS

weapons. It was simply the done thing, you had to carry a tool, pure bravado. The school bogs were laid bare as every chain was detached from its cistern and secreted about our persons, as were our favoured inner tube coshes, steel combs, iron bars and, perhaps the most sinister weapon of all, Jif lemon bottles filled with bleach.

The journey down had been uneventful. A few cans of Double Diamond had calmed our nerves – nerves about Torquay, what a laugh, but we were nervous. We didn't know what to expect. We had heard rumours that Argyle would turn up and there was a lot of bad blood between Rovers and those Union Street arse bandits since our game at Home Park back in April. It was a game that I had attended together with the rest of the Henbury kiddies and which had seen us nervously hanging on the shirt tails of our elders as we battled firstly on the concourse of the station, secondly on the green parkland surrounding Home Park and thirdly on the concrete terraces of the ground itself, before repeating the acts, in reverse order, all the way back to the station.

The 'E-for-B and 'en-bury' chant was becoming as well known at Eastville as the original 'E-for-B and Georgie Best' chant was at Old Trafford, and what's more we were beginning to get our faces known and accepted with kiddies from other districts. We had a good crew, but we weren't in the same league as some of the others. Lockleaze, Fishponds and Kingswood were all well represented, but there was no ill feeling. We were all together, we were the Tote. We were a young, up-and-coming crew. Some of the Lockleaze lads were 18 and older, veterans of the early days, who proudly sported the impressive mutton-chop sideburns that had been popular with the more mature skins and which only Waddsy of our own crew was able to boast. And then there was Andy Phelps.

Big Andy, or 'the Bear' as Villa fans had begrudgingly

BOOTED AND SUITED

nicknamed him, was a legend, our out-and-out leader. He, along with Brian Willis, had created 'the Tote End' back in January 1967 following an FA Cup clash with Arsenal that not only attracted a 35,000 attendance, but also saw the first full-scale invasion and occupation of the covered home terrace of the ground by visiting fans. Andy vowed that the Tote End would never be taken again, well not without a fight anyway. Over the years we did our best to live up to Andy's promise.

Andy was a paradox. When just about every other member of the Tote was a spawny-bollocked pubescent skinhead, Andy was 20 years plus, built like the proverbial brick shithouse and, what's more, a greebo – a great ambling hulk with hair down on his shoulders, wearing dirty jeans and a leather jacket. To get a nod of recognition from the big man was a great accolade in itself. What were we, who prided ourselves on our appearance and our manner, doing, being led by him? But led we were, and whenever Andy was around you felt safer, invincible; he was our talisman.

There were others of equal standing, the delightfully-named 'Iron bar 'Arry', of whom I had heard a lot, but seen little and the very real Pete Kimble, a huge hairy docker from Avonmouth, bigger even than Andy. The skins were led by characters such as Dobbsy who, oddly enough, like Andy came from south of the river, and Rob Boyle from Eastville. Rob was a main face among the skins, a clever, well-educated individual who went on to become a teacher. Always looked smart did Rob, checked Ben Sherman, long black cardigan, thumbs hitched behind bright-red braces, the shiniest pair of cherry-red Doc Martens protruding from razor-sharp, mustard-green Sta-Prest; pure class.

'All right, young uns?' said Rob. He stood there, filling the void left by the now absent door that had been unceremoniously wrenched from its fixings by one of his young entourage.

'Yeah, fine, Rob, an' you?' I replied, chest puffed out with pride.

OUT TO IMPRESS

'We got to be up for it today, Argyle are on their way. All stick together. OK?'

'Yeah, no worries.'

'Good, see you later.'

There's something about arriving in a small town on a train. As soon as the town was in sight and the train started slowing, down came the windows and out went the heads. 'BER-RISTOL, BER-RISTOL, BER-RISTOL!' we chanted, terrifying some old geezer tending his vegetables in his back garden. We couldn't wait to get off; the doors flew open and we were out and running on the platform. It started going off straight away, a porter got a whack, suitcases got kicked over, a window got smashed. We weren't off the station yet and the aggro was already going off. Fucking marvellous!

Outside the station there was a welcoming committee of coppers, but they were taken by surprise – football intelligence was still in its infancy. They'd got a lot to learn. The law couldn't handle hundreds of yobs arriving all at once; one meat wagon and a dog handler weren't going to control this lot. As we exited the station heading for the seafront, a lone Triumph Herald trundled around the corner straight into us. Unwisely it stopped, its bewildered middle-class and middle-aged occupants looked at first mildly annoyed and then terrified as the horrific situation dawned on them. We surrounded the car and quickly got it rocking until it eventually keeled over, the smashing of the windows being greeted with howls of laughter from the baying mob.

Straight along the seafront we ran, shouting, abusing everyone in sight. All eyes were on us, total and utter disgust, the locals' chins dropping on to their scrubbed pavements, in awe at this heathen mob from that ungodly city of Bristol. This was a laugh all right, but it was a bit easy. 'Where's the opposition? Where's the Devon skins?' At last we spotted some, three skins, one tall,

BOOTED AND SUITED

tasty-looking geezer, two smaller cohorts, about our age. No hesitation, we fired straight in. The two smaller ones scarpered straight away. I couldn't believe it when the big one stayed put, well up for it. At the last moment he turned and legged it – unfortunately for him, straight into a lamppost. In went the boots – we were fighting with each other to get the boot in first. Just as I was priming the leg for a full swing there was a whack on the back of my head.

'Get off, you tossers!'

It was Rob Boyle.

'Leave him alone for fuck's sake, he's on his own.'

Rob was punching and kicking now, pulling us all off. We stood back amazed, wondering what his game was.

'Get up, mate, sorry about that, they're just a bunch of wankers.' He handed him back his Wrangler jacket, which someone was determined to relieve him of. Rob was right, it was bang out of order. It was a sharp lesson to us all. We were tough, we liked a ruck, but this was not on.

'Any of you lot do that again and you'll get a hiding from me, all right!' shouted Rob.

We skulked off... time to find a pub.

That wasn't difficult. By now Torquay was overrun with Tote Enders, every pub was full to overflowing, ideal for spawny-bollocked 14-year-olds to hide in dark corners clutching oversized glasses of Tavern Keg; four pints later we were arseholed. The trek to the ground was as eventful as the trip from the station, a milk float overturned, gallons of gold top running down the gutter, broken glass everywhere, a workman's hut thrown over a wall, 50 foot drop on the other side wrecking several cars.

The game itself was an anticlimax. We took their end – the aptly named Cowshed – no sweat. Christ, even a bunch of one-armed dwarfs could take their end, it was hardly an achievement. Time to start on the coppers.

OUT TO IMPRESS

'What's a matter with you, screw? What's a matter with you?' We chanted to the tune of Rolf Harris's 'Tie Me Kangaroo Down Sport'. Who thought up these songs? Did they sit in their bedrooms composing football songs for a living? Sad bastards.

The law fired in, truncheons drawn, and everyone just got stuck in. No organisation, no thought, no worries, you just did it, it was natural. Nobody thought they were doing anything extraordinary or bad; you were a teenager, you were a football fan, *ergo* you fought. If you couldn't scrap with a kiddy just like yourself, who thought exactly the same way as you did, lived the same life, who could you scrap with?

The law took a bit of a pasting. It was years before they would get organised enough to control the hooligans on the terraces. In the meantime, their only effective weapon was the dog. It was a common sight on the terraces in the Seventies: bloody great hairy Alsatians, usually accompanied by bloody great hairy coppers, for it was a proven fact that dog handlers always had beards. The dogs had the right effect, calm was quickly restored.

The game fizzled out to a 1–1 draw. Only one Argyle fan turned up, a mixed-race kid, about as common in Devon as silverware in Rovers' trophy cabinet. Before the twat could finish, 'ARGYL...' he was blatted with a fist the size of his head from Andy Phelps. The poor sod was knocked out cold with one punch. I would see this repeated many times over the years. Andy was never one for hanging around weighing up the options, never one to put the boot in. He didn't need to – one punch was usually enough. It's funny the number of towns and football clubs we visited, the names of which I never quite heard in full, 'Mansf...' Blat! 'Wals...' Blat! 'Bourne...' Blat! Awesome.

After a few more pints, and a quick grope with a couple of local skinhead girls who thought us Bristolians were ace, it was back on the train for a leisurely trip back to Bristol. A leisurely trip of ripped-up seats, broken toilets, smashed windows and discarded light bulbs. The communication cord was pulled more times than an adolescent's penis and fires were started with alarming frequency. We would have put them out but all the fire extinguishers had been thrown through the windows. To top it all, a group of lads had attacked the buffet car, whacked the steward selling drinks and pinched his money and stock, resulting in discounted Mars Bars and Double Diamond doing the rounds.

The last game at Eastville in 1970 was against Swansea Town on Boxing Day, a bitterly cold day when no buses ran and which presented us with a grim, four-mile trek from the Arctic-like northern hinterland of our Henbury council estate. By the time we arrived at the ground, we were frozen solid and even the flask of whisky that Lil had purloined from his old man's drinks cabinet didn't warm our spirits. The Tote performed as usual, giving the sheep-shaggers a right hammering at the Open End. I couldn't be bovvered. It was too cold and I was going down with flu. Anyway, I didn't want to mess up my crombie that my old lady had bought for me for Christmas – not a real genuine Abercrombie, just one of those from Keedons for £12, everybody wore them. The game was crap, 0–0. We had a couple of rum and blacks in the White Swan before trudging back home. I was pissed right off, and what's more it had started to snow.

On the whole, though, 1970 had been good, real good. I had made away trips to Luton, Bournemouth, Reading, Plymouth, even Aldershot, and of course Torquay, and came out relatively unscathed, while even the vicious battle at the Gloucester Cup match at Ashton Gate, which had resulted in over 40 youths being arrested, left me unmarked (due in no small part to me keeping my head down and my mouth shut). So what if it wasn't Arsenal or Liverpool? A fist or a boot delivered by a Janner hurt just as much as one delivered by a Scouser and wallowing as Rovers did in the relative obscurity of the Third Division meant

OUT TO IMPRESS

we had to make the most of our chances of aggro whenever we could. My efforts to climb the ladder of recognition with my peers and make a name for myself were beginning to pay dividends, I was at ease with my identity and my appearance and even my musical tastes were more than being catered for. The music of that year was legendary in its simplicity. Skinheads were not complex creatures and the raw, basic music from North America, and more importantly the West Indies, appealed to our own even baser instincts – 'Give Me Just A Little More Time' and 'You've Got Me Dangling On A String' by Chairmen of the Board and Steam's 'Na, Na, Hey, Hey, Kiss Him Goodbye', which became one of football's quintessential anthems, had made the Top 10 in January and vied with reggae's relentless onslaught on the charts by the Trojan and Pama record labels.

The much-plagiarised favourite of all football 'Ends', 'Liquidator' by the Harry J. All Stars, had first entered the charts in November 1969 and stayed there right through to March 1970, while the heartfelt 'Young, Gifted And Black' by Bob & Marcia peaked at number 5 in April. The band who were responsible for labelling the new West Indian sound 'reggae' or 'reggay' as in 'Do The Reggay' back in 1968, Toots Hibbert's Maytals, reached number 47 with 'Monkey Man' and Nicky Thomas's superb 'Love Of The Common People', which in the 1980s launched Paul Young's solo career, reached number 9 in July. Amazingly, Symarip's quintessential bovver boy record 'Skinhead Moonstomp' failed to make the Top 50. Then again, it was in good company – neither did 'Johnny Too Bad' by The Slickers, with its foreboding message to all rude boys, or one of the earliest 'version' offerings, 'Version Girl' by Boy Friday.

With many of its releases unashamedly aimed at the still-growing and predominantly white skinhead movement, Trojan and its myriad offshoot labels (there was even one named Agro and a Jamaican session band called The Aggrovators) had released

BOOTED AND SUITED

no less than 70 singles that year, selling a staggering 250,000 copies in the British pop market alone and as an independent label had a track record that was second to none. For all of reggae's chart success that year, however, there was one record that stood head and shoulders above anything that Jamaica, or more correctly Neasden, could offer, and that was Freda Payne's 'Band Of Gold', which reached number 1 in September and stayed in the charts for 19 glorious weeks.

Tamla Motown, the label that had first came to prominence back in the Sixties when the mods were causing mayhem in Brighton, also had a number-1 hit in 1970 with Smokey Robinson's 'Tears Of A Clown' and other Top-10 hits with Edwin Starr's anti-Vietnam classic 'War' and the Temptations' amazing cacophony of sound 'Ball Of Confusion', while 'It's All In The Game' and 'Still Water' by the evergreen Four Tops proved that the demise of Detroit was still some way off. The summer, however, had been dominated by one home-grown record, the irritatingly catchy 'In The Summertime' by Mungo Jerry, which stayed at number 1 for seven long weeks and was finally knocked off by Elvis Presley's 'The Wonder Of You'.

As far as music was concerned, 1970 was a year of incredible diversity, from Lee Marvin's tiresome 'Wand'rin' Star' to Jimi Hendrix's awesome 'Voodoo Chile'. Like my new life on the terraces, the music of the 1970s would have no dull moments. I had just boarded the roller-coaster ride of my life and right here, right now in December 1970, at the age of 15, the ride was still heading up its first innocent incline.

9

A Welcome in the Hillsides

Jesus loves the little skinheads
All the skinheads of the world
In their braces and their boots
And their hair cut to their roots
Jesus loves the little skinheads of the world.

Popular terrace song – Sung to Ray Stevens' 'Jesus loves the little children'.

The year 1971 carried on where 1970 left off, with the Tote End's reputation now growing by the week. Another visit by Aston Villa in January saw a mass battle as soon as Villa came off the train in Stapleton Road – the road outside the Black Swan was littered with broken bottles, bricks and two tons of shit the warring tribes had kicked out of each other. We were having a field day, the papers were full of us, and we loved it.

'We are superior! We are superior!' It was an odd, almost childlike chant sung by a ferocious and vociferous band of Preston North End skins who caught us unawares, arrived early

BOOTED AND SUITED

and infiltrated the Tote End on a Saturday in early April. Not only had the shaven-headed, baggy-white-trousered Lancastrians set up camp on our home terrace, they had also desecrated the ground by spraying 'PNE Skins' and daubing huge, cartoon-like Doc Marten illustrations all over the back of the Tote. They had got a result, but one that, like their childlike chant, was about to come to an end with a well-thought-out double-pronged attack as the half-time whistle blew. The decoy assault, of which I was part, fired in from the right-hand side; the Preston lads, as eager as us to prove their worth, took up the challenge, oblivious to the larger mob attacking from behind. The pincer movement caused disarray, they fled on to the pitch, bloodied, battered and beaten, there was only one thing we could chant: 'You are inferior! You are inferior!' I had never heard those bizarre chants before, and what's more I never heard them again.

The following weekend was Easter. Things were really looking up: Rovers had put a good run together and we decided to go on our travels again, this time abroad... Wales. Due to a lack of cash we had to journey by the most horrendous mode of transport known to any self-respecting hooligan – the supporters' club coaches. Still, there was a wagonload of us as we set off from Eastville, raring to have a go and give the Taffies a right kicking. The sun was shining and my Monkey boots couldn't stop dancing – Dave and Ansel Collins were at number 1 with 'Double Barrel' – God truly was a skinhead!

Although reggae was very much skinheads' own music, soul and, to a lesser degree, Motown was also still popular, especially with the skinhead girls in the dancehalls and youth clubs. But much as I enjoyed tapping my boot to Arthur Conley and Junior Walker's offerings, tracks by Diana Ross and Stevie Wonder left me cold. I knew what I really, really wanted: moon-hopping, boot-stomping, unsophisticated reggae. Reggae's popularity had peaked in 1970, but it was still having a huge influence on us a

A WELCOME IN THE HILLSIDES

year later and when 'Double Barrel' hit number 1 in March it proved that skins were still alive and kicking, literally.

It was proving difficult, however, to hear and buy up-to-date reggae. Radio One and the charts were dominated by drippy, hippy crap, with Marc Bolan and T.Rex having a field day. 'Ride A White Swan' irritated the fuck out of me. It was too catchy, I almost liked it – pity it was sung by some druggy Yeti. As relatively young skins we had dipped out on the gems from a few years earlier and we had to rely on the superb *Tighten Up* and *Club Reggae* compilation albums, which could still be bought for under a quid; what a bargain. Buying singles was an expedition in itself. RCA Records in Picton Street was a regular hang-out for skins...

'Got "Hijacked" by Jo Gibbs, Roy?' I would ask the shop's owner, as regular as clockwork, every Saturday morning.

'It'll be in a week on Monday,' was Roy's stock answer.

The trouble was, every time a classic record came in, it would be snapped up straight away by the highest bidder. I discovered RCA was still going strong in the early Nineties, and I thought I'd give it a go.

'Got "Hijacked" by...'

'It'll be in a week on Monday,' replied Roy, not even bothering to look up from rolling his fag. I got the message, I never did get the record.

Skins had developed an affinity with reggae and its predecessor rock steady, much as the mods had been associated with soul and ska. There was a brashness about reggae that was particularly well suited to skins – unpretentious, basic and at times downright fucking ugly, the two went hand in hand and, in cities with a large immigrant population, such as London, Birmingham and to a lesser extent Bristol, there were even black skinheads. In fact, many of the skins' early fashions were plagiarised from their teenage black counterparts. Pork-pie hats and tight-fitting mohair suits with trousers finishing just above the ankle had long been a favourite with the 'rude boys' back in Jamaica. Just why white, working-class youths from council housing estates took to black music from across the Atlantic remained a mystery, but I for one wasn't about to buck the trend. I was a stereotypical skin and I was listening to my stereotypical music. I longed to visit the Bamboo Club, the legendary West Indian club in the St Pauls district of Bristol where Jamaican legends such as Owen Gray, Alton Ellis and The Skatalites had performed, but I knew that at 15 and dressed as I was the chances of that happening were as likely as that of Enoch Powell visiting his local curry house for a vindaloo. Not that we were racist — far from it. In fact, no skinheads that I knew back then were, not as far as West Indians were concerned at any rate; admittedly there were attacks on Asians and the term 'Paki-bashing' had, unfortunately, entered the English language by the early 1970s, but black skinheads were often involved alongside their white counterparts in such attacks, so the race card was a difficult one to call there.

The truth was, a lot of skinheads were just plain 'bad lads' and the attacks and insults on lone Asians, like the assaults on lone greasers or homosexuals, were more about following the herd and proving one's so-called 'hardness' than they were about making any kind of political statement. Politics, at least in the early years of this particular youth cult, was not something that skinheads gave a fuck about.

Thinking back, a fair proportion of skinheads at some time had tried queer- as well as Paki-bashing; there weren't too many Pakistanis in Henbury so we had to make do with queers. I only tried it the once — that's the bashing, not the queer bit. I went to the bogs at the bottom of Cheltenham Road with Nicky Pullin, a lad from Horfield I had first met during the brawl against Preston. The plan was for Nicky to wait inside the toilets while I stood outside, waiting for Quentin Crisp or whoever to turn up. I know public toilets are meant to be shitholes but this one truly

A WELCOME IN THE HILLSIDES

was. What made homosexuals want to have sex in a dirty, filthy, piss-and-shit-ridden public convenience was beyond me. It confirmed my prejudices – they deserved a good hiding; nicking their wallet would be a bonus. Quentin eventually turned up. He was a big old boy and stared me right in the eye; he knew what was coming, in fact he might even have welcomed it. He had obviously made an approach to Nicky.

'Chris, now, get the fucker!' Nicky screamed from inside the shithole.

I waited.

'Now! Fucking get in here!'

I carried on waiting... I stifled a laugh.

'Get your fucking hands off me, you queer bastard! Browner, get in here now!'

I could still hear Nicky's squeals as I boarded a passing 77 bus. I chuckled to myself, leaving Nicky to his fate. He might still be in there now for all I know.

I'll state the bleeding obvious: South Wales is one tough place. Decades of sweating, toiling and breaking your back in steel mills, coal mines and docks had produced a belligerent and pugnacious population, if there is one thing the lads from the valleys enjoy more than fighting with each other, it's fighting with the English.

We arrived in Swansea, cocksure and itching for a fight. The Tote End, however, got there in dribs and drabs, not en masse as at Torquay. This was the trouble with coaches, especially those run by supporters' clubs. With no organisation and no leaders, we were feeling apprehensive.

Swansea was far removed from cosy Torquay. Rows of red-brick-terraced houses, steelworks, docks, a perfect breeding ground for rough, tough aggro merchants. We weren't to be disappointed. Waddsy took the lead as usual.

BOOTED AND SUITED

'Let's find a pub and lie low for a bit, see what turns up.'

None of us was in the mood to go looking for trouble, not yet. This was the first time we had felt vulnerable. On our own turf, Eastville, we were a match for anybody, knowing there was a mob behind us; here we were isolated, we stuck out like a bulldog's bollocks. I nervously fingered the lock knife I had tucked away in the silk lining of my suede bomber jacket. If I had to, really had to, I would use it today. My hands shook and my balls shrivelled up to the size of frozen peas. Andy, where are you?

After several rounds of 'Sorry, lads, you're too young', we managed to find a pub not too far from Swansea's ground. Waddsy went in first – he always did, he looked the oldest. We followed him, as casually as you could with your balls tucked neatly up in your stomach.

'Light split,' said Denny, an octave lower than his normal speaking voice.

'Are you boys old enough?' asked the sheep-shagger of a landlord.

'Yeah, we're all 18,' replied Waddsy. This was a joke and the landlord knew it. At a push I could pass for 17, but Lil didn't even look 15, 12 more like it.

'All right, but sit over in the corner, an' no trouble.'

We all trooped over to one corner, our eyes fixed on our pints, not daring to look around.

'It'll be all right,' I piped up, 'the rest will get here soon, and we'll sort this place out.'

Everybody nodded their agreement, not believing me.

The pub was virtually empty – a few pensioners smoking roll-ups and reading their papers, while over by the fruit machine a couple of local lads, dressed in regulation football gear of Levi's, boots and identical Harringtons, and each sporting neat, close-cropped hair, warily eyed us up. They had clocked us straight

A WELCOME IN THE HILLSIDES

away. There were six of us, Henbury's finest four plus a couple of eager lads from Yate who we had just met and who had tagged along for the crack. The Taffies whispered something to each other and made a quick exit. Something was brewing.

'Let's go after the bastards,' said Benny, ever mouthy, ever stupid.

'No, leave it,' said Waddsy, 'we only just got here, it'll be all right.'

Ten minutes passed. Every time the door opened we braced ourselves and let out a small sigh of relief when another pensioner came in with his dog. Finally, the door opened with a bit more effort. A dozen of them filed in silently. We made eye contact. We knew most Rovers kids and these didn't fit the bill.

'My mate got a hiding in Bristol at Christmas,' mouthed Sheep Shagger No. 1, easy 18 years old and twice the size of all of us put together.

'So fucking what?' I answered. I couldn't believe I'd said it, I regretted it straight away.

I was still sat down, easy pickings. He jabbed his fingers straight into my eyes – the pain was unbelievable. I screamed in agony and put my hands over my face. Then I felt a whack across the side of my head; the punches fired in thick and fast. The others copped it as well; we didn't even put up a fight, it was a poor show. It was over in a split second. In fact, it could have been a lot worse – they realised we were only kids, and they thought a slapping was good enough. We thought they would leg it, but they stayed, ordering pints and glowering at us, chucking beer mats every now and then, daring us to make a move for the door. The landlord didn't give a fuck, he'd obviously seen it all before. But they were soon to regret not making a move when they had the chance.

Keith Hurt appeared at the door – quiet, unassuming, bespectacled Keith Hurt, one of the meanest bastards north of the river. Behind him, a never-ending stream of Tote Enders entered the smoky pub. The cavalry had arrived!

'Who did that nipper?' asked Keith, showing genuine concern – my eyes were now blooded and streaming.

'That fucker over there.' I fingered Sheep-Shagger No. 1, who was by now cacking his pants.

Keith always believed in action speaking louder than words. 'Like beating up little kids, do you, cunt?'

I felt offended at being called a little kid; 'nipper' I could handle, but 'little kid' made me squirm. Still, this was well worth it. Keith didn't fit the bill of your average football hooligan. Buddy Holly-style glasses, pink sweater and beige cords. Highly polished Doc Marten shoes were his only concession to skinhead fashion. He grabbed No. 1 by the throat, kneed him in the bollocks and twatted him on the way down. Most of the Tote Enders were still at the bar, getting their first drinks in, but as soon as they realised aggro was about they fired in. Lesson number one – get the fuckers on the floor; lesson number two – put the boot in. You couldn't keep us off. I was up for revenge. I dived through the mêlée and stamped on No. 1's head – by now he was crying like a baby. I fingered my knife again – no, I didn't have the bottle, just give the fucker a kicking. We were all there now, Benny and Lil going for some of the smaller ones, Lil at last blooding his virgin boots; he was grinning from ear to ear. Waddsy smacked a glass over one of them who was fighting just to get out of the door. Somehow the Taffies managed to scramble out of the pub; beaten and bloody, they had been given a good larruping. 'COME AND HAVE A GO AT THE TOTE END AG-GERO!' rang in their ears. Revenge was sweet.

It wasn't to last. We were still a bit wary on the way to the ground. There had been several scraps, all quickly broken up by the law, nothing too serious. But at the ground there was total confusion. We were trying to find their end, we always went on

A WELCOME IN THE HILLSIDES

the opposing fans' end – this was the only way to establish our reputation – but unlike most grounds, Swansea's mob was based on the large enclosure on the side of the ground. We ended up on the open terrace with Swansea prison right behind us, about 200 of us here, but our main mob was at the other covered end, facing us.

'Come and join us, come and join us, come and join us over 'ere!' bellowed our comrades directly opposite. We didn't really need the invitation, we were off on to the pitch like a shot. The rest followed. The sheep-shaggers, thinking we were coming after them, raced on to the pitch. We met on the centre circle and the Tote poured on from the opposite end – it was chaos. All swift stuff, punches, kicks, jump in with a high kick first, aim for the stomach or the bollocks, do some damage, then leg it. The law joined in, dogs, horses and a few hundred yobs all trying to kick lumps out of each other. Wonderful stuff!

Calm was restored in time for the kick-off. I was slung out of the ground by the law, along with a few dozen others. Bollocks, I thought, I haven't come all this way to spend a Saturday afternoon wandering round this dump. I spotted a St John Ambulance divvy.

'Where's the First Aid Post, mate?' I asked, pointing at my eyes. They were still streaming and giving me a lot of grief.

'Not out yure, boy,' he said, 'it's back in the ground.'

'Whaat? The copper told me to come out 'ere,' I protested.

'I'll take you in,' he said, holding my arm like I was some sort of wounded soldier.

Perfect result, back in the ground, no worries, even had a bit of Germoline rubbed around my eyelids by some young Welsh tart who felt ever so sorry for me. I quickly rejoined the thronging mass on the terraces. Rovers got off to a flying start, we were 2–0 up by half-time and the two sets of fans kept up a never-ending tirade of abuse at each other, separated by a long line of coppers and their mean-looking Alsatians. The chants got more and more abusive. Then we went too far. There was always one chant guaranteed to get all Taffies absolutely raving, including the coppers, and as soon as we started singing it, we regretted it. 'ABERFAN, ABERFAN, ABERFAN...' it was bang on half-time, always an edgy period and this was like a red rag to a bull. They came pouring up the steps behind us, brushing past the ineffectual coppers, who I'm sure actively encouraged them.

They were armed with bricks, bottles and metal bolts, and we dropped like flies. Angus, a thick-set older geezer from Lockleaze, had been standing next to me. Now he slumped to the terrace, a pair of scissors poking out of his shoulder blades, blood oozing through his Fred Perry. The Tote fought back, but the Swansea mob were now coming down the terraces at us, always an advantage. The law finally decided to step in, dogs and truncheons quickly restored order, but not before the Celtic warriors had inflicted severe damage on the English invaders.

On the pitch Rovers won 3–1; off it, a bloody score draw. It was now going into extra time. It went off again, furious hand-to-hand combat in the back streets around the ground, three-way fighting, the Tote, the Taffies and the coppers. I even managed to grab a black-and-white Swansea scarf in the melee, a prized battle colour to be added to my growing collection. The air was full of sirens, barking dogs and that roar, building up to a crescendo: 'Come on then!' the old favourite, ''Ave the bastards!' Total chaos and total violence.

But now we had a problem, a big problem. We had to get back to the coaches and no one remembered where they were parked. I tied my newly acquired souvenir around my waist, under my jacket. We found a small knot of Rovers fans waiting on a corner; they all looked anxious.

'You waiting for the coaches?' We didn't really need to ask. We recognised them from the journey earlier.

A WELCOME IN THE HILLSIDES

'Yeah, they should be along in a min...'

'Fucking hell, look at this lot... leg it!'

As soon as they spotted us they roared, that guttural roar. It reminded me of the film *Zulu*. We scattered in all directions – we were way outnumbered. Me, Waddsy and Benny legged it through some large iron gates, round a corner, desperately looking for somewhere to hide. It was an industrial estate, a gasworks. I was shitting it, my heart was thumping, my legs turned to jelly and my balls returned to frozen peas mode. I prayed to God that the sheep-shaggers had carried on down the main road. No such fucking luck. They must have known we were running into a dead end. There were buildings, offices, around us. Benny and I pushed open a door; a security guard sat there with his feet up, reading a paper.

'Help us, mate, they're after us!' I screamed.

'Fuck off, English twats,' came his sympathetic reply. I got the distinct feeling he wasn't going to come to our assistance.

I slammed the door behind us. Outside I could hear the sounds of violence, someone was getting a right hiding. Waddsy! He was still out there! Fuck it, we had to help him.

I opened the door again, and ran out, ready for it. I must have been mad. Benny was right behind me. These were evil bastards and armed to the teeth. I kicked out at one, but it was a waste of time; say your prayers, Browner, I said to myself. Waddsy was on the floor, foetal position, trying to protect his head, getting a kicking. They then turned on me, and an iron bar smashed against my skull; I went down like a sack of shit. Then the boots came in, one caught me right in the face. That warm, sweet taste filled my mouth. I started blubbering, snot, tears, blood.

'Leave it, leave it please, please,' I snivelled, 'I've had enough...'

'No you fuckin' ain't, you English cunt!'

I could hear their grunts, every time they kicked; like a boxer expelling air at every punch, they really meant it. I could smell them, smell the polish from their boots, even taste it.

Their job done, they made a hasty exit, no doubt off to find further prey. A stillness and silence came over me; the only sound was my own pathetic snivelling and the bubbling of blood from my battered nose and mouth. I barely knew what was happening, where I was, what I was doing. Then a dawning awareness of events came to me. I was in the back of an ambulance heading for Singleton Hospital.

The waiting room was like a battle zone. There were beaten and bloodied kids everywhere, stab wounds, split heads, bodies pummelled with bricks, bottles, the lot. Fairly even numbers too – at least we had given as good as we got. Waddsy was there, grinning, hardly a mark on him, nice little stab wound on his side, blood staining his best Ben Sherman.

My head was stitched up and bandaged, my body was aching like fuck and my lip felt as if it had grown to the size of a rugby ball. I'd been given a right kicking, my skull had been fractured – something really to boast about – and my face looked a right mess. Look on the bright side, Browner, I thought to myself, you're going to have a tidy scar at least, something to show off at school.

There were a couple of Tote Enders there that I knew. We even started laughing and joking with the Swansea kids who were in there – nice lads really, just like us. Took one kid's phone number, promised I'd keep in touch, never did. He had been slashed across the face with a knife – he was going to have a lovely scar. I was jealous.

We all started singing the bow-legged chicken song, the standard football-hooligan anthem. Welsh and English skinheads united, having a crack together... the hospital staff were bemused and bewildered; they didn't understand. Books would be written by experts, psychologists would try to analyse us,

A WELCOME IN THE HILLSIDES

World In Action and *Panorama* would make documentaries about us and questions would be raised in Parliament. We would be studied and various theories would be put forward by the great thinkers of the nation as to why young men caused trouble at football matches. I could have saved them all a lot of time and effort. It was quite simple... we enjoyed it.

April 1971. Hundreds of miles away in Carlisle, a boy was born in the same month that I was receiving a hiding in Swansea. No doubt he came into the world kicking and screaming, maybe even puking and shitting. My contemporaries and I had been causing aggro in Baghdad while the future self-styled England's number-one football hooligan was still in his dad's bag.

10
Front-page News

I hate summers, for obvious reasons. Somehow I couldn't get excited over cricket, but the summer of 1971 was a good one. Although the generic term 'skinhead' was still the norm, the hair length and the fashion was changing with alarming speed; you could almost hear the hair growing in Willesden and sure enough it was quickly spreading to the rest of the country. There were very few truly shaved heads even in 1969 and now, two years on, the blokes, as in the mode of Arsenal's darling of the North Bank, Charlie George, were even beginning to adopt the feather cut that had been popular with the sorts.

The last 12 months had seen the emergence of a more toned-down and conservative version of the skin; we had grown our hair and donned our brogues. By 1971, 'suedeheads' had become the more common moniker, although 'smoothies', which referred as much to our style of clothes as our hair length, was also being bandied around. 'Brolly boys' was yet another tag given to us by the more sensational tabloid newspapers, due to our penchant for umbrellas with sharpened tips, which had become the most recent addition to our armoury. Richard Allen was not slow to catch on. His latest literary offerings featuring the antihero Joe Hawkins, *Suedehead* and *Skinhead Escapes*, were again selling millions and storming up the best-sellers list in WH Smith, much to the disgust of our English teachers.

Ben Shermans were still popular, but the checks and stripes were out. It was now plain black or white, or even chocolate brown, Fair Isle sweaters were confined to the back of the wardrobe and braces were given back to your old man quicker than you could say 'Austins'.

Mr Zeus, Harry Fenton, Beau Brummel and Austins were well up there for the smart gear. Stone-Dri, Keedons, Rodney Thomas and even Millets sold the basics. But Austins was always the clothes shop for the suedeheads; you could walk through one door a yeti and come out the other end smoother than a snake's bald bits. Abercrombie overcoats, Prince of Wales and dog-toothed check jackets, iridescent Tonik strides (as with crombies, not the real thing as made by Dormeuil, but a perfectly respectable imitation made by Levi's and CTs), Oxford bags, the full bollocks. There was fine attention to detail: tie-tacks inserted not through a tie but into your breast pocket holding in a silk handkerchief or a three triangular version in your club colours mounted on a piece of card, embroidered football club badges and coats of arms or your own initials stitched on to box-vented Barrathea blazers. The girls looked little darlings in their two-tone Trevira suits and patterned stockings. The boots were in their death throes, OK for on the terraces but the pubs and clubs were having none of it. Brogues had become popular with the suedeheads and were still much in evidence, as were tassled loafers, basketweave style 'wegians' and 'bovver mocs' – heavy, thick-soled leather moccasins, the forerunner of the platform shoe.

We all had part-time jobs. Nothing special – I worked in the Gateway supermarket stacking shelves, as many Mars bars as you

BOOTED AND SUITED

could nick and 'titting off' the checkout girls in the storeroom being the only bonus scheme on offer. Still, the extra bit of money enabled us to go into town once or twice a week if we were lucky, to our favourite haunt, the Locarno.

The Bali Hai was exactly like it sounded: plastic palm trees and dusky maidens painted on the walls. You could even smell the exotic aromas wafting in from paradise, or was it 'that great smell of Brut'? It wasn't a sun-drenched south Pacific island, but a Sixties-built pile of shite called the New Entertainment Centre in Frogmore Street. Still, it did for us on a Monday night with no football for a couple of months.

There had been some cracking records that year, not least The Elgins with the rereleased 'Heaven Must Have Sent You' and The Tams with 'Hey Girl Don't Bother Me' which likewise had first hit the charts during the previous decade. Reggae was still making an impression with 'Monkey Spanner', Dave and Ansel Collins's follow-up to their number 1 of March, reaching number 7. Motown continued to perform well, with 'Just My Imagination' by The Temptations; which more than made up for that God-awful 'Chirpy, Chirpy, Cheep, Cheep' by Middle of the Road, a massive number-1 hit. Chairmen of the Board, the skins' erstwhile favourite band, were still belting it out with 'Everything's Tuesday' and 'Pay To The Piper' and one of the greatest records of all time, by one of the greatest artists, 'Move On Up' by Curtis Mayfield, made the summer of 1971 one to remember, musically at any rate. And just when you thought it couldn't get much better, an album of epic proportions was released.

Marvin Gaye's *What's Going On* broke all the rules, as far as soul music was concerned. It was a radical and challenging piece of work. Its jazz underpinnings, unconventional tracking and biting political commentary, especially relevant to the US's continued involvement in Vietnam, summed up the tumultuous

FRONT-PAGE NEWS

early Seventies through the eyes of a disillusioned Afro-American. Its relevance to white British kids was negligible; we just liked the music. To quote Smokey Robinson on the legendary album, 'It was funky as the devil... it made musical history'.

On the dancefloors, reggae was still going strong, despite the fact that, for a short time the previous year, the Top Rank had banned the popular West Indian music due to its association with the skinhead movement, something which the manager, Nick Pennycott, vehemently denied, claiming that the music was merely 'out-of-date', extraordinary really when you consider the amount of reggae in the charts at the time. The rerelease of '54–46 Was My Number' by The Maytals got us all stomping and singing along, as did Jimmy Cliff's 'Come Into My Life' and Winston Groovy's 'Please Don't Make Me Cry', while old ska and rock steady favourites such as 'Guns Of Navarone' by The Skatalites, 'Wet Dream' by Max Romeo, 'John Crow Skank' by Derrick Morgan and 'Al Capone' and 'Big Five' by Prince Buster were all as popular as ever.

The Locarno wasn't a place for the intellectual, the educated, the hippies; it was a place of simple pleasures. The Tote was well represented, as was the City's East End, In fact, at times it was more like a football crowd. Violence was as common at the Locarno and the Top Rank as it was at Eastville or Ashton Gate, sometimes even more so, the dancefloor substituting perfectly for the terraces. We always wondered why we were referred to as football hooligans. We were hooligans plain and simple; football just happened to be our most convenient stage.

The city centre wasn't a place for the faint-hearted either. On Friday, 14 August, a young copper was savagely beaten up by a mob of twenty skinheads. Twenty-one-year-old PC Brian Langhorne was found lying in the gutter in Small Street suffering from a fractured skull and concussion. The very next day saw the

BOOTED AND SUITED

start of the football season and a visit to Ashton Gate by Millwall brought about a mass brawl in North Street, Bedminster, after City fans smashed the rear window of a passing coach. The following week, the Centre was the scene of a pitched battle between skinheads, bikers and coppers. Hundreds were involved; in Rupert Street a biker was knocked off his machine by skins armed with paving slabs, only to be rescued by firemen who themselves came under attack. The inevitable revenge mission came about the following week, with a gang of 70 Hells Angels rampaging through the Centre, only to be broken up and moved on by the newly formed Special Task Force, tagged 'The Bovver Squad' by the local press.

The good citizens of Bristol were justifiably terrified and the local press were having a field day. Just to prove how horrified they were, the *Western Daily Press* ran a three-part exposé of how they had infiltrated the 'violent world of the football hooligan' entitled 'The Lore of the Tote End Mob'. We loved it. If the Tote End had been on a recruiting drive we couldn't have written a better piece of publicity, it was music to our ears:

MEET THE TOTE END MOB, third in Soccer's League of Violence [newspapers loved these leagues of violence, see Chapter 14]. *Bristol Rovers are their idols. And if the team gets beaten on the pitch this screaming army of followers will win on the terraces.*

Behind the goal, at the popular end of every football ground in the Third Division, is their battlefield. Here they wage war on rival skinhead supporters, awarding their own fearsome points system. And this young mob, with their steel-capped boots and cropped hair proudly boast: 'We are third in the league.' But this league of terror has nothing to do with sport. It causes havoc to every club in Britain which is fighting the new frightening wave of football hooliganism 1971–72 style.

FRONT-PAGE NEWS

We lapped it up. Sales of the *Western Daily* went through the roof – everybody kept a copy of it in their back pocket. It did more for our self-esteem and reputation than any 'Keep off the Tote End' graffiti spray-painted on a wall outside Stapleton Road station ever could.

The articles appeared in September – the football season was only a month old and already we were making the headlines. We had beaten City on and off the pitch at Ashton in a pre-season friendly, giving the 'boys in suits' a right larruping on the East End and in the streets of Bedminster. The first round of the League Cup saw us playing at Exeter, scrapping all night and 18 arrested. Our first decent away game was, of all places, Torquay again. Following the violence from the previous season the game was played on a Saturday night, but this just resulted in more aggro due to a larger intake of alcohol. The authorities really had their finger on the pulse for that one.

However, back in Bristol at any rate, the police were beginning to get their act together and acting on a tip-off from northern police they stopped and searched three coachloads of Middlesbrough fans who had arrived for the game with City in the early hours of Saturday morning. Ten were arrested as an assortment of weapons, which the local press described as 'terrible', were confiscated off the coaches, the armoury consisted of, among other weapons, two hatchets, five metal-filled rubber coshes, one wooden-handled cosh with a metal tip, one meat skewer, one meat hook, lavatory chains with metal nuts attached, knives and studded belts. A police spokesman at the time, Superintendent Callaghan, commented in the *Evening Post* with almost childlike bewilderment 'the two hatchets were new and bought for a specific purpose – and that wasn't for chopping wood or cleaning their fingernails, it must have been for some more unlawful purpose'.

Due to the late stay in Torquay (those girls were very

BOOTED AND SUITED

hospitable again), we missed the football special back to Temple Meads. There were about 20 of us and the law escorted us to Newton Abbot on a local train where we had to wait for the main line train from Plymouth: It was to be a long night.

The first train that pulled in was a local flyer heading for Plymouth. The windows came down... 'ARGYLE, ARGYLE, ARGYLE, ARGYLE!' It was full of the bastards, one of our old enemies. We knew we only had a few minutes to act, as the train would be pulling out soon. We scrambled around for anything we could chuck – bricks, bottles, a bucket was quickly emptied of sand and thrown at the sitting target. Some Argyle fans got off and jumped on to the railway lines; we took up the challenge, but no sooner had it started than it was over again, a nice little rumble, no real damage, a few bloody noses and broken windows. The train pulled out, skinheads bidding their goodbyes as only they can:

'Yeah! I'll fucking see you at Eastville, you Devon cunt!'

'Come 'ere an' say that, you Bristol wanker!'

'You're 'ard now the train's leaving, tosser, just fuck off back to your sailor boyfriend!'

Two fingered salutes and gallons of saliva accompanied our pleasant little tête-à-têtes.

'That was a laugh,' said Harvey, our biggest lad. He was one of the first on to the railway lines, his pristine made-to-measure crombie now looking decidedly the worse for wear, with a big rip up the back.

'Your mum'll kill you when she sees that.' I gestured to his back.

'Bollocks. I'm dead,' replied Harvey. He was over six feet tall, a great lump of a rugby-playing, up-for-it, 16-year-old Tote Ender, who happened to be shit-scared of his mum.

The action continued. We decided to have a wander around Newton Abbot; our train wasn't due until gone 12. The trouble with small country towns is they've got no class. No class meant no skins. No skins usually meant one thing: greebos!

Skinheads didn't like greebos. For one they were usually bigger than us, and for two they were usually tougher than us – one-to-one against a greebo would usually result in one beaten and bruised skinhead. Tonight would be no exception. They spotted us as we came out of a chip shop, and started to chant:

'Skinhead, skinhead over there, what's it like with no hair? Is it hot or is it cold, I don't know 'cos I'm not bald!' It was a playground chant, and they sang it just like little schoolgirls. Only these schoolgirls were dressed in dirty denims and leathers and slumped on big, ugly Triumphs.

'Go fuck yourself!' shouted Jock, still dressed like a skin from a few years back, quarter-inch-wide red braces, bleached Levi's one inch shy of big black, steel-toe-capped industrial boots. Jock was a couple of years older than us, but not any wiser. He might have looked the part, but like the rest of us he was no match for a big, hulking greebo.

'I'll have you, you little runt!' The yetis were off their bikes and reaching for their chains in a flash. We all looked at Jock. 'Run!' he whispered through gritted teeth. We didn't have to be told twice, once one starts to run you all run; survival of the fittest. We headed back for the station, cod and chips flying. We outran them but they weren't giving up easily.

Back at the station we regrouped and all came out of the station together. But there still weren't enough of us; it was a Mexican stand-off. We outnumbered them two to one, but they had the weapons. And they wanted Jock.

'Come on, you with the mouth!' taunted one of the greebos, pointing at Jock, 'I'll twang those braces round your arse, you little...'

Jock didn't need the invitation, he went for him straight off. Typical Scottish, I thought, never needed much of an excuse for

BOOTED AND SUITED

a scrap. It was no contest. Jock put up a good show, but the greebo gave him a pasting. The law arrived – as usual, never around when you want them – by which time Jock was rolling around the ground in agony. This was serious. He was in a bad way, crying out in pain and clutching his sides. The greebo was arrested, Jock ended up in hospital with a broken pelvis and we skulked off back to Bristol on the milk train. Harvey's mum was not happy.

Back to the *Western Daily*:

> *I have learned the codes of hatred of the so-called supporters, who set themselves up as guardians of their team's honour ... why they have to organise special task forces for away matches; what happens when they take over other supporters' territory; and the meaning behind their constant chanting ... To the Tote Enders their weapons and the cunning tricks to get them into the ground are essential in their deadly serious war on the terraces. The idea is to take over the popular end of every ground in the Third Division. The home team's young hooligan fans defend, the visitors attack.*
>
> *Aston Villa top this league of violence; Notts County, fresh to the Third Division, come second with a quickly established reputation.*
>
> *Word has got round to the boys from the Tote End and they are preparing with relish for their visit to Nottingham on Saturday...*

Thanks to the *Western Daily Press*, an army of low-lifes and desperadoes were heading north. New recruits were taken on, all eager to get a slice of the action thanks to our new-found celebrity status. Boots were polished up and we were armed to the teeth, looking forward to an away victory and moving up the league to second position. Unfortunately Notts County hadn't followed the script.

'Nay, lad, you won't get any trouble here. Notts fans are as good as gold,' the landlord of the Magpie informed us with

FRONT-PAGE NEWS

immense pride. 'Forest are the trouble-makers and they're all away today. See you later, me ducks.'

You can stick your ducks up your northern arse, I thought.

The few yobbos that County had were quickly dealt with; we chased them right out of the ground. It was pathetic. Still, we learned a new song from one lone smoothie who decided to stay and chance his arm: 'Bertie Mee said to Bill Shankly, have you heard of the North Bank of Highbury, Shanks said no, I don't think so, but I've heard of the Tote End Aggro, la, la, la, la, la, la...' An all-time favourite, right up there with 'I was born under the Tote Bar'. Songs and chants were all part of the ritual, as important as the dress code we all rigorously followed. It was a long way to go, however, just to learn a new bloody song. We trooped off home, Rovers had won 3–2, but it didn't make up for a disappointing day, even if we were second in the league.

The season progressed. Football violence was now an epidemic, going off at virtually every ground in the country; it became the norm. We had trouble wherever and whenever we wanted it, which was often, from Bournemouth to Blackburn, and Walsall to Wrexham. We stomped and pummelled across the country. Reading was a particularly good shout. Having chased the bastards right through the town centre, we caught up with them in the local graveyard – very appropriate.

Rovers found glory yet again in the League Cup. Cup games against teams from a higher division were always something special. It was OK wrecking a provincial town like Shrewsbury, but mixing it with the big boys was something else. We visited QPR in the fourth round on a Tuesday evening; West London was in for a shock. Never mind 'Rodneeeee' (QPR's star player, Rodney Marsh), 'Haroooooold' (our own flying winger, Harold Jarman) rang out from all around the ground.

There was a record in the charts at the time, 'Tap Turns On The Water', by CCS who were fronted by blues man Alexis

BOOTED AND SUITED

Korner. It was a dire song, with some dodgy lyrics about seeing your sister in the raw. However, it was perfect for adapting by a drunken horde on a day trip to the Smoke:

Tap turns on the cider,
see the cider flow,
cider makes the Tote End,
watch the Tote End go,
we all come from Bristol,
come from Bristol town,
we all come from Bristol,
so get your knickers down!

Loftus Road roared with laughter; they laughed on the other side of their faces when we took the place over, chasing them first off their end, The Loft, then after the game following it up with a good hammering all the way back to Paddington. The looks on their faces! They couldn't believe a bunch of swede-bashers could be so vicious, especially the ones who, after chasing a gang of locals into a block of flats, grabbed one and threatened to throw the terrified wretch off the balcony, his pleas for leniency echoing around the grim tower block – it was our turn to laugh. Mercifully he was let go, much to the disgust of some of the less compassionate pursuers. Rovers drew 1–1, Harold scoring a screamer resulting in a victorious replay in front of over 24,000 at Eastville, where we gave the geezers from the Smoke another good kicking, bumble-bee tank tops and all.

The quarter-finals in November paired us against Gordon Banks's Stoke City at Eastville. This was to be one of our biggest tests. Stoke City were a big First Division side, over 33,000 packed into the ground; Rovers' anthem 'Goodnight Irene' could be heard all over East Bristol. Eastville never looked or smelled better, the gasworks were working overtime and it was raining

FRONT-PAGE NEWS

again, that relentless rain that got right through your crombie and chilled your bones. The Tote End, though, was steaming; it was so packed the coppers couldn't get a look in. The Stoke fans, a section of whom were known as 'The Family', had filled the right-hand side of the Tote. They'd arrived early and were well encamped; we couldn't budge them.

They were the biggest and ugliest bunch of fans you could ever wish to meet — we had our work cut out. Andy made a move and singled out the biggest fucker of them all.

'Fuck me, wouldn't mind him full of threepenny bits!' commented Lil about the monster that dominated their boys.

Andy sidled up to the monster and swung that infamous arm, landing that infamous punch. I winced. The monster didn't though, he just looked at Andy and smiled. Andy landed another. The monster smiled again, or was it wind? Either way, Andy knew when he was beaten; he made a swift exit. Ball-bearings and lighted bangers were chucked with frightening ferocity, but still they wouldn't move. It was time for some terror tactics.

'I'm gonna grab a fucker!' This came from Ricky Lee, a tasty piece of work from Southmead. We had known Ricky for some time. He was older, though not much bigger than us, and had a reputation for being a bit of a nutter after he had attacked Reading's end several years earlier, virtually single-handedly. Like Andy and Rob Boyle, Ricky was someone we looked up to.

Ricky was also a man of his word. He slowly worked his way through the crowd, determined to get to his prey. He picked out a Stoke fan, another gruesome son of a bitch who had been mouthing to us all night across the gangway. Shaven headed and as spotty as Benny, he deserved to get a slap for being so ugly.

'Oi, ugly!' shouted Ricky. This description could have fitted half of the Stoke fans, they all looked Mongoloid. Must be all that in-breeding in the Potteries, I thought.

Sure enough, Ugly took the bait: 'Fuck off, you southern poofter.'

Ricky had him in his sights, but he needed a diversion. The law had forced a gap between the two sets of warring fans, the gangway being a no-man's land. Ricky pushed against the coppers and we all joined in. A huge shove was now developing behind us, tumbling down the terraces, falling, spilling over each other, the coppers turned trying to stem the tide. But we were determined to breach the long line of dark blue. It gave, the law forced us back, but their line had broken. Ricky was through and we swiftly joined him, quick punches, arms flailing at 90 miles per hour, punching down on to unprotected heads. It was quick and effective. Ricky grabbed Ugly round the neck. Forcing his head down, he pulled him towards us, punching expertly with one fist as his other arm kept a vice-like grip around his neck. He was dragging him backwards. Fist-fights were going off all around, the coppers powerless to stop it; the constant chant of 'A-G, A-G-R, A-G-R-O, AGRO!' rang in our ears. The Rovers fans around us could see what was happening now. Eager to be part of Ricky's rumble, they closed ranks, engulfing the powerless Ugly under a torrent of blows and kicks. He was screaming in terror now – everyone was determined to give him a hiding. He went down, the worse place he could have gone. The boots went in, mercilessly and relentlessly. We whooped like savages – we were savages, and Ugly was our victim. Finally, he disappeared. For all I knew or cared, he could have been ground into the litter and squalor of the Tote.

Rovers lost 4–2 – we were totally outplayed – but the bovver didn't stop after the game; we clashed again outside the White Swan. A Stoke fan suffered a severe beating and lost an eye as a result. A police horse was stabbed, throwing its rider high in the

FRONT-PAGE NEWS

air; Stapleton Road was wrecked; cars had their windows smashed and others were overturned. Terry Conroy, Stoke's flying winger, tore Rovers apart that night; off the pitch, the two sets of fans did their best to tear each other apart. It was a night of sheer wanton violence; we were in our element.

11

Strides and Shooters

Henbury School had by now had enough of Dennis Wardell and his cronies, and the inevitable happened. Waddsy and Benny were expelled for their umpteenth misdemeanour. The school authorities had seen Denny as the head of a troublesome subculture and his expulsion was swift. I never saw him again. Benny joined the army, carrying on being a hooligan and now getting paid for it. His predilection for queer-bashing found greater rewards serving in Her Majesty's forces than it ever could on Civvy Street.

The expulsions had the desired effect: the school returned to normality and I returned to my O levels. We were now leaderless, a pack without a top dog, but it wouldn't last. We were in our last term at school; bigger and better things were on the horizon.

January 1972, third round of the FA Cup – an absolute belter, away to Leeds United, the cream of British football, Billy Bremner, Norman Hunter, Jackie Charlton et al. This would be our real moment of glory, aggro in Yorkshire under an iron-grey

STRIDES AND SHOOTERS

sky. The Tote was on a roll, nothing could stop us now, we were in the big league... somehow I didn't believe a word of it.

We poured off the trains, hundreds, thousands of us, eager and willing. All the kiddies were there: Ricky Lee, still basking in the afterglow of the Stoke match, his faithful sidekick, Sparky, so-called for his ability to 'spark out' an opponent with one punch; tall, wiry, up-for-it Tom Slick. Dependable, classy Rob Boyle, Tim 'Nobody run' Bass, and the irrepressible Andy Phelps and his very own motley crew, 'The Tramps', made up the rest.

There were a lot of mixed loyalties in the air for this match. Leeds United were a big club, they had a large following among the Tote, together with Chelsea (my other team), Manchester United, West Ham and many others. Everybody followed another club, though somehow I couldn't imagine many Leeds fans' other team being Bristol Rovers. We spotted them first on wasteland off Elland Road. Wasteland off Elland Road? The whole fucking town was wasteland. Still, their kiddies looked smart, lots of baggy check strides, Rupert Bear-style, bright yellow with bold black lines, cracking sheepskin coats – they needed them, it was as cold as buggery up north. Shoulder-length hair, not a skin in sight; the times they were a-changing. Boots were still in evidence, highly polished and highly-used too by the look of them. These were class kiddies all right and they knew it. They deserved a lot of respect... didn't get it though, got a good kicking instead.

'Go for the big kiddy over there.' Tim Bass was ordering us around as usual. Tim shouldn't have been a hooligan – not because he wasn't up to the task, far from it, but blokes named Tim, Nick or Simon just couldn't be thugs. Thugs had names like Dave, Steve, Andy or, at a push, Chris. But Tim? No, that was the name of the school swot. There was another reason Tim shouldn't have been a bona fide hooligan: his old man was a copper. Didn't do him much good, though. Tim on his day was up there with the best of them. Seeing Tim being chased down Stapleton Road by his old man was a sight to behold, but it didn't do Tim's reputation much good.

'Nah, leave it out, he's got a walking stick, poor bastard couldn't leg it if he tried,' Harvey replied charitably. Or did his comment have something to do with the fact that tied around Harvey's ample waist, underneath his crombie, was his white, blue and yellow Leeds United scarf? The big smoothie smiled at us, and muttered something under his breath; somehow I didn't think it was 'Thanks'. We left him alone to hobble along Elland Road with half a dozen of his mates, all grinning at us from the other side of the road. I got the feeling this wasn't the last we were going to see of them.

The closer we got to the ground, the more menacing it got. Following the skirmish the law arrived and escorted us all the way to the ground, no stopping, no pubs, no drinking, fuck all. These coppers were professionals, they were used to large-scale aggro, not poncing around with amateurs from some sleepy holiday resort. We got off lightly, a few bottles and bricks coming our way and the odd rush, but the law held firm. We got into the ground in one piece, and all breathed a long, stone-cold sober sigh of relief.

Elland Road was the first big ground most of us had been to. It showed too – we were in awe. We thought about having a pop at the Gelderd Road End – yeah, fucking right, thought about it for a millisecond. Some poor bastards had a go and barely lived to regret it. Still they got a good reception when the law escorted what was left of them around the edge of the pitch, to the comparative safety of the 'away end'. Somebody should have told the Leeds fans this was the away end; there was as many of them as us in there.

'Ay up, ay up, ay up, ay up, ay up!' we goaded them. No bollocks, they really did speak like that. We took the piss out of

STRIDES AND SHOOTERS

their poncy nickname: ''Ere, mate, is that right a female Peacock is called a Pea-cunt?' I shouted, pleased at myself, especially when everybody roared with laughter, including the Leeds fans. Various comments about relationships with whippets and pigeons, answered by tractor and manure retorts – we knew it was about to go off, and we didn't have long to wait.

They scored an early goal, the first of four. The Tote surged towards the Leeds fans who were packed in front of us; no divided loyalties now – it was us against them. Harvey made a beeline for the kiddy who had been genuinely admiring his embroidered initials on his crombie, a popular fashion in Bristol that had not yet spread to Yorkshire; it wouldn't have looked right on their sheepskins anyway. The law moved in fast, breaking it up with truncheons and dogs, and it was over before it started. A dozen or so arrests later, including Dobbsy, later to be fined an ineffectual £5, and a peace of sorts was restored by half-time. Rovers lost 4–1; we didn't expect much more. We were an average Third Division team, they were one of the top teams in the country. Our only thought was getting back to the safety of the station. We decided to leave before the final whistle.

'Let's get the bus back, I don't fancy that walk,' Lil suggested. We didn't need much persuading. 'Good thinking, Lil.'

The buses were lined up ready and waiting. So were the Leeds fans. We kept our heads down and our collars up and arrived at the station in one piece. Judging by the state of some of the Rovers fans arriving at the station afterwards, we were the lucky ones. The long slog from the ground had taken its toll on some of the Tote Enders. We regrouped – we needed to – they were coming up the subway opposite us, hundreds of them, like a swarm of ants. I couldn't believe it. They had beaten us 4–1, what more did they want, blood? Obviously they did. They danced through the traffic, an orchestrated move, obviously practised many times before. We were pinned up against a side entrance to the train station, heavy metal gates barring our way to the safety of our train.

They fired in; we were in disarray. 'Nobody run!' This came from Timmy, who had decided to make a stand. We joined him — safety in numbers. The ones who did run were like headless chickens, running through the traffic, back towards the ground, to be engulfed by even more Leeds fans swarming up the road, car horns, bottles smashing, shouts, screams, the sounds of violence. The ones who stayed were holding their own. We had no inferiority complex — we were as good as them, if not better. And in the end we did all right — I copped a Yorkshire twat right in the bollocks, and got smacked around the head for my sins.

Then I spotted him, the smoothie with the walking stick. Except the walking stick had now miraculously changed into an eight iron golf club. Amazingly, he had also been cured of his limp. He was now chasing some unfortunate Bristolian back down Elland Road, swinging the club through the air and whooping with delight. The sound of iron striking bone brought back memories of my trip to Wales and I winced in shared pain as yet another skull was cracked in the name of football. The gates behind us opened. The police tried to break up the violence and herded us on to the platform, but it wasn't over yet. There were no definitive lines between the fighting fans and chaos reigned; innocent bystanders were now embroiled in the fighting. We headed for the comparative safety of the train. Well, we thought it would be safe at first...

'Bollocks, they're on the train. Get the fuckers!'

These bastards were relentless in their quest for aggro. They had an insatiable appetite and we were the main course on their menu. We steamed in, but it was nightmarish trying to fight in the confined spaces of the compartments. Windows were smashed and a fire extinguisher was let off. The Tote was regrouping as more and more of us piled on the train, weapons

STRIDES AND SHOOTERS

being drawn. Knives, chains, sharpened steel combs, they were all out, slashing and gouging. We eventually forced them off, together with the local constabulary, who had evidently seen it all before. There was, however, one last parting shot. Literally.

We settled down in a relatively unscathed compartment – me, Harvey, Lil, Mogger, Terry 'Arkle' Macallum (so-called for clearing a fence at Shrewsbury with one prodigious leap. I'm not sure if he was chasing somebody – more likely, knowing Terry, somebody was chasing him) and Johnny 'Blue-Eyes' Watt.

'Good crack, eh, boys?' said Arkle.

'Yeah, brilliant.'

'See me belt that big fucker!'

'Yeah, what about me, I got a right kicking.'

'I caught one right in the balls, went down like a bag of shit...'

All the usual self-congratulatory bollocks, each one of us trying to top the other, stories sure to be embellished over the years. The train slowly pulled out. We felt pleased with ourselves, and relieved to be leaving relatively unscathed.

We all gathered around the window to bid our final farewells to the Yorkshire toe-rags, still massed on the platform.

'Give us an RRRRRR!' we started to shout. 'Give us an OOOO!' But we were stopped in our tracks. Johnny Blue Eyes spotted him first: 'Watch out, that little fucker's goin' to chuck summat!'

He reached inside his crombie, which must have been one of the last ones left in Leeds. We expected a bottle, or a brick; we braced ourselves, or rather shat ourselves, when we saw the black barrel of a gun coming out of his pocket.

'FUUUUUUUUUCK!' we screamed in unison. 'He's got a fucking gun!' And he was pointing it straight at us, a black, stubby-barrelled gun. No, this ain't happening, I thought, but it was. He fired just as we all dived for the floor, the crack of the gun and the crack of the window happened simultaneously. We

135

BOOTED AND SUITED

were showered with glass, somebody evacuated their bowels; we were shot at, fucking shot at by some 16-year-old little runt who was out to make a name for himself. Why us? I thought, why waste it on a poxy load of fans like us? You could understand it if we were Manchester United or Liverpool. Maybe he did it every week, maybe aggro like this happened every week in the First Division. Maybe it was time to call it a day, I thought.

We picked ourselves up in utter silence. It stayed like that for a couple of minutes. We were in shock. Then, the door of our compartment flew open. Tom Slick stood there. 'What the fuck happened here?'

'Nothing much,' I replied. 'We were just shot at, that's all.'

'Yeah, right,' answered Tom, he turned and walked away. 'Lying bastards.'

12
New Faces

After our sobering lesson in Yorkshire, we settled down to more mundane matters. But games against the likes of Rochdale, Mansfield and Port Vale somehow didn't have the same appeal; without Waddsy on board, life seemed a bit dull. The Locarno was still an attraction although, sadly, with the demise of skinheads came the demise of good reggae. Eric Donaldson was singing forlornly about his 'Cherry Oh Baby' and Dennis Alcapone did his best Prince Buster impersonation on 'Alcapone Guns Don't Bark'. These and an absolute classic, 'Scorpion' by Lloyd and Carey, were the exceptions that proved the rule. Dennis Alcapone and his predecessors and great rivals King Stitt and U-Roy, who was known as 'the Originator', were DJs of immense talent and originality and were the creators of the style of reggae music known as 'version'. Version involved the DJs singing and talking in rhythm over instrumental versions of the popular hits of the day and even remixing them to form what was to be known in later years as rap. These artistes were the forerunners of the latter-day toasters, boasters and rappers; anyone who thinks rapping started with The Sugar Hill Gang in the USA is very much mistaken.

BOOTED AND SUITED

The style and subject matter of Jamaican music was changing as fast as our own fashions were. No longer were they empathising with white British youth, no longer were they singing about stomping and girls 'Whining And Grining', but about Babylon and Ras Tafari, Lord of Lords, King of Kings, going back to Africa and smoking da weed. It was totally alien to us council-house kids who had taken this music from an island none of us knew about to our hearts. I consoled myself with my own King of Kings, Al Green — that Reverend sure could sing. The girls liked him too — great to work your leg up into their fanny when you danced; you got a stiffy and they got all moist, hand down their knickers in the photo booth if you were lucky.

Motown was dying on its feet, although sweet lyrics were still on offer by the likes of Donnie Elbert with 'Where Did Our Love Go?' and 'I Can't Help Myself'. Sly and the Family Stone performed their masterful 'Family Affair' while Isaac Hayes was coming on like a real bad-ass mother — or so he said, what the fuck it meant nobody knew — providing the excellent soundtrack to *Shaft*. We watched *Shaft* and *Superfly* (featuring another cracking soundtrack, this time courtesy of Curtis Mayfield) at the Orpheus in Henleaze, because we thought we had to. We all tried to act like big, cool, John Shaft, even donning long black leather coats and polo-necked sweaters like his. The metamorphosis of the skinhead was now all but complete.

By the summer of 1972, the cult, in southern England at any rate, had all but disappeared. But it wasn't as if skinhead values had disappeared with the skinheads themselves. Skins, by way of suedeheads and brolly boys, had now fully evolved into smoothies. Admittedly, a lot of new smoothies were kid brothers who had been too young for the skinhead movement, but by and large smoothies were all ex-skins, so it wasn't as if we were about to change our outlook or the way we acted. Scratch away at any smoothie with his shoulder-length hair and his bumble-bee

NEW FACES

striped tank-top and you'd find a dyed-in-the-wool skinhead who, given half the chance, would still participate in aggro and bovver.

The ubiquitous tank-top had appeared at the tail-end of 1971 and was now part of our standard dress code. Tank-tops came in a variety of bright colours, were usually striped and proved to be a natural successor to the popular Fair Isle sweaters of a few years earlier. Plain black vest tank-tops were also customised with iron-on transfers of Popeye and 'Tote End' or your postcode, as in 'BS' in the top corners and '10' in foot-high figures in the centre. This certainly made you stand out in the crowd and also guaranteed you a hiding from an inhabitant of BS9 or BS11 if you were unlucky. That proved to be the case for me one evening when, on leaving the Locarno, I was set upon by a disgruntled Southmead smoothie, an assault that put me in the casualty department of the BRI thanks to a lethal kick to the head from a heavy loafer.

Our shirts now possessed large, rounded 'fly-away' collars. One particularly popular design came in dark brown with a contrasting cream 'yoked' top running across the shoulders, while our straight-legged Toniks had disappeared in favour of high-waisted 18" bags. The tight Levi's or Wrangler jeans had given way to wide, baggy jeans, a popular make being 'Skinners', available not only in blue denim but brilliant white and purchased from Mr Zeus on the Centre. If you couldn't run to the cost of a pair of white Skinners then a pair of ex-naval baggy strides as worn by those 'superior' Preston lads the previous year would suffice. Fringed and buckled stompers which had appeared in early 1972 were now being joined by elevated wooden-soled or plastic imitation 'madcaps', large, highly polished toe-capped shoes in a variety of colours. Even the old mod favourite the suede desert boot had made a bit of a comeback.

BOOTED AND SUITED

The hair was long, centre parted and blow dried and curled up in the style of Brian Connolly from the glam rock band Sweet. Suddenly, from getting our barnet shaved in some backstreet barbers we were booking appointments with Tina, Tracy or, worst of all, Jason at Guy Fawkes in St Nicholas Street. Getting your hair cut by some tart was an embarrassment, only mildly compensated for by them sticking their tit in your ear. We were actually paying to get our hair washed before we had it cut — what was the world coming to? In a short space of time your average white working-class kid had evolved from a tough, macho deserter from the British army into a limp-wristed, lily-livered poof, but I always believed in never judging a book by its cover. Our title and fashion had changed, but our outlook hadn't.

Hand-made three-piece suits were as popular as ever, but they were now 'bastardised' in more outrageous ways than you could think of. Jacksons in Broadmead on an early Thursday evening was the place to be. The made-to-measure suits that were ordered on the previous Saturday would arrive in all their glory.

'Look at the width of the lapels on that!'

'Fucking hell, half tulips, ace.'

'Nice stitching.' Stitching was all important, contrasting red, yellow or blue stitching and in varying width of stitches with every possible attention to detail. We posed and preened ourselves like a bunch of strutting peacocks.

The vents on the jackets were getting bigger and bigger, sometimes half the length of the jacket. Buttons on the cuffs went from a standard three to a dozen, going all the way up to the elbow.

'Bet the poor bastard Yid tailor was up all night sewing the buttons on that fucker!'

Tonik suits, black suits, brown suits, cream suits, white suits, even yellow suits, the lot — we were dictating fashion, fashion wasn't dictating us. 'Budgie' jackets were all the rage, so-called

NEW FACES

after the character played by Adam Faith in the ITV series of the same name. He was a right tasty geezer. I had bought one such jacket in Hummingbird on Park Row; a year or two earlier no self-respecting smoothie would have been seen dead in a 'jitter' shop like that. The jacket was brown and black suede, big, wide, rounded lapels, obscene really. We wore what we wanted. We were getting more outrageous, and glitter and glam rock was upon us. David Bowie was giving his all as Ziggy Stardust, Slade had abandoned their somewhat questionable skinhead roots, Roger Daltrey had long given up being a mod and Gary Glitter was about to unleash his brand of tacky showmanship upon us. I embraced the fashion but I couldn't take to the music, apart, that is, from Ian Hunter's Mott the Hoople, who had a cracking hit with Bowie's 'All The Young Dudes', which appealed to my sense of style in 1972, and 'All The Way From Memphis' and 'Roll Away The Stone' the following year. Apart from these all-too-infrequent offerings, there was little that stirred my soul. I immersed myself in Sixties ska and stayed there until it was safe to come out – it took a while.

We were getting to look more and more like the hippies we despised. There had even been a sighting of an Afghan sleeveless coat on the Tote End. The kiddie wearing it still had his Doc Martens on, though – some things never changed. The platform shoe might have ruled the dancefloor but the Doctor was still doing a roaring trade with the lads on the terraces – even if they were now being sprayed gold or silver. The general moniker of smoothies was all-encompassing, although the label 'Boot Boys' was also in common use, especially by the media, and was an obvious reference to our favoured footwear and the association with our earlier years. 'Boot Boys' was seen spray-painted on walls more than 'Skins' ever was and became synonymous with stating your territorial claims and your allegiance to your football club: BS10 Boot Boys, Knowle West Boot Boys, Tote End

BOOTED AND SUITED

Boot Boys, or just as commonly the abbreviations, T.E.B.B. We ruled, we dominated, Tote End Rules, OK? was spelled out on every wall. Why it was queried I never knew; it was an undeniable fact. R.A.M. baffled me for a while. Steve Bould and Gary Mallett were the kiddies responsible: Redland Aggro Merchants, all two of them.

'Kiddies', a peculiar expression, peculiar to Bristol. The Cockneys had their geezers, the Northerners had their lads, we had our kiddies. Nice kiddy, hard kiddy, smooth kiddy, gert big kiddy – you would only hear that in Bristol. I met Phil Gordon Hampshire for the first time on 3 April 1972 at Villa Park. It was the start of something big; we were to become top kiddies.

That day, though, didn't belong to Hampshire. Mogger became the name of the day. I had known Mogger since the late Sixties. We had gone to school together and he had been a fanatical Rovers fan since as long as I could remember. As a youngster he was a Rovers ball-boy and a bit of an 'anorak' judging by his collection of programmes and autographs, but now like the rest of us he was more interested in rucking. He did have one other interest though – a young girlfriend from Westbury called Jackie. It was a teenage love affair, nothing spectacular about it, and, like all our liaisons with girls at the time, he didn't let it interrupt his long-term love affair with Rovers or the Tote End.

Mogger had been with Jackie for about a year. She was a pleasant enough sort, not quite my type but she had a face that only a mother, or a Mogger, could love. Still, there's no accounting for taste. Jackie had recently spent a weekend in Weymouth, that familiar bolt-hole for all Bristolians, where she met a young Brummie chap called Mick who, of course, was a Villa fan. Now Mick had taken to writing to Jennie long and explicit love letters; the love letters, of course, found their way into Mogger's grubby mitts. Mogger was usually quite a placid

NEW FACES

chap, but with raging hormones inside him and revenge on his mind, there was only one course of action.

Mogger, together with trusty sidekick Terry, caught the early train from Temple Meads and headed straight for Mick's house in Brum. There, they proceeded to smash every window in the grimy Coleshill council house before exiting smartish for Villa Park pursued by one angry Mick and his old man, no doubt questioning Mogger's parentage all the way.

Terry couldn't stop laughing as they retold the story time and time again to us when we met up in the pub in Aston later. 'You should have seen his face, poor bastard was still in his pyjamas!'

'Ugly twat as well, don't know what she saw in him. Still with a bit of luck we'll see him again later, finish him off then, won't we?' boasted Mogger, looking at me for support.

'Don't look at me, it's your argument, not mine,' I replied.

'I don't think so,' said Mogger. 'I've written him a letter telling him all about my crew and how we're goin' to sort him out. I even said, "Watch out for Chrissy, he's got a knife and he's goin' to slit your throat from ear to ear!"'

'Thanks a bunch, tosser!' I replied, not believing him for one minute.

'We've got the Holte End in our hands, we've got the Holte End in our hands, we've got the Holte End in our hands!' We had too! I had never seen so many Rovers fans at an away game, there were thousands of us, many more than at Leeds. Our main mob was facing us at the opposite end of the ground, but about 500 of us had infiltrated the home fans and we had taken the massive, infamous Holte End with surprising ease. We had come charging up the steps at the back, a swift attack, and were merciless in our operation. It had been virtually bloodless, they ran to the far end of the cavernous terracing, stopping to regroup and assess the situation.

We knew we were in an unstable position. It was only 2.45, a quarter of an hour away from kick-off. If we could stay put for the next 15 minutes we would be OK. The law wouldn't dare move us off once the game had started, there were too many of us.

'Is that thunder?' I said to Lil, knowing deep down that it wasn't.

'With the weather like this?' he asked.

He was right, you didn't need to be a meteorologist to know there wasn't a cloud in the sky. It was the sound of a thousand pairs of heavily booted feet charging up the stairs to reclaim their territory.

They appeared behind us, coming up the same steps and emerging through the same tunnel we had exited not ten minutes before. They also came from our left and the mob that we had just chased off to our right had now recovered. Absolutely incensed, they attacked with real venom, a three-pronged attack that left us with only one way out – the pitch. We fought as much as we could, we could see our comrades-in-arms at the open end facing us desperately trying to get on the pitch and help us out, but the law massed in front of them held firm. To coin a phrase, we were fucked.

'VILLA, VILLA, VILLA!' It rang in our ears, it was deafening. We were fighting just to get away. Most of the Tote managed to get on the pitch – most, but not all. About 20 of us were stranded, surrounded, engulfed by this huge mob of enraged Brummies, baying for our blood for daring to take their famous end. The Rovers fans who were now on the pitch got brave again; they stood and taunted the Holte End as they slowly sauntered across the pitch back to their adoring worshippers at the open Witton Lane end. 'We took the Holte End, we took the Holte End!' they chanted. 'Shut the fuck up, shut the fuck up,' I chanted to myself, I didn't want the Brummies antagonised any more. We were cut off from safety, the law couldn't get anywhere near us,

NEW FACES

and I now knew how the Christians must have felt shortly before the lions tucked in. The whistle went for the kick-off. This was it, we were dead.

I looked around, carefully avoiding eye contact with the Holte Enders. I was looking for friendly faces. There weren't many. Lil, Harvey, Gerry Bays, the Barrett brothers from Lockleaze. Not many others I recognised. No Andy Phelps, no Dobbsy, no Ricky Lee, no Mogger or Terry for that matter — it was a sorry-looking bunch. Nobody dared say anything to each other. An uneasy peace set in, there was the odd 'sheep-shagger' comment and other references to various illegal acts on farms, but generally the atmosphere became less threatening. Both sets of fans realised the situation. They could have given us a right hammering if they had wanted, but they were above that — nice kiddies, really!

'Where yo from in Bristol then, mate?'

A variation on 'Have you got the time, mate?' I thought. This question was usually the prelude to a right hook. They didn't really need to hear your accent, it was just a polite way of going through the structured formalities of violence.

'Oi! Oi'm talking to yo!' the Brummie continued, poking me in the ribs at the same time. Perhaps he was just trying to be friendly.

'Embree,' I replied. Henbury, really. He probably wouldn't understand anyway.

'Enbury!' he hollered. 'Do you know a bloke called Mogger?'

I couldn't believe what I was hearing. 'No, never heard of him,' I said, as matter-of-factly as I could.

'Are you sure, only 'e definitely comes from 'Enbury. What's your name then?'

'C... C... Colin,' I answered.

'Well, Colin, if you come across a bloke called Mogger...'

'Or Chris,' his big mate piped in.

BOOTED AND SUITED

'That's roight, or, Chris, because he's the bastard who's threatened to slit me from ear to ear, yo tell them we'll come down to Bristol next game an sort them out, roight?'

'Yeah, roight,' I answered, 'I'll tell him... if I ever meet him, that is.'

The crowd that day was a massive 45,000 plus. The Holte End alone held over 20,000 and I had to stand next to the twat who Mogger was having a running battle with; just my luck, I thought. They were a good-natured bunch for all that, taking the piss the whole game. We even got brave and came out with a weak chant of 'Rovers, Rovers,' when Tom Stanton scored a late goal for us. Villa ran out winners 2–1. I breathed a sigh of relief at the final whistle and my buttocks finally came unclenched. They even shook our hands and wished us luck – they could afford to be charitable, Villa went up as champions at the end of the season. The club would never look back, the First Division and European glory beckoned. This was to be our last encounter with the Villa for a quite a while.

'Don't forget, if yo ever see, what's his name again...'

'Mogger,' I answered, forgetting myself for a moment.

'Yeah, Mogger, yo tell 'im!'

Too fucking right I'll tell him, I thought.

We filed out of the Holte End, relief etched on our faces. But now we had another worry. We were unintentionally part of the Villa fans heading for the Rovers fans at the other end, and clashed head-on underneath the Trinity Road stand, not knowing which way to turn. For once I hoped the Rovers fans would bottle it and run, but no such luck. They fired in, fired in to us who were at the front trying to join them.

'Leave it out, we're Rovers!' I shouted, but to no avail. Nobody could hear, there was too much going on, too much chaos. Villa were now massing, outnumbering Rovers and beginning to get on top. There was a slight lull, we were eyeing

NEW FACES

each other up, waiting for the next move. I spotted Mogger of all people, made a break from the Brummies and ran towards him, inadvertently leading the charge. Villa fired in again – 'Get the bastards!' they screamed, following me towards the Rovers fans. A grinning Rovers fan standing next to Mogger went for me. It was a grin I was to get used to over the years, Hampshire always grinned like that when he was enjoying himself, and was he enjoying himself. Other Rovers fans joined in and started belting me, I broke away and legged it back to the safety of the Villa fans. The law arrived just at the right moment. I could see Lil and Harvey safely among the Tote Enders. That left me the only one stranded. I was in a no-win situation, there was only one thing for it – I turned and pushed my way through the Villa fans and legged it straight out of the ground.

I was on my own now, just part of the huge, heaving mass of Villa fans heading away from the ground, but I had no colours on so I felt comparatively safe. I couldn't see any Rovers fans at all – they were all heading in the opposite direction. I kept my head down and said nothing, praying no one would ask me the time.

I felt that every pair of eyes was upon me; surely I looked and walked different? I felt like I had a sign on my back saying 'Bristolian, kick me hard, please', but I needn't have worried, they weren't interested in me. I followed the signs for the City Centre, walked along the still-to-be-finished 'Spaghetti Junction' and spotted at long last a friendly face, well as friendly a face as Andy Phelps could muster, ambling along with another one of the Tramps, a miserable little wretch from Little Stoke known as Mouse. Apart from Andy, the Tramps comprised Brian Willis, Freddie Dempster, Daryl, Eddie, Chrissy the Biker, Mike the Wrestler, and Jimmy from Yatton (a village on the outskirts of Bristol) who, according to Brian 'falls off walls for tourists', to name but a few. But Mouse was different – he really was a tramp. He was eventually murdered and his body set on fireas he slept on the streets of Montpelier. His murderer was never found.

'Am I glad to see you.' I could hardly contain myself.

'All right, nipper, any trouble?' grunted Andy in greeting.

'Not 'alf, I was... we were... forget it.' I couldn't be arsed, it would take too long to explain. We trudged on to New Street, hardly speaking, Mouse eyeing me up. Now Mouse wasn't the most eloquent of chaps, so I wasn't expecting a deep, meaningful Jimmy Hill-type analysis of the game we had just witnessed when he opened his mouth to speak.

'Lend us a quid,' he demanded.

'Fuck off,' I replied, and they were probably the last words I ever spoke to him.

13
The Divide Widens

I hated Bristol fucking City. I couldn't say their name without using an expletive. What's more, everybody I knew felt the same. I didn't know any City fans and I didn't want to know any City fans. They stood for all the things alien to me: south Bristol fucking toe-rags, ignorant, fickle and disloyal. Hampshire was a man after my own heart: he hated City with a passion. Admittedly, he wasn't much of a Rovers fan either. He was clueless when it came to football; he just loved to hate City fans.

I had now left school and was waiting to start work as an apprentice compositor at a god-forsaken shithole of a printing factory in Avonmouth. If God was to give the Earth an enema he would insert it in Chittening Estate, Avonmouth. I was still working at Gateway in the meantime, filling my pockets with change from the till and my stomach with biscuits from the shelves. The extra money from Gateway meant more time in town. I was now a fully fledged 'town kiddy'. No suburban Old Crow pub for me, pal, give me the Crown, the Rummer or the Bank Hotel any day. It was in 'the Bank' that I met Hampshire again after that eventful Easter Monday in Birmingham. He walked in with Rob Whatley, a slant-eyed, droll fucker, from Lockleaze like Hampshire.

'Two halves o' brown split,' Hampshire requested.

'Come again, love?' The barmaid had heard it all before. Two lads, not yet expert in the fine art of pub etiquette, making total pricks of themselves.

'I said two halves of brown split,' Hampshire repeated, not sure why the sniggers and laughs were getting louder from the more seasoned beer drinkers.

'I heard you the first time, love, it's just that we usually sell brown splits in pints, you know, half of bitter and half of brown?'

'Oh yeah, right, better make it pints then,' mumbled Hampshire, much to the amusement of Brian Willis and the rest of the regulars.

Suitably embarrassed, Hampshire and Whatley skulked over to me and Mogger, pints of brown splits in hand. We were the same age as them and they looked for some sympathy from their contemporaries.

'Half a brown split, what a twat,' taunted Mogger, as sympathetically as he could.

Hampshire was eager to change the subject.

'You two going down the City ground next week?'

We were playing City the following week at Ashton Gate. The Gloucester Cup was upon us, the annual finale to the season, a chance for the fans to prove themselves as the top dogs. It was always a murderous affair – no quarter asked and no quarter given. We had had an average season on the pitch, but a spectacularly successful one off it. Our rucks with QPR, Stoke, Leeds and Villa had hardened us up. We wanted the season to end on a high note – we were right up for it, we knew we had a boring three summer months in front of us and wanted to go out with a bang.

'Too fucking right,' I answered. 'You?'

THE DIVIDE WIDENS

'Yeah, we're meeting in The Star, opposite the ground, put it around. Get tooled up, we're going in big time, no leggin' it like at Villa.' He gave me a sideways glance. 'We'll take the fucking East End no worries, teach them scumbags a right lesson. We're number one in this city, right?'

He was ranting. I had only just met him and I liked what I was hearing. This geezer meant business. He was much shorter than me, but stockier; long, thick black hair, Italian extraction by the look of it, a mean piece of work if I ever met one. I wasn't so sure about Whatley. He just grinned and nodded every time Hampshire opened his mouth, which was often.

I had left school with two items that would keep me in good stead in the future, a clutch of O levels and a metal hinge bracket from the side of a desk. It was about a foot long and solid steel and made the perfect weapon. I stuffed it in the lining of my bomber jacket, praying to God I wouldn't be searched. The Monkey boots were brought out of the wardrobe and polished up. They were like old friends; I swear they smiled at me.

'Where you off to tonight?' my old lady asked, eyeing me up and down.

'Football,' I replied.

'Be good,' she said.

'I will,' I said, with a wink.

Word had got round all right. The Star was packed, Tote Enders everywhere. Hampshire, Whatley, Dobbsy, Rob Boyle and, best of all, Andy and the rest of the Tramps, they were all there; tense, nervous energy filled the air. Ever-watchful eyes stared out of the windows. The City boys were gathering in their pubs. We were on their turf and were expecting an attack. With a few younger spotters outside, dotted along Ashton Road, we were ready and waiting.

A breathless 14-year-old apprentice suddenly burst through the door: 'They're coming now, fucking hundreds of 'em!'

BOOTED AND SUITED

We couldn't get out of the pub quick enough, picking up beer glasses and ashtrays on the way, the familiar guttural roar went up and the two tribes went to war. We clashed head on in the middle of the street. It was an ugly scene, but a scene I was now accustomed to; it held no fears or terrors for me, it was all I wanted out of life. I was in my element. Pick a scumbag out of the melee, go for him, kick him, punch him, flailing arms like windmills. I felt utterly confident, the adrenalin was pumping. I had a superiority complex. No, it wasn't a complex — they were inferior.

I could see Hampshire, he was grinning again. Andy was making them bounce, they had nothing to match him at all. Their main man, Angus, was no more than five foot six in his silver, spray-painted Doc Martens. He might have been an evil little bastard, but he was not in Andy's league; none of them were.

We were doing well, but by sheer numbers they were beginning to overwhelm us. The more you punched out, the more appeared, there seemed to be a limitless supply of the fuckers and, unbelievably, no coppers on the horizon. They outnumbered us, it was a familiar story. I looked around anxiously, but I needn't have worried, everyone was staying firm. It was now the City fans' turn to suddenly looked worried. They were looking past us.

Beyond us, out of our sight, was an enormous horde of Rovers fans charging across Ashton Park to back us up.

'We are the Tote End, we are the Tote End, we are the Tote End of EASTVILLE!' The reinforcements fired in, but the battle was all but over. City ran, we gave chase and whooped our delight: Rovers 1, City 0.

It didn't stop there. We made a beeline for the East End. All colours were hidden; the law were lining up to search us and I still had my bar hidden in my sleeve. I hadn't had a chance to use it in the street-fight. Others hadn't been so reluctant to

THE DIVIDE WIDENS

use theirs; there were some severe injuries. It was too late to ditch the weapon. I held my breath, my balls did their disappearing act once again.

The law were having an off day. Not only had they failed to break up the scrap in Ashton Road, but they didn't seem interested in the hundred or so shifty-looking Tote Enders queuing up to get in the East End (these were the days before crowd segregation or fences, it was relatively easy to gain access to any part of any ground, home or away). We field in quietly in ones and twos; we didn't want to be rumbled before we were all in.

Andy took the lead.

'Get in and move to the back, don't say a fucking word until we're all in place,' he urged.

The East End was long and narrow, a gangway ran all the way at the back with just a small terrace maybe nine feet wide behind it. We positioned ourselves dead centre, right behind the main bulk of the East Enders. Once you had occupied this area it was very difficult for anybody to force you out. We all knew we could rely on each other. If you weren't up for it, you wouldn't be there, it was as simple as that.

We tried to blend in while everybody took up their positions, a few even chanted 'C-I-T-Y'. I couldn't, though, it just stuck in my throat like a ball of phlegm. We waited, all eyes on Andy. Wait for it, wait for it... we had no prearranged signal, we were waiting for something to happen. The scumbags were going to get the shock of their lives. Unintentionally, the catalyst came from them.

'Rovers where are you? Rovers where are you?' they taunted the Rovers fans massed at the opposite end of the ground, their right hands raised, the thumb and index finger joined and giving the universal 'wanker' signal. Not for one minute did they suspect the enemy was in their camp, not two feet from their poxy noses – literally breathing down their necks.

BOOTED AND SUITED

It was instantaneous. 'TOTE, TOTE, TOTE ENDERS! TOTE, TOTE, TOTE ENDERS!' There was a split-second of silence... their jaws dropped quicker than a pair of whore's knickers. Yeah you fucking heard right, Tote Enders on your fucking manor. I pulled out the bar. The tall wanker in front of me didn't stand a chance – I whacked him right across the side of his pockmarked face with all my might, his cheek split open, oozing scarlet – cop that, you tosser! He went down and stayed down.

I felt an immediate rush of blood and adrenalin. I was getting my fix again, we all were, everywhere around me the Tote was having a field day. Small, powerful, pit-bull-like Johnny Budd, arms like Popeye, taking some geezer's head off with one awesome punch; a young lad nicknamed 'Ginger' for obvious reasons, head-butting, his favourite form of attack, breaking the poor recipient's nose like a squashed tomato – Ginge was obviously destined for greater things. It was sheer bedlam, the City fans were frantic. The ones nearest to us were trying to get away but they couldn't escape; it was lambs to the slaughter. The boot was going in on some unfortunate bastard on the ground, the worst place to be. I whacked another one. I could see other weapons being used, bars and sawn-off broom handles mostly. For all the bravado of carrying a knife, it was rare to see one being used. Out of the corner of my eye I could see the law heading for us, truncheons drawn. I quickly discarded the bar. The aftermath of battle lay all around; bloodied bodies, scarves, shoes and youngsters crying. Did I feel sorry for them? Did I fuck, should have gone in the enclosure with your old man, shouldn't you? Besides, he'll be doing the same to us in a few years' time no doubt.

The law had at last woken up. The dogs were barking and the truncheons were swinging. They were nicking anybody, some were still scrapping and kicking as they were grabbed round the neck and wrestled to the ground: 'You're fucking nicked, son!'

THE DIVIDE WIDENS

How many times had we heard that one? I was not to be spared, my arm was forced up my back — shit, it fucking hurt!

'You, out, come on, with me!'

'I ain't done fuck all!' I protested. I was now shitting it. I had been arrested and charged before, but only for vandalism and a bit of thieving as a kid. To be grabbed by a fat bastard of a copper who was determined to snap your arm off was another story,

'Honest, leave it out. Ow! You're breaking my fucking arm!'

'I'll break your fucking neck in a minute, son!'

I was dragged out of the ground, kicking and screaming, I realised there were hundreds of pairs of eyes upon me, eyes full of hatred and venom... and fear. Yeah that's right, I thought, we took your fucking end! I suddenly felt a lot better.

They marched me into their brand-new station which had been built inside Ashton Gate, all breeze block and corrugated iron. It was packed and chaotic, there were as many kiddies as coppers, all shouting and bawling, some snivelling and even some laughing.

Fat copper sat me down and took my details, well Harvey's details anyway. I had practised Harvey's address and date of birth so I knew it off by heart. Harvey had never been nicked — it helped. As the years went by I ran out of people I knew who hadn't been arrested — something about the company I kept, I suppose.

The law were in a benevolent mood. Perhaps they were all Rovers fans. Either way, I wasn't charged. I was searched — bit late now, copper, I thought — and kept in for the remainder of the game. A few were charged and taken away in the meat wagon to spend the night at Bridewell, but all in all we got off lightly, unlike some of the poor bastards on the terraces. I was released after the crowds had gone, with a caution and a slap on the wrist. That will teach me, I thought.

'Good game, son?' asked my old man when I got in.

'Yeah great, Dad, one of the best.'
'Who won?'
'Rovers, Dad, easily.'

I spent the summer as I had the previous summer, wishing it away, counting off the days to the start of the next football season. My year started in mid-August, not January, and ended in May. That meant three months that didn't really exist, three months of sheer boredom.

For all that, the summer of 1972 had been pretty good. After my performance at Ashton Gate I had endeared myself to the Tote End hierarchy. I had now been elevated from nodding terms to full-blown 'All right, Browner.' Hampshire was up there too – the Bank regulars had confined his 'Half a brown split' episode to the vaults, and he and I were now regarded as journeymen, no longer the apprentices of a few years back. We had done our time.

I was now feeling as at home in the smoky bars and pubs of town as I was on the terraces at Eastville. The Tote End was simply a mass of concrete terraces with stanchions, girders and a roof, a very physical place in every sense of the word. 'Tote Enders' merely collectively described the individuals who frequented the Tote End. Anybody could become a Tote Ender, simply by paying 30p and positioning themselves on that west part of the ground. The Tote was something completely different, it was something that separated, segregated and divided us not just from other football fans, but from our parents, our workmates and the authorities. But most of all, it separated us from City fans. There was an East End, but there was no The East, there never would be. There would always be the Tote.

The Tote was now my family; it gave me a sense of belonging. I was a member of a club that I chose to belong to, a club whose rules and ethics I would adhere to for the rest of my life. I had

THE DIVIDE WIDENS

turned my back on Henbury and its clique of mates who would all work at Rolls-Royce or BAC, who would all play football or rugby with the same lads they had known all their lives, who would drink in the Salutation or the Old Crow and who would all date and eventually marry girls from the same street as them. I wasn't knocking it, it just wasn't for me. I couldn't wait to get away. Others stayed put. Mogger was a Rovers fan and Tote Ender through and through, but he wasn't a part of the Tote, neither was Harvey, or Tommo. Surprisingly, Lil was – maybe it was his dysfunctional family. Either way, we made an odd pair: me tall, blond and slim; Lil, short, dark and stumpy.

We had started meeting Hampshire and his mates now on a regular basis. The Bank, tucked away in St John's Lane, was an obvious meeting place for us. You could find a fellow Tote Ender in there most nights of the week. It was small and welcoming, more like somebody's front room than a pub. The jukebox was an added bonus, full of old skinhead classics by Prince Buster and Laurel Aitken from a few years back. The atmosphere and ambience of the Bank was unique, something to be savoured and enjoyed.

The Elephant in St Nicholas Street was an altogether different story. In later years it was to become Bristol's most famous gay pub, but in the early 1970s, when terrace rivalry was reaching its peak, it rather bizarrely catered for both sets of supporters, from the blue and red halves of the city. The right-hand bar was frequented by the Tote and the left-hand by the East End, and rarely would a cross word be exchanged between the two tribes. There was an unwritten law: 'Thou shalt kick the shit out of each on the terraces, but thou shall drink in peace in the Elephant!' It wasn't totally unknown for Rovers and City fans to join forces. I had even known of several Tote Enders who had travelled to Cardiff to help City out against their arch-rivals, and likewise, City fans would frequent the Tote when we played the likes of

BOOTED AND SUITED

Villa and Plymouth. Even at Gloucester Cup matches it wasn't unusual to hear the two mobs chant 'BER-RISTOL' simultaneously, or 'City AND Rovers!', although this was usually instigated by the City fans as a conciliatory gesture for fear of getting a kicking.

The peace was nearly always kept by the robust landlord, Barry, who shaded more than a passing resemblance to Henry Cooper, and his wife Tina, who shaded more than a passing resemblance to the back end of a bus, hence her nickname of 'Mrs Elephant'. They were aided and abetted by the weirdest of weird characters, a man called Stuart, who took it upon himself to dress up as a bunny girl, a cat, or Hiawatha or whatever took his fancy. We always thought he should have been working in the queer's pub down the road, the Radnor, or at least be a City fan, but like the rest of the staff, he wisely stayed strictly neutral on the football front.

After meeting in the Bank or the Elephant it would be on to the more cosmopolitan watering holes like the Lowenbrau Bierkeller, situated below the Mauretania in Park Street, or the Crown or the Rummer in the covered market, where no truces existed. Anything went, and often did. It got so bad in the Crown that they served plastic glasses only. The Rummer was just as bad, both hostelries were dark cavernous cellars, full of dodgy kiddies and even dodgier women, tanked up on snake bites and brown splits. Meeting a tart in the Crown was risky business. You could judge how sophisticated they were by their drinks: light and lime – cheap and all right, cherry b – farts don't smell, port and lemon – use her shit for toothpaste.

The summer was to finish on a right old high. The FA in their infinite wisdom decided to do something for us poor, unfortunate, bored football hooligans who had been deprived of our entertainment for three long months. They introduced a pre-season tournament called the Watney Cup.

THE DIVIDE WIDENS

Rovers at last won some silverware. All right, so it was some Mickey Mouse kick-about, what the hell, it was big at the time and it was on the telly! The first round was against First Division top guns, Wolves. The law were at last getting the hang of this football hooliganism lark and for the first time they segregated the fans, meeting the Black Country boys straight off the train and herding them on to the Muller Road End. The match was virtually trouble-free, until the final whistle that is. With Rovers winning the match 2–0 the Wolves fans were naturally a little peeved, and as if on cue they came charging around the back of the North Stand to do battle with the Tote. We met full pelt in the car park.

'YOU'LL NEVER TAKE THE TOTE END! YOU'LL NEVER TAKE THE TOTE END!'

'Come on then, you bastards, I'll take you all on!' She did too, a right tasty bird, neat blonde feather cut, firing in to us. Bemused and baffled, I gave her a double-take. She gave me a right-hander – fucking hurt as well!

Tina was a bit of a legend; I'd read about her in the *Daily Mirror*. She came from Wolverhampton but she was in fact a Chelsea fan – obviously took her aggro very seriously, prepared to travel a bit to get it. Somebody not as chivalrous as me gave her a smack; she didn't flinch. Tough young bird – didn't see our women, Jill Vickers or Karen 'Strainer' Burton anywhere. Typical women, I thought, never around when you want them. Still, the game gave the Tote some much-needed practice. We had become a bit rusty over the summer months; it was nice of the FA to think of us.

Our reward for beating Burnley away in the next round was a meeting with First Division Sheffield United in the final at Eastville. It was a scorching mid-summer day and ironically, since the competition was for top-scoring teams, the game finished 0–0. The match went into a penalty shoot and Dick Sheppard saved the final penalty, his save signalled a massive pitch invasion, and for once there was no malice intended. He was carried shoulder-high around the pitch and ensured his entry into the Rovers' hall of fame. The mass of Sheffield United fans stood and watched, and even applauded — what sporting fellows! We applauded back. It was a nice touch and, needless to say, something of a rarity.

14

A Bit of Psychology, A Bit of Humour and Who the F**k are Man United Anyway?

Inevitably the hooliganism that had engulfed football for the past few seasons showed no sign of letting up as the 1972/73 season kicked off. Reports of the games in the *News Of The World* and the *Sunday Mirror* now vied for column inches with reports of the hooliganism and with in-depth analyses and interviews of the top hard men of the infamous 'Ends.' The first day of the new season read like this:

> *A half-housebrick drew first blood of the new football season. Victory for an unknown hooligan and mob violence. Agony for a youth who went to seek an afternoon's entertainment. This was the first score for the lunatics in the League of Thugs.* [Newspapers delighted in printing league tables of football violence. This would inevitably lead the fans to try and gain a higher position, therefore perpetuating the violence.]
>
> *Violence and rioting on the terraces was rife on Saturday. The worst trouble was at LEICESTER. Arsenal fans invaded the pitch*

and stopped the game for three minutes. And 36 people were arrested after rival gangs met in bloody clashes. Seventeen will appear in court today. The rest will come before a juvenile court later.

At LEYTON ORIENT, scores of Oxford United fans ran riot in streets round the ground after being stranded in London. Coach drivers returned home empty because of trouble on the way to the game. At YORK, police dogs were called out to quell rioting. There was also trouble in BOLTON and WALSALL. In SCOTLAND, Jock Stein and Willie Waddell, managers of Celtic and Rangers, both declared war on the hooligans. Stein went on to the terraces at Stirling to stop the singing of 'party' songs. Waddell publicly branded the troublemakers as 'drunkards and louts'.

In LIVERPOOL, a gang of more than 100 Manchester City supporters clashed with police outside Lime Street Station. Passers-by ran for cover as bricks flew. A police spokesman said, 'This was pure hooliganism' Eleven fans were arrested and charged with disorderly conduct.

Each scene of violence was highlighted in bold upper-case type — it was easier for the hooligans to identify themselves that way. A quick scan of the paper and no mention of your own mob performing meant you must try harder.

There was also a growing list of 'celebrity' hooligans who revelled in their names and exploits being published in the tabloids. These were people such as Arsenal's Nick 'the Hammer' Russell, who boasted to the press of leading an army of 400 hooligans 'who can dish out more aggro than anyone else in the country'. According to trusty lieutenant Pat Stone, Russell 'never runs, slugs it out with anyone, he's our leader'.

Another was the infamous Jenkins, who led Arsenal's Bromley Boys.

A report in the *Sun* focused on two particular mobs, West

A BIT OF PSYCHOLOGY, A BIT OF HUMOUR...

Ham and Chelsea. The West Ham ringleader, 19-year-old Chris Lightbown, showed an amazing insight into the football hooligan psyche. His comments are as relevant today as they were almost 30 years ago:

> *Chris Lightbown, leader of West Ham's North Bank mob, sees the fights as a sort of fringe football league and is determined to come top of it. Rival Mike Greenaway, a 27-year-old railway clerk who leads Chelsea's notorious* [mobs were always 'notorious'] *Shed gang, is all keyed up to get some Manchester fans who waylaid him and six of his henchmen last season. Why do they do it?* [the shocked reporter asks incredulously]. *Lightbown answers: 'We fight for the pride of our ends — there is nothing else to be proud of in our society.'*

Nice answer, but a bit deep. I still preferred the enjoyment theory.

Lightbown continued with his erudite observations:

> *They will never stamp out football hooliganism. It is going to get more, rather than less. What's so marvellous is that these kids who are doing bum jobs and are said to be idiots can get themselves organised like this and set up a fantastic military strategy that goes into the battle. It is not as simple as it looks. Decoys are planted and flanks formed. It's great to see it. We have been brought up on war psychology so long that it has become part of our culture, and teenagers expect to be fighting. When there are no wars, there will be things like punch-ups at soccer matches.*

Read it and weep, psychologists.

The winning of the Watney Cup was the prelude to a cracking season. Football hooliganism was now our way of the world; it was no longer an unusual event at a game, it was now the norm.

BOOTED AND SUITED

In fact, it was a rarity if there wasn't aggro at a game, any game, from Aldershot to Aberdeen. Every home game brought a new opportunity to defend our end and our honour, and every away game brought a fresh opportunity to gain more notoriety. Visiting fans were now becoming wary of coming to Eastville – it was after all a gloomy, imposing ground in an even gloomier district of Bristol.

There were two main pubs in Eastville, the Black Swan, where visiting fans generally gathered and our favoured meeting place on a match day, the imposing White Swan, a big, dismal and foreboding pub for even home fans to venture in, let alone visiting ones. Its long main bar was full of 'seen-it-all' hard nuts and 'up-and-coming' youngsters trying to make a name for themselves. For good measure a smaller bar at the back usually contained locals who didn't like anybody fucking up their patch and disturbing their game of snooker. The flock wallpaper was peeling off, revealing damp, stained walls and cracked lino that had been laid when the pub was built. It was stained with more bodily fluids than a whore's mattress. The atmosphere in the White Swan matched that of the ground: dismal and uninviting.

Of all the 'up-and-coming' youngsters, none were to quite match Clyde Ogden Smithers. I'm not sure about the Ogden bit, but when it came to Clyde I wasn't sure about a lot of things. It wasn't as if Clyde was a new kid on the block. I had first met him at an away FA cup tie at Telford a few years earlier when, aged just 13, he gave the coach driver a right slapping, knocking the poor bloke out cold with a stonking right-hander. I also had the honour of seeing him perform with his lethal head-butt on the East End the previous season. Clyde was one tough little bastard and as edgy as fuck: say the wrong word, give him the wrong look and you were likely to be on the wrong end of his tough, ginger forehead. He was more commonly known as 'Ginger' or 'Smiffy'; his 'Iggy' nickname would follow later.

A BIT OF PSYCHOLOGY, A BIT OF HUMOUR...

Clyde was a mate of Hampshire's, from Rovers' backyard of Lockleaze. He was smaller and younger than us, but made up for his lack of size by sheer aggression and fanaticism, while his love of Rovers was only matched by his love of West Ham and of a good scrap. Hampshire on the other hand knew fuck-all about football. His lack of passion for Rovers didn't come into it, but he more than made up for it with his hatred of Bristol fucking City. Clyde and Phil together were big trouble. They both shared a common sense of humour and mischievousness. It wasn't evil, it was just their way. Unfortunately, a lot of people took it differently and their behaviour was to get the two of them into a lot of trouble. Clyde was one of those people who could start a fight in a phone-box; however, his own particular brand of 'humour' also shone through.

Over the following years, Clyde's deviousness and wicked sense of humour were to become legendary. He not only succeeded in persuading Don McInnery, a recent release from Horfield prison, to don Clyde's mother's floral blouse and wear it to the pub in the belief that it was 'what all the kiddies were wearing in London', but he also managed to get into a woman's item of clothing himself, this time Grant Davy's mother's favourite dress. Following a drunken night in town with Hampshire, the two of them had found themselves crashed out in Grant's house with Grant only agreeing to let them kip there 'as long as you don't touch any of our ma's clothes'. Clyde's cries of innocence in the morning and of protestations that Hampshire had forcibly dressed him in Grant's mum's best green dress during the night predictably fell on deaf ears. Someone else who was to regret letting the Terrible Two spend the night was Stuart 'Ommy' Holmes, when Hampshire, on finding himself caught short in the night, shit in a shoe-box that he had found in his host's wardrobe only for Hampshire to pitifully blame Ommy's one-year-old baby son for the offending turd. Understandably,

BOOTED AND SUITED

Ommy never saw the funny side. Of all the examples of Clyde's quick-wittedness none more summed it up than an incident that occurred while he and Hampshire were staying in Torquay over a Bank Holiday weekend towards the end of the Seventies.

The dangerous duo had been staying at a cheap and cheerful guest house run by a spectacularly attractive 40-something-year-old. Hampshire, having just emerged naked from the shower, spotted the object of his lust hanging out the washing. Inevitably and embarrassingly, he found his manhood rising to the occasion. Clyde, never one to miss an opportunity, leaned out of the opened window.

'Missus! Missus! Come up here quick!'

'What? What is it, my luv?'

'Can't say, can you just come up here quick!'

'You bastard Smiffy, what the fuck you playing at?' yelled Hampshire. Desperately trying to think of a way out of his enforced predicament, he spotted the near-empty wardrobe and jumped in, just as the landlady politely knocked on the door.

'What is it, luvver, have you got a problem?'

'Yeah, come in, will you,' replied Clyde, mischievously.

She entered gingerly. Clyde pointed to the wardrobe.

'It's in there.'

'What is?'

'Just open the wardrobe, will you...'

It took a lot of persuading for her not to call the law and a long time for Hampshire to forgive Clyde. If he ever did.

Our first game of the new 1972/73 season was at home against Blackburn Rovers. We were packed like sardines into the White Swan, Dandy Livingstone's 'Suzanne Beware Of The Devil', a pleasant enough reggae record that had reached the top 20, jumped and skitted around the inside of the antiquated jukebox in a forlorn effort to be heard above the raucous din of the

A BIT OF PSYCHOLOGY, A BIT OF HUMOUR...

growing crowd. It was an OK sort of record but unashamedly aimed at the pop market and not in the same league as his old classic and all-time skinhead favourite 'Reggae In Your Jeggae'.

'I'm goin' over to the bookies to place a bet, anyone comin'?' Clyde stared at us pleadingly. He looked far too young to get into Len Bryer's, the bookies next to the Monte Carlo café. Perhaps he wanted some back-up from us.

'Yeah, all right, I've never been into a bookies in my life,' I answered truthfully.

'I go all the time,' replied Clyde. I didn't believe him for one moment.

Clyde filled in his betting slip. Carefully following the instructions printed on a notice on the wall, he handed his slip in, clutching his 50p in his hand.

'Have you betted before, son?' asked the overweight greaseball behind the counter.

''Course I have, why?'

'Well, I don't know if you noticed, but we went over to decimalisation a couple of years ago!'

The slip was chucked back to Clyde with disdain. He had filled it in word for word from the notice on the wall: 'No. 4—10 shillings to win.'

Shades of half a brown split, I thought, but I stifled my laugh. It was wise not to laugh at Clyde. We trooped out to a loud guffaw from Greaseball and headed for the ground. Clyde was in a foul mood. I gave him a wide berth for the rest of the day.

Amazingly, for the third year in a row Rovers progressed yet again in the League Cup. We had dumped out Cardiff in the first round after a replay at Eastville. The away tie at Ninian Park had been my first visit to Wales since the Swansea incident two seasons previously and although the game had not been quite as eventful as the game at the Vetch, it was nevertheless a vicious encounter, with running battles on the terraces continually spilling on to the pitch and holding up the game. A contingent from Ashton Gate had even joined us for the evening in a successful attempt to further disrupt Anglo-Welsh relations. The replay the following week carried on where the first one had left off and after sorting out the Taffies in the car park we moved on to Stapleton Road railway station and wrecked the train as it pulled out. Who needed the East End?

After demolishing Brighton 4–0 in the next round, Rovers were paired against mighty Manchester United, except they weren't so mighty now. Best and Charlton were still playing but too many late nights in the company of Jack Daniel's and encounters with ex-Miss Worlds had taken its toll on George and it was a sad Manchester United team who scrapped a 1–1 draw against Rovers at Eastville.

Much to the Tote's disappointment, there was very little trouble in the 33,000-plus crowd; the worst part was getting in. I spent the first half, along with 50 or so others, on the roof of the Tote End watching as John Rudge and Bruce Bannister tormented the ageing Reds' defence. It would have been a famous victory but for Willie Morgan's equaliser in the 87th minute.

The infamous Stretford End were a sad bunch. Far from being the scourge of every terrace in the country, they were a demoralised, weakened mob of half-wits who knew when they were beaten. They stayed put on the Muller Road End and hardly sang a word all night. The Tote, on the other hand, had reached its zenith.

On nights like this you turned your attention to the Old Bill. Not that PC Plod minded – I think they enjoyed it as much as we did.

An addition to the Tote End during the pre-season had been a fully enclosed pen at the rear of the terraces, directly in front of the Tote End Bar. It was about four feet high and enclosed with

A BIT OF PSYCHOLOGY, A BIT OF HUMOUR...

wire mesh. This pen was off-limits for fans, it was strictly for the Old Bill to keep an eye on us and was quickly named the pig-pen.

The singing and chanting was incessant and intense. Songs could usually be segregated into three categories: extolling the virtues of Bristol Rovers FC, extolling the virtues of the Tote End and antagonising the coppers and the opposing fans. The sheer variety and originality of the songs never ceased to amaze me. Many pop songs of the day were quickly turned into football chants. The rereleased Chris Montez song 'Let's Dance' was quickly adapted to:

We are the boys in the blue and white,
We like to sing and we like to fight, so let's fight!

Middle of the Road's insipid hit, 'Tweedle Dee, Tweedle Dum', became:

Oh Tweedle Dee, Oh Tweedle Dum,
We are the Tote End and we never run,
We took the East End, the Holte End and the Shed,
We'll fight the Villa bastards until they're fucking dead!
If you hear the sound of footsteps running,
It will be the East End on the run,
If you hear the sound of footsteps following,
It's the Tote End after 'em!

However, for sheer originality, the Tote's adaptation of Lee Marvin's 'Wand'rin' Star' took some beating:

I was born under the Tote End bar,
I was born under the Tote End bar,
who's the greatest player?
Brucie is his name,

> *and if you come to Eastville,*
> *you won't go home again...*
>
> *Knives are made to stab with,*
> *guns are made to shoot,*
> *and if you come to Eastville,*
> *you're gonna get me boot!*
>
> *Knives are made to stab with,*
> *trains are made to wreck,*
> *and if we see a City fan,*
> *we'll break his fucking neck!*

To wind up the coppers, the favourite (sung to the tune of 'The Camptown Races') was:

> *Who's that twat with the big black hat,*
> *Dixon, Dixon.*
> *Who's that twat with the big black hat,*
> *Dixon of Dock Green.*
> *On the beat all day, on the wife all night,*
> *who's that twat, etc.*

They were all being sung that night with a gusto and a fervour I had rarely heard before. And so it went on, the law inevitably moved in and the aggro started, the spittle flew and the truncheons swung. Coppers' helmets started arcing through the night sky, bereft of their badges, which had been wrenched off, taken for treasured mementoes. As each helmet took flight, it was accompanied by cheers from the lawless mob.

'Come to Eastville if you dare, if you dare, come to Eastville if you dare, 'cos we'll sing and fight 'cos promotion's in the air, come to Eastville if you dare!' we chanted, and we meant it.

A BIT OF PSYCHOLOGY, A BIT OF HUMOUR...

But for all these clever lyrics that espoused the virtues of the Tote and Bristol Rovers, there was one that was guaranteed to send a shiver down the spine of visiting fans and coppers alike. It was brutal and straight to the point and it reverberated around every hate-filled ground in the country: 'You're gonna get your fuckin' heads kicked in!'

Willie Morgan's late equaliser was in vain. The following week in the replay at Old Trafford, Rovers surprisingly won 2–1. I didn't go and I was gutted afterwards. The following round we were drawn against Wolves. They exacted their revenge for the Watney Cup defeat, thrashing us 4–0 at Molineux and stoning our coaches. I bet that tart was there again. I didn't go to that game either; this time I didn't give a shit.

15
Celebrity Status

There was a further distraction from the league in November – the glory of the FA Cup. Only this year, it wasn't so glorious. Rovers were riding high in the league and when we travelled to the depressing West London suburb of Hayes in Middlesex, the result seemed a mere formality. Bruce Bannister was scoring with ease and the Tote had been buoyed by further hard-earned victories across our green and pleasant land. It would be a nice little day out. I was now well teamed up with Hampshire, Smiffy and another newcomer, Graham 'Gubby' Raleigh. My faithful sidekick Lil came along for the ride.

I was kitted out in my best football gear. Black all-in-one overalls bedecked with a bulldog's head cloth patch badge on the left forearm and the Bristol coat of arms badge transplanted from my out-of-date crombie sewn on to the left breast pocket. I sported a multi-coloured, scooped-neck South Sea Bubble T-shirt, love beads around my neck and on my feet a brand-new pair of Onitsuka Tiger basketball boots. To top it all, my naturally blonde shoulder-length hair had been enhanced by silver highlights. I looked the business.

CELEBRITY STATUS

The Onitsuka boots were the dog's bollocks. They were fast becoming the 'must haves' for any self-respecting lad about town and came in a variety of colours: red, blue, bottle green and my own preference, brilliant white. There were still a lot of Doc Martens about which were now often spray-painted in a variety of colours and which still kept the 'Boot boys' label going strong, although the skins had long disappeared, leaving the DMs and the denim jacket as the only recognisable legacy from a few years back. Denim jeans were still compulsory wear, but they had now ballooned to hideously baggy widths and sometimes featured tartan turn-ups and piping. Tartan zip-up lumber jackets trimmed with fake fur were also much in evidence, as were Tam o' Shanters. The Tartan influence was down to Rod Stewart and groups such as Slade, who were trying their hardest to reduce the teenagers of Britain into a bunch of illiterate jocks with their renditions of 'Mama Weer All Crazee Now' and 'Gudbuy T' Jane'. It was OK for stomping your feet to in the Crown, but I for one wasn't going to rush out and buy it.

The record charts were still suffering from a dearth of decent music although Alex Hughes, recording under the pseudonym Judge Dread, tried his hardest to keep the sound of skinhead reggae going with 'Big Six' and 'Big Seven', both of which were Top 20 hits during 1972. Over the years Alex Hughes had numerous jobs associated with the reggae scene, from working as a nightclub bouncer and DJ to being employed as Prince Buster's bodyguard – ironic considering the Prince's own expertise in the boxing ring. Alex eventually tried his luck at performing the music he so obviously loved and over the following four years he achieved a further seven Top 30 hits, many of which featured suggestive nursery rhyme-style lyrics chanted over rather tame reggae backing tracks. Undoubtedly 'Big Six' and 'Big Seven' were the best of the crop although none of them came within touching distance of Prince Buster's humorously disgusting 'Big Five' from the previous decade, which was still as popular as ever in the dancehalls. Alex's alias likewise originated from Prince Buster's Orange Street studio during the rock-steady period where the draconian Judge Dread passed sentences of four hundred years' imprisonment and five hundred lashes on rude boys Two Gun Tex, Adolphous James, Emanuel Zachariah Zakipon and my own favourite, the snivelling George Grab-and-Flee for the crimes of 'robbing school children', 'killing black people' and 'burning homes.' Perhaps the courts in Britain could have learned a lesson from the Judge as the boot boys, the Seventies version of the rude boys, carried on their reign of terror, although most of us drew the line at the aforementioned crimes.

There was still the odd little soul belter like 'Here I Go Again' by Archie Bell and the Drells and Billy Preston's funky instrumental 'Outa-Space', which reached number 44 in the charts and made me realise why The Beatles had insisted he played keyboards on 'Get Back' some three years earlier. Roy C's 'Shotgun Wedding', which had originally been a hit way back in 1966, had been rereleased in time for Christmas and went to number 9, but generally I was not impressed on the music front. It didn't seem to bother most of the Tote Enders, though. Judging by the number of Noddy Holder lookalikes parading around with scarves tied around their wrists, I was obviously in the minority.

Surprisingly, on arrival in Hayes we were welcomed by a fair reception from the locals, who as it turned out were a right old mixed bunch. Chelsea and QPR fans were in the majority and there was even a small number of Brentford lads, not to mention one or two die-hard Hayes fans themselves. What's more all of them were vying with us to take each other on. Smart geezers too, even wearing a smattering of Onitsukas; obviously had class like me, I thought. Obviously twats who deserved a kicking, thought Hampshire.

CELEBRITY STATUS

He wasn't to be disappointed. It went off all around the ground – not that it was much of a ground, more of a municipal playing field with a bit of a covered terrace down two sides. There was one particularly huge bastard, wearing a Chelsea scarf round his puffy, pseudo-Cockney neck.

'CHEL-SEA, CHEL-SEA, CHEL-SEA!'

The fat git was relentless, he stood there at the front of his cronies, about a dozen of them, at the back of the terrace.

'Come on then, have a pop!'

He motioned to me, the familiar way, arms by his bloated side, hands beckoning me on. I was directly in front of him, my back to the pitch. I'd had a few pints beforehand, but I wasn't that pissed. He was a big fucker, after all. I knew my limits.

'Go on, sort the fucker out!'

It was one of the QPR lads, egging me on.

'You know him?'

'Yeah, Chelsea twat, 'e's a tosser though, all mouth!'

'You whack 'im then!'

'It's not me 'e wants a pop with, though, is it?'

He was right. For some reason the fat bastard was determined to have me. His eyes were riveted on me.

'Come on,' he hollered at me, 'you with the poofy beads!'

I couldn't lose face. I was a lot of things, but a poof I wasn't. The QPR kiddy was still egging me on. Hampshire was there, grinning.

'Go on, Browner, it's you he's after.'

Before I had a chance to weigh up the options he launched at me, charging down the terrace. I managed to land a punch before he could, straight in his beer-filled stomach, he doubled over, winded. Like a lot of fat bastards he was fit for fuck all. As his hulking mass almost engulfed me I gave him another whack in the face. He lurched over on to one side, his bloated body twisting at an acute angle from his tree-trunk-like legs. He

BOOTED AND SUITED

crumpled to the concrete terrace and let out an almighty scream which almost drowned out the equally almighty crack as his leg snapped under him.

'Aaaarghhh! I've broke my fucking leg!!'

He lay there clutching his leg, which was now distorted and looking almost remote from his body.

'He's broke his fucking leg!' squealed the QPR kiddy.

I stood there motionless.

'I've broke his fucking leg!' I barely whispered it. I was lost for words.

Fat bloke just lay there, sobbing,

'You've b-b-broke my f-f-fucking leg!'

By now, everybody had got the message, I was even waiting for it to be announced over the tannoy. His Chelsea mates had summoned the St John's ambulance crew and fat bloke was stretchered off around the pitch to the cheers of the Tote End. For my sins I was thrown out of the ground by the law – as usual they hadn't a clue what had gone on, I was so full of myself I felt like telling them, just to get my name in the papers, but I thought better of it.

It was no great hardship getting thrown out – Rovers that day were a disgrace. For my efforts I had become an instant celebrity, unlike Don Megson, who as manager of Rovers had to put up with the ignominy of being dumped out of the FA Cup. It was an eventful bitter-sweet day, the sort of day that I was to become accustomed to over the years.

The rest of the season fizzled out in the same way as the previous ones. Rovers flattered to deceive. We had a few more good trips away. Bournemouth proved to be a decent one – getting there early and wrecking the pier, the large steel dustbins being manhandled over the railings and making a spectacular splash as they nose-dived into the English Channel. I got pulled in by the law for that one…

CELEBRITY STATUS

'We had a witness, son, woman saw a lad in a check jacket smashing a window on the pier.'

'Pick any one out of a hundred,' I answered sarcastically. They knew I had a point and reluctantly let me go. I met up with the others on the way to the ground.

Tote End Boys we are here, wo-ohh!, wo-ohh!
Tote End Boys we are here,
To shag your women and to drink your beer!

An old favourite on away trips was quickly adapted in honour of recent events...

Tote End Boys we are here, wo-ohh!, wo-ohh!
Tote End Boys we are here,
To shag your women and wreck your pier!

Don Megson more than made up for the Hayes debacle when, in March, he signed a tall, bustling old-fashioned centre forward from Sheffield United called Alan Warboys. Sir Alan became an instant hit. He teamed up with Bruce Bannister and the dangerous duo of Smash and Grab was born. Maybe if Megson had signed Warboys earlier on in the season, Rovers would have gained promotion. As it was we headed for our final game at Chesterfield with just the remotest chance of going up. However, as it turned out, Bristol Rovers and their fans were to hit the headlines for an altogether different reason...

16
Like Clockwork

It was customary, if not compulsory, for it to go off at the last game of the season, and the end of the 1972/73 season would be no exception. Coincidentally the last away match of the previous season had also been against Chesterfield and, true to form, we had had a large-scale bundle that day. We headed for Derbyshire mob-handed, eager to carry on where we had left off 12 months earlier.

Johnny O'Shea and Brian Willis had organised and filled two Tote End coaches and we met on the Centre full of optimism and bravado. There was one small problem: Big Andy wasn't coming.

'You're doing what?' bawled Brian, not believing what he was hearing.

'I'm going to work. I told you, I just started this new job in Avonmouth and they want me in today,' Andy pleaded. He had turned up just to see us off and wish us luck. He was even clutching his sandwiches that his missus had made for him.

'Tell you what, any chance of a lift down the "mouth"?' he asked.

'You got a fucking nerve, yeah, all right... jump on.' Brian had resigned himself to losing his right arm for the day.

LIKE CLOCKWORK

After the obligatory 'another 50p off everyone an' we can go' from Johnny, we set off down the Portway heading for Chesterfield via Avonmouth.

'Just 'ere will do, Drive,' Andy motioned as we pulled up by the Miles Arms, one of Avonmouth's more salubrious drinking establishments.

'Where do you think you're fucking going?'

It was Freddie Dempster, one of the few who could tackle Andy on a good day. He made a lunge for Andy.

'Get the fuck off...!'

It was too late for Andy. By now it had dawned on Brian and Daryl what Freddie was playing at. The three of them grabbed the big fellow.

'You're not going anywhere – apart from Chesterfield that is. Carry on, Drive!'

Andy howled his protest and tried his hardest to dislodge the trio, but they held firm. The driver put his foot down and headed north. Andy begrudgingly surrendered to his obvious fate.

'I didn't like the fucking job anyway.' He spat as he nonchalantly threw his sandwiches out of the window.

The hundred or so on the two coaches were the core of the Tote. That was all we needed and if you had the right lads behind you, you didn't even need that. Twenty lads all sticking together could do more damage than two hundred tossers who would leg it at the first sign of aggro. Everyone who was anyone was there, and with Andy on board we felt confident of a result. Myself, Lil, Hampshire and Smiffy were now well up the pecking order, which meant we could sit near the back seats, which were customarily reserved for Andy and the rest of the Tramps. The eager youngsters filled the front seats. John O'Shea, the organiser, sat by the driver, keeping a vigilant eye on the passengers and his deposit that would be forfeited if the coach got wrecked.

BOOTED AND SUITED

'Eight-pinter today, lads!' Stefan Collier opened his carrier bag, took out a flagon of 'Natch', popped the top and took a long draught.

Steff was a top kiddy from Banjo Island, that mysteriously named place more properly known as Cadbury Heath, a real solid one hundred per cent Rovers area. He was accompanied by, among others, Alan Roberts and David 'Edgar' Ellery. I had known these lads for a couple of years. They were decent, dependable kiddies who you could rely on and, like a lot of Tote Enders, they had a keen sense of humour. Stefan always judged the distance of an away game on the amount of alcohol he could consume. By the time we had got to Gloucester most of the coach had had a belly full of alcohol already, it was ten o'clock in the morning and the driver was already getting it in the neck to pull over for a piss stop.

'All right, but make it quick!'

'Come on, girls, you coming?'

This was aimed at the three Tote End girls who had come along for the trip – Jill Vickers, Jane Murphy and Nicki Laurie.

'Fuck off, you pervs, we'll go when you've finished,' mouthed Jill.

The three of them patiently waited, cross-legged, we trooped back on, shaking our members in full view of them. 'Go on, Jill, show us your twat!'

'Fuck off, Hampshire, you're the only twat around here.'

The girls now took their turn and clambered over a gate, stumbling across the ploughed field, and duly did their business. Unfortunately they hadn't bothered to check the hedge behind them, where a six-foot gap gave the hundred leering Tote Enders an uninterrupted view of their sliced beef curtains.

There had been a bizarre and sinister change in fashion and youth culture over the past 12 months. It was blamed on a joint attack

LIKE CLOCKWORK

on British sensibilities by a freakish American rock singer named Vincent Furnier, better known as Alice Cooper, and the eventual release of the classic, but very controversial Stanley Kubrick film *A Clockwork Orange*. Young men up and down the country had taken to wearing make-up. It was worn not in the same way as women wore make-up – to make themselves more alluring – but in such a way as to make us appear more menacing, more evil. Unfortunately this wasn't just a fashion or a mere fad, it was something altogether more malevolent.

Alice Cooper first entered the charts in 1972 with 'School's Out'. He was back in the charts as we headed for Chesterfield with 'No More Mr Nice Guy'. It summed up myself and my contemporaries perfectly.

Whereas Alice Cooper and his snake and whips were purely theatrical, the menace of *A Clockwork Orange* was very real indeed. After much deliberation by the British Board of Film Censors the uncut film was eventually released in December 1971 with an X-certificate, Many provincial councils, however, refused to allow the British-made film to be shown in their local cinemas due to its graphic scenes of rape and violence – one scene shows a gang rape set to music by Rossini and another a vicious mugging to the tune of 'Singing In The Rain.' Eventually Kubrick himself pulled it from British cinemas in 1973 after the film had been linked to a number of horrific incidents, including the rape of a 17-year-old Dutch student in Lancashire by a gang chanting the words to Gene Kelly's jolly show tune. A judge in another case spoke of the 'horrible trend inspired by this wretched film'. The film remained banned in Britain for the next 27 years. However, what was really disturbing about the film was that it was supposedly portraying Britain in the future, when casual violence and gang warfare were a way of life for Britain's youth. It was a true tale of life in Britain all right – but 1970s style.

In the manner of Malcolm McDowell's gang leader, Alex, and

his assorted Droogs, disorder reigned as innocent citizens were set upon in random and unprovoked attacks of 'ultra violence'. Tramps in particular (one is set upon in the film) came in for unwarranted attention as delinquents the length and breadth of the country mimicked both Alex's actions and his vocabulary with his boasts of going to 'tolchock some old veck in an alley and viddy him swim in his blood'. Ludwig van Beethoven topped the album charts as thousands of adolescents clamoured to buy the soundtrack of the most controversial British film ever made. As the awesome effect of Clockworkmania raged, the strains of 'Singing In The Rain' echoed out from every football terrace in the country as a prelude to violence. I rushed to buy Anthony Burgess's original 1962 book but its bleak vision of Britain in the supposedly not too distant future and its use of the bizarre Nadsat teenage vocabulary made it demanding and laborious. I consoled myself with Richard Allen's latest best-seller, *Smoothies*, which, if the cover and the title were anything to go by, should have mirrored my lifestyle to perfection. But sadly, like all Allen's other offerings apart from *Skinhead*, it missed the mark by a mile.

Myself and a number of other young smoothies sported false eyelashes and heavy black mascara as we arrived in Chesterfield. Our minds were as warped and twisted as the town's famous spire – and with our white overalls, white strides and single, solitary black leather-gloved hands we all thought we looked the epitome of terrace fashion culture. Brian Willis and the rest of the Tramps thought we looked total prats.

To everyone's regret, Chesterfield itself was a big disappointment. We took their home end, the Spion Kop, with ease. It seemed their lads had learned their lesson from the previous year and gave us a wide berth and plenty of respect. After a minor scuffle that saw the Tote chalk up yet another away victory, I was ejected from the ground for my part in the pre-match skirmish. I was skint and cold and headed back to the coach for some kip.

LIKE CLOCKWORK

Rovers scraped a 1–0 win. The other results didn't go our way and so we were destined to spend another year in the backwater of the Third Division. We left Chesterfield and dejectedly started our long journey home knowing that our season was over and that we had a boring couple of months ahead of us. However, the events of the following few hours ensured that 28 April 1973 would go down in the annals of Tote End history. For reasons that will become apparent the name of the town and its police force shall remain nameless – it all started when some bright spark suggested stopping off at a town that we had often visited in the past and whose football fans were known to have a small but tasty mob. In fact they had surprised us with a ferocious bit of aggro a couple seasons back. It was to be a night that Alex and his Droogs would have been proud of.

'Coming, Browner?' Hampshire asked as we pulled into a car park round the back of the Co-op, the largest and, judging by the rest of the place, the most fashionable store in town.

'Nah, I'm skint and fucked. I'll catch up with you later.'

I couldn't be arsed, really. I had drunk too much earlier on in the day and was feeling like a bag of shite. I felt sure I had a cold coming. Good old Steve Edwards had lent me his classic sheepskin coat to keep me warm. Steve was a real gentleman. I had never seen him get into trouble and he would rather talk his way out of a fight or just walk away. I admired him for that. I wished I could do the same, but it wasn't in my nature. Once that red mist appeared in front of my eyes I knew my fists would do the talking. Most of us thought that way – Steve was just the exception that proved the rule.

Five of us stayed on the coach. Like me, the other four were either skint or fucked, or both. We let the others go off and enjoy themselves if that was possible in this dump. It was like many other Northern towns, small, grimy and tough, populated with not-so-small, grimy and tough coal-mining hard-nuts – and the lads were even worse.

BOOTED AND SUITED

'Ay-up, I think we've got company.' Roger Bell had spotted a coach pulling in, followed by another, and another, and another...

'Fucking hell, look at this lot.'

By a bizarre coincidence the local team had likewise had a chance of promotion, this time from the Fourth Division, and like us their results had not gone in their favour. Their fans were now arriving back *en masse* from their fruitless journey to Cambridge. The coaches parked and immediately disgorged their disgruntled passengers. They eyed us up and quickly spotted the 'Sparkes of Bristol' logo on the side of the coach.

'What are we gonna do, leg it or stay on the coach?' Roger was getting nervous. He was only a young lad and needed some assurance.

'Judging by this lot, I think we'd better leg it!' I replied.

We had no option: the mob were heading for us and we could see them picking up bricks and bottles. I opened the fire exit at the back and jumped out, the others quickly followed. We ran as a rain of bricks descended on the coach, smashing the windows with fearsome thuds.

They were on us like a pack of wolves. A half brick hit me on the back — luckily, Steve's sheepskin softened the impact. Micky Cole, wearing his white butcher's coat, a common sight on the terraces that season, daubed with 'Tote End Boot Boys' wasn't so lucky. A brick hit him on the back of his head, pole-axing him and sending him collapsing to the ground like a dead-weight. They followed up with the boot, going in with murderous accuracy. Micky was getting a right kicking and I was powerless to help. I felt sick with fear and loathing; I was desperate to help but at the same time I was even more desperate to get away.

As I was beginning to fear for Micky's life, the law arrived. A panda car screeched into the car park and signalled the end of Micky's beating. The local lads scattered in all directions, except for one big, sneering bastard who cockily sauntered away.

LIKE CLOCKWORK

'Oi, you, stop!' the copper shouted somewhat optimistically.

I had never heard anybody say 'Certainly officer' at that request and this bloke was going to be no different. I had a brick in my hand – this will fucking stop him, I thought. I chucked it and caught him square in the back; he crumpled to his knees.

The copper made his move and grabbed him round the neck, forcing his arm up in customary fashion. 'You're arrested, son!'

I turned my attention to Micky. He was struggling with his breathing and he had an ugly gash on the side of his head. He was bleeding heavily and the bile that had been rising in my stomach finally made its appearance – I vomited over the tarmac.

I didn't wait to hang around. I needed to find the others quickly and legged it just as an ambulance arrived to take Micky to hospital. The rest of our crew weren't hard to find: the town had a large market square in its centre with a profusion of pubs, I just followed the noise. I burst through the doors and all eyes were on me.

'Come on, we've got trouble!'

They didn't need to be told twice. The pub emptied speedily; we were out for revenge. What followed next was described in the *Bristol Evening Post* as THE BATTLE OF THE YOBS. Three hours of intense violence and wanton destruction – cars, shops and offices were damaged as our two mobs took turns to attack each other. Bricks, dustbins and youths were thrown through windows, cars were overturned and the final tumultuous battle took place in the market square, where wooden stalls were smashed up and used as weapons. Ten Rovers fans were arrested. I was one of them.

'Name?'

'John O'Shea.' I had given up using Harvey's name and address – I had overused it in the last year or two.

'Really, is that why one of your mates shouted "Drop it, Chris, it's the law"? Give us your real fucking name, sonny.'

'Chris... Chris Brown.' I was fucked, I had been caught

redhanded chasing a local kiddy. It hadn't helped that I was brandishing a three-foot length of wood, nails still intact from where it was wrenched from a market cart. We went through the preliminaries. The law were in no mood to argue – the station was overrun with delinquents all proclaiming their innocence,

'I didn't do fuck all.' This came from 'Edgar' Ellery, one of the Banjo Island boys.

"Swan' I, copper.' The Bristolian equivalent of 'It wasn't me, officer.' Others weren't so blasé. A few were even muttering something about wanting their mums. Before banging me up in the cells, the copper looked me straight in the eye.

'What the 'eck dost thou look like, son?'

'What do you mean?'

He reached out and pulled my false eyelashes off with a vicious tug. 'Fuckin' southern poofter,' he said as he shoved me in, slamming the heavy steel door behind me.

I had been charged with possessing an offensive weapon and threatening behaviour. Like most of the others I was to be released on bail to appear at a later date; another four lads were kept in custody. All I was concerned with now was getting out of this shit-hole and getting home, although I wasn't looking forward to explaining to my old man and old lady what had happened.

'C'mon, coppers, you've charged us now, when you gonna let us go?'

'When we've got rid of your coaches, that's when.'

'What? How we supposed to get home?'

'That's your fucking problem.'

The bastards meant it too. Our coaches, although severely damaged, were waiting outside for us, but the wonderful local police decided that arresting us wasn't enough. They escorted the coaches out of town on to the motorway and only then did they let us go.

LIKE CLOCKWORK

'Thanks for fuck all,' I muttered. The coppers took a real and perverse pleasure in our predicament. Here were six young men, no money and miles from home, and not a clue how to get there. What a bunch of bastards, I thought, as they opened the cell doors and bade us farewell.

'Right, Chris, they finally let you go then.' It was Steve Edwards.

'What are you doing here?' I couldn't believe what I was seeing.

'You've still got my sheepskin,' shrugged Steve, looking a little embarrassed.

'I would've given it back to you, you daft bastard.'

Steve must have been a sandwich short of a picnic. I gave him back his sheepskin, shaking my head. I was lost for words. The daft sod would rather be stranded 200 miles from home rather than not get his sheepskin back. It was a nice coat, but not that fucking nice. We trudged off into the cold night air. It was one o'clock in the morning; we had a long night ahead of us.

We had walked for miles, optimistically thrusting our thumbs out every time a car went past. We knew we would be out of luck – who in their right mind would stop for a bunch of thugs like us? After walking for two hours we were still a long way off the motorway junction. Even then we doubted if anyone would give us a lift; cars were now as rare as a brain cell in Steve Edwards' head.

'Fuck this for a game of soldiers, I'm gonna nick a car.' It was Barry Cooper, a lad whom I had met for the first time that night. Barry was from the City heartland of Hartcliffe, where handbrake turns and hot-wiring cars were on the school timetable. If anyone knew how to nick a car it would be him. I didn't even know how to drive, let alone how to break into a car and start it up.

'I dunno, we're in enough trouble already,' I replied.

BOOTED AND SUITED

'Yeah, well we're not going anywhere at this rate are we, who's up for it?' Barry asked. We huddled in a circle in the middle of a nowhere road in the middle of a nowhere county. It was gone three and it had started to rain. It seemed a tempting idea.

'Come on, next house we come to we get the car, all right?' Barry suggested. We muttered our approval. I was still dubious, so was Jeff Shellard, a *Clockwork Orange* clone from Barton Hill. Jeff was decked out all in white and heavy black Doc Martens. He stood out like a bulldog's bollocks. He didn't want to risk another run-in with the law.

The next house we came to was perfect. It was big and detached and had a long driveway leading to the front door. Parked on the gravel drive was a roomy Austin Cambridge, perfect size for all of us to squeeze into. But I was still wary...

'Tell you what, I'll stay out here, just up the road a bit. Keep an eye out for any traffic.'

'Yeah, me too.' Jeff sidled up to me.

'Good thinking, we'll push the car out of the driveway and on to the road and start it there, right?' Barry was taking control; it was OK by me.

Jeff and I waited with bated breath. We positioned ourselves about 50 yards away, just far enough to make it look like we were having nothing to do with it. The whole thing took an age. We could see Barry expertly get into the car, and the other four started pushing it out on to the road. We could now hear Barry starting the engine.

'Come on, come on, you bastard, start the fucking engine,' I murmured through gritted teeth. The engine turned over, and over. 'Come on, come on!' Before it had a chance to kick into life a large van came hurtling round the corner – a fucking coppers' van!

It screamed to a halt parallel with the Austin Cambridge. The

LIKE CLOCKWORK

coppers flew out and dragged Barry out of the car before he had even realised what was happening. The others legged it in all directions, some running straight for us.

'Run, it's the fucking Old Bill!' one of the lads hollered as he headed our way.

'I know, I know, it's fuck all to do with us, right?'

'Just fucking leg it, Chris!' Jeff shouted at me.

'No, just carry on walking. The law don't know we're involved, trust me!'

The lad ran straight past us, pursued by a copper who caught him with a flying rugby tackle. He frog-marched him back past us towards the van. The copper gave us only a cursory glance.

'Told you, Jeff, we're getting away with it!'

I spoke too soon, another copper was heading towards us armed with a ferocious-looking Alsatian.

'You two, come here, you're nicked!'

'We're nothing to do with it, honest, honest, we...'

The copper was having none of it.

'Yeah, fucking heard it all before, move it. You lads have really dropped a bollock!'

He motioned with the dog. The Alsatian could hardly contain its excitement, its barking was relentless. Another copper joined the first one. We could hear dogs barking in the nearby trees – one of the lads had tried to escape into the woodland. I didn't reckon he would be in there for long. The coppers hauled us back to the van and then, amazingly, dragged us across the road into the driveway of the house. By now all the coppers were laughing; there was a private joke going on, and we were the subject of that joke. As they hauled us towards the house I spotted the cause of the coppers' mirth. A light had now come on in the house, and another light had appeared over the front door, a big blue rectangular light with the words 'POLICE' emblazoned across it.

The front door of the country police station opened up. Its

frame was filled with a brick shithouse of a bloke dressed in jeans and a white T-shirt. He gleefully pulled us through the door one by one, through the reception area and into a small cell. He held a large American night stick in one hand which he rhythmically, and menacingly, slapped into his other huge, open palm.

'Face up against the wall, you dozy fuckers!' said the Shithouse.

We obediently did as he told us. I had never been so scared in my life. I looked around at the others. Poor Steve Edwards had pissed himself, the urine making a large dark patch in the front of his Levi's.

'You'll do more than piss yourselves when I've finished with you!'

My head was in a spin. The situation still hadn't quite registered with me. Who the fuck was this thug? What was he doing in this house? It dawned on me that not many people had a cell in their house. He was a copper and we had tried to nick his fucking car! The others looked as mystified and dumbfounded as me. They had pulled all seven of us in, including Edgar Ellery who had legged it into the woods.

Before I had a chance to fathom out what was going on I felt the baton smash against the back of my legs. I let out a cry and slumped to the floor. The copper grabbed my hair and yanked me back up. Spinning me around, he punched me in the face. I began snivelling.

'Leave it out, copper, you'll fucking kill hi...' pleaded Jeff. Before he had a chance to finish the sentence, one of the other coppers grabbed Jeff's head and smashed it against the wall. Jeff slid down the wall leaving a smear of blood from his nose, which had been broken by the impact. It was now bedlam as the rest of the coppers fired in to all of us. By now we were all screaming, but to no avail. These coppers wanted blood – ours.

After what seemed like a lifetime of a beating they departed,

LIKE CLOCKWORK

but the Shithouse quickly returned and doused us with a bucket of freezing cold water. A mop followed.

'Clean this fucking mess up!' he hollered. 'Or you'll get another beating!'

He retired to tea and digestives with his mates. We could hear them laughing and retelling the events of the last hour over and over again. For all my misdemeanours and wrongdoings over the last few years, I had never lost sight of the fact that what I was doing was breaking the law. I knew the difference between right and wrong – my old man had seen to that. Unbelievably, I still had respect for the law – until that night. My attitude to the police would never be the same again.

We were taken to a nearby police station, where thankfully the coppers believed my and Jeff's story that we wanted nothing to do with stealing the car. The other five, including poor Steve Edwards, had backed us up and they were charged with 'Taking and Driving Away' or 'Tickling Dogs Arses' as it was more commonly known. Taking away? Barry Cooper hadn't even started the engine, let alone driven the car away.

The fact that Jeff and I were apparently innocent of stealing the car had a sobering effect on the coppers. While they locked up the others in the cells we were treated to a warm office and a decent cooked breakfast. Embarrassingly for the coppers, the two who were not charged were the two who had taken the severest beatings. My head felt like it was hanging off, my nose and lips were split and I had a nasty bruise coming up on my eye. Jeff hadn't fared a lot better: his nose was swollen to twice its normal size and his large rabbit-like teeth had pierced his lips and left a nasty gash. The cops now embarked on a damage-limitation exercise and ensured we got our story right.

'If anybody asks, lads, tell 'em you got the injuries at the match, OK?'

'Yeah, OK. Just get us home, will you.'

BOOTED AND SUITED

Somebody did ask. It was a superintendent who had been briefed on the night's events. I gave him the rehearsed reply.

He winked at me. 'That's right, lad, you stick to that story and you'll be all right.'

The whole fucking lot were in on it. I had heard stories of police brutality and beatings in Bridewell before. I hadn't quite believed them – naively, I thought the law weren't like that. I now knew better.

After releasing us on the Sunday morning, the coppers at least had the decency to arrange our journey back to Bristol. If only those bastards the previous night hadn't wanted to prolong our ordeal we wouldn't have been in this situation. They drove us to the local railway station and put us on the first train back to Bristol. My thoughts were now on my parents. Because they weren't on the phone the law in Bristol had been contacted and despatched to my house to get the money off my old man to pay for the train fare. I was now not looking forward to getting home...

'You lying bastard!'

'Honest, Dad, that's what happened!'

'You got that beating from some other toe-rag like you, not the police!'

My old man would have none of it. In his eyes and those of most of the older generation the law were whiter than white. He gave me another whack for my troubles. My older brother, Mike, looked on in disgust.

'How can you do this to our mum? I thought you had got over all this, it's about time you grew up!'

My mum was distraught, she had been awake all night – she hadn't stopped crying since the law had knocked on the door at seven o'clock. I vowed to call it a day, my football hooligan days were over for a while. After all, it was the close of the season.

The Gloucester Cup Final against City took place just three

LIKE CLOCKWORK

days later, despite my absence. In revenge for the previous year's onslaught by Rovers fans the City fans rampaged along Stapleton Road after the game and caused thousands of pounds worth of damage (a huge sum bearing in mind the already dilapidated state of Stapleton Road). Following on so swiftly after the 'BATTLE OF THE YOBS' it caused more predictable headlines in the *Evening Post*, Rovers Supporters' Club Chairman Eric Godfrey leading the chorus for the 'Bring back the birch' brigade. It would be to no avail – violence bred violence, the cycle would go on.

17

All Mouth an' No Trousers

The Top Rank in Nelson Street had been the favourite haunt for Bristol's white working-class kids since the mid-Sixties. Its heady mix of cheap alcohol, even cheaper women and predominantly black dance music made it an irresistible magnet for hundreds of factory-weary council house inhabitants on a Saturday night in pursuit of instant gratification.

The city of Detroit was still trying to keep its name on the map with the magnificent offering from The Temptations, 'Papa Was A Rolling Stone' (sadly their last top 40 hit in the Seventies). The Detroit Emeralds' 'Feel The Need In Me' and 'You Want It, You Got It' were also riding high in the charts. The O'Jays followed up their previous year's hit, 'Back Stabbers', with the massive dance favourite 'Love Train' and the odd Northern Soul track by Dobie Gray and Robert Knight also made an appearance. Big, bad Barry White entered the charts with 'I'm Gonna Love You Just A Little Bit More Baby' in June – it was the first of ten consecutive Top 30 hits for the 'Luurve God', whose girth almost matched his ego. Reggae proved it could still do the business with a stunning offering, Zap Pow's classy 'This Is

ALL MOUTH AN' NO TROUSERS

Reggae Music', which surprisingly failed to make an impression on the charts.

Two funky belters did manage to make the charts however, Timmy Thomas's 'Why Can't We Live Together' and Chairmen of the Board's 'Finders Keepers', but *the* dance record of that period, if not the decade was released in 1973. It became the benchmark for the burgeoning funk music that was beginning to find its way into the British dance scene. 'Soul Makossa' by Manu Dubango, an obscure African guitarist, struck a chord with me the first time I heard it. It never featured in the British charts, yet it turned out to be one of the most influential records ever made, being one of the first truly 'disco' recordings.

By the end of the decade The Bee Gees were widely being regarded as the best disco group in the world. Seven short years previously they had been scoring hits with mawkish ballads such as 'New York Mining Disaster 1941'; how times had changed. Records such as 'Soul Makossa', however, were still only a glimmer of light in a dark musical world. Sadly for me, in mid-1973, Britain was still firmly in the grip of glam rock. Roxy Music, Gary Glitter, Elton John, Slade, Sweet and the high priest of glam, David Bowie, were still churning out hit after hit featuring banal lyrics about spacemen wearing lip gloss and the like, although, admittedly, there was the odd classic as far as rock music was concerned, as in the case of early punk rocker Lou Reed, with his timeless 'Walk On the Wild Side'.

Perhaps surprisingly, glam rock was going down a storm in the clubs; it was loud and aggressive and suited the times. It even got to the point where Elton John's 'Saturday Night's All Right For Fighting' and Sweet's 'Ballroom Blitz' were banned for causing too much trouble. Likewise, Gary Glitter's 'I'm The Leader Of The Gang', with its thrashing chorus of 'Come on, come on, come on' could have been written specifically for the football terrace gangs. It didn't take long for one of his other hits, 'Hello,

BOOTED AND SUITED

Hello I'm Back Again', to be adapted to 'Hello, Hello, Tote End Aggro', which was always the overture to a good ruck, whether on the terraces or on the dancefloor.

Jeff Beck's 'Hi-Ho Silver Lining', although a few years old, was still a favourite and was another song that always caused mayhem. Positioning ourselves on the balcony of the Top Rank we would wait until 'Hi-Ho Bristol City, everywhere you go now baby!' could be heard from somewhere among the throbbing mass below. We would descend on the unsuspecting group from behind, glasses in hand...

'And it's Hi-Ho Bristol ROVERS, everywhere you go now baby!' The attack would be short and sweet, reminiscent of our assault on the East End the previous year. Injuries would be severe – broken beer glasses rarely did anyone any favours. Of course, it worked both ways. It was unwise to visit the Gents alone, when a 'Glasgow kiss' from an enraged East Ender would often be the sequel to splashing your boots.

A new club opened that summer, Scamps in the Pithay. Scamps promised to be a sophisticated, more intimate nightclub. It was the forerunner of smaller, members-only clubs such as Shades and Maxims, which would eventually proliferate in Bristol and sound the death knell for the bigger, older dancehalls such as the Top Rank, the Locarno and Tiffanys which stood as it did, isolated at the top of Blackboy Hill. The writing was on the wall – within a year of Scamps opening the Top Rank had shut for a major renovation. It reopened as Bailey's; the dancehall era was over.

Our first visit to Scamps was an eye-opener in every sense. I queued up with Gubby, Lil and Hampshire, the usual Saturday night foursome. I was wearing a dark brown zip-up velvet bomber jacket, brown bags with one-inch turn-ups, patch pockets on the back with contrasting yellow stitching and a brown shirt furnished with small yellow stars and yellow buttons and piping. On my feet were my pride and joy, my favourite metallic blue two-inch soled platform shoes I'd purchased from Hummingbird. The shoes were cool but they weren't a patch on the brand-new pair of blue and orange platform shoes that Hampshire was wearing. They looked expensive and were a welcome change from the 'wet-look' cream-and-chocolate stack-heeled brogues that he customarily wore and that his old man, Bert, amusingly called his 'Charlie Corolli' shoes.

'Nice shoes, Hamps.'
'Yeah, got 'em last night.'
'Last night? Where from?'
'Beau Brummel on the Centre, opened late especially for me.'
'I never knew they opened late.'
'Yeah, like I said, just for me.'

The ape-man on the door was welcoming but adamant: 'Sorry, lads, you gotta have a tie on.' Gubby, Lil and I were suitably dressed but Hampshire was wearing his favourite flyaway collar shirt with a penny farthing pattern on it, and no tie.

'Come on, I've got an idea,' said Gubby. That was a rarity coming from Graham. Good-looking smooth bastard he might have been but intelligence was not a trait Gubby was known for.

'I'll pull the lining out of my tie and we'll use that.' It wasn't a bad idea. Gubby carefully pulled the stitching apart from the join; he was left with two ties, two very short ties, but nevertheless two ties. Unfortunately there wasn't enough material to go around the neck, so after carefully knotting them and positioning them under their collars, they kept them in place with their chins.

'That looks pretty good, we'll get in no sweat.'
'Evening, lads.' It was the same bouncer, totally oblivious to the quick change act.
'That'll be a quid, my love,' said the middle-aged tart on the desk.

BOOTED AND SUITED

'How much? 'S only ten bob round the Top Rank!' said Hampshire, raising his chin in alarm, only to see his customised tie fall to the floor, directly at the feet of the apeman. We conceded defeat and headed for the Top Rank with its unsophisticated Wills' cigarette factory girls who gave away both their fags and their favours for free. Scamps would have to wait another week for the honour of our company.

After another stimulating evening listening to Hampshire's standard chat-up line of 'Did yer' 'air get wet this morning?' which, when met by a querying 'No?' brought the retort of 'What did you do, piss through a straw?' and adding to the profits of Courage's brewery, we staggered towards the foul-smelling hot-dog stands and their even fouler-smelling proprietors with their 'plen-tee onions' on the city centre. On the way we took in the arguing couples, the brawling youths, the alcohol-induced piles of vomit and the recently boarded-up window of Beau Brummel.

A crowd of nearly 20,000 turned up at Eastville in early August to see Rovers play against First Division West Ham United in their defence of the Watney Cup. The London club's followers were among the most feared set of fans in the country. I was determined to be on my best behaviour – I was due in court the following week. The rest of the Tote were determined to show the Cockney geezers that the West Country wasn't populated by straw-sucking tractor drivers. Predictably the violence was incessant, the boys from the Chicken Run had infiltrated the Tote End and the first 45 minutes matched the ferocity of the Stoke game two years earlier. At half-time Steff and Alan Roberts were on the prowl, mustering up support for a determined attack on the infiltrators who were firmly encamped on our territory.

We gathered at the top of the steps leading on to the Tote, another mob assembled at the other gangway on the far side; it

ALL MOUTH AN' NO TROUSERS

was to be a two-pronged attack. I was in two minds about the plan: I was wary about getting nicked again, but the mouthy Cockneys deserved a whacking. I wanted to knock their 'Hampstead Heath' down their big, fat 'North an' Souths'. Clyde was also wary, but for different reasons. Tied around his neck was his Rovers scarf and on the lapel of his jacket was the cross-hammered badge of West Ham. Talk about a rock and a hard place.

Before anyone had a chance to plot our next move, Alan had a rush of blood.

'Come on, lads, let's get the bastards! CHARGE!'

Alan fired in, not considering the consequences. Events had overtaken us, there was no time to think; we followed up in a fierce phalanx. Alan struck a geezer with a cracking punch. He slumped to the terrace and Alan rapidly followed up with a vicious kick to the head. The law were on him in a flash; mayhem now ensued as our second column attacked from the other side. The law responded in large numbers, mounted police and dogs adding to the chaos and confusion, the fighting fans spilled on to the pitch, followed by a police horse and its rider who expertly jumped the perimeter fence.

Peace was eventually restored. Alan and six others were arrested, but he had done enough to write his name in to the Tote End book of fame. It was odd, away from football he was one of the most mild-mannered and polite men I had ever met and his face was never short of a smile. He eventually emigrated to Australia with his wife and boys, who were all blissfully unaware of Alan's notorious past.

I appeared in court just two days before the start of the new season. I was fined £25 and put on probation for six months; it could have been a lot worse. In court I approached a local lad, an apprentice coal-miner. He looked vaguely familiar.

'All right, mate?' I asked him as I sat down.

BOOTED AND SUITED

'Yeah, 'n' you?'

'Not bad. What you being done for?'

'GBH, did one of your lads. Would've got away with it too, but as I was leggin' it, some bastard clouted me with a brick an' I got nicked.'

'Bastard, innit,' I replied, barely containing myself.

He got six months. I laughed my bollocks off.

Due to the timing of my court appearance I missed the start of the new league season. As my mates rampaged through Bournemouth on the first game of the season, watching Warboys and Bannister spectacularly carrying on from where they left off with their Smash and Grab act, I was helping my old man in the garden.

To rub salt in the wounds the lads stayed on in the South Coast for the Bank Holiday weekend. There was havoc on the seafront and in the Bournemouth nightclubs as both sets of fans tried their utmost to kick the shit out of each other.

Chelsea had always been my 'other' team. I had seen them a couple of times at Stamford Bridge a few years earlier. One game in particular, against Arsenal stuck in my impressionable mind, not for the huge 50,000 plus crowd and the stunning winning goal by John Hollins, but for the viciousness of the incessant brawling on the Shed and below the Matchstick stand. Chelsea in the early Seventies were the Manchester United of the south, a big, glamorous club with stars such as Peter Osgood, Ian Hutchinson and Alan Hudson gracing the pitch as well as the Kings Road and in the close season they enhanced their celebrity status by signing Bristol's very own glamour boy Chris Garland from the Shit across the river. Part of the transfer deal was for Chelsea to play at Ashton Gate in a 'friendly', although, in retrospect, 'friendly' seemed an incongruous description of the event itself.

There were quite a number of Rovers fans who also followed

ALL MOUTH AN' NO TROUSERS

Chelsea and through the hooligan network we had arranged to meet the hard-core of Chelsea's notorious Shed in the Star at Ashton before the game. I had turned up with Hampshire and a pocket full of lead 'quads', metal pieces used in type-setting, that I had 'borrowed' from work. They would be ideal for chucking at the East Enders from a distance and would cause maximum damage.

Jeff Shellard had also turned up, with his appropriately named mate, Roy Savage; they were both dressed up in full-on *Clockwork Orange* gear. Jeff, like me, obviously hadn't learned a thing from his court appearance and Roy was still boasting of his exploits at Bournemouth, where his performance with a carpet knife had left a local fan in stitches. Roy really was a character. He was more commonly known as Rod, due to his uncanny resemblance to Rod Stewart, his spiky red hair was nicely set off by his long, black false eyelashes, but there was something missing – this was the first time I had seen Rod not wearing his trademark tartan scarf.

The Rovers/Chelsea lads who had arranged the meet were also there. Pete 'Egghead' Daniels, and Bob 'China' Head took great delight in introducing us to the top Chelsea geezer, a short, stocky, balding thug whom I had read about just 12 months earlier. I was in awe.

'Nice to meet ya, lads,' said Mike Greenaway as he shook our hands.

'Egghead tells me some good fings about you boys. I hear you 'ad a bit of a rumble against the 'Ammers, that right?'

'Yeah, we've had our moments,' I replied. 'Did you ever get those Man U kiddies?'

'Eh? Oh, yeah in the paper like. Yeah, too right.'

Here was a legendary figure and I was making small talk with him. The thing that struck me about Greenaway was his age. Everybody I knew to be involved in football violence was either a teenager or in their early twenties at most. I was staggered to think that this overweight railway clerk, wearing a natty check sports jacket, could be involved in aggro. The tell-tale signs were there, though: huge shovel-like fists and a nose that had been broken more times than Beau Brummel's window.

There were about 50 of us in total, about half and half Rovers and Chelsea. It was agreed we would infiltrate the East End in ones and twos, the Bristolians ahead of the Cockneys. Once inside, we would all meet up on the back terrace. It had proved successful the previous year in the Gloucester Cup and we were eager to show our London counterparts we were as good, if not better than them at causing 'a rumble'.

This time, though, the City boys were ready for us. No sooner had we got on to the terrace than they were on us. They had spotted me and Hampshire.

'It's fucking Rovers, get the bastards!'

The Chelsea lads were still filing through the turnstiles. They could see the situation developing and promptly made a 'U'-turn and legged it big time. The City fans couldn't care less whether we were Chelsea or not, they were just intent on getting the intruders off their patch. 'You'll never take the East End, you'll never take the East End!' they roared, and for once they were right. We knew when we were beaten. Hampshire and I had taken too many whacks.

'C'mon let's get out of here!' I urged. Hamps didn't need telling twice.

We fled back to the turnstiles with the East End on our heels. Luckily, the law were on hand to get us out.

'You dozy Cockney bastards, get up the other end,' said the copper opening the gates. It wasn't until we were all outside that we announced who we really were.

'Come and have a go at the Tote End ag-ero! Come and have a go at the Tote End ag-ero!' It was easy to chant now, we had a 12-

ALL MOUTH AN' NO TROUSERS

foot-high steel fence between us. I chucked over a few lead quads for good measure, then we licked our wounds and headed back to The Star. As we passed the Park End, the terrace reserved for visiting fans, we spied Greenaway and his oppos at the back of the terrace. He looked at us in dismay and maybe even a hint of shame; I returned his stare with one of disgust.

'That lot aren't worth a J. Arthur Rank,' said Hampshire in his best Cockney rhyming slang. He was right. With the absence of the infamous Shed, the City boys had giving us a right hiding. And what's more, Chelsea had lost themselves a fan.

18
We're on the Telly!

Rovers had stormed through the division like a dose of diarrhoea with daps on, and we arrived in North Devon for our FA Cup game against non-league Bideford undefeated in the league. It had been going off all morning as every car and coach brought more and more Tote Enders to the dour shipbuilding town on the Bristol Channel. I had travelled down with Hampshire and Egghead in an ancient Morris Minor driven by Southmead's finest, Ricky Lee.

The yokels tried their hardest, but experience shone through. The local police were bemused by it all – poor bastards were more used to herding up runaway sheep than hooligans from the big city. In the ground the atmosphere was simmering; one of the farmer boys pulled out his mum's best carving knife and waved it at Ricky.

''Ave summa dissun, you Brizzle basars!' yokel grunted, not bothering to remove the straw from his mouth. I didn't want to question his parents' sleeping habits, but I could see he had two thumbs on one hand.

A huge, ruddy-faced copper made a move for him. 'Now

WE'RE ON THE TELLY!

we'em 'ave nun a that, young Eric, take that 'ome an' give it back to yer mum!' The copper cuffed Eric around the ear and made him put the knife back in his pocket. It was now our turn to be bemused and bewildered. Somehow I couldn't see that scene being repeated at Eastville.

Prior to the kick-off, a local fan ran on to the pitch, determined to grab his 15 minutes of stardom. Carefully placing his scarf on the centre spot, he proceeded to bow down and kiss his prized possession to the cheers of the gathering farmers and shipwrights. Larry Bird, a permanently denim-clad accomplice of Steff from Banjo Island, was having none of it. He had arrived in Bideford on his Lambretta scooter and dashed on to the pitch to redress the balance still carrying his helmet. Oblivious to the fast-approaching Larry, the yokel continued to do his press-ups and kissing act, each smacker being greeted by a loud cheer from the assembling crowd. The yokel took a smacker of his own as Larry swung his helmet and brought it down with a thud against his skull. All hell was now let loose as a full-scale pitch invasion ensued. In the confusion and near riot that followed Larry and his battered helmet made their triumphant and rather fortuitous escape back to the safety of the terraces. Rovers made amends for their non-league debacle the previous season with Smash and Grab bagging a goal apiece and Rovers were in the next round.

The following week we were on our travels again, this time to the genteel Sussex town of Brighton, where ol' big mouth himself, Brian Clough, had just been appointed as the new manager of Brighton and Hove Albion. It was now December and Rovers had gone an incredible 18 league games without defeat. The team and the Tote Enders were on a roll. The national papers, however, rather than concentrating on how well Rovers had been doing, were full of Cloughie,

BOOTED AND SUITED

who was confidently predicting an end to the Rovers bandwagon. There had been rumours that the game was to be televised. The Tote was determined to put on a good show for the cameras and shut Cloughie's big orifice up once and for all.

It was the sort of cold, dismal winter morning that made you want to stay in bed with your hand wrapped around your cock rather than get up at the sound of a sparrow's fart and trek halfway across the country just to see your team more than likely get beaten. Nevertheless, I was one of a hundred hardy souls who patiently waited at Lawrence Hill for Johnny O'Shea's coaches to arrive. It was seven in the morning and I was wearing only a brown skinny-ribbed sweater featuring a yellow five-pointed star on it, a flimsy gold-coloured satin jacket that was so thin you could piss through it and my faded baggy Falmers jeans. I was beginning to regret confining my crombie to the back of the wardrobe. My Onitsuka Tigers likewise did little to keep out the frost that had formed on the pavements overnight. To top it all, most of us had hangovers from a typical Friday night out; the foul sounds and smells of young men belching and breaking wind filled the cold morning air.

'The next bastard who says we're not real football fans I'm gonna whack!' said the newly nicknamed Iggy.

I agreed, you had to be a bloody fanatic to stomach what we put up with; for people to question our motives or our intentions was an insult. We were football fans of the finest pedigree, prepared to take our allegiance to our team to the limit, often risking life and limb in the defence of our club's honour. Well that was how we saw it, anyway. We were convinced we were of a high order, fighting a true and noble cause. As the sleet began to fall I realised my mind was full of bollocks. I wanted my bed.

WE'RE ON THE TELLY!

Clyde's new nickname, Iggy, had come about through a rather convoluted route. A ropy ex-skinhead tart named Leslie, who had made the papers a few years back when she had been savagely beaten by a gang of Hells Angels in a Bristol café, had taken a shine to Hampshire, obsessively following him round the pubs and cellar bars and even buying him a Tam o' Shanter cap (which he refused point-blank to wear). Leslie herself was the original Iggy, although where she got her nickname from nobody knew. She wasn't a bad-looking old bird, but one thing that put Hampshire off was the large and unsightly mole complete with hairs bristling out of it on her chin; the offending spot therefore became known as an 'iggy'. Clyde, unfortunately, was in possession of a rather large 'iggy' of his own. Before he knew it, Clyde had progressed from 'Smiffy' to 'Iggy'; the nickname stuck.

After a small-time altercation with a couple of Southampton fans during our piss-stop in Salisbury, we arrived in Brighton just in time for the pubs to open. We had done a minor tour of the seafront, which had yielded little in terms of entertainment, and had ended up in a large pub close to Brighton's ground. Like the rest of Brighton it was dull and depressing. I was convinced it was going to be a bad day. Half a dozen brown splits later the world seemed a better place, though not for little Norman Macallum, younger brother of Arkle, who had been unceremoniously dragged from the crapper with his trousers and pants round his ankles by Iggy, who by now was firmly established as the head of jolly pranks. Our howls of laughter quickly turned to howls of revulsion, however, as we discovered Norman had not quite finished his bowel movement.

Even with Norman's deposits the pub had now become a warm and inviting place. Exiting it gave us a cold, sharp reminder of what a dreary place England could be in December, but we were now buoyed up and the adrenalin was pumping again, we progressed to the ground in small groups, determined to enter Brighton's end and prove our mettle once again. The law, however, were ready for us. Crowd segregation was now becoming the norm at football grounds and the more obvious Rovers fans were quickly herded us and escorted to the 'away' end of the ground. Those of us that were left were subjected to body searches and threats of having our boots taken off us or, as had been the custom for years, our laces removed for the duration of the match. This was not an idle threat – I had seen many fans stood on cold, concrete terraces in their bare socks over the last few seasons. I was thankful I was wearing my Tigers.

'How many of us are in here?' I asked Little Bado who, paradoxically, was a six foot plus lump of a bloke from Hillfields. I looked down at his feet. Like me, Bado was wearing a pair of Tigers. The classic tan-coloured suede bomber jacket he was wearing confirmed the fact that he was an ex-skin.

'About ten, I think.'

'Fucking great, we'll get a right kicking.' My depression still hadn't lifted.

'Nah, it's all right, the rest of 'em said they'll come across the pitch as soon as there's a goal'.

Pitch invasions were becoming more and more commonplace. It was an obvious reaction to crowd segregation. Put us all on one end together and we'll just have a pop with each other; segregate us, *ipso facto* you'll get pitch invasions. Either way your average hooligan was going to have his rumble, whether the law liked it or not. There had been some spectacular ones in recent years, at places such as Manchester United, Liverpool and most famously at Leeds. There, the game against West Brom came very close to be abandoned, as thousands of young delinquents battled

WE'RE ON THE TELLY!

it out on the centre spot. There was only ever going to be one conclusion to this – fences to keep us caged in like wild animals.

The ten had now become three: me, Bado and his mate Stuart Holmes who, like Bado, hailed from the same grubby council estate and who was to later unwittingly feature in Hampshire's infamous 'shit in the wardrobe' episode. I didn't know them that well but they had a look about them that said they were the reliable sort. I had also seen big Barry Waller come through the turnstiles with Brian 'Clint' Butterfield but we had lost them in the crowd. That was a shame. Brian, although a bit of a mouthy git, was generally up for it and good for a laugh, although often his words spoke louder than his actions. He also had more nicknames than Iggy. Apart from Clint, due to his liking for a small cheroot, he was also known as Toblerone Head, due to his triangular-shaped bonce, and Thrush, due to him being an irritating cunt.

Barry, however, was a totally different animal in every sense. His disarming, somewhat childlike grin, disguised an awesome battler of a man. He was up there with Andy Phelps and Pete Kimble as big men of the Tote End. If any of these were around the world seemed a somewhat safer place. Still, for the time being we had to do without them.

Although we fancied ourselves as being brave, we were not stupid. We positioned ourselves just behind the goal, close to the edge of the pitch; if it was going to go off we would be able to make a quick exit across the pitch to our comrades positioned at the opposite end. We were also in a perfect spot to be picked up by Brian Moore and his *Big Match* cameras, which sure enough had turned up to see Cloughie's boys give the upstarts from Bristol a right whupping.

As the teams emerged from the tunnel we made our presence felt: 'The Rovers!' clap, clap, clap, 'The Rovers!' It brought an immediate response from the Brighton lads, who menacingly moved down the terraces and took up their position behind us.

'Why don't you fuck off down the other end?'

'Why don't you go fuck yourself, you fucking Spannerhead,' said Bado.

Succinct and to the point. I liked Bado's style.

Within four minutes Rovers had decided to rewrite Cloughie's script. Bruce Bannister had put us one up with a wonderful trademark finish. The goals flowed – three, then four; the abuse mounted; we stood fast. The Tote stayed put at the other end – they didn't want to risk being ejected from the ground and miss out on this glorious goal-fest, and who could blame them.

By half-time Rovers had hit five. Apart from the odd globule of spit and verbal abuse the Brighton fans left us alone. The only hint of trouble came when the ball flew into their mob and, for obvious reasons, they refused to give it back. Bado was eager for the action to continue and took it upon himself to retrieve it. He plunged headlong into the disgruntled mob, dispersing them like a wolf harrowing a herd of sheep. He emerged grinning from ear to ear, clutching the ball. Before throwing it back on the pitch, he kissed it.

Often when a team hits a hatful of goals in the first half, the remaining 45 minutes are an anticlimax, but on 55 minutes Sir Alan Warboys hit his second of the game. This was all too much for the disheartened Brighton fans, who finally decided to have a pop at us. I took a clout to the back of the head, we exchanged a quick flurry of blows, made our apologies for leaving early and swiftly legged it on to the pitch. A quick dance with Sir Alan followed before we leaped into the safety of our cheering compatriots.

The final score was 8–2 to Rovers; Brighton were lucky to get the two. 'Smash' Warboys hit four and 'Grab' Bannister hit three.

WE'RE ON THE TELLY!

Rovers' reserves had beaten City Reserves 6–1. Cloughie was lost for words. It didn't turn out to be such a bad day after all.

I watched myself on *The Big Match* the next day; my Tigers looked good. Funnily enough, Brian Moore didn't even mention them.

Rock music, and in particular the sort offered by the ubiquitous Slade, was still pre-eminent in the British charts in early 1974. The Wolverhampton outfit had scored a mammoth hit with 'Merry Xmas Everybody' over the Christmas period, a song that both amused and annoyed me at the same time. Its musical content left a lot to be desired but Noddy was such a performer I couldn't help but admire the gormless-looking twat. Christmas had also been a good period for Rovers as, fresh on the heels of the Brighton hammering, they put four past Southend and another four past Plymouth on Boxing Day in front of a crowd of 22,000 at Eastville.

The Argyle fans turned up in numbers as usual and the inevitable aggro ensued. Argyle were one of the few teams in the Third Division who could put up a good showing against the Tote, but even on one of their better days they were no match for us. A huge police presence on the Tote End was the only thing that kept us from battering the Devonians like a piece of Brixham cod. Outside of the ground they were not so lucky, the ambush and attack had been planned with military precision. The length and breadth of Stapleton Road was turned into one long battlefield, with human debris littering its squalid pavements.

'Argyle Mental Terror' screamed the graffiti spray-painted on the walls of the Concorde cinema adjacent to the ground. It wasn't far from the truth, although 'Argyle Mentals Terrorised' probably would have been more appropriate. Oddly enough the wording stayed for years; week after week I passed it on my way to the ground. It was never defaced or altered and seemed to be an indelible reminder of those darker days when British football, even society, was firmly in the grip of the yob, when anarchy was threatening to take over, when it even seemed appropriate to boast about one's insanity and to proclaim it in four-foot-high letters.

Rovers went into January still in top spot and still undefeated. The home game against second-place Bournemouth was to be one of the stiffest tests of the season. John Bond's outfit from the South Coast had come a long way from the opening day of the season when Rovers had hammered them 3–0 and they were up for revenge. Surprisingly, so were their fans, who up until that season had never had much of a reputation. They arrived in Bristol in large numbers full of optimism; they were to get a rude awakening.

I entered the White Swan to be greeted by Hampshire.

'Where the fuck have you been? We've had the bastards already.'

'Bit early, innit?' It was only midday, visiting fans usually didn't arrive until about one.

'Couple of their coaches were here half an hour ago, must have been their main kiddies. Sorted 'em out though, no sweat. Me and the Barretts smashed the coaches' windows as they parked up.' Stuart, Colin and Gavin Barrett were a troublesome trio of brothers from Lockleaze. They were always accompanied by, among, others Clyde Hardy and Gary Sheen, collectively known to the rest of us as 'The Barretts.'

Hampshire was chuffed to bits. I don't think there was anybody in the pub who hadn't heard the story. I bought him a pint to shut him up. By two o'clock the White Swan was full with the usual crew. We were still reliving the Plymouth game and Hampshire was still boring us with his smashing tale when one of the young lads came running in.

'Bournemouth are on the Tote, they've fucking taken it!'

WE'RE ON THE TELLY!

We couldn't get out quick enough. We stormed across the road, eager to displace the intruders who had dared to take out patch. It wasn't as if it was Villa or City we were up against, just a bunch of Tory-voting beach boys who only worked in the summer. We made a quick detour down Napier Road, where a convenient alleyway between the terraced houses gave us a near-perfect view of the covered terrace.

Barry was raring to go. 'They're fucking on there all right, loads of the bastards! Everybody get in and meet at the bogs, then we'll all steam in together, right?'

Barry didn't need to tell us twice. But it was no good everybody entering in dribs and drabs, we needed the full mob. By the time we had assembled we were up for it, my heart was pumping like a steam engine and the red mist was descending. The law were in a quandary; they didn't know whether to try and hold us back or escort the Bournemouth fans off of the Tote. We were overwhelming them as each click of the turnstile brought in another impatient Tote Ender who was hell-bent on doing his duty.

Barry made up the Old Bill's mind for them,

'Come on, let's do the fuckers.' He said it slowly and matter-of-factly. It was more a statement than an instruction.

The familiar guttural roar went up again. Fuelled by alcohol and adrenalin we charged up the terraces leading to the usurpers with Barry a full five yards in front of us. So much for us all steaming in at once; Barry was determined to be the first one in. A splinter mob emerged from the top entrance, their silhouettes outlined against the weak sun of a January afternoon. Bournemouth's moment of glory had come to an end. The few who stood and fought soon regretted it as we fired in with our customary ferocity. The majority of them headed for the pitch or to the back of the North Stand enclosure, where a third formidable mob of irate Tote Enders exacted their own form of retribution. The battle was short and brutal; we had claimed our territory back. There was only one thing left to do: announce to the watching TV cameras just who the fuck we were:

'We are the famous, the famous TOTE END!'

Rovers won 3–0, Warboys, Bannister and Johnny Rudge doing the business in front of 21,000. Despite, or maybe even because of the result, the violence kicked off again after the game. The aggro was now becoming as predictable as the results, but there was still no strict pattern to it. There was never anything planned, it just seemed to be an inevitable consequence of the day's events. We had won easily against our nearest rivals, but clearly that wasn't enough to satisfy the bloodlust of the mob. A headlong collision with a breezeblock left one luckless Bournemouth fan in hospital after having the temerity to walk past the White Swan. An empty car parked in Stapleton Road was overturned and all the windows kicked in; the unfortunate owner must have regretted leaving the sticker innocently proclaiming 'Another Ford from Lex Motors, Bournemouth' in the rear window of his treasured Consul. We had become a devious rabble, whose pursuit of aggro was bordering on the perverse. The sad thing is, I didn't see anything wrong with it at the time.

The Drawbridge on the Centre was packed with jubilant fans. As we settled down to watch *Match Of The Day* on the TV, the Tote End came over loud and proud. We never looked or felt better in our lives. I bought the Saturday football paper, the *Green 'Un*.

''Ere, Hamps, listen to this: "Two Bournemouth coaches were seriously damaged when they came under attack from bricks thrown by Bristol Rovers fans earlier today..."'

'See, told you,' gloated Hampshire for the umpteenth time. I carried on reading.

WE'RE ON THE TELLY!

'Police are looking for a number of youths, including Phil Gordon Hampshire, of...'

'Let me look at that!' He ripped the paper from my hands. For one brief moment he believed me; for the first time that day, he was quiet.

19
When the Lights Went Out

January, that most miserable of months, was made even more wretched by the Arab oil embargo that had begun the previous year and had made the national coal miner's strike of that winter particularly biting. The country was plunged into darkness, literally, as the strike forced factories to operate three-day weeks and civilian Britain was periodically reduced to going about its business by candlelight.

As Edward Heath's government did their best to commit, political suicide, football, the only really important thing in my life, carried on regardless. Matches were played on a Sunday for the first time in history in an effort to avoid the inevitable power cuts. Our new-found fame on *Match Of The Day* and the Sunday fixture ensured a mass exodus of Rovers fans to Aldershot the following week. The streets north of the River Avon were deserted as a fleet of coaches and cars headed along the M4 for the army town. Ricky Lee's Morris Minor did the honours again and transported myself, Ricky, Lil, Hampshire and Steff to the dull barrack town where the locals were unprepared for the mass invasion that was about to hit them.

WHEN THE LIGHTS WENT OUT

We arrived ahead of the coaches, outriders to the forthcoming mass of expectant Bristolians.

''Ow many of you boys are coming up today then?' queried Soldier Boy as we entered the first pub we came across, a grubby little boozer standing opposite the quaint floral display that, curiously, was the main entrance to Aldershot's ramshackle ground.

'About eight thousand, why, what's it to you, bladderhead?' answered Ricky in his usual confrontational manner.

'Eight thousand? You're 'aving a laugh, you ain't got that many fans! Anyway we'll sort you out no worries.'

'Oh yeah, you an' who's army?' I replied. The joke was missed on him. Even allowing for the fact he was a squaddie, this one's IQ was not even running at room temperature.

'Yeah, well everybody's turning up today, including Pompey and Millwall.'

'Big fucking deal, we're shitting ourselves. Look, pal, I could listen to you for seconds, but in the meantime, let us get a pint, will you?' He grunted a parting farewell and reluctantly shuffled away, his knuckles rasping loudly against the linoleum floor as he departed.

'What d'you reckon then, Millwall coming or not?' Lil queried, ever the worrier.

'Could be Basingstoke's only down the road, and that's full of Millwall fans,' I answered. We weren't unduly worried, even allowing for Millwall's fearsome reputation. We knew we were a match for anyone on our day – and today was going to be one of our days.

Hampshire suddenly looked up from his pint, which was forming ripples of vibration as he spoke. 'What's that noise?'

Ricky's prediction of eight thousand fans coming from Bristol looked increasingly plausible as a faint rumble coming from outside rose to a huge crescendo. A convoy the likes of which

BOOTED AND SUITED

Aldershot had not seen since the war passed within feet of the pub, its windows rattling in alarm. Soldier Boy pressed his face against the glass.

'...Forty-three, forty-four, forty-five...' he finally gave up counting, whether through exhaustion or numerate ignorance I wasn't sure. He turned and faced us, his jaw now in close proximity to his knuckles.

'Fuck that for a game of soldiers,' he blurted out, rather aptly. He put his pint down slowly and left the pub. No doubt he went back to his barracks to change his trousers.

As we queued to enter the ground it became apparent that we weren't going to get in. Aldershot was overrun with Bristolians who were eagerly anticipating another goal flurry from our Dangerous Duo. We did a Smash and Grab act of our own as the chain-mail fence surrounding their end was ruthlessly torn down. I was helped over the fence by one very ignorant Aldershot fan.

'Better watch it today, there's fucking thousands of the bastards here!'

'Who're you calling a bastard?' I asked.

His quizzical look rapidly gave way to a look of fear as the sudden realisation hit him, almost as quickly as my fist did. I caught him with an adroit punch to the nose, the familiar crack signalling a perfect hit. His look was almost indignant, he responded with a similarly deft punch that made my lower lip double in size; the warm, unmistakable taste of blood filled my mouth. He looked at me pityingly.

'Fight fair next time, you bastard,' he said matter-of-factly.

He turned and casually walked away. It had never crossed my mind ever to fight fair. I always believed in getting in my strike first. It was a sobering message; I felt a pang of guilt.

Naturally, my guilt didn't last. We entered their end to be confronted with thousands of Tote Enders who were firmly

WHEN THE LIGHTS WENT OUT

encamped on the home fans' terrace, as well as three-quarters of the rest of the ground. The Tote Enders were clearly enjoying themselves, the tell-tale sign of police helmets spiralling through the air was testament to that, as was the familiar sight of hundreds of toilet rolls littering the goalmouth.

'What's it like to, what's it like to, what's it like to see a crowd? What's it like to see a crowd?' we taunted the overrun Aldershot fans, who had by now resigned themselves to watching from the safety of the High Street.

By half-time Rovers were coasting. We were three up courtesy of you-know-who and all the signs pointed to another Brighton. But the second half saw a fight back by the plucky Shots who brought the score to 3–2. Rovers were on the rack and the Aldershot fans rallied as they sensed an upset. They had mustered outside the enclosure and began throwing missiles through a gap at the top of the corrugated iron cladding that made up the back of the terrace. A familiar face appeared through the gap to add his saliva to the constant barrage coming through at us. It was Soldier Boy himself, probably wearing a fresh pair of strides. His great lump of a meathead filled the opening. He couldn't have made the invitation clearer if he had held up a sign saying 'Hit me hard please.'

Gary Sheen, one of the Barrett entourage, didn't need to be asked twice. He took a running jump and landed a perfect punch to the squaddie's grinning face. It took a second for the blow to register. Then, the eyes rolled upwards and Soldier Boy's smile turned distinctly lop-sided as his head slowly sank from view. The lights stayed on long enough for another Rovers victory; unfortunately, for Soldier Boy, they went out quicker than a striking miner could say 'Tories out!'

The general election the following month brought about a Labour victory, which ensured that the lights came back on, but they were soon dimmed for me again when I heard my favourite record label, Trojan, had gone into liquidation. Along with Pama, Trojan, which itself was a subsidiary of Chris Blackwell's innovatory Island record label, had been the label responsible for introducing most white working-class kids to reggae. Its decline and eventual disintegration in 1974 paralleled the decline of skinheads, an inevitable conclusion to the transformation in reggae music that had taken place in the previous few years.

When Bob Marley's Wailers signed to Island records in 1972, it signalled the beginning of world recognition for 'roots' music. It was the birth of a new, internationally oriented form of reggae that had moved far away from the dancehalls, which themselves were in a serious slump due to the emergence of the discos.

The Wailers' debut album on Island, the stunning *Catch A Fire* and the soundtrack to the classic Jamaican rude boy film *The Harder They Come* starring Jimmy Cliff, turned white, middle-class kids on to reggae for the first time in their dreary lives. Hippy types from Redland and Clifton, who had been previously weaned on Island's Fairport Convention, Traffic and Free, were now buying reggae. Up until the early Seventies, black harmony groups were almost entirely associated in the rock world with soul, which by this time couldn't have been more unfashionable. Rock critics deemed that any music deserving to be taken seriously had to be made by self-contained bands featuring a lead guitarist and 'meaningful' lyrics. What's more, 'progressive' music appeared on albums that had taken years to be conceived and produced, and certainly not on 45s that had been churned out overnight in some backstreet studio in Kingston, Jamaica.

The demise of the label that had meant so much to a generation of British youths passed by without so much as a one-line obituary in the papers. Its final, defiant parting shot was a

WHEN THE LIGHTS WENT OUT

huge number 1 for Ken Boothe, a reworking of Bread's vintage hit 'Everything I Own'. But to me it was an archetypal 'pop' record that had typified the insipid and vapid Trojan releases of the previous couple of years – it couldn't have got further away from 'Skinhead Moonstomp' if it had tried.

20

One Team in Bristol

Rovers' unbeaten run in the league finally came to a halt in early February when we lost away to Wrexham 0–1. It proved to be the start of a slump that threatened to put paid to the team's hopes of promotion, but much to the relief of the Tote Enders by late April the Holy Grail was there for the taking. All we had to do was gain a point at Southend on our final away game of the season.

Southend was a bastard of a place to get to at the best of times, especially with the Shrimpers playing their home games on a Friday evening. And with no official transport available due to the untimely wrecking of a football special the previous week on our visit to Tranmere, it meant only the truest of true blues were to make the trip.

I phoned in work sick – losing a day's pay seemed a small sacrifice in order to see Rovers gain promotion for the first time since the Fifties. I hitch-hiked to London with my old oppo Mogger. We crossed London courtesy of London Underground, caught a mainline train at Stamford Hill, jumped off the train at the unmanned Prettywell Station one stop short of Southend's

ONE TEAM IN BRISTOL

main station and were drinking in a pub on the Kursaal just six hours after thrusting out our thumbs on the M4. Total cost of transport, a big round fuck all.

Rovers gained the precious point in front of 2,000 or so delirious Bristolians, the final whistle signalling a huge collective sigh of relief and the inevitable pitch invasion. As we danced on the pitch and sang our tribal songs exalting our heroes my thoughts were now no longer of Walsall, Halifax or Aldershot, but of more exotic football locations such as Sheffield Wednesday, Sunderland and Bristol fucking City. I couldn't wait.

We were still in celebratory mood when we met City in the end-of-season ritual of violence known as the Gloucester Cup. Normally it was a case of lighting the blue touch paper and retiring to a safe distance, but this time there was no such thing as a safe distance.

City had always seen themselves as the superior team in Bristol. Our promotion now pitched us into the same league as them. We had the chance to prove our mettle once and for all. On and off the pitch the blue half of Bristol was preparing for battle.

There had been a few run-ins before the game. We had clashed along Coronation Road but the law were out in force; they were becoming as expert at breaking up the trouble as we were at causing it. They were still on to a loser though; where there was a will there was a way.

We entered the East End in our customary ones and twos, but instead of congregating at the back of the terrace as we had done in previous years we split up and foisted our way into the East Enders. We were scattered across the terracing, about 70 of us in total, just enough to do the business. The seeds had been planted, we were ready to erupt into life and cause mayhem. And we didn't have long to wait. It was time for big, bad Bobby Doughty to make his entrance.

BOOTED AND SUITED

Bob had burst on to the scene that season. He had been a fringe member of the Tramps for a number of years but up until the previous few months I had rarely seen him in action. Bob, like his sidekick Paul Sweet, was a genuine biker. Resplendent in full-blown leathers and denim, he made an awesome sight. The City fans had no answer to the Rovers bikers and tramps, they were too intent on looking tidy and getting their creases right in their flares. I suppose Hampshire and I were of their same ilk, but I was as pleased as a dog with two cocks that I was on Doughty's side and not the other way round.

There were just ten minutes to go before kick-off and the mass of Rovers fans had filled the open end terrace opposite us once again. I was in position with Hampshire, Iggy and Lil who, disappointingly, had brought his younger brother Mick with him. I had nothing against Mick — far from it, we had all witnessed the lad's prowess with his fists on the Tote End — but he was only 15 and tonight was not the night to introduce him to the East End. They were as pissed off as a whore on blob with us getting promotion and were just as determined as us to prove who was number one in Bristol. All around I could see faces that resembled bulldogs licking piss off a thistle. We could barely contain ourselves as the familiar chant of 'Rovers where are you? Rovers where are you?' went up.

'I'll fucking show 'em where we are,' said Iggy impatiently, ever eager for the aggro to go off.

'Wait for it, Clyde,' said Hamps. 'You know what Andy and the others said, ten minutes after kick-off. Until then, not a fucking word.'

The game kicked off to a mighty roar. We were conscious of a thousand pair of eyes upon us. I shivered with fear and excitement, my teeth began to chatter and my balls said cheerio to the rest of my body for the umpteenth time in their career. Just as the East Enders settled down for what they thought was going to be a quiet night, a huge leather-clad figure hauled himself up on to a crash barrier not ten yards away from us. It was Doughty right on cue.

'THE ROVERS! THE ROVERS!' the bellow was animal-like, in a way that only Doughty could deliver. The fist raised in a call to arms had the desired effect, it was like a flag dropping at the beginning of a race. For a split second there was a silence, a silence of incredulity, a silence that was finally broken by the shrieks of dismay as the awesome truth suddenly dawned on the hapless City fans: the Tote End was back.

I announced my arrival by smacking the geezer behind me with a perfect right, followed by a perfect left. We all fought in exactly the same way, our fists flailing like windmills. It was the most effective way of fighting in the confined spaces of a football terrace, a technique we had mastered over the years, and was a common sight on terraces the length and breadth of Britain. Our surprise attack had the desired effect. The East End was in disarray as more and more Tote Enders joined in the attack. We had infiltrated good and proper, from every angle they came under assault. It was awesome to see such chaos caused by so few. The City fans could not determine from which way we were coming, and neither could the law. No sooner would they move to one skirmish than it would go off again somewhere else. We just kept on lashing out, as much as in self-preservation as anything else. We just had to keep the momentum going. Mick was doing his big brother proud and he was loving every vicious minute of it.

We battled our way to the centre of the East End to be joined by the rest of the jubilant Tote Enders. The City fans were spilling out away from us and we now had a distinct gap between us. The law moved in and surrounded us, but it was too late, our mission had been accomplished, we had taken the East End with consummate ease. We triumphantly revealed our colours as hitherto hidden scarves were unveiled and hoisted aloft as a sign of victory. It was time to proclaim our superiority,

'Hello! Hello! Rovers are back! Rovers are back!'

An uneasy calm descended for the remainder of the first half. The City fans had resigned themselves to the squatters that had taken over their abode, we were congratulated on our achievement from our associates massed at the opposite end, who celebrated our exploits by systematically breaking the flagpoles at the rear of their terrace and hurling the debris on to the pitch. To top it all, Rovers took the lead through Dave Staniforth; those bulldogs were licking piss again.

The retaliation when it did come was not quite what we expected. A hefty platform shoe came flying through the air from somewhere among the mass that surrounded us. It hit Mick of all people, catching him full in the face and creating a hideous gash on his cheek. The East End roared their approval and a full-scale onslaught stared us in the eye. Barry Waller was not amused.

'Who the fuck did that?' Barry asked Mick, as if Mick would know. It was not as if we were on first name terms with the Shit from south of the river.

'D-don't know, s-someone just chucked it.' Mick was trying his hardest to put on a brave face. Tears would not have gone down well with Lil or the rest of us.

Barry reacted in the only way he could. Reminiscent of his performance against Bournemouth earlier on in the year, he charged at the encircled mass with a frenzy that bordered on the hysterical.

'Come on, you bastards, I'll take you all on! Come on, who wants some!'

We fired in behind Barry. The coppers again were powerless to stop us, we were intent on proving our worth and Barry was not going to be stopped. He bulldozed through their terrified fans, who again began to scatter in the face of such a massive onslaught. Barry made it easy for us, we simply picked off the human flotsam that he was leaving behind him in his wake. One geezer just stood there, his arms by his side, eyes transfixed like a rabbit caught in the headlights of the juggernaut that was Barry Waller hurtling towards him. He was pole-axed with a single punch of epic proportions, Mick meting out his own form of retribution with a swift kick to the unfortunate victim's motionless body.

'Come on, where's your boys?' Barry threw down the gauntlet, but there were no takers. By now the City fans were making their way to the exits and the law were making their way for us. A few arrests were made but the police were just intent on getting rid of us. The battle was over, we had done enough; our mission was accomplished.

The Old Bill herded us up and escorted us around the edge of the pitch for a well-deserved lap of honour. Our reunion with our brethren at the opposite end was like a joyous homecoming of the troops. We were cheered every step of the way and as we were reunited with our brothers-in-arms they roared their approval: 'One team in Bristol! There's only one team in Bristol!' I caught a glimpse of Lil who was embracing his younger sibling, the two of them were beaming from ear to ear.

'It don't get much better than this, Mick,' said Lil proudly, 'you done good.'

Mick, despite his injuries, smiled back and winked. He knew he had 'done good'; he knew he had arrived.

21

From Miami to Philly, via Sheffield

I had been dating a cracking sort named Karen off and on, since my school days. She was a stunning blonde with legs that finished where hopefully only I knew. She was also insecure and demanding due to a luckless childhood in Plymouth that involved too many friends called 'Mandy' and 'Dexy'.

I remember the day that she started at our school, she had been despatched to the local 'naughty girls home' to get away from her unfortunate past. Hundreds of pairs of lusting eyes belonging to pupils and teachers alike watched her every move as she cast her spell over us all and sent hormones raging through the roof as if they were on speed.

I was already 'knocking off' Cheryl, one of the till girls from the local Gateway supermarket who lived in neighbouring Lawrence Weston (it was a compulsory rite of passage that Henbury boys 'knocked off' Lawrence Weston girls and in so doing endured the wrath of older brothers from that gritty, tough district) when a friend of Karen's approached me at the school gates.

FROM MIAMI TO PHILLY, VIA SHEFFIELD

'Yer, my mate fancies you, wanna go out with 'er?' This was a common way of being 'asked out' in those days, you got your mate to do the dirty deed.

'Eh, what? No thanks, I'm already courting. Who is it anyway?'

'Karen.'

'What Karen with the...'

'Yeah, Karen with the...'

Cheryl quickly became a distant memory as she was handed back, slightly soiled, to her thuggish guardian angels.

Back in those gert lush schooldays Karen was a top skinhead sort of the highest order, she took the cult to her heart, even naming her pet rabbit 'Bovver'. She looked a dream – neat blonde feathercut, black and white checked Brutus shirt slightly on the small side to accentuate her pert breasts, tiny pelmet-length bottle green Trevira skirt and cute tassled loafers made her a sight to behold; what's more she must have learned a few tricks from her rabbit – I thought I had died and gone to skinhead heaven. But now, three years on, things were different. The promotion season had taken a heavy toll on our relationship. Karen's spectacular looks and figure I could handle, her moods and obsessive behaviour I couldn't.

Deep down she knew she couldn't compete with the one and only true love of my life and after a row that bordered on the murderous and a visit to the casualty department of the BRI she hit me with the immortal line that I 'loved Bristol Rovers more than I loved her'. There was only one reply I could offer, and it was as brutal as it was untrue: 'I love Bristol fucking City more than I love you.' The inevitable ultimatum came. Either I finished my love affair with Bristol Rovers and the Tote End or my relationship with a gorgeous, leggy 17-year-old, blue-eyed, blonde nymphomaniac was over.

I sure was going to miss her.

BOOTED AND SUITED

As was customary for promoted football teams, Rovers took themselves off on a celebratory tour of the Far East and Australia. As I was now a single man again I went off to Weymouth for a week in a caravan with Harvey and the boys from Henbury. It was a typical British holiday week, as typical a week for a group of 18-year-old adolescents as was possible. Too much alcohol, too much fighting and not enough women. I was beginning to regret my decision over Karen; the only action I had that week was with Pam – as in 'pam' of my hand.

Still, the music, unlike my sex life, was on the up. Black music was shaking off the shackles of 'elevator music' as typified by tight harmony groups such as The Chi-Lites and The Delfonics and getting decidedly funkier. Gil Scott-Heron's 'The Bottle' was the first release on the embryonic disco-funk label Salsoul Records and caused a stir with its tale of alcoholism in the city, as did his menacing masterpiece 'The Revolution will not be Televised.' Maceo Parker's magnificent 'Soul Power' proved there was life after James Brown, who himself set everybody dancing with 'Funky President.' Oliver Sain got everyone 'bumping' with 'Double Bump' and The Blackbyrds made us all 'Do It Fluid'. There was even a chart hit for those old Motown boys The Isley Brothers, with 'Summer Breeze.' Beginning of the End got to number 31 with the rereleased 'Funky Nassau', all horns and guitar riffs, and there was some perfect smooth soul by William de Vaughan with 'Be Thankful For What You've Got' and Marvin Gaye with the super-sensual 'Let's Get It On'.

The Sound of Philadelphia, spearheaded by Harold Melvin and the Blue Notes and MFSB (Mother, Father, Sister, Brother; or was it Mother-Fucking-Sons-of-Bitches?), made a welcome change from the drivel that the Scottish teenybopper group of the day, The Bay City Rollers, were churning out. The old Sixties

FROM MIAMI TO PHILLY, VIA SHEFFIELD

showman Don Covay managed a minor hit with 'It's Better To Have And Don't Need.' It was no 'See-Saw' (his vintage hit from a decade earlier) but it proved that good music and good lyrics were still around. It sure beat 'Shang-a-fuckin'-Lang', by a long shot.

The Bay City Rollers had taken the tartan fashion started by Rod Stewart and Slade to the extreme, resulting in an army of prepubescent schoolgirls bedecked in baggy calf-length white sailor trousers adorned with tartan piping. Bright red braces, tartan scarves and rainbow-coloured socks completed the fashion disaster, which was in truth a parody of the skinhead gear of a few years earlier.

My own ensemble was changing again. The platform shoes, although still very much in evidence, had developed into huge, heel-less Frankenstein-style boots. The effort to walk in them was immense. Only slightly more uncomfortable were the wooden-soled clogs that had made an appearance that summer – all right for poncing around on the dancefloor but a complete waste of time when it came to giving somebody a good kicking. Knitted, diamond-patterned twin-sets and cardigans, once the preserve of your old man and old lady, were surprisingly popular, and the only jacket to be seen wearing that summer was a single-breasted, two-buttoned velvet jacket, either bottle green or navy blue, worn, of course, with the fly-away collar of your cheesecloth shirt firmly on the outside.

We entered the Music Box Disco in Weymouth, teetering on our clogs that were thankfully hidden from view beneath our bottle-green jumbo cord flares with their three-inch waistbands. A heady mix of Cossack hair spray, Hai-Karate aftershave and a dash of Clearasil surrounded us, and we felt we were the epitome of Seventies fashion, smooth, suave and sophisticated. The days of sharp suits and even sharper haircuts had long gone. Bad taste was not in our vocabulary; perhaps we should've taken a longer look in the mirror.

The huge hit of that summer came from the new Jayboy label from Miami, Florida. 'Rock Your Baby' by George McRae went straight to number 1, due in no small part to the Radio One disc jockeys' strike, which resulted in punters buying the music they heard in the clubs and discos and not the usual diet of glam rock and teenybop nonsense that had dominated the charts for the last few years.

'Rock Your Baby' was a massive hit that turned out to be a very significant record, being as it was the first 'disco' record to get to number 1. George McRae's stablemates at Jayboy, the Hues Corporation, also had a top ten hit with 'Rock The Boat'. Before the summer ended the Jayboy houseband KC and The Sunshine Band, fronted by Howard Casey entered the charts, scoring a massive dancefloor hit with 'Queen Of Clubs.'

Miami's influence on dance music over the next 12 months was immense, with further hits for Little Beaver with 'Party Down' and more chart success for KC with 'Sound Your Funky Horn' and 'That's The Way (I Like It)', which put the sunshine sound of Florida firmly on the map of dreary Britain. Ironic really, considering that this new-found leader of dance music was in fact a white, ex-DJ with a somewhat limited musical ability. Britain's response to this new disco phenomenon was the embarrassingly awful 'Kung Fu Fighting' by Carl Douglas. Unbelievably, it reached number 1. Still, there were much better things on the horizon – across the Atlantic, funk was beginning to flex its mighty muscles.

As the new football season kicked off, 'Machine Gun' by the Commodores a hunk of pure instrumental funk, stood proudly at number 20 in the charts. The Commodores would have another big hit later on that year with the impressive

FROM MIAMI TO PHILLY, VIA SHEFFIELD

'Brickhouse', but it would be all downhill from there as Lionel Richie came to the fore and the funk took the back seat. Still, it was good while it lasted. Another band who were seriously funky in their early years but who, perhaps understandably, changed both their sound and their image to suit the more commercial sounds of disco as the decade progressed were Kool and the Gang. The band were named after group leader Robert 'Kool' Bell and started out life as a jazz combo in Jersey City. In the early Seventies, the band applied the same structures of a jazz jam session to the funk groove, allowing the horn players to play blues changes over a relentless bass and guitar combination. This kind of formula emphasised instrumental precision and it soon became obvious that Kool and the Gang were a much tighter outfit than a lot of other funk bands of that era.

The band broke through to the mainstream American audience in 1973 and to the more discerning British funkateer the following year. It was during this period that the band laid down some of their all-time best recordings. 'Funky Stuff' hit Britain's shores in 1974 and was quickly followed by 'Hollywood Swinging' and 'Jungle Boogie' – all of which featured on their superb *Wild And Peaceful* album. Unfortunately, the latter failed to make an impact on the album charts due to the continual presence of such Seventies 'giants' as Elton John, Mike Oldfield and The Carpenters.

I looked forward to the forthcoming football season in the way that an eight-year-old kid looked forward to Christmas. The first away game of the season was against Sheffield Wednesday at Hillsborough, a big team with a big ground, and even bigger supporters.

No sooner had we disembarked from our coaches than they were upon us, a mass of denim-clad boot boys. Somebody had forgotten to tell the Yorkshire lads we were now in the mid-Seventies. They reminded me of their near neighbours, Leeds United, with whom we had a slight altercation a few years earlier. The only difference was that, to a man, the Wednesday fans' Doc Martens were spray-painted gold. Suddenly my Tigers felt as much use as a Durex machine in a monastery.

We had a good turn out. A lot of the old faces had turned up to see Rovers' first appearance in the Second Division since the early Sixties and as well as Andy, Dobbsy and Kimble there were a number of fresh-faced eager lads all willing and able to make a name for themselves. The mischievous Barretts had turned up with a relatively new addition, Tony Stone, otherwise known as 'Os' for his affiliation with Chelsea and 'Gout' for reasons that I never found out. Os sported blue spray-painted Doc Martens that at a glance marked him out as a Wednesday supporter, but the ice-blue zip-up satin bomber jacket in the same style as my gold one singled him out firmly as a soft, southern smoothie and made him an obvious target for the Owls' boot boys. After a flurry of punches that had 'Welcome to the Second Division' written all over them, their mob quickly dispersed. They were no more than a reception party, on observation duties to see what the new boys of the division had to offer. On this showing we were to be in for a tough season.

As more of our fans arrived, though, we regained our confidence. Our optimism rose with our intake of alcohol. By the time their next attack came crashing through the doors of the large Victorian pub we had occupied, we were back to our awesome best, a mass barrage of glasses saw them make a swift exit, quickly followed by a hundred or so Bristolians including Os, who had by now wisely decided to remove his jacket. We soft southern smoothies were to be no pushover.

FROM MIAMI TO PHILLY, VIA SHEFFIELD

Our success even revived our humour: 'WEDNES-DAY! WEDNES-DAY!' chanted the Owls fans as we entered the ground, 'SATUR-DAY! SATUR-DAY!' we taunted back. Somehow the Owls fans didn't get the joke. After erring on the side of caution we decided to enter the terrace reserved for away fans, the Leppings Lane End. The welcoming committee was back. The Owls fans were waiting for us.

'Got t'time, John?' asked an Owls fan as he sidled over to John O'Shea. The ritual was about to begin. John was ready for him.

'How do you know my name's John?' queried John.

It took the wind out of the Owls fan's sails.

'I fuckin' guessed.'

'Well, guess what the fucking time is then,' replied John. He always fought with his mouth rather than with his fists – unlike myself and Hampshire who firmly believed that a punch in the mouth was worth a thousand words.

John's retort had the desired effect. The Owl opened his mouth hoping for something equally witty to come out. Nothing did. He skulked away, mumbling. All I could hear was references to intercourse with sheep. Very original.

After a few clashes that resulted in no more than bruised egos, the law moved in and escorted the Wednesday fans out of our terrace and back to their own huge end opposite us. The bleak Yorkshire hills behind it gave the immense terrace a grim backdrop. The ground was prodigiously large, about as far removed from Aldershot as you could imagine. We were no longer a big fish in a small pond. If anything, the reverse was true. Rovers scored their first goal in the Second Division for 12 years courtesy of Gordon Fearnley, an underrated journeyman of a player who lived forever in the shadows of Warboys and Bannister. At times he had the touch of a genius but more often than not he failed to deliver. Wednesday equalised and the game was petering out to a 1–1 draw when, with ten minutes to go before the final whistle, their gold-plated boot boys decided to make a move.

'They're leaving early, aren't they?' I motioned to Hampshire at the mass exodus opposite us.

'Probably on the night shift down t'pits,' replied Hampshire casually.

Something told me these boys weren't about to start digging for nutty slack. My fears were confirmed as the Owls fans streamed through the unguarded open gates behind us, the law having long departed and leaving us painfully exposed and severely outnumbered. They fired in without hesitation and met with little resistance. It was safer to play dumb than to hit back.

'Where's t'Bristol fans?' The Tyke accent cut right through me. He stood there grinning, a six-foot slag heap of bearded Yorkshire grit. 'Hast thou seen any?'

I was wearing my blue-and-white scarf, no wording just colours, same as the Owls. Mercifully he thought I was a Wednesday fan.

I tried my best Yorkshire accent: 'All t'gone,' was the best I could come up with.

'Pity, I've got this fer 'em.' He opened up his Levi's jacket to reveal a wooden-handled axe. He patted it affectionately. 'Later, me beauty, later,' he said soothingly. I looked at him and smiled. This fucker gave me the willies. I couldn't get out of the ground quick enough.

The journey back to Bristol was a long and cold one – the bastards had put the windows through on our coaches. I curled up on the seat with Jane Murphy's comforting breast firmly in my right hand and went to sleep, longing for visits to Torquay.

Within a fortnight we were playing one of our old rivals from the Third Division from a few years back, Luton Town, whose

Above: Some of the 'Never' gang, 1969 – Fairfax Street, Bristol.
Photo Courtesy of Lloyd Sutherland

Below: *Bristol Evening Post* and *Western Daily Press* headlines, 1969–1971.

Above: The 'truce' between the 'Cropheads' and the 'Greasers' – 24 July 1969. It goes without saying that the truce didn't last. Lloyd Sutherland can just be seen, third from the left at the front. © *Bristol Evening Post*

Below left and right: 'Stop and search' is nothing new. The Bovver Boys arrive at Weston-super-Mare, August Bank Holiday 1970. © *Bristol Evening Post*

The Bovver Boys and Girls meet on the beach at Weston. It doesn't take long before it kicks off – August Bank Holiday 1970.

© *Bristol Evening Post*

Above: The Tote End. It might not have been the Kop or the Shed, but it did for me during the 70s.

© *Alan Marshall*

Below: The 'Chaps' at the Arnolfini, 1977. A couple of my old mates Jeff Shellard (*2nd from left, standing*) and Roy Savage (*third from right, picking his nose*). Vernon Jozefowicz (RIP) on the far right was also one of the 'Never' gang.

Photo courtesy of Tim Williams

FROM MIAMI TO PHILLY, VIA SHEFFIELD

shabby Kenilworth Road ground was home to the obnoxious Oak Road Boot Boys. I had travelled to Luton with the Rovers back in the late Sixties. It was one of the grubbiest towns I had ever visited, dirty and unfriendly, a tired little town, full of tired little people. It was not a place I cared to visit again, especially for a mid-week League Cup game that carried little importance so early on in the season. Nevertheless, the knot of kiddies I was performing with were determined to go and put on a good show. Nobody liked Luton, it was just another name on the long list of clubs to visit if we were to carve out a name for ourselves, a compulsory rite of passage for any crew determined to make the headlines.

Much to Hampshire's disgust I decided against the outing.

'Come on, it'll be a good crack, we've got Sheener's van from work and Jimmy White's driving. Everyone's going, we'll have a good mob.'

'Nah, I'm skint, I'll see you down the ground Sat'day against the Villa. You can tell us all about it then.'

'Fucking tosser, always knew you were a wimp.'

I felt guilty, but unlike Hampshire I was still serving my apprenticeship at work. I was only taking home £10.50 a week; Hampshire was on big money working for SWEB and without a care in the world. If he lost his job he could pick up another, labouring jobs were two a penny. I was determined to see my five-year apprenticeship through. I was halfway there, but I'd already been warned about my behaviour following my court appearance the previous year, and a series of scraps with other apprentices hadn't done much to endear me to the management. Another incident and I would be out on my ear. My old man wouldn't be amused.

Andy Greaves, a fellow apprentice at work and a fringe member of our crew, whose only claim to fame was smashing the Radnor's windows (the only queer pub in Bristol at the time – it was something to do with proving his sexuality) came in the following morning brandishing the *Western Daily Press*. He could hardly contain himself.

'Browner! Browner! Read this!'

He thrust the front page of the *Western Daily* under my nose.

'Read it! It's got to be Hampshire!'

Under a headline that screamed SOCCER HOOLIGANS RUN RIOT IN LUTON was an all-too-familiar tale of violence and mayhem. 'Fifteen arrested, thirteen charged with breach of peace, two actual bodily harm, offensive weapons, fans running amok', it was the language of the tabloid describing the actions of the yob. It could have been written in the Fifties describing the Teddy Boys in the dancehalls or the Sixties of the mods and rockers at Brighton. It just happened to be the Seventies and therefore it had to be football hooligans.

I read the article over and over again. There was no mention of names just the graphic details of the violence: 'the group of fifteen ran amok, armed with pieces of wood torn from fences, some with nails sticking through. They were looking for trouble...'

I felt sick in my stomach, then a shudder of relief shook my body, the realisation that it had very nearly been me. I didn't know whether to laugh or cry.

'Well, what do you reckon, Hampshire or not?' asked Andy.

'Oh that's Hampshire all right, bet you a pound to a pinch of shit.'

Oddly enough, when I read the *Evening Post* later on in the day there was no mention of Hampshire. All the rest were there, the full role call of my mates from the Tote End: Iggy, Gerry Smith, Gary Abbott, John. O'Shea... John O'Shea? John I knew wasn't going and if he was he wouldn't get into trouble. John was too sensible. For John O'Shea of Lawrence Weston read Phil Gordon Hampshire of Lockleaze, nice try, Hamps, but it didn't work.

FROM MIAMI TO PHILLY, VIA SHEFFIELD

The lucky ones got fines and probation, Iggy even got acquitted. The rest, including Hampshire, got three months in Hollesley Bay DC. The unfortunate Jimmy White, the innocent driver, got sentenced to a spell in Bedford prison due to his age. A certain William George Mercer of Luton got a very sore head and a trip to hospital due to his insistence on incessantly head-butting several pieces of wood.

The close call had a sobering effect. I breathed a long, hard sigh of relief and vowed to stay clear of trouble. As I smacked one of the Villa fans who dared to venture on to the Tote End within 24 hours of my mates being banged up, I made sure there were no coppers in sight; henceforth, caution would be my middle name.

The next few months were noticeably quieter without Hampshire's presence, although games against the once great Manchester United and our first encounter with the bad lads from Millwall helped to alleviate the depression. We were more than holding our own against the big boys and the routine of gratuitous violence continued unabated. It would take more than a few derisory custodial sentences to halt the tide of violence that was swamping the nation both on and off the terraces. These were dark days for Wilson's new Labour Government: not only were the youth of the country doing their utmost to tear each other apart, but both inflation and unemployment were on the rise. The IRA were determined to do their bit and brought their murderous campaign of indiscriminate bombing to the British mainland, which included a bomb exploding in Bristol's Park Street. Just as 1974 came to a close and you thought it couldn't get much worse, Mud got to number 1 with 'Lonely This Christmas'.

I met Hampshire for the first time after his release in the popular Dunlop's pub on the City Centre.

BOOTED AND SUITED

'How was it then, Hamps?' I couldn't hide my guilt about not visiting him.

'All right,' he shrugged.

'Any regrets?'

Remorse oozed from every pore of his body.

'Yeah, wish I had belted Mercer harder.'

22

A Momentary Respite and a Musical Interlude

One consequence of Hampshire's incarceration was my renewed acquaintance with the enigmatic Karen. My head told me I should stay well clear but unfortunately my lower regions told me otherwise. What's more, I was getting blisters on the palm of my right hand and my eyesight was failing. The Tote End's loss was the dancefloor's gain, as Scamps, Bailey's and the newly opened Maxims on Park Street vied for my attention. For the first time since I had learned to tie the laces of my bovver boots, football was taking a back seat. Oddly, the lure of the terrace had lost its attraction since Rovers had gained promotion, proving that the thrill of the chase far exceeded the thrill of the kill. I even relented and took my trophy girlfriend to her first match. Thankfully it finished in a dour 1–0 win against a dull Bolton side on a miserable winter's day and had the desired effect. She never wanted to go to a match again.

A disappointing mid-season with such low-lights as a 1–4 home defeat against the Shit from across the river and numbingly dull 0–0 draws with such greats as Orient and Blackpool proved that life in the higher division wasn't all it was cracked up to be.

BOOTED AND SUITED

The City game had been a major let-down, with Eastville resembling a police state, such was the law's determination to avoid the aggro that had marred the previous season's encounter. The huge blue line had proved effective; barely a punch was thrown as the two mobs were kept well apart. The highlights of my week were now becoming the almost nightly visits to the pubs and clubs of the Centre. I was resplendent in my newly acquired handmade, cream double-breasted box jacket and chocolate-brown, monstrous 24-inch bags. A brown velvet dicky-bow and white shoes completed the Forties Humphrey Bogart look that was becoming *de rigueur* for the ever-so-trendy Way-In crowd on College Green and the gangster-themed Broads in Knowle. The Way-In, as well as being the trendiest pub around, was the favourite haunt of Bristol's notorious gay icon, Sapphire, an attention-seeking black cross-dresser whose trademark was a bright-yellow star dyed into his neatly coiffured afro. Sapphire loved the attention and for a short time was a go-go dancer at Bailey's where his gyrations thrilled and entertained the crowds. None more so than Phil Hampshire, but that's another story.

If the football was proving to be an anticlimax, at least the music was going from strength to strength. This year, 1975, saw some cracking music, not least from the Average White Band doing a passable impression of James Brown's musical sidekicks Fred Wesley and Maceo Parker. The AWB's February hit 'Pick Up The Pieces' belied the fact the band originated on the mean streets of Glasgow rather than the mean streets of Chicago; at least it proved Scotland wasn't all Bay City Rollers and Rod Stewart. Other home-grown bands to get in on the act were the Northern Soul imitators Wigan's Chosen Few with 'Footsee' and Wigan's Ovation with 'Skiing In The Snow', paying homage to the home of Northern Soul, the legendary Wigan Casino.

As the year progressed, couples across the country bumped in

A MOMENTARY RESPITE AND A MUSICAL INTERLUDE

tune to Van McCoy's 'The Hustle', a lame disco hit that nevertheless filled the dancefloor as did Bill Curtis's Fatback Band with 'Keep On Steppin'. James Brown and his 'above-average black band' The JB's, enhanced his 'Godfather of Soul' reputation with 'Get Up I Feel Like Being A Sex Machine', a cracking follow-up to his superb 'Payback' of the previous year. Moody funk poet Gill Scott-Heron followed up his success from 12 months earlier with the thought-provoking 'Johannesburg', which proved that funk could make bold, political statements as well as being decidedly danceable.

BT Express's 'Express' was a huge hit in the clubs and the single featured Parts 1 and 2 on the A- and B-sides, which enabled the DJs, who were now becoming as well known as some of the artistes, to mix two discs on separate turntables to extend the length of playtime. This was specifically aimed at the emerging dance culture and ultimately paved the way for the extended 12-inch dance versions that were to become the norm in later years. 'Express' featured a wonderful string and brass combination, something that was to become synonymous with the disco/funk music of that era. 'Always There', a beautiful brassy instrumental by Ronnie Laws, just oozed laid-back coolness as did Joe Bataan's instrumental version of Gil Scott-Heron's 'The Bottle'. The obscure Oliver Sain was back with his jazzy instrumental 'Bus Stop', a track that was among the first to feature whistles; it wouldn't be long before every disco hit seemed to include them and every serious dancer sported them. George 'Bad' Benson even managed an appearance in the UK Top 30 with the mighty 'Supership'. Hamilton Bohannon had no less than four disco hits in the space of eight months, while Donald Byrd and the Blackbyrds had two hits with 'I Need You' and their first and only British chart entry, 'Walking in Rhythm'. The list, like the new 12-inch records, went on and on.

The most unexpected dance hit of the year, however, was

'Makes You Blind'. What made it so surprising was that it was a B-side. Even more astounding was the fact that it was made by the Glitter Band, now thankfully liberated from their embarrassing 'leader' Gary Glitter. Even my first musical love, reggae, made a comeback with Susan Cadogan sweetly singing 'Hurts So Good' and Bob Marley and the Wailers with their live recording of 'No Woman, No Cry' opening the eyes and ears of a completely new audience. If the football was no longer giving me the adrenalin rush, the music certainly was.

The music itself was still relatively hard to come by, for while the trendy kids of the Seventies were listening to the funkiest street sounds around, Radio One was still churning out its daily diet of hackneyed, bromidic pap that appealed as much to your parents as it did to your kid sister. There were number-1 hits for Tammy Wynette this year with her country-and-western smash (or was it 'some cunt from Weston' as Iggy so eloquently put it) 'Stand By Your Man' and 'Hold Me Close' by David Essex – hardly uplifting anthems.

The Abba phenomenon had kicked off the previous year when their atrocious Eurovision Song Content winner 'Waterloo' rocketed straight to number 1. The four members of the group looked like they were straight out of a Swedish blue movie, with Agnetha and her perfect arse being the star turn. Amazingly, by the end of 1976 Abba had become the world's best-selling group. Otis Redding must have been spinning in his grave.

While the uninitiated listened to Dave Lee Travis, who was as amusing as a dose of clap, the cognoscenti among the nation's youth religiously tuned in to Robbie Vincent's Soul and Funk show at six every Saturday evening, which provided us with our weekly fix from across the Atlantic. If it wasn't for his show I would have been as ignorant as the rest of the country; until then I had thought the magnificent Ohio Players were an American baseball team.

The Ohio's first album on the Mercury label, after spending

A MOMENTARY RESPITE AND A MUSICAL INTERLUDE

many years on Chicago's Westbound, was the quintessential *Fire* – which, if released by a white rock outfit, would have been known as a 'concept' album. Its menacing title track was perhaps their most recognisable song: a heavy guitar riff and simple, ominous, yowling lyrics featuring the vocals of lead singer Leroy 'Sugarfoot' Bonner. The Ohio Players' trademarks from the earlier Westbound recordings were all there: uncluttered, doom-laden sounds, provocative photos of naked women on the cover and a no-star approach – all the tunes were listed as written and produced by the whole band. The single 'Fire' was destined to become one of the all-time funk favourites and before the year was out the band had released the equally impressive album *Honey* which included their biggest hit to date, 'Love Rollercoaster' (successfully revived in 1996 by The Red Hot Chilli Peppers), plus the seriously funky 'Fopp' and the magnificently deranged ballad 'Sweet Sticky Thing'. The obligatory naked babe on the cover, this time sensuously dripping with sweet, sticky honey, simply added to the band's appeal. The Ohio Players were one of the most innovative and imaginative bands of this era. Their music would influence numerous acts to follow in their funky footsteps.

The only other national radio DJ of note was the eccentric Emperor Rosko who, since the Sixties, had been at the forefront of bringing American soul music into Britain. Rosko's style, heavily influenced by the California DJ Wolfman Jack, couldn't have been further removed from the Hairy Cornflake (as DLT insisted on calling himself).

Closer to home, DJs such as Paul Russell, Seymour, Superfly, Paul Alexander aka Maceo and the evergreen Jason did their best to bring the sounds of Chicago and New York into the pubs and clubs of Bristol. For sheer fanatical promotion of funk music in Bristol, however, no one was more zealous than the Ashby brothers, Adryan and Steve.

BOOTED AND SUITED

I remembered Steve from the Elephant several years earlier, where Iggy consistently wound him up with his request for the non-existent 'Funky Milkman' by The Nurdlers. Steve's funkiest record at the time was 'Higher and Higher' by Jackie Wilson. He led a precarious existence back then, keeping one eye on his precious records and the other on the not-so-precious clientele, the threat of a major ruck never far away. By the spring of 1975 Steve and Adryan's weekly appearance at the new Guildhall Tavern in Broad Street was bringing in a veritable army of young soul boys and girls. The two brothers had always appeared under the name of ASA Enterprises but, taking advantage of a teenager's natural desire to belong, kept the initials and changed their name to form the Avon Soul Army.

New recruits for the Army signed up every week. The only qualification required was to have soul coursing through your veins – not difficult for me when I had been reared on the Stax and Atlantic labels of the Sixties. The alternative? Well, there was no alternative: Status Quo, Suzi Quatro, 10cc or Queen versus Isaac Hayes, James Brown or Marvin Gaye. No contest. We even had our own T-shirts, natty white or yellow with a helmeted soldier squinting through the sight of a rifle, complete with the Avon Soul Army logo. Thankfully, the ASA crossed the football divide – the T-shirts were as popular on the Tote End as they were at Ashton. It didn't quite unite us but at least it gave us some common ground. The Soul brothers even laid on Saturday lunchtime sessions specifically for the football fans. Trouble was rare, due to the fact that we were more interested in listening to the music rather than kicking lumps out of each other – which was more than could be said for what was happening at the football grounds of our green and pleasant land.

After 30 or so years, I managed to catch up with Seymour at his impressive home on the Gloucester Road. I reminded him of the

A MOMENTARY RESPITE AND A MUSICAL INTERLUDE

time I made a trip to London and bought some vinyl for him and even recalled the records: 'Spiderman' by Ramsey Lewis, 'Wipe your Feet and Dance' by Wee Willie and the Winners.

'Can you remember, Seymour?' I asked, hoping for a flicker of recognition.

'Can't say I do,' he answered. My ego was well and truly deflated.

I was once again joined by Lloyd who had helped me track down Bristol's early boot boys and who grew up with Seymour in and around the St Pauls district of Bristol. Another old-time mate of theirs, Anthony, also turned up. Anthony was a bit of a star on the dancefloor in his day. He introduced himself by saying that Donny Hathaway's 'The Ghetto' was one of the all-time classic records, ever. Hard to disagree on that front, so his credentials were in no dispute. Seymour, like Lloyd, had arrived from Jamaica when they were both no taller than one of Duke Reid's sound system speakers. I recalled seeing and listening to Seymour (and his cohort and stepbrother Mike, who everyone knew as 'Superfly') in the mid-Seventies, in the cellar bar of the Rummer hotel in the fruit market and later at the Blue Lagoon club off of Newfoundland Road. I was interested in how the two made their debut on the soul scene – it was probably these two guys, alongside Paul Russell and the Ashbys, who were the main proponents of funk music in Bristol; quite a legacy, quite an influence. Without these soul brothers, there may never have been the Pop Group, Tricky, Massive Attack or even Portishead – I suppose three out of four ain't bad.

As it turns out, their debut was relatively inauspicious. Seymour 'my own name was cool enough, I didn't need to change it' and Superfly's first '100% soul' night was in 1973 at the not-so-legendary home of funky music, Bishopston rugby club. (The club, who they both played for, was and still is, slap bang in the middle of the tough Lockleaze council estate.) The

BOOTED AND SUITED

duo had tired of hearing the same old soul tracks in the city dancehalls. Motown was upping sticks, heading for Tinseltown and forgetting its heritage, while the legendary southern soul labels of Atlantic and Stax were becoming a dim and distant memory. Across the pond, Sly and the Family Stone, Parliament and Curtis Mayfield were getting decidedly dirty, making music that was so bad, it would come round and burgle your house when you were out. The boys tapped in and Bristol got its first taste of the funk – the night was a sell-out and a roaring success. 'It all kicked off – not in the trouble sense, it went really well,' Seymour recalled with pride. From then on, they just put the word around and the offers flooded in.

They made a point of approaching pubs and clubs that were struggling to pull in the punters. 'I would make them an offer, say they could keep the bar takings, but I would keep the door.' A shrewd move. Although the places would be rammed, many of the punters were there purely for the music and the beer was a side issue – hardly surprising when you think fizzy Breaker lager or warm Toby were the drinks of the day. As well as the money from the door, Seymour and Superfly provided their own door staff – the incomparable Lloyd Russell and Florey Downer, two lads who would go on to be champion kickboxers. Needless to say, no one took liberties, the nights were nearly always trouble-free. The Stonehouse pub, The Rummer, The Granary, even The Salutation in my neck of the woods Henbury (which wasn't so trouble-free), hosted the funk brothers and, before the decade was out, the two made the Blue Lagoon and the Princes Bar off of Park Street home to the funkiest sets in the West Country. The Dug Out, which in later years was to become the birthplace of the Bristol Sound, was another venue in which they appeared but Seymour wasn't too impressed with the clientele. 'All they wanted was Nutbush City Limits', which reminded him of the time he saw Ike and Tina Turner perform live. 'We saw her

A MOMENTARY RESPITE AND A MUSICAL INTERLUDE

somewhere – there was no one there, we just went to the front and looked up her skirt.'

In the early days, they hired their decks from Bristol Sound System on Kellaway Avenue. In later years, Superfly made them himself and they bought their vinyl from all over. Seymour worked for a cash register company which took him round the country and enabled him to hear the latest imports. From Liverpool to, of all places, Swindon, he would hear tracks and buy them on the spot. Locally, Revolver on The Triangle and the aforementioned RCA in Montpelier were sources for imports but in the main, Blues & Soul and Contempo in London fed the hunger of the funketeers. Seymour recalled that there was often nothing clever or sophisticated about his record buying. 'I would go to London, Contempo in Piccadilly. Jeff [the owner] would get a container load of records at the airport, not knowing what they were and just put the records on in the shop and people would just buy them.'

If they were lucky they would be able to catch a bit of Wolfman Jack on the radio direct from California but it wasn't until later years that Greg Edwards and Robbie Vincent spread the gospel of funk to the nation via Radio One. There was none of the elitism and egotism that marred the Northern Soul scene; Seymour didn't quite think he was on a mission but he felt honoured to be both hearing and playing records that were not commercial or mainstream. 'We thought we were privileged, having this music. Once it got in the charts, you didn't want to know it. We would have white label records, but we weren't precious about it: if someone wanted to know what the record was, we would tell them. There's nothing like coming up with a big thick wad of 12-inch records and albums and you knew that nobody else has got them.' Quite a difference from the scene in the north of England and, for that matter, the ska and reggae scenes of earlier years where the DJ's would often scratch off the

BOOTED AND SUITED

labels to preserve their identity and thus enhance their own reputations. They stuck to the funk, they had no desire to play reggae – either dub or old skool. 'You would hear that in the Blues parties in St Pauls, but we were town kids, we only wanted the funk.'

The duo and their growing number of fans would also go further afield to put on a show – sometimes with their own dance troupe which included Anthony and his monstrous flares (made by his dad). Seymour's set went down a storm when he performed at the famous Goldmine, Canvey Island one night. Anthony's moves on the floor, less so – the trio laughed out loud but declined to go into further detail – perhaps it was the flares. A trip to the roughhouse town of Lydney in the Forest of Dean caused a right old ruckus. As Seymour recalled, it was 'real redneck country', Lydney's the sort of place where the youngsters give 'high sixes' – you get the picture. Surprisingly, the music wasn't a problem; the locals loved it but the competition announced by Superfly, with a ten-pound prize for the best dancer, didn't go down so well when he declared the winner and handed over the prize – a ten-pound bag of dirt. Predictably, it 'kicked off afterwards' with the disgruntled rednecks – the kickboxers earned their money that night.

A regular gig in their early days was at the Mecca in Frogmore Street, or the 'Bristol Entertainment Centre' as it was also known. The huge, concrete, Sixties-built monstrosity consisted of, among others, the legendary Locarno, the Mayfair Suite and the Golden Lounge. It was at The Golden Lounge that the lads had one of their better and more memorable experiences: meeting Miss World on her tour of the Mecca empire was part of her prize, although it's not sure who was more impressed, Seymour on meeting Miss World or Miss World on meeting Superfly. If that rated highly on Seymour's best memories of the Seventies, one of the worst was when he his house was broken

A MOMENTARY RESPITE AND A MUSICAL INTERLUDE

into and his prized collection of vinyl was stolen, Seymour recalled the occasion, which was just after he had got married to his wife Julie (who he had known since he was 13).

'We were in bed when it happened. I used to come in at night and just leave my records in the hall. They also nicked the stereo. Anyway, two weeks later, I was speaking to someone at a hi-fi place in Newfoundland Road, they told me I looked down. I said, "Yeah, someone has nicked my records."

'He told me that, if I had gone in five minutes earlier, I would have seen the guys trying to sell my kit. I went outside and caught this chap, but he said he was selling them for someone else. They had already sold some in a shop in City Road. I was going to give him a good kicking but my dad came round the corner and talked me out of it, as he said I would get into trouble. So I marched him to the police station. I went in the next day but they released him as there was not enough evidence. I managed to find out where he lived, went round his house with a mate to sort him out and get my records back. But he was a dosser and he just shot off – I ended up having to buy some of my own records back.'

As well as risking the wrath of Ike Turner by looking up his missus's skirt, Seymour recalled seeing other musicians perform live back in the Seventies. He was more impressed with the likes of the Ohio Players and Isaac Hayes. 'That was a fantastic show. We hired a van, went to London Hammersmith Odeon, full orchestra behind him – we were all wearing full-length leather John Shaft coats.' Other performers who impressed the 'bad muthas' of Bristol were Earth, Wind and Fire, who they thought were 'absolutely brilliant – show full of magic', George Benson and James Brown. He regrets never having seen Luther Vandross perform live, as he and Donald Byrd were two of Seymour's all-time favourites. One of my own favourites, Parliament, also rated highly with Seymour, although he was not too sure on

BOOTED AND SUITED

George Clinton as a performer. 'Too many bad drugs' was his view of the P-Funkmeister.

Although Seymour was still into his music and liked many of today's artistes, he regrets the demise of vinyl, feeling that CDs and downloads have 'cheapened' music. He loved the feel, even the smell of plastic wax, loved reading the cover notes on a new LP, admired the artwork. 'Vinyl was tactile – you could really "feel" it', something that he feels is now lost with the music of today. 'You even get CDs free with the Sunday papers now,' he wailed.

He had a point, and I felt it hard to disagree with him. Having said that, he loved listening to Last.fm on his PC and the ease of downloading long-lost, hard-to-get tracks. Like all of the guys I interviewed back then, I finished with the hackneyed question of whether he had any regrets about those days. 'Only not giving that bloke who nicked my records a kicking,' he answered with a smile.

23
Back in the Old Routine

The terraces were still a simmering cauldron of violence, with pitch invasions and missile-throwing – most notably darts and snooker balls – replacing the toe-to-toe rucks of the previous years. Due to my involvement with the blonde bombshell, my excursions to the nation's theatres of hate had been somewhat curtailed. And with Hampshire still lying low since his release from Her Majesty's holiday camp, the opportunity to perform had been severely restricted. The final months of the season, however, pitched us against the big boys of Manchester United and Notts Forest at home and – the icing on the cake – Cardiff and City away. I was determined to make up for lost time. As with our previous meeting with the Manc boys, the encounter on Good Friday was somewhat of an anticlimax. Most football fans were now begrudgingly following the Old Bill's directives and would, albeit reluctantly, encamp on the 'away' terrace. This is turn resulted in 'home' fans moving from their customary terrace behind the goal and setting up position as close as possible to the intruders, namely the side enclosures or seated stands, which were usually occupied by the more law-abiding supporter and dads with their kids.

The unfortunate consequence of these posturing manoeuvres was to involve innocent victims, something which thankfully up until then had been a rare event. No matter what the law came up with, the thugs would have their way. Rovers fans were no different. A new mob had been formed, the old Tote End was still the place to be, the atmosphere could not be matched, but there was now a fresh alternative: the North Stand. There was a small bonus as well for occupying that part of the ground – the bar opened at half-time and lukewarm, comforting Double Diamond flowed freely to those sharp enough to get there before the masses descended.

Despite the United fans' notorious reputation, the game itself passed off with little trouble, a Bruce Bannister goal securing a point against the eventual champions of the division. As was becoming customary, however, the trouble went off after the game, the squalid streets of Eastville replacing the terrace as the stage for our thuggery. We gathered in Robertson Road behind the White Swan, another mob mustered 50 yards away in St Marks Road, just as the unseasonal snow began to fall.

'Here they come, fire in when I say, right?' Hampshire was back, barking his orders, this had been his first game since the Luton incident; we had missed him.

The United fans were being escorted down Stapleton Road by the law, blue lights flashing heralding their arrival, motorcycle outriders at the head, ringed by dog handlers with their fearsome Alsatians, horses thrown in for good measure. As ever there would be some stragglers; if they were anything like us, it was a deliberate ploy. We weren't disappointed and neither were they. They were looking for us as much as we were looking for them. The last of the law had passed, they were on the opposite side of the road to us, 50 or so of them, their hardcore. Big, uncompromising long-haired northern bastards, no colours to be seen, as contemptuous in their own appearance as in their attitude to us, arms thrust deep into their jackets, collars turned up in an attempt to keep out the snow. Other unfortunates were just wearing T-shirts — at midday, when they had arrived, there had been brilliant sunshine — the vagaries of British weather. We were about to add more misery to their day and let them pass, knowing that our other mob, headed up by Ricky Lee, would be watching from the shadows not 20 yards away.

'Come on then, you bastards!' Hampshire roared.

We emerged from the doorways and gardens of Robertson Road, a salvo of bricks announcing our presence. We clashed in the middle of the road, and passing cars quickly accelerated and slid in the slush to avoid the ensuing battle. The United boys proved their pedigree and stood firm.

'U-ni-ted! U-ni-ted!' They took up our offer; lesser crews would have legged it. We traded punches and kicks, the grunts and curses growing with the violence. I took a kick, a bad one right in the bollocks. I slumped over the bonnet of a parked car; I was winded and in severe pain. More punches rained down on my head — this was not going to plan. I could see the others performing better than me, not least Ricky Lee, whose arrival with the rest of his crew had ensured we had the upper hand at last.

I recovered from my ignominious predicament and, although the wind had been taken out of my sails and my voice had raised an octave, I managed to retaliate with a few consolatory punches, not least on the twat who had landed the offending blow on my crown jewels. The wail of the sirens signalled the imminent arrival of the law and the two mobs dispersed. There were minimal arrests and walking wounded only. Apart from one poor bastard, who had copped a brick full in the face, honours were even.

We had earned the respect of one of the top mobs in the country. We retired to the White Swan to analyse and recount our experience. Our reputation had been enhanced.

'What's it like to be back, then?' I enquired of the beaming Hampshire.

'Like I've never been away,' he replied.

Within a fortnight we were off across the river again. City, unlike us, were having a storming season and were pushing for promotion. Ashton Gate was packed with almost 30,000 fans, and the atmosphere, as ever, was electric. Again, we erred on the side of caution and opted for a quiet evening at the open end. The law and the East Enders still hadn't forgiven us for our foray the previous season, with Barry Waller and Bob Doughty the top of the City boys' 'most wanted' list.

The final whistle signalled the inevitable pitch invasion. It wasn't as if it was unexpected – the baiting by both sets of fans was relentless. The disrespect for each other was mutual – the love of your own club was now secondary, the hatred of each other was all-consuming. Manchester United v City, Liverpool v Everton, Spurs v Arsenal were not in our league. This was up there with Rangers v Celtic, but without the religion and the dour Scottish wit.

We squared up to each other on the halfway line, but the huge police presence managed to keep the majority of the warring armies apart. We both made strategic withdrawals and the battle-plans were redrawn; we met again later in Coronation Road, this time minus the law.

Doughty was at the head, Mike the Wrestler and Paul Sweet were also in attendance – a fearsome trio. I tucked in behind with Hampshire and Iggy and a shedload of others I knew only by nods and winks. We didn't need to know each other's names –

BACK IN THE OLD ROUTINE

the knowing smiles were enough to tell me I was in good company. Across the road, trying to be nonchalant about their appearance but not succeeding, were Andy and his Tramps, their very presence instilling me with confidence. The City kiddies were waiting. They surged out of a side road, a big crew, many more than us. But this wasn't about numbers – the awesome physical appearance of Doughty, Mike and Sweet, resplendent in their motorcycle gear, was enough to put them off their stride. This triumvirate made the Horsemen of the Apocalypse look like outcasts from a gymkhana. The battle was lost for the boys in suits before it had even started.

The yell of 'Get the bastards!' quickly turned to 'Fuck it, it's Doughty!' as they realised that they were out of their league. None of them were keen on making that much of a name for themselves, their screams filled the air as they tried to retreat, but for one luckless City fan the swishing of Doughty's motorcycle chain heralded excruciating pain, as Bob's favourite weapon wrapped itself around the unfortunate's neck. Bob wrenched him to the ground and followed it up with a swift kick. Mike, hot on the heels of Doughty, landed a murderous kick with his steel-toe-capped motorcycle boots to the youth's head. I feared for his life, I could hear the sound of bone smashing. His body was lifeless, not a sound emerged from his gaping mouth, which was now filling up with dark, oozing blood, the boot still going in on his unconscious body as the rest of the pack fired in. I felt sick and exhilarated at the same time, but it was all going off too quickly for me to feel sorry for the poor bastard. I smacked one fleeing City fan round the back of the head. He stumbled and fell and more lethal kicks hit home. We were well on top. The brave ones tried to stand and fight but the sheer terror that filled the younger ones was enough to spread alarm through the rest of them. Despite the pleas of 'Stand and fight, you bastards, no one run!' by their more experienced boys, the struggle was lost. They scarpered with their bodies as badly battered as their pride.

A wave of euphoria engulfed me, but it was rapidly replaced with a feeling of guilt. I knew such feelings of remorse wouldn't last, they never did. I knew I was doing wrong but it was hard to stop doing something I enjoyed so much. The unfortunate thing for football was that I was not the only one who felt this way. I was one of thousands who felt the same, including, for some unfathomable reason, the unlucky sod whose head was now split like an over-ripe melon and whose bodily fluids were now making a mess of Coronation Road.

The season wound down with a home game against Notts Forest and an excursion to Cardiff, when the old boys from Henbury reformed for the day. The inevitable ruck with the sheep-shaggers erupted on a garage forecourt but came to an abrupt end when a pair of Stilsons came to my old chum Harvey's assistance. The home game against Forest was notable for its endless brawls and pitch invasions, one of which was led by Lil's younger brother Mick and his cohort Matthew 'Maff' Simmonds, now both firmly established as promising young Turks in the Tote hierarchy. In the year since Mick's initiation to the Tote he had made quite a name for himself, but even he was being surpassed by Maff, whose reputation had been enhanced after he was the victim of a serious stabbing in a fairground brawl that had threatened his life.

The favourite hypothesis of the time from the so-called experts – i.e. the misguided psychologists, the misinformed theorists and the mistrustful politicians – for the upsurge in youth, and in particular football-related, violence was that the perpetrators of the heinous crimes were the results of an underprivileged upbringing and, more often than not, broken homes. Mick Warbutton and his brother Lil made a

BACK IN THE OLD ROUTINE

nonsense of that theory with their well-educated, comfortable middle-class background in leafy Westbury-on-Trym. Maff, the son of a nuclear physicist, whose sister was a concert cellist, whose detached, family house in Henleaze occupied more acreage than the street in which I lived, destroyed it lock, stock and fucking barrel. No, the experts were looking too hard again.

Further afield, all-conquering Leeds United reached the European Cup Final. Their opponents were the German champions Bayern Munich and the game was played in beautiful, unsuspecting Paris. Unfortunately, the museums and architectural delights of the French capital had little appeal for the culturally deficient northerners and the French authorities were totally unprepared for the invasion, which reminded elderly Parisians of a little visit by Hitler's stormtroopers some 35 years earlier. Some woeful decisions by a partisan referee ensured the Germans won 2–0 and signalled the systematic dismantling of the Parc des Princes stadium by the disgruntled Yorkshire fans. 'The English disease', as it had now been appropriately tagged, was becoming a major export, one that was set to hang around for the foreseeable future.

And so the season finished on a relative high. A mediocre season on the pitch, an average one off it with a few spectacular peaks – bit like the girlfriend, really. It was the summer of 1975 and Hampshire and the rest of my single mates took themselves off to Benidorm. I had to make do with a fortnight in Newquay with Karen. No great hardship, admittedly, but as much as I enjoyed sampling the delights of the Cornish Riviera with its fish and chips and Starlight lager, it hardly compared with San Miguel and dusky señoritas. The holiday was yet another nail in the coffin of my turbulent relationship with Karen and as the summer ended and the new season loomed, our squabbles and ultimatums predictably started again. The spectacular rows of the previous year, which had cumulated in the trip to the casualty department, were now becoming a regular occurrence. The age-old battle of the sexes that must have started in prehistory was raging again. The choice was simple: go out with your mates clubbing, or stay in the cave in front of the fire with the wife and the sabre-toothed tiger.

I had chosen the former, but not without a struggle. The final calamitous row ended with me storming out of Karen's flat and with her once again querying my parentage. My reply to her question 'Do you really love me?' was the romantic 'I shag you, don't I?' As I dodged the tirade of insults and pans that were coming my way, I couldn't help feeling that I must have unwittingly touched a nerve. I made my way back to the bus stop shivering from the bitterness welling up inside me. Then I realised it wasn't just that – I really was bloody freezing. I had left my favourite hand-made, full-length black 'John Shaft' leather coat back at her flat.

'Will you open this fucking door and give me my coat!' I shouted through the letter box. My incessant bell-ringing and door-kicking had had no effect – Karen was in no mood to cooperate. I was giving up hope when, finally, the window opened.

'You want your coat, do you? Well fucking have it!' she shouted.

It slumped to the ground in front of me, £50 worth of David Ferrari's finest leather slashed to ribbons. My world had fallen apart. I was now bereft of my coat and of my girlfriend. I cried all the way home. I loved that coat.

The 1975/76 season dawned and I found myself mercifully free of the attentions and confinement of the female of the species. This enabled me to pursue more manly pursuits, namely football, fighting and drinking with no particular emphasis or

BACK IN THE OLD ROUTINE

preference for one over the other. Indeed, my usual Saturday pastime was a combination of all three. The start of the new season brought about a nationwide ban on coach companies carrying 'unofficial' supporters to away games. It was an unworkable and unsuccessful attempt to avoid trouble and had little effect, as determined fans simply hired self-drive transits and minibuses. The ban was soon revoked and the hooligans were once again free to travel the country in search of their fun.

By the end of the first month of the football season it was apparent to all and sundry that the football hooligan problem was no passing craze. The violence kicked off all around the country, with stabbings, beatings, pitch invasions and train vandalism as conspicuous as ever. Our first away game of the season took us to Oldham, where three coachloads of 'unofficial' supporters sporting the home colours of blue and white amazingly infiltrated the home terrace and caused chaos. The highlight of the day was finding myself unintentionally positioned next to an obnoxious northerner whose oversized mouth worked overtime in berating and insulting my fellow Tote Enders, who were for the most part situated behind the luckless oaf.

'Come on then, 'ave a go, you southern poofs!' It was the usual stereotypical stuff from the northerners. Why they assumed all southerners were handbag-carrying homosexuals was beyond me. No different than us assuming all Cockneys were mouthy and all Taffies were sheep-shaggers, I suppose. Not that those two statements were incorrect, of course – they were both indisputable facts.

The oafish unemployed northerner (for it was also a fact all northerners were on the dole) carried on with his relentless diatribe. 'You're 'ard when thee's in a gang, ain't thee, come 'ere an I'll give thee a right battering!'

He stood there, nonchalantly leaning back on the barrier, his right fist punching his open-palmed left hand, inviting all-comers to have a go, quite oblivious to the increasingly agitated southern 'poofter' at his side.

I could take it no longer. I tapped him on the shoulder. Indignantly he reeled around to face me, his piggy eyes meeting mine for a split second before my forehead smashed into his nose. He reeled backwards in pain and shock and struggled to find his feet, but it was a fruitless attempt. His legs finally gave way and he slumped to the terrace, where he became easy pickings for the same mob that he had been insulting not ten seconds earlier. I turned back and watched the football. The law moved in and made their customary arrests of no one in particular – just the poor unfortunates who happened to be there. That was their problem, being in the wrong place at the wrong time, just like the Oldham fan, who by now was being stretchered off to have his nose stitched back together at the local infirmary.

Our first clash of the new season with City at Ashton on 30 August brought about numerous pre- and post-game clashes. Eight arrests were made in total, a pitiful amount considering the number of fans who had battled with each other on the streets of Bristol that day.

Ted Croker, the FA Chairman, called upon Harold Wilson's government to get tough with the louts who were spoiling the beautiful game. In later years Croker famously told Margaret Thatcher to get '*her* hooligans out of *his* sport', and he rightly refused point-blank to acknowledge us as football hooligans, despite the boasting chant of 'We are the famous football hooligans' that was heard at every ground in the country. The Government's response was for the Lord Chancellor, Lord Elwyn-Jones, to issue a directive to magistrates instructing them to make offenders report to police stations and attendance centres on Saturday afternoons or force them to do community

BACK IN THE OLD ROUTINE

work, as the derisory fines being handed out were clearly having no effect on ridding the game of this evil.

As ever it was a futile attempt. For every thug that the authorities managed to get off the terrace there were another dozen or so waiting to take their place. Hooliganism was far too glamorous and appealing a lifestyle for Britain's youth to give up. The threat of painting some old biddy's outhouse or digging up their garden hardly proved a worthwhile deterrent when glory and respect from your peers beckoned.

24

Changin' Times

Away from football, the nightclubs were now in their heyday. Funk was the dance music of the Seventies and by 1975 it was well on its way to reaching its zenith. Local clubs such as Raquels in the Entertainment Centre, Tiffany's on the Downs, Vadims on Queens Road, Maxims on Park Street and the Carousel near Bath all competed with each other to bring the best in dance music to its devoted and enthusiastic fans. The dance generation rang the latest changes in both fashion and new moves, with blokes both wanting and willing to show off both their wardrobe and their wiggles on the dancefloor.

Baggy bowling shirts complete with American team logos and loud, garish Hawaiian shirts, bought either second-hand or from Bristol's trendy new clothes boutique, Clobber, rapidly replaced the fly-away collar, fitted shirts and tight, star-patterned sweaters of the previous years. The outrageously wide flares were also on the wane, at least with the newly emerging, funkateering soul boys, who had started wearing peg-style trousers known as 'Zooters'. These were the complete opposite of flares, with heavy pleats at the top, gathered in with a belt and tapering to a

CHANGIN' TIMES

tight fit at the ankle, reminiscent of the 'Zoot' suits of the 1930s as worn by your old man when he was strutting his stuff to Ambrose and his band. Pointed winkle-pickers and open-toed sandals, both leather and, more oddly, plastic, completed the ensemble which, although popular with the southern trendies, was virtually non-existent north of Watford. Clobber, which had a sister shop in Newport, South Wales, was owned by a smooth, trendy geezer named Alan, who had once played in Andy Fairweather-Lowe's band, Amen Corner. Alan and his shop manager Richard played a major role in dictating and influencing fashion in Bristol during the Seventies, and their independent, alternative stance made a welcome change from the mass high-street stores, such as Austins and Burtons.

Many of the southern youngsters who sported the new change in fashion were drawn not only to US contemporary funk but also to Northern Soul, whose followers had long worn oversize shirts emblazoned with badges proclaiming 'Keep the Faith' and 'The Torch All Nighter' and which portrayed the clenched black fist that was synonymous with the US Black Power movement. But whereas the southerners' taste in trousers and footwear had shifted dramatically, the northerners clung on grimly to their high-waisted, monstrously wide flares and flat-soled moccasins. Northern Soul was a genre of soul music that had been around since the Sixties. This distinctive music with its emphasis on the back beat and its fast, energetic pace, survived in its own small pockets, where it created its own charts. In the north of England, where skinheads had taken longer to die out than in the south, clubs in places such as Stoke, Blackpool, Manchester and Wigan continued to play predominantly Sixties soul music and it was in these clubs that the music was to survive for a good many years. One club in particular, the Wigan Casino, became famous when the media cottoned on to the fact that young people could enjoy themselves all night without having to resort to smashing the

BOOTED AND SUITED

place up. Coaches from Bristol, South Wales and the rest of the country regularly journeyed to Lancashire, where the alcohol-free environment — milk and Lucozade, being the favourite drinks, admittedly laced with uppers of varying descriptions — ensured all-night music throbbed to 2,000 or so devoted worshippers.

Northern Soul, although an important part of the British dance music scene, failed to stir much passion in me, as I could not see the attraction of ancient recordings of obscure and often long-dead artists (in order to retain their kudos, jealous and over-protective DJs such as Ian Levine would often remove the labels of the records they were playing). Like glam rock, Northern Soul was for me at any rate, past its sell-by date although its devoted and passionate followers loyally 'kept the faith' until it finally closed its doors on 20 September 1981. However, the burning question on most southern soul boys' lips remained: 'Who the fuck was Major Lance?'

The significance of the extravagant back-flips and characteristic side-to-side shuffling of Northern Soul's fanatical followers and their legendary 'All nighters', where the only white powder needed was talcum powder for the dancefloor, should not be dismissed. Many years later the dance moves resurfaced in the form of breakdancing and the all-nighters developed into 'raves'. The legacy of Northern Soul lived on.

OK, I got it wrong here. After years of indifference and ignorance towards Northern Soul I've had a 'road to Wigan pier' moment. Thanks to Goldmine, Kent Records and Fopp record stores, I can now boast a veritable feast of 'essential floorfillers' and 'best of the Blackpool Mecca scorchers' in my CD collection. Thankfully, I now do know who the fuck Major Lance is, not to mention J J Barnes, Betty Everett and of course the truly wonderful Frank Wilson (memo to self — add 'not

CHANGIN' TIMES

appreciating Northern Soul' to my list of regrets). So as a small apology to all you Northern Soul fans (not just the original aficionados of the Seventies but, like me, the recently converted), the following has been written by Tim Williams, a Bristolian soul kiddie, who unlike me, cast off his southern funk prejudices and headed north towards Mecca.

Torquay, Bournemouth, Newquay. We went south, we never went north. Luckily for us the girls of the North also headed for the deep South come summer holidays, finding the coastal delights of Bridlington and Morecombe utterly resistible, though those far off places always performed with pluck on It's a Knockout.

Neil Emery met a girl from Ashton-in-Makerfield at Curly Neill's on Paignton seafront. Ashton is basically Wigan but with more trees, syllables and a couple of hyphens. Neil said his farewells and set off for Lancashire to see his new love just as the Wigan Casino was completing its first year at the centre of the Northern Soul scene.

In the Sixties, soul was the sound at the heart of all Britain's cities. Young moderns drove scooters and danced to the sounds of Stax, Atlantic and Tamla Motown. Bristol was no different with soul nights regularly kicking in late and within a hop, step and a back flip of Beau Brummels. In the South, however, people are always trying to sniff out the next big thing and scenes evolved often before they had really taken root. Before you knew it London's mods had added a flash of paisley and a neckline of worry beads to deepening sideburns. Wispy beards were only months away and soul was filed away for collectors only until the South got its groove back through James Brown and many former jazzers in bad afros.

But the North kept faith and that rallying cry passed from soul centres across and around the Pennines. From The Golden Torch in Hanley near Stoke to Va-Vas in Bolton and the Twisted Wheel in Manchester.

BOOTED AND SUITED

Music-wise, the paisley push for world domination had already overrun Detroit and a number of Berry Gordy's stalwarts like The Temptations succumbed. Holland, Dozier and Holland chased off by Norman Whitfield. Motown's was a closed book, a finite catalogue. Luckily for the soul scene in the North of England, every town across America had its own version of the Motor City's finest and Roulette, Chess, Okeh and the rest provided barely diminishing pickings through until the current day.

By the time Neil disembarked at Wigan Central, the Northern Soul crown was shared between the Casino and the Highland Room at the Blackpool Mecca. The latter, where the music came from wannabe/soon-to-be impresario Ian Levine ran to normal hours and featured more modern 'chuggy' dance tunes, some of which were being produced by Levine himself. The Casino, where Russ Winstanley and Richard Searling played the discs relied upon out and out stompers where the line between soul and a catchy tune with a northernish beat often blurred. Tobi Legend and Frank Wilson were pure soul make no mistake, unlike Gary Lewis and the Playboys and (gulp) the theme from Joe 90.

The Casino, like the Twisted Wheel before it, was an all-nighter and to get in you had to be a member. Days after Neil's return from the first anniversary night a clutch of the curious, mainly from Brislington filled out the joining form in Blues and Soul. *The magazine came out every other week and was essential reading for anyone with a passing interest in the soon to go overground northern scene. Dave Godin, the Londoner who initially coined the name 'Northern Soul', wrote a regular column but it was Frank Elson's words, often sprawling across four or five pages, that were at the core of the journal. Elson simply reported on where he had been since the last issue, who else had been there, who had DJ'd and which records they had played. It was an insight into another world where the faith had been well and truly kept.*

Blues and Soul *also featured an advertisement for a record shop*

CHANGIN' TIMES

in Nottingham called Selectadisc that ran a mail order service. Southerners playing catch up could get 'I'll always need you' by Dean Courtney, 'I can't help loving you' by Paul Anka and 'Tainted Love' by Gloria Jones for 85 pence each. Cheap as it seems now, but this was nearly 35 years ago and 85 pence bought a small family saloon or a fortnight in Lloret de Mar.

The first Saturday after the arrival of the small blue membership card, I packed an Adidas sports bag and left home, Temple Meads and the South behind me. Neil, the veteran of one Casino visit and the (by now) former beau of a genuine Wigan girl led the way closely followed by Trapper John, Dave Moore, Dinger Bell and myself. Others subsequently made the trip. Elmer? Icky? Hard to recall across the expanse of time. A couple who certainly went were Richard 'Loony' Lane and his soon-to-be wife Mandy. They usually brought a cassette player so that scratchy versions of big Northern sounds could be enjoyed throughout the long day's travel and the unavoidable Sunday return journey. Loony was also from Briz and he was never called anything but Loony... except to his face. If you accidentally called him by his nickname it was odds on you would find out very quickly why he was called it and then you would find out if there was much of a queue in casualty that day. I am feeling furtive just typing his nickname, in case he finds out.

You took the train to Birmingham New Street, where you changed for Crewe. By that middle leg of the trip, more and more soul fans filled the carriages. You met Reg from Hemel among those who actually came from the North, or at least, the Midlands.

By this time, Northern Soul was already responsible for two hit records. Record companies were always looking to turn a quick buck on the back of any fledgling scene, no matter how obscure or localised. So 'Love on a Mountain Top' by Robert Knight and 'There's a Ghost in my House' by Motown honky house boy R Dean Taylor, both 'discovered' by Northern DJs, broke on to the Radio 1 playlist and became UK hits. All right? Not 'alf!

BOOTED AND SUITED

The final stage of the train ride was Crewe to Wigan, a route that got busier the later the hour. Once we arrived in the hometown of George Formby we caroused a great many pubs, all bereft of the north's soul fans — they were at the Mecca or some other regular time Northern Soul night, no doubt scoring pills to sustain them through the long night ahead.

At midnight, the Beachcombers opened. This was a spacious, dark, cavernous room that opened at an ungodly hour to provide refuge for the gathering hordes two hours before its next-door neighbour finally opened up for business. Beachcombers played top Northern sounds, allowing people to practise their spins and flips before hitting the hallowed dancefloors of the Casino. On my first visit I passed out, probably through too much beer and not enough food. I lay just inside the doorway and people stepped over me in their baggy hordes until I was able to stagger to my feet again. Passing out at the Beachcombers was commonplace, like buying a coffee or asking for the time.

Some people resisted the allure of the Beachcombers in order to start queuing for the Casino, for despite it being for members only and holding about 1500 people, not everyone got in. The queue was a terrifying place. Sardines would not have put up with it. The more experienced hoisted their Adidas bag up on to one shoulder to avoid losing it underfoot. They could then concentrate on trying to breathe. It was always a massive relief when at 2am the doors finally opened. The first noises heard from within were the door staff imploring people to stop pushing. This was like telling weeds to stop growing or Roger Whittaker to stop whistling.

There was never any hesitation. People had come to dance and that's what they did from the moment they got beyond the paydesk and could see Winstanley lining up the next 45 or acetate. Walking too close to the speakers rendered industrial hairspray redundant. The place stank of Brut and though the great scent diverted the smell, sweat was everywhere, hence the ubiquitous Adidas bags all

CHANGIN' TIMES

packed with spare bowling shirts. Because the Casino was so vast, there was plenty of room for everyone, which was a good thing because, unless you could spin like Robin Cousins, you needed a bit of room. Even then, you were more likely to stop by careening into someone else and, amazingly, that person would invariably help you stop and even offer tips on how to achieve a more abrupt stop next time. It was friendly with no booze or edge. Girls danced a completely different dance to the boys, scooting on their heels powered by short chugging arm movements into slowish heel spins that sent pleated skirts ever outwards. The gymnastics were left to the boys. And in this post-hip hop breaking world, the tricks seem kind of tame and military like something from the Edinburgh tattoo. But back then, there hadn't been anything like it since the Jitterbug. One guy could drop below knee height and not repeat a move in 90 seconds. And everyone was in the know. They knew just when to clap during 'Cochise' by Paul Humphrey and 'Thumb A Ride' by Earl Wright Orchestra. Some songs had just a single handclap sequestered into a middle eight but when it hit it was like indoor thunder. Spins, back flips and tricks generally had their own musical countdown. You could feel a break coming when everyone was going to hit the deck or the people around them, but in a friendly way. This was before talcum powder so it was just down to flat leather shoes to provide ballast beneath Karmen Ghia's, the bowling shirt and the beret, clipped to the back of the head with unseen clips or hatpins. Mr M's was a side ballroom where they only played oldies. It was magic with a single black glove. The faith.

This scene had to be worth money and the record companies grew restless trying to gain the rights to the UK release of some obscure soul gem from Chicago. So they started to make their own using white, UK-based session musicians. 'Footsie', many sides that bore the name Simon Sousson and 'Goodbye, Nothing To Say' by Nosmo King' shamefully played to death at the Casino by compliant DJs

BOOTED AND SUITED

with a share in the takings. Though no one ever owned up to Wigan's Chosen Few and their dire version of the Invitations dancer 'Skiing in the Snow'.

It was these UK-produced releases that were at the fore as the scene broke its groundings and went national. DJs around the country accepted their free copies and artlessly programmed in a Northern sequence whether they were in Southend or Southmead. Bristol joined in gainfully and even got its own all-nighter/all-dayer when Kojak brought his Inter City Soul Club to the Sterling Suite at Yate. The heavy curtains kept the light out if it was an all-dayer and Yate out whatever the time. Elson came though he hated Kojak. Northerners came. We copied their accents.

All-nighters at Wigan finished at eight in the morning when hundreds of people walked to the local swimming baths for breakfast and more Northern Soul. The bastards were all in on it. But after Yate it was a drive back to town in someone's Allegro with Tony Haneley ramming the bumper from behind with his. Not quite so friendly as the Casino.

Better all-dayers were held at Tiffanys, courtesy of Kojak, with Edwin Starr performing his Ric Tic classics one Sunday. We had seen him during the night at the Casino and caught him again at six in the evening on the downs, twice in 24 hours with agent 00 soul. He was impressed and we were wired.

But soon, another magazine hit the stands to rival Blues and Soul. Black Music was about funk, the music beginning to take hold. Southern Soul? I went to the Black Music roadshow at Crackers in Wardour Street the night after we saw BT Express at the Hammersmith Odeon. But that's another time and place that we moved on to, not keeping the faith. But you can get it back. Just connect a deck to your sound system or computer and put on 'If You Ask Me' by Jerry Williams or even better 'Get Out' by Harold Melvin and the Bluenotes. Then close your eyes, smell the Brut and try another kitchen spin. Bliss.

CHANGIN' TIMES

South of Brum, however, in clubs such as The Goldmine in Canvey Island and Lacy Lady in Ilford, DJs like Chris Hill and Froggy ensured the funk just kept on coming. 'Do It Any Way You Wanna' by Peoples Choice was the major hit of late 1975; the stompingly good 'Wipe Your Feet And Dance' by Wee Willie and the Winners was a dance sensation and 'Latin Hustle' by Eddie Drennon was a huge hit in the clubs, eventually breaking into the Top 20 in February of the following year. My own personal favourite, 'What's The Name Of This Funk (Spiderman)' by the old ivory-tinkler Ramsey Lewis, featured high in the Avon Soul Army charts, but sank without trace as far as Radio One was concerned. Some of the better-known performers who also made an appearance were the Isley Brothers with 'Fight The Power' and The Miracles, sans Smokey, with 'Love Machine', which even managed to get to number 3 in the national record charts in early 1976.

Other funk bands that featured in the national charts were Banbarra, who had a minor hit with 'Shack Up' and ex-Animal Eric Burdon's War, with two hits – 'Me And Baby Brother' and 'Low Rider' (amusingly resurrected in the Nineties for a Marmite Ad), both recordings featuring Lee Oskar's amazing harmonica skills. While Bill Curtis's Fatback Band, with five Top 40 hits including 'Yum, Yum' and 'Do The Bus Stop' from September 1975 to August 1976, could possibly lay claim to being the most successful funk band of the Seventies. Their sell-out live appearance at the Colston Hall unleashed a thousand or so harmonised black and white whistle-blowing teenagers on to the unsuspecting City Centre.

Paradoxically, though, while dance music was spawning some of its all-time greats it was also spewing out some of its all-time disasters. For while funk was still the music for the serious clubber, disco music was making a name for itself in its own right, for all the wrong reasons. Donna Summer, Tina Charles and Silver Convention with their Biddu/Moroder-created Eurotrash all undeservedly gave dance music a bad name. To add insult to injury, the gay scene, which had always had a large influence on dance music, laid claim to disco as its very own; they were welcome to it. Funk, after its brief incursion into the UK mainstream charts, wisely went back underground leaving the charts to their bland diet of Abba, The Wurzels and Demis Roussos, who all had number-1 hits in early 1976.

Was it any wonder that Malcolm McLaren, who, along with Vivienne Westwood, had been arrested the previous year and charged with a breach of public decency after selling T-shirts featuring trouserless cowboys with their penises touching, was waiting in the wings with his enfants terribles The Sex Pistols?

I was now part of an ever-increasing circle of mates with similar tastes, views, humour, opinions and backgrounds. Whether at Eastville or the City Centre we would meet in the same pubs, drink the same drinks and fight the same fights; we were indivisible and indomitable in our quest for the crack. For life was just that: a crack. Everything we did was without malice or spite – apart from when we played City. We rarely harmed anyone who wouldn't have done the same to us, given half the chance.

Our struggle continued through the 1975/76 season against other similar-minded lads the length and breadth of England. Sunderland at home brought an invasion of long-haired shipbuilders, who themselves looked like they had been welded and riveted together in the shipyards of the Wear. Sunderland were still riding high from their FA Cup win against Leeds several years earlier and their arrogance, and ignorance led them to try an assault on the Tote. They stayed put for the whole game, despite our attempts to oust them. One of our star performers that day was Brenton, a black kid from Soundwell who was a workmate of Gary Abbott. Brenton, or 'Beep-beep' as he was

CHANGIN' TIMES

more commonly known due to his wearing of a T-shirt with the Roadrunner cartoon character on it, had been hanging round with us for years. I remembered him from our promotion year, he was one of only a handful of black kids who followed Rovers, it was surprising really, bearing in mind Eastville stadium's close proximity to a large immigrant population. A year or two later Brenton acquired a new nickname following a nasty and racially motivated bloody fight with an ear-munching sailor in Baldwin Street which left him with only the top half of his left ear remaining. From then on, Brenton was often known as 'Eighteen months' as in "Ear and a half".

The northern toe-rags gave Brenton a hard time, their relentless baiting and monkey references only enhancing his, and our, determination to rid our terraces of the northern intruders. A Bruce Bannister goal only minutes before full-time gave Rovers a well-earned win and ensured the Wearsiders had a long and hard journey home. I felt genuine anguish for Brenton, but the abuse didn't seem to worry or affect him. We laughed it off over a few pints later in our new watering hole, the Sceptre in Baldwin Street.

'Yer, see I whack that kiddy today, Browner, gert ugly twat 'e was 'n' all.' Brenton giggled over his lager and lime, his high-pitched Bristolian accent grating like fingernails against a blackboard. We were playing ping-pong on an amazing new TV-like game from Japan; the relentless 'Bip, bipping' of the bats hitting the ball was becoming addictive. Brenton was as good at this game as he was with his fists, and was giving me a right hammering.

'Fucking clever these Japs,' said Brenton, 'what are they going to think up next?'

I liked Brenton. I didn't see his colour as an issue. In fact, I didn't even acknowledge him as being black; perhaps that was a failing. I'd never had a problem with colour, and with my love of

BOOTED AND SUITED

reggae and soul music I guess I even liked blacks before it became compulsory. Admittedly, we usually gave the black kids that we came across in Bailey's and The Rummer a wide berth but that was down to self-preservation rather than prejudice. It was generally accepted, rightly or wrongly, that most black kids carried blades. Brenton was an anomaly. Generally, there was very little integration between white and black kids, although to most white kids' eternal disgust, black kids seemed to attract good-looking, white chicks in the way that flames attracted moths.

'Ain't that that tart Karen you was seeing last year?' asked Hampshire, nodding in the direction of the bar. It was now late February and we were in the Assize Courts in Small Street, an overcrowded, newly refurbished pub, not a beer glass's throw from the Guildhall Tavern. The O'Jays hit 'I Love Music' blasted out from the sound system's immense speakers. I glanced over. She looked as stunning as ever, dressed in a flimsy white satin halterneck-top dress that spectacularly accentuated her curvaceous figure. I felt a pang of remorse. She caught my eye and came over.

'Long time no see. I see you've got a new coat,' she said with a smirk.

Like every other kiddy in Bristol I was wearing a newly acquired zip-up leather bomber jacket. This one would hang around for the rest of the Seventies. As long as Karen didn't get her evil hands on it.

'Yeah, I had to get a new one, remember?'

'Serves you fucking right, you bastard,' she replied. I got the feeling we weren't about to kiss and make up.

'Seeing anyone, or have you and Hampshire married yet?' she asked sarcastically, looking at Hampshire. There was no love lost between them. I knew she was working up to something.

'No, I'm having a whale of a time. How about you?'

CHANGIN' TIMES

'Yeah, met a real nice bloke, treats me proper. I'm with him tonight, I'll introduce you to him later.'

'Look forward to it,' I lied through clenched teeth.

She slid away with a hundred pairs of leering eyes on her.

'Fucking hell, Browner, you packed her in to follow Rovers? I'd sling one up it no fucking shit, she's gert ace.' Brenton had a way with words; put like that it did seem a bizarre choice.

'Yeah, all right, don't rub it in.'

I was beginning to see the folly of my decision. To make matters worse Rovers had just lost to Karen's team, Plymouth Argyle, 3–0; hopefully she didn't know the result. Just when I thought things could only get better she reappeared with her new boyfriend, somebody we all knew only too well.

'Chris, have you met Lenny?'

Lenny Silvester thrust out his huge black hand to shake mine. He could barely contain himself; he smirked from ear to ear, his gold tooth flashed menacingly.

'All right? I've heard a lot about you,' Lenny began.

'Right,' I grunted a reply, 'yeah, likewise.'

I shook his hand begrudgingly; my blood ran cold. Lenny was one bad mother. We all knew him, a drug-dealing, knife-carrying, woman-beater. But worse – much worse – a no-good City fan.

'See ya later,' he grinned, and walked away with Karen draped on his arm. She was clinging on to him like a leech. I felt like vomiting.

'Not if I can help it,' I muttered. My anger and disgust was welling up inside me. 'Come on, we're fucking going,' I said finally, 'this place stinks.'

'That bastard will have her on the streets in a fortnight,' said Brenton. If he was trying to console me, it didn't work. If he was trying to wind me up, he succeeded. I spent the rest of the night drinking myself stupid. I took out my anger on some hapless

BOOTED AND SUITED

bastard who accidentally bumped into me in Scamps, but all the rucks in the world wouldn't change the way I felt that night. The seeds of hate were being sown.

Easter 1976 came and the end of the football season loomed. Rovers' season was finishing on the crest of a slump and City, unbelievably, were heading for promotion to Division One. The game at Eastville on Good Friday drew a crowd of over 26,000. The City fans were full of themselves – they had a right to be, they were heading for the high life of the top division. Promotion for City was to become a watershed event from which Rovers, and more importantly their fans, took a long time to recover, if indeed they ever have. The dire 0–0 draw was only enlivened by the incessant baiting and battling of the fans: ten ejections, eight arrests and four lads in hospital, one of whom was a 17-year-old Rovers fan who had the misfortune to come across eight City fans after the game. They set upon him mercilessly and broke his jaw.

The following day Rovers were at home again, this time against Southampton. Rovers won a thrilling game 2–0 with the old hero of the Tote End skins, Frankie Prince, bagging a brace. Whether as a hangover from the previous day's violence with City or as a result of the game being the last home fixture of the season, the violence kicked off again, if anything worse than the previous day's events. One incident in particular hit the headlines for its sheer brutality. An up-and-coming crew from Kingswood led by wily youngster Rich Nunn (yet another Bristolian whose passion for the Blues of Eastville was matched by his passion for those of the Fulham Road) encountered a number of Saints fans on the forecourt of a petrol station in the shadow of the M32 flyover. The incident quickly escalated from obscene name-calling and customary 'come on then' hand signals to a vicious, bloody, brick-

CHANGIN' TIMES

throwing assault that left one stricken Southampton fan unconscious and choking from his own blood on the back seat of his mates' car, which by now was wrecked. It never crossed Rich's mind, or the minds of any of us for that matter, that his actions could cause so much anguish and pain. The lad survived, just, but remained brain-damaged for the rest of his life.

Rich was arrested on the spot and served six months in DC for his crime. To horrified innocents he should have got more. Rich's contemporaries all thought he was unlucky to get caught.

All round it was a black Easter. While Hampshire and I were having an alcohol-induced minor disagreement with each other in the Poor House in King Street – which left Hamps with a bloodied nose and me with a gashed eyebrow – our old mate Gubby was involved in a car smash in Devon that left him fighting for his life. The good-looking bastard never lost his looks but the accident ensured he wouldn't dance the 'Funky Chicken' again. In another, unrelated car smash on the outskirts of Torquay, the darling of the Guildhall Tavern girls and all-round nice geezer, Gary Mallett, was not so lucky. Gary died, leaving his Redland Aggro Merchant accomplice, Stevie 'Little Ipswich' Bould, distraught and the Tote End and the Avon Soul Army with one less foot-soldier.

Two awesome records featured strongly in the Guildhall charts that Easter: Juggy Jones's 'Inside America', which even made a brief entry into the UK Top 40, and Donald Byrd's groundbreaking record 'Change', which climbed to the top of the funk charts. At the top of the national charts for a staggering six weeks were Brotherhood of Man singing Britain's Eurovision Song contest entry 'Save Your Kisses For Me'. The two records were poles apart, but in their own way they were both perfect examples of Seventies music. Donald Byrd's

BOOTED AND SUITED

influential jazz-funk masterpiece summed up all that was good about the music of the era, and Brotherhood of Man... well, that was just shite.

25

The Temperature Rises and the Bomb Drops

The summer of 1976 became legendary. It would long be remembered for its oppressive heat wave, when hose pipes were banned, tarmac melted and temperatures and tempers rose to boiling point. The music suited the heat. The Ohio Players released another scorching album, *Contradiction*, on which the funk was nastier than ever, with tracks such as 'Tell The Truth', and the eerie 'Far East Mississippi'. The inevitable single release from the album, 'Who'd She Coo?', was pure pop-funk and deserved a showing in the charts alongside James Brown's 'Get Up Offa That Thing' and The Isley Brothers's 'Harvest For The World', though sadly it didn't get one. Someone else who appeared in the charts in the summer of 1976 was the lounge lizard himself Bryan Ferry, with his biggest hit to date, 'Let's Stick Together'. Ferry had temporarily abandoned the rest of Roxy Music, who had declined with the demise of glam rock and glitter the previous year. He was becoming something of a fashion icon with British youth, his androgynous look of the early Seventies having now given way to a leaner, meaner image with sharp suits and a penchant for

BOOTED AND SUITED

American military khakis as worn by Glen Miller 30 years earlier. Ferry had even taken to wearing the soul boys' favourite footwear, the plastic sandal, and the boys in turn donned the khakis.

Blue denim was as popular as ever, for shirts as well as for jeans, which for the soul boys anyway were erring towards a more slimline straight-legged style, while the rest of the nation were still firmly clinging on to the hideous baggy flares as made by Falmers. FU's labelled all-in-one bib-and-braces purchased from Jean Machine matched with V-necked, collared T-shirts were also much in evidence and, teamed up with the smarter, shorter hairstyles, thankfully gave us all a respite from the era that taste forgot. Unfortunately, facial hair, for the lads anyway, was becoming increasingly popular, with every spotty-faced 17-year-old attempting to grow a droopy moustache and sideburns.

The soul boys, whose numbers had increased dramatically in the last year and who included my old chum Harvey, sporting the heaviest of heavy fringes, were now the dominant force among the club-goers in Bristol and became synonymous with the ever burgeoning dance scene. Although I was very much part of their music scene, the soul boy fashion, in relation to the clothing at any rate, was passing me by. In fact due to their penchant for the ubiquitous plastic sandal the soul boys became the subject of much derision. They quickly became known as 'Kit kiddies' or 'Jelly heads' due to their peculiar head movement action while dancing; it wasn't really an insult, more a simple observation.

Jelly was just the latest in a long line of prefixes that had been added to 'heads' throughout the Seventies, from the more obvious skinheads and suedeheads, to the more insulting and obscure spanner-, bladder-, div- and nuggetheads. To call someone merely 'a head' was an insult in itself as it referred to

THE TEMPERATURE RISES AND THE BOMB DROPS

the recipient's mental health, as in 'headcase' or 'head-banger'. A motley collection of such 'heads' met on a sultry June evening to celebrate one of their own's imminent wedding and, more importantly, indulge in several hours of drinking, singing, fighting and sundry misdemeanours. In other words, a good old-fashioned English stag night.

Andy Pridholm, one of Iggy and Hampshire's old muckers from Lockleaze, was marrying Diane, an attractive enough sort whose features were substantially enhanced by the fact that her mother owned the Star and Garter pub in St Pauls. The evening had started well enough with Grant 'don't touch any of our ma's clothes' Davy fascistically chairing several games of 'buzz' and 'fizz buzz', which fuelled our lust for a good night out and a 'crack' if it came our way. It was inevitable that it would. Take 20 or more fit young blokes. Add copious amounts of alcohol, a dash of female company and a generous heap of gloating City fans headed by our old chum Lenny. Let them simmer in a red-hot pub for an hour or two and it doesn't take a Fanny Craddock to turn out the perfect recipe for aggro.

The inevitable eruption happened in Nelson Street, within a few hundred yards of Bristol's Bridewell nick. Lenny and his cohorts had been baiting and berating us relentlessly in the Guildhall and then in the newly opened Wheatsheaf pub situated, appropriately, beside the Magistrate's Courts. The spark came from Egghead, the Chelsea kiddy, who by now had just about been forgiven for his debacle with Greenaway and the rest of the Shed at Ashton a few years earlier.

'Go fuck yourself, you black bastard.' The emphasis was firmly on the last two venomous words that spewed out of Egghead's mouth, aimed firmly in the direction of Lenny Silvester. Ironically, Egghead was standing next to Brenton at the time who, fortunately, either missed or chose to ignore the odious insult.

BOOTED AND SUITED

'What did you fucking say?' said Churchill, one of Lenny's sidekicks, who we had all had run-ins with in the past. Churchill was a nasty, tasty squat little bastard who, like a lot of City's main boys, had started off following the Rovers years earlier. Now, due to City's change in fortunes, he had nailed his colours firmly to a different mast.

'You fucking heard, Churchill, you turncoat bladder!' Hampshire joined in.

It was about to go off; it was that split second before the ruck starts when your eyes are darting everywhere and your heart is pumping, anticipating who's going to make the first move. Predictably, it was Hampshire. He lunged at Churchill and the two fell to the ground in a mass of swirling arms and thrashing legs.

The rest of us clashed head-on in the centre of the road. I went for Silvester; my months of anger had reached boiling point. I was no match for the heavily built pimp on my own, but luckily I was joined by Iggy and Lil, who didn't need to be asked twice to join in. Brenton went for one of their black kiddies, who earlier had called him a 'Coconut': I feared that his next move was going to be for Egghead.

By sheer numbers we dragged Lenny down to the ground. He was fighting ferociously to get back up, the inevitable boot was going in and the grinning 'Moggy' Moran managed to straddle the flattened Lenny. Moggy's superiority came to an abrupt end, however, as an unknown assailant emerged from the ruckus and jabbed a knife into his side, sending him spinning off of the prostrate Lenny.

All around young men were battling and swearing; passers-by were now joining in and adding to the chaos; bottles smashed and cars beeped their horns, Hampshire and Churchill were continuing their one-on-one tête-à-tête, Moggy was propped up against a parked car – amazingly the

THE TEMPERATURE RISES AND THE BOMB DROPS

grin was still fixed on his face – nursing nothing more than a flesh wound.

The sirens announced the arrival of the law. Everyone, including the leaching Moggy and the pummelled Lenny, acted the innocent. It was impossible for the law to work out who were the instigators and who were the victims; we were all guilty – Rovers, City, black and white. The two mobs faced each other across the narrow street, the law clueless as to the reasons or motives for the scrap. We carried on trading insults and threats, but it was now entirely academic. We had all had our excitement for the evening and reluctantly we dispersed into the night.

We all knew, however, that this wouldn't be the end of the matter. We would all have to watch our backs in the future, this feud was going to run and run throughout that long, hot, sticky summer and beyond. A turf war had begun.

Given the ill-feeling that was brewing among us, the irony of some of the titles in the charts at the time struck home like a knife. Freddie Mercury's Queen were riding high with 'You're My Best Friend', War's 'Why Can't We Be Friends?' and the legendary disco hit 'Young Hearts Run Free' by Candi Staton signalled the start of the rollerdisco craze. I guess the records suited the climate and the times for the rest of the world, but somehow the message of friendship and togetherness was lost on me.

If ever there was a year that could be judged as a landmark time for music, then surely 1976 was it. The all-encompassing tag of 'disco' was becoming a misnomer. What made a disco record spectacularly good or, conversely, embarrassingly awful? How could Isaac Hayes's first hit since 'Shaft', the 100-mph 'Disco Connection', be classed alongside Tina Charles's 'I Love to Love'? Was The Bee Gees' hit of the summer, 'You Should Be Dancing', really in the same category as 'I Need It'

BOOTED AND SUITED

or 'Real Mutha For You' by Johnny 'Guitar' Watson or 'I'll Be Good To You' by Brothers Johnson? Dance music was becoming a victim of its own success; it wouldn't be long before every Tom, Dick and Leo Sayer were making disco records and giving dance a bad name. Disco died for me in 1976 with the likes of Tina Charles's 'Dance Little Lady, Dance' and Abba's 'Dancing Queen', although, according to the record books at any rate, it would take another year before disco was even born, in the form of Robert Stigwood's *Saturday Night Fever*.

The issue of what constituted good and bad records, or indeed whether they were even funk or disco, suddenly became irrelevant when two albums of immense quality and breathtaking musical artistry for all us funkateers hit our shores. These albums were to challenge Donald Byrd's 'Change' as the finest examples of Seventies funkiness. Brass Construction, with their unimaginatively titled *Brass Construction*, and Parliament, with the awesome *Mothership Connection*, both touched down in Britain in the summer of 1976, although both had been released the previous year in the US. The two albums, which, together with virtually any track by James Brown, must be the most heavily sampled records in recent years, had a huge impact on dance music that is still being felt to this day.

With their cosmopolitan mix of hard funk, big band jazz, Latin salsa and delicate Caribbean upbeats, Brass Construction had a profound effect on the music of the 1970s. They managed to couple dancefloor cool with commercial common sense and masterminded a brand of sophisticated pop funk that, mixed with mainstream jazz and African folk, appealed greatly to the discerning British clubber of that era.

Led by keyboards player and singer Randy Muller, Brass Construction became a leading group in the disco movement of

THE TEMPERATURE RISES AND THE BOMB DROPS

the Seventies. Muller originally formed the band in Brooklyn, New York, as Dynamic Soul, mixing funk, salsa and reggae rhythms with a more orthodox jazz line-up to create a highly danceable sound. Renamed Brass Construction, the nine-piece group was signed by United Artists in 1975. With infectious rhythms and minimal, chanted vocals, the group's first single release, the magnificent 'Movin' grabbed us all by the throats and became a firm favourite with the Guildhall crew; its infectious rhythm topped the R&B charts and even managed a brief stint in the UK national charts. It was followed by 'Changin' and both featured on the seminal album of that summer that bore the band's name.

George Clinton had formed the five-man doo-wop group The Parliaments way back in 1956 although it was not until 1967 that the renamed Parliament had any hit of note, with 'I Wanna Testify'. It was around this time that the group picked up a band for their shows. This was the era of the free-loving, drug-influenced hippy movement of flower power and the resultant band were named 'Funkadelic' by the band's bass player Bill Nelson, a name that suitably reflected the funky, psychedelic times. Funkadelic's music, like that of The Ohio Players, became instantly recognisable, with heavily guitar-oriented solos and instrumental pieces replacing the brassy horns of some of their contemporaries. The sound was greatly influenced by Jimi Hendrix, while still being firmly rooted in the R&B and gospel traditions. Sly Stone's fusion of styles and enlightened lyrics were another big influence, as were The Beatles, with their predilection for innovative studio experimentation. The result was a thick, complex, loud and in-your-face sound that was heavily psychedelic and very rock-oriented, with a heavier basis in blues than anything else.

If Sly and the Family Stone were the Beatles of funk, then Funkadelic were the Rolling Stones, a chaotic, rebellious

BOOTED AND SUITED

travelling riot of sound with deep and disciplined roots. The overall vision was undoubtedly George Clinton's, a man who from the very beginning envisaged his own musical empire, with a number of groups under his creative direction. Clinton's charisma, wit and willingness to experiment made the entire P.Funk (Parliament/Funkadelic) collective movement possible.

Parliament were used as the main outlet for the five singers. Plenty of doo-wop and gospel-influenced vocals resulted in some beautiful, if occasionally bizarre, harmonies. Horns were more prominent, with the occasional solo (*Mothership Connection* at times sounds like a jazz album). Keyboards and bass are the dominant instruments, with the guitars being left to drive the riffs.

In 1972 several members of the movement left due to financial disputes and drug-related problems and Clinton decided to move away from the psychedelic sound and lifestyle and tried experimenting with the sound of the group. The result was the introduction of two significant new players, the one-time New JBs brothers, William 'Bootsy' and Phelps 'Catfish' Collins. Bootsy was to become a big player in the history of funk, but he left after the release of their first album under the Funkadelic umbrella, *America Eats Its Young*, only to rejoin later, evolving into a witty, much-imitated, spaced-out, bass-playing superstar.

In 1974, a new era began. Parliament were reactivated and two original JB members, Maceo Parker and Fred Wesley joined the ever-growing funk mob. Fred and Maceo created a new dimension to the group, adding a whole new sound to Parliament and eventually going on to anchor Bootsy's Rubber Band. Fred did most of the horn arrangements on many classic tracks, again bringing the discipline of his background with James Brown that Bootsy and Catfish had also experienced. The fact that both had a great love of jazz also influenced the sound,

THE TEMPERATURE RISES AND THE BOMB DROPS

adding another layer to the blues/funk/rock/soul/gospel stew that was P.Funk.

The opening narrative on the first track of *Mothership Connection*, 'P. Funk (Wants To Get Funked Up)' sets the scene, explaining that the listener is now tuned in to radio station WEFUNK, home of the extraterrestrial brothers, home of the P.Funk, the Bomb. Clinton's character 'Sir Lollipop Man' lays on rap after rap about the miraculous qualities of P.Funk. Clinton goes on to denounce his contemporaries such as the Main Ingredient and the Doobie Brothers as being cool but not being in the same league as P.Funk.

'Give Up The Funk (Tear The Roof Off The Sucker)' became the biggest hit from the album, but in many ways it's probably its weakest track. A pure dance track, it features a clever drum intro with the horns and keyboards swelling into the main body of the song, but unfortunately it tends to get a bit repetitive. The album ends with 'Night Of The Thumpasorous Peoples', a crazed chant song that is once again dominated by the inventive Bootsy Collins. Two other horn masters who featured on the album along with Fred Wesley and Maceo Parker were the Brecker brothers, Michael and Randy, who themselves had had a hit of their own that year with 'Sneakin' Up Behind You'.

Mothership Connection quite simply took all us funkateers' breath away, its divine grooves were in danger of being worn out in the Guildhall by Adryan and Steve, and every track became an instant classic as far as we were concerned. For us it was the most important album of the Seventies, certainly the most groundbreaking since Marvin Gaye's *What's Going On*. It was a culmination of a superb team of musicians, vocalists and conceptualists who were all working at their peak; an avant-garde funk album that broke all the rules and wrote a few of its own; a concept album free from any of the restraints associated

BOOTED AND SUITED

with that genre; a brilliantly fused assortment of funk, jazz, gospel, Motown, science-fiction, sex and drugs. In short, it was the genesis of a freaky universe that sprang full-born from George Clinton's mind, the simultaneous coming-of-age and birth of P.Funk, the Bomb.

26

Dark Days, Darker Deeds and a Savaging by Sheep

As City and their jubilant fans lined up against the aristocrats of Arsenal at hallowed Highbury, Rovers were losing to bland Blackpool at home in the more humble surroundings of Eastville. The old ground was beginning to show its age and the depression that had hung over Rovers fans since City's promotion was reflected in the abysmally low gate. While Paul Cheesley's head was making a mockery of Malcolm Macdonald's 'Supermac' moniker and rocketing City to the top of Division One – albeit for only a week or so – and City took on the likes of Liverpool, Leeds and Manchester United, Rovers were slugging it out against Oldham, Hereford and Orient. None of us even bothered to turn up for the next home game. Instead, we headed to Weymouth for the Bank Holiday weekend in Harvey's classy 1600E, one of Dagenham's finest, to get away from the City fans and for a final curtain-call on that long, hot, summer. The Labour Government, in its infinite wisdom, appointed Dennis Howell as Minister of Drought; we arrived on the South Coast to a torrential downpour that lasted for three days. I vowed to never vote Labour again.

BOOTED AND SUITED

The Vic Bar on the esplanade was our first port-of-call, as it was for many of the thousand or so other Bristolians who habitually visited Weymouth every Bank Holiday. There were lots of familiar faces, both friendly and not so friendly. As I downed my first pint of the weekend, Rog Mitchum and his Kingswood mates nodded their greetings to us across the crowded bar.

'Right, Rog, how's things?' I asked.

'Could be better, how many boys you got?' queried Rog. I knew something was brewing, even without their figurehead, Rich Nunn, who was now halfway through his six months' stay in Usk Detention Centre for the incident with the Southampton fans, the Kingswood lads were still a formidable crew and rarely shied away from a bundle.

'Hamps, The Captain and Harvey. Brenton and the others will be here later, why?'

'Good, there's a load of City lads in the disco in the back bar. Have 'em or what?'

'Fuck's sake, Rog, only just got 'ere. What's the hurry, we came down 'ere to get away from them wankers.'

Rog was keen to prove that even without their main man they were still capable of performing.

'Look, if we hit them now they won't bother us for the rest of the weekend, right?'

He had a point.

'Maybe. Who is it anyway, know any of 'em?' I was still wary of Silvester and his knife-wielding crew.

'No, none of the usual lot. Some big kiddies though, been singing ever since we got in 'ere. Go take a look.'

'C'mon, Hamps, back bar now, full of City, let's take a dekko.'

'Yeah, alright.' Hamps was never worried. Just point him in the right direction, say 'City fans', and he was off quicker than shit off a shovel.

We entered the large room. Steam was rising off of the

DARK DAYS, DARKER DEEDS AND A SAVAGING BY SHEEP

assembled sodden bodies, the dancefloor was packed with a right assortment of characters: young fleshy tarts enjoying the last few days of their holidays, determined to score with the long-haired locals sporting painfully large flares and even more painful faces. There was even a sprinkling of jellyheads dressed in box jackets and straight-legged jeans with three inch turn-ups, their heavy fringes swaying in unison as they nodded their heads to Wild Cherry's 'Play That Funky Music'. Harvey, who was decked out in his best 'kit kiddy' gear including an ice-blue zipped-up box jacket, couldn't wait to get his plastic sandals on the dancefloor. Hampshire and I had other ideas though.

You couldn't miss them. Up at the bar a mob of about 20 arrogant, ignorant City boys, bawling at the tops of their shifty voices.

'Hi-ho, hi-ho we are the City boys! Hi-ho, hi-ho…!'

We didn't recognise any of them. They were big enough lads, but you could just tell they weren't up to much. The way they looked, dressed, behaved, there were no tell-tale signs of them being 'kiddies'; you just get to recognise the look of kids who are up for it, and these definitely weren't. They continued with their battle song…

'…and if you are a Rovers fan, surrender or you die, we will follow the City!'

'We'll sort them out no sweat,' said Hamps. 'Let's go back an' finish our pints, we'll 'ave 'em later.'

'C'mon, Harvey, let's go back with the others. Harvey? Harvey?'

It was too late. Harvey was nodding furiously like a toy dog in the back of a car, his plastic sandals shuffling from side to side to the record that had taken us all by surprise that late summer, the surprisingly good 'Jaws' by the soundtrack legend Lalo Schifrin. Harvey was lost in a wave of funk with his heavy-fringed soul-mates. I felt like joining in, but a glance from Hamps and rolled-eyes skywards told me not to.

BOOTED AND SUITED

'Fucking ponce,' said Hamps, ''bout time they played some Slade, innit.' There was no educating some people.

'Well, what do you reckon?' asked Russ Furnell, one of Roger's fresh-faced sidekicks from Kingswood. Like the rest of them, he was younger than us and more eager to prove himself.

'Yeah, fucking cracking record, must get it some time,' I replied.

'Nah, not the fucking music, you twat, the City kiddies!' said Russ, taking a serious liberty with me.

'Oh them. Nothing to worry about it. Let's have a few more pints and wait for the others.'

The others duly arrived – Brenton, Egghead, Gary Abbot and Steve 'Big Baz' Perrin, a docker from Lawrence Weston who was an old mate of Pete Kimble. We could still hear the wankers singing every time there was a lull in the music. The City hadn't been in the First Division five minutes and you would have thought they were in fucking Europe; time to teach them a lesson.

We headed for the back bar en masse, the older kiddies at the front with Rog, Russ and John Roberts, the younger brother of my old mate Alan and the rest of their eager crew impatiently bringing up the rear. A nice match of experience and fiery apprentices, we steamed through the double doors with only one thing on our mind. The two ineffective bouncers made their excuses and left as we steamrollered through the crowd and headed for our prey. Their singing came to an abrupt halt as a glass smashed against the wall above them; the fleshy tarts screamed in terror as their newly acquired boyfriends ushered them to safety.

'We are the famous, the famous Tote End!' Our entry was proclaimed like that of a prize fighter entering the ring. Our assault met with little resistance and our fists met with only slack-jawed opposition; our young accomplices were thriving on

DARK DAYS, DARKER DEEDS AND A SAVAGING BY SHEEP

it, delighted to be associated with their older mentors. The victims were not in Silvester's league and it turned into a rout. The attack was over as quickly as it began, as the bouncers returned with reinforcements to quell the disturbance. We had already done enough – the parquet dancefloor was awash with blood, spilled alcohol and broken glass, all-too-familiar signs of all-too-familiar violence. We left the bar as rapidly as we had entered it, our task complete. Rog Mitchum sustained the only injury of note, a swollen and bloodied nose courtesy of a well-aimed bottle.

As we exited the bar, sirens announced the arrival of the law. We mingled with the bedraggled holidaymakers and their whinging kids and departed into the miserable Bank Holiday crowd feeling both victorious and vindicated. Our weekend was off to a good start, despite the weather.

We eventually found a comfortable B&B for a bargain £5 a night, run by Mrs Hunt, a timid, mousy woman who proudly announced we were to be the first guests in her newly decorated best room. No sooner had my drunken, throbbing head touched the pillow later that night than the double bed started rocking and moving uncontrollably. I knew I had had a lot to drink but this was way past the familiar spinning-room experience. I fumbled around and switched on the bedside lamp, which was now lying askew on the shag pile. Hampshire was standing at the foot of the bed with the bottom end of it raised aloft, doing his best Keith Moon impersonation.

'C'mon, you fucking bassars!' he was rooted there, stark bollock naked, off his trolley and grinning, a sure sign of trouble.

'Leave it out, Hamps, I'm trying to get some fucking kip!'

'C'mon, wankers! Want some?'

Hampshire was living out his fantasy of being a wild rock star again, only for some swanky Beverly Hills hotel, read the Sea View guest house, Weymouth. I took up his challenge and in the dim light grabbed the nearest item of furniture, a solidly built bedside chair, which I proceeded to bring down on his mentally deranged head.

The light came on and froze the moment in time.

'Boys, boys, boys! What's going on? Stop it at once!'

It was Mrs Hunt, curlers, dressing gown and all, looking horrified at the sight of two naked adolescents trying their utmost to kill each other.

'It was him,' we both muttered sheepishly, our little riot at an abrupt end. The Captain and Harvey had slept through it all. The next night we slept, rather uncomfortably, in a railway carriage on a siding in Weymouth station.

One hundred or so miles away from sodden Weymouth, London's Notting Hill annual street carnival turned into a full-scale riot that year when the law moved in to stop the event after a spate of muggings and street crimes had put a bigger dampener on the event than the rain. With uncompromising dub reggae blasting from the mobile sound systems as an appropriately apocalyptic backdrop, the black kids attacked the unprepared and belligerent law with rocks, bricks and bottles. Ultimately, the law backed down and beat a hasty retreat. The black kids won the day; relations between British white authority – 'Babylon' – and, more specifically, between the police and Britain's Afro-Caribbean community would take a long time to recover. If indeed it ever has.

On a damp evening in the autumn of 1976 we faced the geezers from Chelsea, who had been relegated the previous season. As I no longer had any allegiance or commitment to what was at one time my 'other' team, I looked forward with relish to the clash at Eastville with the cocky Cockneys. Predictably they approached the game with the same enthusiasm as us and, taking advantage of the fact that both

DARK DAYS, DARKER DEEDS AND A SAVAGING BY SHEEP

sets of supporters sported the same colours (scarves were still worn by the majority of fans, though they were often kept out of sight), they infiltrated the Tote End an hour before kick-off. Two hundred or so tasty geezers set up camp, smack bang in the middle of our territory. The Cockney geezers had taken a severe liberty.

Not only had they taken the Tote, they had also smashed up the White Swan. This was serious business. They had done our pub and taken our end. We were squeezed in at the front of our own terrace, evicted from our own patch by a mob who didn't look like they wanted to move on. There was no singing from them, no shouting, no banter, nothing. They just stood there, eyeballing us with arms folded and arrogant smirks, the sort of smirk that Cockneys had made their own over the years, inviting us to have a pop. They didn't need to announce who they were, they stood out like a collective group of bulldog's bollocks. It was 7.15, a quarter of an hour before kick-off. Unbelievably not one punch had been thrown in anger. But that was all about to change. As we debated and discussed our tactics, assessed our numbers and looked for a weak spot in their defence, a breakthrough landed literally in our lap.

''Scuse me, mate, let's get through.'

The unmistakable, grating Cockney twang cut through the damp night air like a knife. God knows where he was from – anything east of Swindon was Cockney to most Bristolians, and Bristolian this geezer definitely wasn't. As if the accent wasn't enough, the small rampant lion lapel badge affixed to his tidy leather bomber jacket confirmed my suspicion.

I didn't bother to answer him. I simply swung my fist as best as I could in the cramped surroundings and landed a weak punch on the side of his head. He retaliated with a better-weighted blow that caught me out and the two of us grabbed each other and danced around in a flurry of blows. The spark had ignited the fuse; it kicked off all around. I was in severe danger of getting a pasting. I felt an arm around my neck that tightened like a vice; a clenched fist then started pummelling my face. Fuck it, he must have a few mates. I managed to break free and blindly swung a punch at my new assailant who, to my horror, turned out to be Hampshire.

'Wha-the-fu... sorry, Browner!'

It was total chaos and confusion all around as the Tote now retaliated against the uninvited guests and tried its utmost to rid itself of the squatters. We succeeded, but only with the help of the law, who had arrived in numbers with dogs and drawn truncheons. It was like the old days, the old end hadn't seen action like this on its decrepit terraces for a number of years. For some of the younger Tote Enders, it was the first time they had experienced terrace fighting on their own turf. We had recovered our pride, but only just. To rub salt in the wounds, the following night's *Evening Post* reported our plight with journalistic glee:

Tote End pride will take longer to repair than the damage to Eastville's dressing rooms following a coup by Chelsea fans last night. It will take the proud Tote Enders a long time to live down the fact that their territory was taken over by three coachloads of Chelsea fans. The Chelsea fans were eventually rounded up by stewards and police for their own protection and escorted to the Muller Road terrace. It was while they were being escorted that they smashed £40 worth of windows at the back of the South Stand. 'The lads who came by coach had the specific intention of taking over the Tote End,' said Peter Terry the Rovers secretary. 'The Chelsea lads took up position under the Tote End some time before the game. As the crowd grew so they became more and more outnumbered and we realised there could be a lot of trouble if we didn't get them out, we virtually rounded them up like sheep, the only problems were that they were not quite so docile!'

DARK DAYS, DARKER DEEDS AND A SAVAGING BY SHEEP

If we had been taught a bit of a lesson by the Cockney geezers at least it was by a firm with a decent reputation. City's East End, on the other hand, were getting a slapping of their own by the not-so-notorious hard men of Ipswich. In their quest for action the Ipswich lads had arrived in Bristol a full seven hours before kick-off. They clashed with City in the streets of Bedminster, leading to 17 eventual arrests, the majority of whom were from sleepy Suffolk. City's gloating fans had been given a sharp lesson that life in the First Division was not going to be a bed of roses.

27
Doing Something Outrageous

Bristol football fans weren't the only ones who were feeling hard done by. Life in Britain during the tail end of 1976 was no picnic for many of Britain's disillusioned youths either. The economy was in a state of collapse, inflation was going through the roof, unemployment was rocketing and incidents of racial conflict were on the rise. In response to the troubled times, and as a two-fingered rejection of the mega-rich rock dinosaurs such as Pink Floyd and The Eagles who were dominating the album charts, and the insipid disco dross that was engulfing the singles charts, Malcolm McLaren, co-owner with Vivienne Westwood, of the King's Road fetish clothes shop 'Sex', had organised a music festival for Britain's desperate and forgotten youth at Oxford Street's 100 Club. The festival featured groups with limited musical ability, bizarre, often offensive names and an even more bizarre and offensive dress sense.

The riot at the Notting Hill carnival during the August Bank Holiday was particularly influential on this emerging group of oppressed youngsters who had been dubbed 'punks'. The new

DOING SOMETHING OUTRAGEOUS

movement's combination of music and politics represented a whole new sphere of youth culture. While punk itself was often identified with political apathy, black youth had shown that politics and music could be explicitly combined. Later that year, blacks and punks united in a group called 'Rock Against Racism', a movement based on the principle of furthering political goals through music.

West Indian musical subculture had influenced white working-class youth since the mods first latched on to Prince Buster's 'Blue Beat'. But this new youth movement was about far more than donning a pork-pie hat in homage to your hero. This was about mixing with the young black community and adopting their beliefs and values – uncompromising rebelliousness and subversiveness. More importantly, black youth had already combined politics and music in a way that rock'n'roll had never done, demonstrating that the ideology of punk could extend beyond fashion and shock tactics.

Whether the music was a product of disillusioned youth, or whether the behaviour of the youths was prompted by the music remains a grey area. Either way, punk rock had reared its ugly head. It came into the world kicking and screaming and spewing forth profanities. It was born of desperation and disenchantment from the mean streets of inner London by way of New York, or so we were led to believe. Or was it cleverly nurtured and cultivated by the manipulative brain of Mr McLaren for the sole purpose of selling more clothes in his Chelsea store? Whatever the reason, punk rock, with its bondage trousers and ripped T-shirts featuring anarchistic messages had arrived, and this newborn pug-ugly, Mongoloid offspring of somewhat dubious parentage was not going to go away.

'Is she really going out with him?' was hardly a sentence suggesting rebellion and anarchy, but those seven softly spoken words from The Damned's Dave Vanian heralded the dawning of the new movement. The landmark 'New Rose' is generally accepted as the first ever British punk single and was released in October 1976 on the Stiff record label, whose legendary strapline was the unforgettable 'if it ain't Stiff it ain't worth a fuck'. Music, and for that matter the Establishment, was totally unprepared for the revolution that was about to begin.

As to who first labelled this cult with no name 'punk rock', and just who laid claim to being the first punk rock band, remains open to question. Certainly many American artistes, most notably Television, The Modern Lovers, Lou Reed, Iggy Pop, the Patti Smith Band and Richard Hell and the Voidoids, paved the way with their unpretentious, high-decibel outbursts and eccentric stage presence, while The Ramones could lay claim to the first record with punk rock in the title – the incredibly commercial 'Sheena Is A Punk Rocker'. Unquestionably The New York Dolls (managed by Malcolm McLaren in the twilight of their career) with their glam rock/androgynous Ziggy Stardust look and shambolic stage presence, had more influence on the British punk movement than most die-hard Anglo punks would give them credit for.

If the American influence contributed the bizarre behaviour of Iggy Pop, Britain's offerings to this musical melting pot were the more musically literate 'pub rock' bands in the mode of Ian Dury's Kilburn and the High Roads, Wilko Johnson's Dr Feelgood and the veritable rocker Nick Lowe. All contributed to the emerging British scene that by the tail end of 1976 had already seen bands such as The Buzzcocks, Eddie and the Hot Rods and The Clash making their stage debuts. Steve Jones was another 'pub-rocking' guitarist. Jones struck up a friendship with drummer Paul Cook and in 1974, together with a couple of other mates, formed a band known as The Swankers. McLaren took Jones, who was a regular visitor to his Sex shop, and the rest of the fledgling band under his wing and changed their name first to The Strand, and then to the more provocative Sex Pistols.

DOING SOMETHING OUTRAGEOUS

McLaren was eager to advance his theory that a band could appeal to the record-buying public purely because of their crudeness and utter musical ineptitude, a theory that he had already tried out Stateside with The New York Dolls, though with limited success. Glen Matlock, a journeyman bass player, who had previously worked in the shop, was recruited to play alongside the band's rather out-of-depth singer Wally Nightingale. The latter was shortly to leave the band to be replaced by someone who gave more credibility to McLaren's outlandish theory than even the ever-optimistic Malcolm could have envisaged.

The story goes that John Lydon, resplendent in verdant-green hair and even greener teeth, wandered into McLaren's boutique wearing a Pink Floyd T-shirt with the words 'I HATE' scrawled above the logo in biro. After a brief audition involving Lydon singing along to Alice Cooper's 'Eighteen' on Sex's jukebox, McLaren signed him on the spot, renaming him 'Johnny Rotten' after a comment by Jones ('You're rotten, you are'). The Sex Pistols and Malcolm McLaren were on their way. The Pistols, with their apolitical views and a genuine contempt, even hatred, of other bands, became the most talked-about band of the Seventies.

The group played their first real gig on 6 November 1975, at St Martin's College of Art, Charing Cross Road, as support band for the rock'n'roll outfit Bazooka Joe, one member of which was a young Stuart Goddard, aka Adam Ant. It was hardly an auspicious start, with the members of Bazooka Joe literally pulling the plug on the Pistols, who had the audacity to 'borrow' the headliners' equipment. After a succession of appearances at other home-county art colleges, the reputation of the band was starting to precede them and by the time they played Ravensbourne College of Art, Chislehurst in early December, the Pistols found themselves with an adoring band of young followers known as the Bromley Contingent. The fans were as colourful and unpredictable as the band and included among others the stunning Siouxsie Sioux and a young, sneering Elvis-clone, William 'Billy Idol' Broad.

Further, increasingly chaotic live appearances followed. In March 1976, the Pistols appeared at the famed Marquee Club, supporting Eddie and the Hot Rods, where Lydon threw both a fit and numerous chairs, resulting in the Pistols being banned from the legendary venue. The Nashville in West Kensington, where the blood flowed as frequently as the beer, became a regular slot for them, but it was the punk festival organised by McLaren at the 100 Club in September that saw the Pistols garner the first of many screaming tabloid headlines. On the second night of the festival a young female fan was blinded in one eye after a bottle was smashed near her face. The culprit was one John Beverley, who, at the time, apart from being a great friend of Johnny Rotten, had no connection with the band whatsoever. Nevertheless, the Pistols, who had appeared on stage the previous evening, but were in fact over 150 miles away in Cardiff when the incident occurred, were blamed. The adverse publicity, however, had little effect on the record labels, who were now firmly convinced that punk rock was about to become the 'next big thing'. Within a month, the Pistols had signed for Britain's biggest record label, EMI.

The turning point for the band's career was undoubtedly their infamous and chaotic appearance on the Thames TV programme *Today*, fronted by the odious Bill Grundy. The Pistols, together with Siouxsie Sioux, who had now formed her own band, called The Banshees, had been playing to the cameras all evening and there had already been odd mutterings of 'shit' and 'wanker'. Then, in reply to Grundy's request for the band to 'say something outrageous' at the end of the interview, the intoxicated Steve Jones offered 'you dirty fucker'. This was a deliberate jibe at Grundy, who had made sexual innuendoes to Siouxsie earlier in

DOING SOMETHING OUTRAGEOUS

the interview. The comment was hardly worthy of Oscar Wilde, but it endeared the Pistols to white working-class kids who saw the band's behaviour as the perfect escape from the mundanity of everyday life. The Pistols simultaneously delighted the teenagers and outraged their parents, a sure-fire winning combination, and with the tabloid press the next day screaming such headlines as PUNK FILTH (*Daily Express*) and THE FILTH AND THE FURY (*Daily Mirror*) the Pistols became anti-heroes and rock icons the likes of which Britain had not seen since the Sixties. McLaren's script was being followed to the letter. Bill Grundy disappeared into TV obscurity but his contribution to the British music scene of the Seventies, albeit unintentional, should not be underestimated.

Despite, or maybe because of the Pistols' appearance on Bill Grundy's show, their first and only single on the EMI label, the gloriously irreverent anthem 'Anarchy in The UK' with its opening lines 'I am an anti-christ! I am an anar-chist!', entered the British charts on 11 December, just a week or so after the notorious programme. It may not have been the first punk rock record to be released but it was certainly the most momentous.

The final piece in McLaren's jigsaw fell into place when Glen Matlock left to form The Rich Kids in early 1977 to be replaced with the bottle-throwing John Beverley, aka Sid Vicious. Sid had been a friend of Lydon's for years and like Matlock before him had worked in McLaren's shop. Undoubtedly Sid was the least talented of the band, but if his musical ability was in doubt his street credentials were beyond question. His CV carried a list of assaults and felonies that compared favourably with even the meanest Tote Ender. No sooner had Sid joined the band than Rotten was arrested for possessing amphetamine. This was the final straw for EMI, whose factory workers had even refused to handle and package 'Anarchy In The UK'. The company promptly dumped the group because of their outrageous behaviour and the adverse publicity they had attracted to the label which, until then, had boasted Freddie Mercury's Queen as their most outrageous act.

A&M were the next label to chance their arm with the unpredictable Pistols, but just a week after signing a £75,000 non-returnable advance outside the gates of Buckingham Palace (McLaren always had a keen eye for a publicity opportunity) they too parted company. The Pistols then agreed their third record deal in six months when they signed to entrepreneurial ex-hippy Richard Branson's newly formed Virgin Records. Branson rashly agreed to McLaren's idea of a boat trip down the Thames past the Houses of Parliament to promote his fledgling band and their new, genuinely outrageous single 'God Save The Queen'. The trip aboard the ironically titled *Queen Elizabeth* ended in predictable chaos when a mass brawl broke out during 'Anarchy in The UK'. As the 200-odd passengers disembarked, the police waded in with truncheons drawn, reminiscent of scenes on the Saturday football terraces, and promptly arrested ten members of the party, including Malcolm McLaren and Vivienne Westwood. 'God Save The Queen' was already at number 5 in the charts at the time of the boat trip and despite a nationwide airplay ban (John Peel was the only Radio One DJ to play the record), it went unofficially to number 1, according to the *NME* and *Melody Maker* charts. However, it was officially kept off the top slot by Rod Stewart's 'I Don't Want To Talk About It'. After all, they couldn't have the Pistols at number 1 with that song during Jubilee week, now, could they?

Curiously, for all the subversive 'destroy' and 'exploited' rhetoric of the punks, the one message they promoted was that you didn't have to comply or be a genius to succeed. Indeed, although 'ambition' was hardly a word you would associate with punks, their ideology of 'do anything you wanna do' spawned numerous successes from the do-it-yourself generation. Instead of being told what they had to wear or what they could or could

DOING SOMETHING OUTRAGEOUS

not get musically excited about, anyone with any balls or sense of independence could make it happen by forming a band, creating a fanzine or even starting their own record label.

By the end of the 1970s, Margaret Thatcher had become Britain's first woman prime minister; her ideology likewise supported free enterprise and saw the rise of the entrepreneur. She didn't realise it at the time but Thatcher had more in common with Johnny Rotten than she thought. As well as their do-it-yourself philosophy, neither of them could sing, both of them ranted and shouted obscene statements at adoring, mesmerised audiences and, to top it all, they both had appalling teeth.

I would be lying if I said I was a convert to the new rebel cause. I had no desire to wear ripped, soiled T-shirts held together with safety pins and, like most white, British working-class kids, I had always taken a pride in my appearance. My hooliganism was a natural extension of the great strength of the British people, heroism in the face of adversity. It was lads just like me and my mates who had fought at Agincourt, Waterloo and the Somme and my allegiance and my pride was in myself, my football club and my country. Punks, whether rightly or wrongly, were being portrayed in the tabloid press as unpatriotic, workshy degenerates, due in the main to their outrageous irreverence to the Royal Family and their inclination towards extreme ideology and anarchy. I didn't want any part of it.

Sid Vicious's penchant for wearing the Nazi swastika and The Clash's prophetic masterpiece 'White Riot' even had the paranoid press convinced that most punks were in fact Hitler-worshipping fascists. In fact, members of the Pistols and other punk bands were attacked on numerous occasions by various outraged groups from both ends of the political spectrum. The extreme far-right, in the form of the racist National Front and the British Movement, were offended by the punks' abuse of the Union Jack and by their anti-royalist lyrics, while the extreme left-wing Anti-Nazi League were convinced that punks were supporters of the NF due to their Union Jack T-shirts (even though they were usually ripped or bore the legend 'Anarchy') and Nazi regalia. The fact that many punks also flirted with Communist symbolism seemed to be an irrelevance that could be conveniently overlooked. The riotous, anti-social behaviour and almost weekly clashes between the punks and the born-again rockabilly teds on London's Kings Road throughout 1977 at last gave the tabloids an alternative to the terrace terrors, who by now were becoming yesterday's news. More fuel was added to the flames that were beginning to engulf Britain. If 1976 was the year of change, 1977 was the year of chaos, for UK fashion, music and politics.

It would be a while before I danced the pogo, spat a globule of phlegm in appreciation or even embraced the punk ethos. I shared my old man's sardonic view of it all: he raised his eyes skywards after reading yet another shock horror exposé about punks in the *Daily Mirror* and uttered the immortal line, 'I'll tell you now, son, if you come home with a bloody safety pin through your nose, I'll give you a clip round the bloody ear…'

28
Do Anything You Wanna Do

My teenage apprenticeship years were now behind me and, like the rest of my mates, I had grown more cocksure and arrogant as the Seventies progressed. Alcohol was vying with Hampshire as my best mate and Karen was now a dim and distant bad memory. Brief liaisons and furtive encounters with the opposite sex suited my lifestyle and, as Hampshire put it, sex was all right but it would never beat the real thing.

I could also take or leave the Rovers. It wasn't as if I had run off with another mistress but by 1977 our relationship had hit a low spot. The deadly duo of 'Smash and Grab' were no longer; Bruce Bannister had been transferred to Plymouth Argyle the previous December and his sidekick Alan Warboys had left for Fulham in February. My jig with Sir Alan on the pitch at Brighton was like my relationship with Karen – an event that, given time, I would forget. Warboys's last goal for Rovers came in the home game against our old friends from across the bridge, Cardiff City, on 15 January, and was a game not remembered so much for the quality of football as for the vicious fighting before the game. The murderous volley of bricks and debris that a group of

BOOTED AND SUITED

Cardiff fans threw at the Tote End from outside the ground resulted in numerous injuries, including a severe head wound to a young girl.

Somehow the spark between myself and Rovers was no longer there. We had become bored with each other's company and even though I still made the effort to visit every fortnight or so, it was becoming an obligatory duty, like going to your gran's, rather than the adrenalin-filled buzz that it had been in previous years. Eastville was becoming grubbier by the week. The once-elegant old lady was now turning into an old scrubber and we were all in the grip of deep depression brought on by City's continuing progress in the First Division. What's more, the rigorously enforced crowd segregation had done nothing to improve the ambience. If it wasn't for the regular bonfires that were started by torching the accumulated rubbish on the terraces the atmosphere on the Tote End would have been flatter than a witch's tit.

Was it any wonder the depressed, exploited white punk rock trash felt at home at Eastville? Before the 1976/77 season came to an end, leather-jacketed, glue-sniffing, shock-haired teenagers were a common sight on the dingy Tote. Just as the kit kiddies were associated with the City slickers across the river, the Tote became a home for the unloved and the dispirited. A sizeable number of punks were disillusioned soul boys anyway. The ubiquitous 'mohair' fluffy jumper as favoured by many punks was a refugee from many a soul boy's wardrobe and bondage trousers owed more than a passing resemblance to the 'Smith' workman jeans complete with loops and buckles as worn by many poseurs in the Guildhall that same year. The footwear, likewise, was a bastardised mix and hangover from every youth culture that Britain had produced, a smattering of plastic sandals as worn by Johnny Rotten, a hefty dose of Fifties brothel creepers and winkle pickers and more pairs of Doc Martens, as worn by their

DO ANYTHING YOU WANNA DO

older brothers on the terraces a few years earlier, than you could shake a tin of Evo-Stik at. Joe Strummer of The Clash even sported a bright-red pair of Onitsuka Tigers as worn by yours truly on that memorable day at Brighton. Punk fashion, like its music, owed more to its past than it would dare to admit.

A stag night reared its ugly head again, this time the groom-to-be was Baz Perrin. If Andy Pridholm's the previous year had been eventful, what with its racial undertones and the stabbing of Moggy, Baz's in March made not only the local, but also the national papers, with the *Sun*'s rather understated headline STAG NIGHT — WHAT A WOW.

The Webbington Town and Country Club was a favoured venue for Bristolian stag nights. It stood in deepest rural Somerset and thus lured the easily impressed and wonderfully obliging girls from the dreary towns of Bridgwater, Taunton and Weston. The evening had started off quietly enough with early drinks in the Long Cross pub in Lawrence Weston for the north-west Bristol contingent before meeting up with the rest of the tribe in Canons on the Centre. Baz was a well-known and respected figure and consequently a 50-strong mob, which included Hamps, Iggy, Mick Warbutton and myself, boarded the coach in high spirits in anticipation of an enjoyable and incident-filled evening. We were not to be disappointed.

It started off as a harmless and somewhat predictable prank — predictable in as much as we had seen Hampshire dancing around with his trousers and pants round his ankles many times before. However, it quickly degenerated from a bad-tempered pushing and shoving contest between out-of-depth bouncers and determined thugs, into a full-scale, ferocious riot that resulted in the aforementioned bouncers having to resort to locking themselves in the women's toilet to avoid a severe beating. Even the use of a fireman's axe on the locked door failed to extricate the terrified bouncers from their sanctuary. Damage, both to property and personnel was severe – glasses, tables, chairs and even beer barrels were thrown through the air, through windows and at people in a ferocious act of hooliganism that bordered on the insane.

By the time we had boarded the coach and started on our journey back to Bristol the law, inevitably, were on their way. A frantic chase through the country lanes that bordered the Webbington eventually saw the coach brought to an abrupt halt and an escort to the police station at Burnham-on-Sea, where long and intense interviews established only that no one had seen or heard anything and that no one had caused any trouble. Admittedly, during the subsequent court appearances it became clear that this wasn't entirely the case, as statement after statement came to light from witnesses who had miraculously remembered the events of the evening. No doubt their memories had been jogged by the threats from the law of manslaughter charges after one of the injured bouncers eventually died, although at his inquest it was proved that his death was not a consequence of his injuries. The collective sigh of relief was heard across the length and breadth of Bristol.

We weren't the only ones making the headlines. Chelsea's fans, who by 1977 had found themselves being tagged as among the worst set of fans in the country, were making the most of their enforced excursion into the Second Division. One game on 12 March at Cardiff, who themselves were up there with the big boys when it came to hooliganism, saw one of the most ferocious battles between two sets of football fans ever to take place on the British mainland. Around 6,000 Chelsea fans travelled to the Principality, nearly half of whom could be described as 'lads'. Their numbers were swelled by a number of Swansea fans who were more than willing to team up with the Cockneys to have a pop at their long-time bitter enemy. The fighting after the game

DO ANYTHING YOU WANNA DO

in particular reached epic proportions, with the Chelsea fans and their allies tearing down iron fencing to battle with the Cardiff lads. Numerous arrests were made, as up to 5,000 fans fought with each other. Remarkably, considering the numbers involved, there were reports of only two stabbings.

The following May, with Chelsea heading back to Division One, their fans were at it again, this time at Wolverhampton. Although there was a ban on Chelsea supporters travelling (due in no small part to the trouble at Cardiff), over 3,000 travelled to Molineux to witness their impending promotion. More than 20 arrests were made before the game, and incidents of hooliganism and violence were reported throughout the Black Country town. At one particular flashpoint, the Molineux Hotel, a mounted policeman and his horse were brought down to the ground by fighting fans. In total 76 fans were arrested and 23 were treated in hospital for stab wounds.

Like our night out at the Webbington, our forays into the city centre pubs were now becoming eventful, to say the least. After a brawl that culminated in a vicious glassing of an ex-City player in the Guildhall Tavern by one of my compatriots and a further glassing of the then current City goalkeeper, Ray Cashley, in Platform One, it was safe to say we were not exactly being welcomed with open arms in those particular establishments. At the time it seemed of little significance but in fact it had a huge impact on my musical tastes. The Guildhall in particular had been a bastion of serious funk music. Without the Ashby brothers' weekly dose of music therapy my tastebuds were in serious danger of degenerating.

As much as commercially driven disco funk was having a major impression on the charts in 1977, with bands such as Heatwave, Trammps and Earth, Wind and Fire, classy funk like T-Connection's 'Do What You Wanna Do', an awesome never-ending, stitch-inducing 12-inch slice of funk, was becoming a rarity. The emergence of gay icon disco stars such as Donna Summer, Andrea True and Cerrone was beginning to turn me away from dance music. I hadn't bought a record since John Handy's cool, laid-back belter 'Hard Work' came out the previous November and with electronic, studio-produced, banalities such as Meco's 'Star Wars Theme' filling the disco dancefloors I wasn't about to rush out and spend my hard-earned 75p on another dance record for some time. It wasn't as if I had given up on funk music or that it had disappeared overnight; it was just that it was harder to come by and I couldn't be bothered to look for it. Funk was going the same way as reggae – the brash, enthusiastic music had given way to the twin evils of commercial disco drivel and obscure, pretentious jazz fusion. Suddenly I could see the appeal of Mr Rotten and his cohorts.

What would seem like a 180-degree turn in my musical tastes came about through our latest excursion to Weymouth during the Queen's Silver Jubilee celebrations in early June. While the jubilant kilted clansmen from north of the border were busy digging up the sacred Wembley turf after their 2–1 win over England, we more refined Englishmen were toasting Her Majesty's health in the appropriate surroundings of the Victoria Bar. Although the tropical heat of the previous summer was not to be repeated, The Stranglers raised the temperature with 'Peaches', a superb and bizarre sexual offering, with obscure references to girls getting out of their cli-tor-is-es and being on the end of skewers.

The Stranglers' little peach was more than matched by the debut offering by a pseudo-mod band from Woking, The Jam. 'In The City' was a magnificent and uncompromising record which was clearly and unashamedly influenced by early Who material from over a decade earlier. It was an intensely likeable number

DO ANYTHING YOU WANNA DO

and was quickly followed up by 'All Around The World', a song that spurned the punk oratory of 'no hope and no future', with a dismissive:

> *What's the point of saying destroy*
> *Want a new life for everyone.*

Like all of The Jam's early offerings, 'All Around The World' featured a throbbing Bruce Foxton bass line that provided a suitable backdrop for Paul Weller's throaty vocals, while Rick Buckler's precise, machine gun-like drumming completed the powerful, cohesive unit. The Jam were a total anomaly to the rest of the punks, their neatly styled haircuts and mohair suits more reminiscent of mid-Sixties Carnaby Street than late-Seventies Kings Road. Whereas Johnny Rotten and his lackeys dismissed their musical predecessors with sneering disdain, The Jam openly acknowledged their influences and inspiration, with The Kinks, The Beatles and Wilson Pickett all receiving credit and surfacing one way or another in future Jam releases. Their critics labelled them revivalists and conservatives, but for me, along with The Clash, Squeeze and Elvis Costello, The Jam penned and performed some of the quintessential British rock classics of all time. It was a shame Weller eventually disappeared up his own arse and instigated the break-up of the band just when they were at the height of their musical inventiveness. As Bruce Foxton bitterly commented in later years, 'There were actually three people in The Jam. And two of them weren't Paul Weller.'

And so, great British rock music, the likes of which hadn't been heard for a considerable number of years, blasted from the jukebox of the Vic Bar to a new, recently recruited audience, the younger members of whom even sported spiky (by way of Vaseline – hair gel was still a long way off), dyed hair and *de rigueur* torn T-shirts. Punk rock had reached the masses. 'Walking on the beaches, looking at the peaches!'; punk rock was alive and well and living in Weymouth.

I had lost count of the number of pints I had drunk or spilled – the front of my Union Jack T-shirt was testament to that fact. I felt and looked a mess. From a lean, fit, sharp-suited smoothie of just five years earlier I had degenerated into a 13-stone, beer-swilling misogynist; my eyesight was failing and my bladder was permanently full. I was too old to be a punk and too young to be part of the Establishment. I drunkenly sneered at Mick Warbutton and Maff Simmonds who, along with their latest punk recruit, Dave 'Haggis' McDunn, were resplendent in the obligatory punk gear of lurid T-shirts and leather jackets, randomly covered in cheap badges proclaiming 'Destroy' and 'Anarchy'. The three of them were perfect examples of no-hope, white, middle-class England. Mick's elder brother Lil, my old oppo and soul mate from the glory days of the Tote, was now living in London. In the following years he would leave these shores for his great adventure around the world. It would ultimately take him back to his birthplace of North America where, tragically, he was to meet an untimely and tragic death through heroin.

'You look a fucking state, Browner,' proclaimed Mick.

'You've got a fucking cheek. Have you looked in the mirror lately, you cheeky bastard? Not to mention the stink; you smell like an anchovy's twat!'

I knew Mick was right. However, I was determined to get my act together, stay out of trouble and save up a few quid. Me and Hamps had been toying with the idea of legging it off to America for a while. By 1977 Britain was a desperate place full of disparate people, governed by a Labour Party that was at loggerheads with its trade union bankrollers and who had used the International Monetary Fund to bail it out as if it was some kind of backstreet pawnbrokers. What's more, too many of our mates were spending too much time in Her Majesty's hotels, and I for one didn't want to join them.

We staggered out of the Vic into the fresh night air, a chaotic jumble of drunken young men. There were about ten of us, our ears ringing from a pummelling by The Jam. Our speech was slurred and incoherent.

'Goin' fer chips?'

'Nah, les's go to a fuckin' club.'

'Bollocks to a fuckin' club, I'm goin' back to kip.'

'S'com'on, coupla a tarts over there. WHOOOA! DARLINGS! SHOW US YER TITS!'

Hampshire had taken up his customary drunken stance, strides around his ankles and cock in hand.

''Ave summa dissun, you old scrubbers!'

'Piss off, hummingbird dick!'

We skulked off, wandering aimlessly, hands deep in pockets, elbows thrust out, enticing passers-by to collide with us and spark off a scrap. Two steps forward, one step back, on the pavement, in the gutter, in the road. Our invitations to have a pop went unanswered despite our pleas of 'Come an' 'ave a go at the Tote End agg-ero!' For neither rhyme nor reason, nor because of any deliberate intention, we ended up on the shore of The Swannery, Weymouth's boating lake, adjacent to the fairground.

'Let's get the boats out!'

We giggled like schoolgirls.

I stayed on the shore with Rich Nunn, who since his release from DC vehemently vowed he would never get in trouble again, and Hampshire, who was still smarting from his mauling by the tarts. Apart from the odd mutterings of 'Fucking hummingbird dick', he was uncharacteristically quiet. He was also terrified of water. The rest of the lads had managed to untie a couple of boats from their moorings and were now trying their utmost to drown each other or knock each other senseless with flailing oars. We heard a car make an abrupt halt behind us. A suntanned little geezer, decked out in a pristine white, short-sleeved shirt and a navy hat complete with braided anchor, forced his way between us.

'I've bloody had enough of you yobbos getting my boats out every week, get back 'ere before I call the law!'

I gathered he was the admiral of the wretched fleet. He stood there, hands on his hips, a tight roll-up in his swarthy mouth. 'I won't tell you a-bloody-gain, get out of my...'

The splash was somewhat muffled as, before hitting the water, he cracked his head on the wooden jetty. The admiral's descent into the murky water was as undignified as it must have been painful, his hat pathetically floated away into the night. Rich was now standing on the very spot that not two seconds earlier the admiral had occupied. His grin was getting wider the further the admiral's hat floated away. It had been a powerful and enthusiastic shove and had only just beaten the ones that myself and Hampshire were about to deliver. So much for Rich staying out of trouble.

'Come on, you lot, get out before the law gets 'ere!'

The others were now making a hasty move for the shore. Our very own captain, Grant Davy, who had gained his nickname 'Captain Bullshit' from his exaggerated tale-telling, even made an heroic, though unsuccessful, attempt at rescuing the mariner's cherished headgear. But it was to no avail. The hat disappeared below the surface, causing even more anguish for the distraught boat owner, who now sat on his backside with the water lapping round his chest, red oozing from an ugly wound on his forehead and tears rolling down his tanned but bloodied cheeks.

It wasn't long before the law caught up with us. We were back on the promenade heading for our guest house and a welcoming bed when we heard it: 'You lot stop there!'

The weary-looking copper emerged from his panda car. Sat in the back with a blanket wrapped around him was the bedraggled admiral.

'Do you lot know where the boats are?' asked Plod.

'What, the ferries?' asked Hamps nonchalantly.

'No, not the ferries, the smaller boats, the...'

'The fishing boats in the harbour?' Hamps carried on with his act.

'No, not the fishing boats, the rowing boats in the...'

'What, not the fishing boats?'

'No, I said not the fishing boats, but the rowing boats in the...'

'What boats then?' The tables were being turned.

'The boats in the Swannery! The rowing boats! Plod was losing his patience.

'Oh, the rowing boats in the Swannery!'

'Yeah, the rowing boats in the fucking Swannery, you know them?'

'No.'

The exasperated copper turned to the admiral.

'Recognise any of 'em?'

The admiral was too dazed and confused to identify anyone. He shook his head. The only physog that had registered with the ancient mariner was our own captain Grant Davy, who luckily had taken another route back to the safety of the guesthouse. Grant was distinctive with his balding head and trimmed black beard. He also wore a 'Starsky'-style chunky cardigan that was as noticeable as it was tasteless.

'All right, fuck off out of it, smartasses.'

'Happy to be of assistance, officer,' Hamps answered with a final flourish. The smile was back on his face again; the tarts' insulting words had long been forgotten.

BOOTED AND SUITED

Whether through curiosity or the bloody-minded desire to prolong someone else's misery and misfortune, we found ourselves back at the Swannery the following afternoon. The admiral was nowhere to be seen, probably back at home nursing his battered pride and his even more battered head. The Sunday lunchtime session in the Black Dog and the Vic had once again whetted our appetite for a maritime adventure, and no sooner had we launched the rowing boats, legally this time, than the first childish splashing began. The splashing soon became a soaking, which quickly became a deluge. The prank had rapidly degenerated into a drunken, full-scale naval battle with oars, seats and various bits of flotsam and jetsam launched between the assorted craft. Hamps, being a non-swimmer, was unamused – in fact, he was terrified – and, when 'Haggis' McDunn succeeded in capsizing his boat and sending Hamps plunging into the murky water, I saw fear on his face for the first time since I had known him.

'Fuck's sake save me, save me, I'm drowning!' screamed Hampshire. The terror in his voice and eyes was genuine.

While everyone else thought Hampshire's predicament was hilarious, Gary Abbott, realising the seriousness of the situation, rowed towards Hamps and thrust out an oar. Hamps grabbed at it desperately, pulled himself to the safety of Gary's boat and pledged his lifelong gratitude to Gary, who shrugged in his quiet, unassuming way. The boating lake now resembled a scene from the Battle of Trafalgar and a sorry bunch of shabby, bedraggled individuals came ashore to face the wrath of son of admiral.

'I don't fucking believe it, last night my old man ends up in hospital, now you fucking lot wreck our boats! That's it, I'm packing it in!' He threw his hat in the water in disgust, no doubt to join his old man's on the bottom of the lake. It had been a bad 24 hours for the boating fraternity of Weymouth. And their hats, for that matter.

DO ANYTHING YOU WANNA DO

We stumbled across a launderette, and way before some red-bracered London ad-man thought up the idea of a poncy male model getting his kit off to the sound of Marvin Gaye's 'Heard It Through The Grapevine', we stripped and dried our gear off in the tumble dryers, which in the case of Larry Bird, included not only his customary Levi's jacket and jeans but also his ancient Doc Martens. As the tumble dryer clanged and rattled under the internal kicking it was receiving from Larry's size tens, we settled down to watch *The Golden Shot* on the portable telly which had thoughtfully been installed by the proprietor to keep his clientele happy. We sat there in our Y-fronts, cosy and warm, watching sexy Annie Aston making a fuck-up with her maths on the telly, not a care in the world, radiating with that dull Sunday afternoon glow that follows from too much alcohol. We all had stupid little grins on our faces; even Hamps had recovered from his near-death experience. My dissatisfaction with life was disappearing fast.

In response to the thoughtful, hand-scrawled 'If any assistance required, please ring bell' message on the wall, Larry's intellectually challenged army mate, Dave Stanton, whom we had only met that afternoon, promptly obliged. Not a quick ring, as a normal, polite citizen who frequented the launderette would give, but a long, harsh, hard ring that only terminated when a disgruntled, tousled-haired manager opened a door at the rear of the launderette. The door had only opened a fraction; it was evident the man was not at all amused about his Sunday afternoon activity being interrupted, and obliging assistance was the last thing on his mind.

'Wass want?' he grunted.
'Gotta light?' asked Dave, holding up his bedraggled fag.
'You fucking what?'
'You 'eard, gotta light?'

BOOTED AND SUITED

'You mean you've made me put me beer down, take me 'and off me bird's tit and miss *The Golden Shot*, just for you to ask for a fucking light?'

'Yeah, fucking right,' answered Dave matter-of-factly.

The door opened a fraction more. He was a big geezer and filled the frame. He glanced at the rest of us, but even in our underpants, or maybe because of our underpants, we were a fearsome sight, and he thought better of it.

'Go fuck yourself,' he said, before slamming the door in Dave's bemused face.

'Charming,' said Dave.

We could hear Disgruntled Bollocks stomp back up the stairs, to his warm beer and even warmer tit. But Dave was not finished. He pressed the bell with venom once more. The stomp returned, louder and quicker; the door burst open. The manager stood there, veins visibly throbbing on his forehead.

'Well, 'ave you got a light or ain't you?' Dave offered up his fag again.

'That's it, get the fuck out of 'ere before I call the law, and take your fucking spawny-bollocked mates with you!' He gave Dave a dismissive shove in the face and turned and stomped back up the stairs, throwing in a final 'fucking Bristolians', before he disappeared.

'Whaa-at? What did I say?' Dave looked at us incredulously as we rolled around the floor laughing like drains. He looked at Larry for some support, but Larry was laughing with the rest of us. We dressed quickly, savouring the delight of warm clothing against our skin. As we left the launderette I heard the sound of a machine start up again. It was rumbling and clanging incessantly. My first thought was that Larry had put his Docs back in for a final warming, but the noise was different this time – louder, more metallic and decidedly angry. I turned and focused on the offending machine. It wasn't a tumble dryer, but

DO ANYTHING YOU WANNA DO

a washing machine. Dave leaned against the machine with a smug grin on his face. Through the glass door of the washer I could see the remains of the telly crashing round as it started its first spin cycle.

'I'll give 'im fucking Bristolians,' smirked Dave.

The onslaught of punk continued to fuck up Radio One's summer. While the ubiquitous Radio One Roadshow, hosted by the likes of the painfully untalented Paul Burnett and Dave Lee Travis, continued to play the latest chart-toppers by Hot Chocolate and Brotherhood of Man in sunny Skegness, the new wave, as it was now usually known, was changing tack and beginning to reveal greater depth. From the sublime and musically subtle US offerings of Jonathan Richman's 'Roadrunner' and Mink de Ville's 'Spanish Stroll', to The Stranglers' threatening 'Something Better Change' and The Adverts' reactionary 'Gary Gilmore's Eyes' (a reference to the double murderer who was executed by firing squad in the US that year), the music was now beginning to appeal to a wider audience than that which punk had attracted. The Sex Pistols, determined not to be outdone by the rash of new releases, had their third hit single of the year with the rough and raw 'Pretty Vacant'. The best the dance scene could offer was Donna Summer's mind-numbingly repetitive 'I Feel Love' and The Floaters' inane 'Float On'. If I needed any further convincing that my love affair with dance music was over, the Rods released 'Do Anything You Wanna Do'. Punk music was not known for its profound lyrics, but this one certainly hit the target...

> Don't need no politician, tell me things I ought to be.
> Neither no optician, tell me what I ought to see.
> No one tells you nothing, even when you know they know.
> They tell you what you should be, they don't like to see you grow.

BOOTED AND SUITED

Forget the spitting and pogoing, forget the bizarre fashion and McLaren's posturing. This record more than any other that eventful year summed up what punk music was all about. Elvis Presley, probably the most successful singer in popular music, who cribbed and plagiarised throughout his entire career and who didn't know the difference between a decent lyric and a double cheeseburger, died from overeating and drug addiction in the same month that the Rods savoured their one and only Top-ten hit.

A considerable number of Rovers fans now counted themselves as punks, and duly found themselves classed as outcasts in the trendier drinking haunts of their own city in the summer of 1977. The great unwashed were as welcome as a turd in a swimming pool at places such as the Assize Courts Tavern and the Wheatsheaf and after a ferocious Friday evening of bloodletting and glass-throwing that left both the optics and the landlord's nerves severely shattered, the licensees banned all punks until further notice. The punks weren't exactly crying in their snakebites – it wasn't as if glitterballs and chrome fittings featured highly in their prerequisites for a good night out. The sad and tired Locarno, now minus the plastic palm trees and renamed The Studio, which had once reverberated to the sounds of Wilson Pickett and Otis Redding, and the grandly titled Bristol Exhibition Centre (a disused warehouse on the now defunct docks) more than adequately catered for the discerning punk. A stage, a decent sound system and a cheap bar enticed them in their hundreds to hear uncomplicated loud rock music played by unskilled but enthusiastic musicians, uncompromising bands performing in uncompromising venues. The two-fingered 'V' was well and truly being shown to Pink Floyd, Fleetwood Mac and the rest of their self-indulgent contemporaries.

I was never a punk – at 21 I felt I was too old and too set in my ways. Nevertheless, I would willingly sport a token safety pin

DO ANYTHING YOU WANNA DO

to show my affiliation with the culture, which I was totally absorbed and fascinated with. I revelled in the young punks' sneering disregard for authority and their attitude of 'doing their own thing'. It was a very British movement and, contrary to popular belief, I could see that punks were the new young patriots, indulging in the very Britishness of punk's mannerisms, clothes and music, the three key ingredients to a credible cult. Punk's origins may have been in New York's CBGB's club in the Bowery or London art colleges and may have ended with professional punks in Trafalgar Square posing for tourists for a tenner or in haute couture Milan fashion houses, but it was honed and shaped in the back streets of Britain. It was the last in a long line of mass teenage cults, from the Teddy Boys of the Fifties who beget the mods and rockers of the Sixties, who in turn beget the skinheads, suedeheads and smoothies of the Seventies. The punks were the last generation of great British rebels.

29

No Fun

The banning of punks from the city-centre bars and clubs effectively forced them into less fashionable pubs in the outlying districts. Landlords of drinking houses in Redland, St Pauls and Barton Hill suddenly found themselves benefiting from the actions of their beleaguered colleagues in the LVA. And with the association between punks and Rovers fans, we found ourselves becoming increasingly outnumbered by City rivals in our traditional watering holes.

Although we were unaware of it at the time, the turn of events were to have far-reaching consequences – the inexorable decline of Rovers fans' dominance on the streets of Bristol was on its way, due in no small part to our taste in music and to a volley of beer glasses thrown at the optics in the Assize Courts Tavern one Friday night. The Yanks have an expression for it: 'Shit happens'.

Eyes bored into us wherever we went. City's mob was swelling by the week as they continued to enjoy life in the First Division. Our previous superiority was under serious threat and it was with great reluctance that we decamped from our established stamping ground of the city centre and started meeting in the Black Horse in Redfield. The choice of the Black Horse did not come about by accident. The landlady, Shelly Collett, was related to Hampshire's mate Jeff Vickery, brother of ex-Tote End boot girl Jill and wife to our own crew's Baz Perrin.

We took to the Black Horse instantly. It was the sort of pub where the first question on a Quiz Night was 'Who you fucking looking at?' It was our home from home, all varnished tongue-and-groove, red-flocked wallpaper and typical Seventies pub mirrors. And Reggie Collett was typical of a Seventies pub landlord. Reggie was a squat, swarthy, tattooed geezer with a street-tough gypsy background, who delighted in telling us of his bare-knuckle fighting days. He was stereotypical of his ilk, shaggy, collar-length hair, droopy moustache and gold medallions; Shelly was a stereotypical landlady, just like Reg but with blonde hair. And without the tattoos and moustache. The Black Horse was a popular pub with Rovers fans and was well known for its cracking jukebox, mainly consisting of classic soul and modern punk, a great combination. It was also well known for an altogether more different reason — the local black community were not welcome.

It wasn't as if this singular fact appealed to any of us in particular. We were all working-class kids from council estates and to a man voted Labour. I was proud of my old man, who had fought Mosley's blackshirts on the streets of Bristol back in the Thirties, ironically not a hundred yards from the Black Horse. But this was the Seventies and things were different, and for me it was decidedly personal. Admittedly, apart from Brenton, who had, fortuitously as it turned out, joined the army in the summer, we weren't exactly bosom buddies with our Afro-Caribbean neighbours from St Pauls. But, even so, none of us was overtly racist. However, events such as the Notting Hill riot in 1976, which had been repeated over the Bank Holiday in 1977, and the spiralling rise in unemployment and street crime in recent years, had had a profound effect on numerous ignorant, white working-class trash who began to query the logic of continued immigration to Britain while the dole queues were still escalating. I was one of those ignorants, although there were also a few personal demons from a couple of years back still drifting through my mind which, try as I might, I could not exorcise.

It did not take long for the ultra-right National Front to discover the Black Horse and, more importantly, its impressionable clientele. Each weekend would bring a rash of leather-jacketed bigots spouting their odious rhetoric to an audience who, unfortunately, were all too willing to listen and believe in the hate-fuelled diatribe. As the evenings wore on and the alcohol and adrenalin combined, the answers to all Britain's ills seemed there for us all to see. The immigrants, the communists, the IRA, the ineffectual Labour government and particularly the NF's very own nemesis, the Anti-Nazi League, were all our enemies, furthermore they were all being orchestrated and manipulated by a world-wide Zionist plot. The only answer was for white youth to unite and fight and join the National Front. Of course, it was all bollocks, but regrettably I, and thousands of other gullible young whites like me, took it all in.

Up and down the country, in pubs not too dissimilar to the Black Horse and hate-filled football grounds not too dissimilar to Eastville Stadium, the NF bullied and cajoled youngsters into joining their odious organisation. The Tote and football in general was awash with the evil of racism. *Bulldog*, the mouthpiece magazine of the Young National Front, was openly sold on the terraces, while badges supporting the NF and the overtly militaristic British Movement were a common sight. The fascists found football grounds a fruitful recruiting ground; the NF sympathised with and even praised the young, white heroes of the terraces, offering them comradeship and encouraging them

NO FUN

to attend antagonistic marches on Sunday afternoons in places as far afield as Lewisham and Bradford. 'There ain't no black in the Union Jack, send the bastards back!' had replaced 'You're gonna get your fuckin' head kicked in!' as the hooligans' favourite chant. Football and I had reached our lowest point.

For the first time in a decade I had not looked forward to the new football season with my usual childlike enthusiasm. Optimism, accelerated by the first skirmishes on a balmy August afternoon at any rate, is something most football fans have in abundance. But as is often the case, once the temperature starts to drop and the autumn rain and mists transform the football stadia of the country into the grey, inhospitable arenas of hate that grounds in the Seventies were, the rose-tinted outlook quickly descends into misery. Ten games on and with only one victory under their belt, Rovers and their long-suffering fans had a long, difficult season to look forward to.

In an attempt to alleviate the gloom, Rovers signed the veteran football nomad Bobby Gould from Wolves. His first game in mid-October against Blackburn Rovers produced an unforgettable hat-trick and culminated in a 4–1 victory. The depressed mass of the Tote End, now devoid of any style or culture but revelling in its own misery, celebrated later that evening by visiting a punk club of legendary seediness, the British Queen in St Pauls, to see an all-girl punk band of equally legendary status, The Slits.

The British Queen, or BQ club as it was more commonly called, was a small, desperately dingy pub off Portland Square run, perversely, when you consider the politics of a sizeable chunk of its clientele, by an affable elderly West Indian named Slim. The latter took great delight in alleviating acne-ridden punks, sporting right-wing regalia, of their hard-earned lucre.

Rovers' punks had taken to visiting the BQ most Saturday lunchtimes before games to hear their very own Roy 'Play Misty

BOOTED AND SUITED

for Me' Savage spin an eclectic mix of music ranging from Lee 'Scratch' Perry's latest dub recordings from the Black Ark studios to the faster-than-a-speeding-bullet 'Shadow' by The Lurkers. The wonderfully romantic 'Shadow' was an endearing three-way punk love story, which in two and a half short minutes told of a boy's undying love for a girl who had unfortunately ditched him for another. Pete Stride's energetic and robust guitar solo led in to Howard Wall's classic line coming from the character of the dumped boyfriend, who threatens to 'shoot that boy in the legs when 'e comes to ring your bell'. Not surprisingly, the record, which was released on the fledgling Beggars Banquet label, never featured on Radio One's playlist. But it will long be remembered as a vintage punk track that did its best to show punk's softer side, admittedly played at 90 miles an hour and at a decibel level that would put Concorde to shame.

If Roy Savage had a softer side, he didn't show it. He did, however, have an uncannily appropriate surname and was born to be a punk. Savage had long lost his Rod Stewart identity, and his predilection for all things *Clockwork Orange* had gone the same way as his tartan scarf and tam-o'-shanter. The 'Play Misty' reference in his pseudonym was due to his fascination with the film of that name in which Clint Eastwood starred as a Californian DJ, and Jessica Walter featured as a crazy, sexually obsessed female stalker. Only Roy knew what connection it had with punk and Seventies Britain. Roy was one weird but very likeable bloke.

The Slits at the time consisted of Ari-Up attempting vocals, Viv Albertine on guitar, Tessa Pollitt on bass and Palmolive on drums, and more than any other punk band they were prime exponents of the principle that rated enthusiasm above talent. In fact, they were to music what Rovers were to the beautiful game. Skill, talent or professionalism were not words that came easy to either. To be honest, neither Rovers nor The Slits could play to

NO FUN

save their lives. Their arrival on stage was greeted with a raucous mix of 'Bobby, Bobby, Bobby Gould', 'Sieg Heil' and, most predictably, 'Get yer tits out!'. It did not bode well.

Almost from the off, trouble started. No sooner had Ari-Up started yelping in her native German accent and the band attempted their reggae-influenced style of punk, than the bottles and glasses started flying. The Neanderthal chant of 'Nash, Nash, Nash-nul Front!' rose from the sweating mass, whose right arms stiffly saluted the steamy air. The Slits, to their credit, carried on regardless, but they were fighting a losing battle. A mass brawl had started in the crowd between the various political factions and the music had become a secondary issue. I was at the back of the crowd observing the unfolding chaos with Hampshire, Roger Mitchum, Rich Nunn and Stuart Clarke. Clarkey was one of Egghead's Chelsea mates who, like him, had shared his allegiance between the Shed and the Tote. I looked at Clarkey, who was carrying a rather self-satisfied smile on his face.

'Bobby Gould has got a lot to answer for,' he said with a smirk. We had instigated the racist chants and were now proudly watching the results of our actions. Two punks from opposite political spectrums were now grappling on stage and the mike stand was wrenched from Ari-Up's hands and flung into the crowd spear-like, with devastating consequences. The Slits could stand no more and Ari-Up lead the retreat to the dressing room with a parting 'You're just a bunch of fascist wankers!' Big bad Bob Doughty grabbed the vacant mike and took the opportunity of spouting his own philosophy to the unruly audience.

'Yeah, um right, National Front, ha! Yeah, Bristol Rovers, er, yeah, Bobby Gould, fucking Rovers, ha ha, cider, yeah, fuck the City!' Words did not come easy to Doughty. Not words with more than two syllables anyway.

Behind Doughty, from the left of the stage, appeared a leather-clad roadie who was determined to rescue the band's precious

BOOTED AND SUITED

equipment from the howling mob. The assembled fascists couldn't believe their luck, for the unfortunate roadie was as black as Newgate's knocker. The rain of glasses, bottles and spittle was immediate and odious shouts of 'Get the nigger' filled the air. The roadie crouched in the corner of the stage, wrapping his arms around his head in a vain attempt to protect himself from the onslaught. It was a cowardly and ugly assault and looked like it was about to get even uglier when a tall, gawky punk jumped on stage and headed menacingly towards the under-siege roadie. He was someone I knew well from the Tote, a wild, unpredictable but frighteningly educated character who, though a fanatical Rovers fan, hailed from the City heartland of Bedminster. Kevin Malloney was the same age as me and had served his apprenticeship with myself and Hampshire. From the early Seventies, he had proved himself to be a wild card and often struggled to control his temper. Kevin's venom was always there, bubbling just below the surface of his sallow skin.

Kevin and I had been involved in a rumble with a group of West Ham fans in a match at Eastville a number of years earlier. It had started as good-natured banter on the steps leading up to the Tote, but had quickly deteriorated into an ugly slanging match. We were heavily outnumbered, but I could see Kevin's rage welling up inside him as each reference to 'Sheep-shagging carrot crunchers' hit home. Kevin exploded and charged up the steps towards the incredulous Cockneys. I followed in the wake of Kevin's rampage and we took down a couple of Hammers before the law moved in and nicked Kevin. Since that day Kevin and I had remained good mates, although there was one thing that cut through our friendship like a knife: Kevin was an extreme socialist and fully paid-up member of the Anti-Nazi League. Naturally, he despised my association with the National Front.

'C'mon, get up!' Kevin yelled at the bloodied roadie, offering his hand in assistance.

NO FUN

'Fuck off, Bristol wanker!' came the ungrateful reply.

'Look, I ain't fucking about, get up before they kill you!' Kevin meant it, the crowd were baying for the roadie's blood.

Kevin grabbed the roadie and manhandled him offstage shielding him from the never-ending hail of missiles, which were now striking his unprotected head. Despite this act of heroism the ugly atmosphere continued. Obscene racist chants filled the smoky air.

'Sieg Heil! Sieg Heil! Sieg Heil!' A hundred right arms thrust into the air, in scenes more reminiscent of Forties Nuremberg than Seventies Britain. It was a disturbing sight that made the hair stand up on the back of my neck; I say that even though, regrettably, I was part of it.

My bladder beckoned me outside. A wall built in Victorian times served as a convenient urinal, the dark stains and foul smell confirming the fact that I was not the first. I stood there holding my breath as firmly as I held my cock, listening to the familiar sounds of disorder emanating from the BQ, casually whistling 'Land Of Hope And Glory' as glass upon glass smashed in tune to Elgar's patriotic offering. Through my drunken whistling I could hear another familiar sound in the distance, faint at first but growing rapidly into the wailing of a police siren. And there was only one place it could be heading. The harsh blue light intermittently lit up the street and tyres squealed on the damp cobbles as the squad car rounded the corner. I dashed back into the BQ, where Roy Savage was trying to restore order. The Clash's 'White Riot' was blaring out. It was not the wisest of song selections.

'Come on, let's leg it, the law's outside!' I shouted above the noise to Hampshire and the others. But it was too late, the coppers were already at the door, truncheons drawn, eagerly awaiting the confrontation and raring to crack a few heads.

As the law moved in we side-stepped them and made for the

BOOTED AND SUITED

toilets, where a battered and graffiti-strewn door led on to the open street. More reinforcements arrived as we casually sauntered across the road to watch the unfolding drama. Half an hour went by before a peace, of sorts, was restored. Each passing minute saw another copper emerge from the BQ with a squealing, snarling youth entrapped in their vice-like grip, which was only released when they were unceremoniously dumped in the waiting meat wagon. An attentive crowd of onlookers had gathered, including Churchill and his City boys. The sound of the sirens had attracted them like flies to the proverbial shit. With so many coppers in attendance there was little likelihood of it going off. Churchill got lippy.

'You an' your punk mates misbehaving again then, Hampshire?'

'Wassit to you, Churchill, you short-arsed cunt? Up for it or what?' Hamps took a step forward.

'Any time, Hampshire, any time – could be sooner than you think', Churchill signed off with a smirk. Something was being planned in his devious little brain. Something we wouldn't have too wait long to find out about.

30
A Day to Remember

It seemed the whole of Britain was in dispute. Thousands of trade unionists fought toe-to-toe with the SPG outside the Grunwick film processing plant for trade union recognition; power workers had once again plunged Britain into darkness; and the firemen refused to put out the raging fires. You didn't fare much better if you were dead – the striking undertakers refused to bury you. But at least you were saved from reading the grim news of the disputes in the papers – Fleet Street was also on strike. As 5 November 1977 dawned, it seemed Guy Fawkes had the right idea. Personally I didn't give a fuck – Saturday meant only one thing and despite Rovers' failings in the league, a visit by a top London crew was always something to look forward to. And today's visit was going to be extra special.

My customary Saturday-morning hangover slowly gave way to the euphoria of knowing this would be an ace day. I stumbled out of bed with a diamond-cutter of a stiffy and shuffled to the wardrobe, incessantly farting and rearranging my balls. Somewhere at the back, gathering dust, were my ancient Monkey boots; it was time for them to get an airing. The rest of

BOOTED AND SUITED

my wardrobe looked decidedly shabby, a proliferation of denim and knitted jerseys. We dressed like the mass majority of youngsters in Britain who, at the latter part of the decade, had long put their brash, colourful past behind them.

There was the odd bowling and baseball shirt as favoured by the jelly heads and I had even succumbed to punk fashion and bought a pair of straight-leg, black needle-cord jeans from Paradise Garage, which, since changing its name from Clobber, now stocked a more diverse range of clothing that attracted a more wide-ranging clientele. But in the main my wardrobe, like that of many of my contemporaries, was awash with faded denim, capped-sleeve T-shirts and polo-neck sweaters. There was not an inch of satin to be found and my velvet jacket had long since found its way to the jumble sale along with my sky-high platform shoes. If you weren't a soul boy or a punk, and the majority of the nation's youth weren't, you were still clinging on to your baggy denim jeans, your grey sweatshirt emblazoned with 'Ohio State University', and your indispensable leather bomber jacket. Discos around the country were awash with that year's colours – dull grey, dull blue and dull brown. Fashion, just like the country, was at a low point. I did have one saving grace, however: a cracking sheepskin coat as favoured by the skinheads at the start of the decade. I had bought it, second-hand, off Stuart Clarke. This was the genuine article, full-length and originally purchased in Petticoat Lane; a real villain's coat. I stood there admiring myself in the mirror, kitted out, booted and ready for action, my blue-and-white quartered BRFC badge nestling alongside a small enamel Union Jack badge in the off-white wool of the lapels, proudly declaring my twin beliefs in club and country.

'Who you looking at?' I queried through gritted teeth at the surly, moustachioed geezer dogging me up. 'Come on then, you Cockney bastard!'

A DAY TO REMEMBER

I motioned with both hands, invitingly twitching them towards myself. It was a scenario I had played out many times over the years, and one not too dissimilar to a scene in *Taxi Driver* involving Robert de Niro's character Travis Bickle.

'Yeah? You fucking want some, do you? Come on, you bladder, have some of this!'

I threw a perfect head-butt at the mirror; my reflection copied me perfectly. I winked admiringly at the arrogant fucker.

It wasn't the first time we had come across today's opponents. In fact, we had clashed several times before and more than held our own. But today was going to be different. The geezers were coming in force, mob-handed and tooled up, and for one of their boys in particular, the barking mad 'Harry the Dog', it was a chance to become a TV star. Every move, every word, every deranged action of this notorious firm was going to be recorded on celluloid for posterity. The BBC current affairs programme *Panorama* was following the boys from South-east London and making a 'hard-hitting documentary' about the scourge of the football terraces – Millwall.

Chelsea, West Ham, Leeds and Manchester United fans – the latter having succeeded in getting their club banned from Europe for causing a riot in St Etienne, France, two months earlier – were among the elite of football hooligans. But right up there at the top of the festering pile was Millwall and any opportunity to have a pop at the top boys was one that most Ends around the country relished.

Rumours had got round about the documentary. In the Black Horse the previous evening's talk was of little else – the football was a secondary issue. A fortnight earlier Rovers had been given a sobering lesson about life in the Second Division by Tottenham at White Hart Lane, a 9–0 defeat featured on *Match Of The Day*. We were lucky to get the nought and Bobby Gould's hat-trick against Blackburn had long been forgotten.

BOOTED AND SUITED

Whether 'F-Troop', 'Half-Way Line', 'The Bushwackers' or 'Treatment' with their bizarre surgical hoods or any of the other assorted 'loonies' and 'nutters' as the documentary quaintly tagged them were following a script or not was open to conjecture. But for some reason, certain members of the aforementioned crews arrived in Bristol suspiciously early. While I was still at home drooling over *Tiswas*' Sally James, praying that her tits would fall out of her denim waistcoat, the boys from Cold Blow Lane were smashing up Stapleton Road and putting Iggy in hospital with a badly slashed arm. They had led a pre-emptive assault on the White Swan as soon as the doors opened.

By the time I reached the Swan, Stapleton Road was swarming with the law. I entered the sorry-looking pub through its side entrance, now bereft of its door which had been kicked off its rusty old hinges.

Hampshire stood at the bar, light split in hand.

'Fucking late, Browner. It's already gone off.'

'That ain't right, what's happened?'

'Bastards got here early. Iggy's in the BRI, stabbed 'im in the arm or summat.'

Hampshire, like the rest of us, had also missed it. Apart from a couple of early morning pissheads, Iggy had been virtually alone. He'd still had his nose in *The Sporting Life* when he got a whack from a couple of kiddies who proceeded to smash a beer glass into his arm; so much for Millwall's reputation as being hard men. A few pints later and Iggy's injuries had taken on life-threatening proportions. The new young lads who were now swelling our ranks listened in awe; by the time we left the pub for the ground, we'd managed to convince ourselves that Iggy was on his death-bed. The alcohol-induced bravado took effect and as we took up our positions on the Tote End, the familiarity with every turnstile, every entrance and every piss-filled corner of that grim terrace filled us with confidence. The Tote End, even

A DAY TO REMEMBER

on the brightest of days at the start of a season, was an unforgiving shithole, but on a grey, murky day in early winter the menace and foreboding hung over it like a dismal, dank fog.

There was little conversation. The odd 'Right, Browner', 'Right, Hamps' and the knowing winks were enough to establish intent and allegiance. Arms were folded across puffed-out chests, hands were thrust deep into coat pockets; some nervously fingering tools that had been surreptitiously smuggled in. The singing and tribal chanting was half-hearted and only instigated by the younger Tote Enders who, though keen, lacked the honed skills of terrace combat, their blue-and-white scarves draped around their young necks or tied around their weak wrists portraying their innocence.

The game kicked off with taunts of 'Millwall, where are you? Millwall, where are you?' echoing around the ground. It was venomously directed at the four hundred or so Lions' fans gathered on the Muller Road End. The North Stand to our left, where a young Dave Ashley and his keen crew were beginning to make a name for themselves, vociferously joined in. We had a good turn out, the best for a number of years – not as big as in the glory days of the early Seventies, but the rumours about the *Panorama* documentary had brought a lot of lads out of retirement. All around I could see kiddies who had not put in many appearances over the last few years. Andy Phelps and the rest of the Tramps had now taken a back seat. Bob Doughty was coming to the fore, not because of his physical presence or stylish prowess like Andy or Dobbsy but more because of his fearsome image. Bob epitomised the Tote End perfectly – part-fascist, part-biker, part-punk and not in the least bit sophisticated.

Harry the Dog, who along with Bobby the Wolf, Mad Pat and Winkle sounded more like star turns from an alternative Camberwick Green, were the top men of F-Troop, the elite and most experienced of all of Millwall's crews. Harry summed up the aspirations and aims of his contemporaries during the documentary and eloquently boasted of how they 'would do a few geezers like, 'cos we're the F-Troop, see what I mean, we love a row, we go a foo'ball'. Not to be outdone, the all-in-black, sunglasses-wearing Bobby the Wolf chipped in with 'an' we won't take it from these northerners like'. Geography, like sartorial elegance, obviously wasn't the Wolf's strong point.

Harry failed in his quest to 'do a few geezers like' as the coach carrying the pride of South London broke down on the M4 and failed to reach Bristol. They arrived late, but were just in time to see Chris the Browner, Mad Hamps and Iggy, now miraculously raised from his death-bed and as eager as a greyhound in a trap, exact revenge on the foolhardy Lions' fans who had dared to venture on to our beloved Tote. The brawl was over in a matter of minutes – the heavily outnumbered Cockneys legged it as a flurry of punches and kicks hit home. We stormed down the terrace and fired in as soon as the interlopers dared to appear.

The fracas was shown in all its gory detail the following week on TV. We watched with glee as the reporter observed that 'without F-Troop the Millwall invaders got short shrift from the home fans [and] the tide of battle turned against Millwall's hooligans.' The weather, the result (Rovers won 2–0) and the performance of Millwall's fans conspired to make a member of Treatment profess that he 'was pissed off and sick as a parrot'. We, on the other hand, were 'over the moon'. Harry the Dog and Bobby the Wolf skulked off back down south with their tails firmly between their legs.

We were buoyed with the result both on and off the pitch and our new-found optimism led us to an overdue incursion into the city centre. There were rumours that the Millwall boys were staying over for the night, and any chance of prolonging their misery seemed too good to turn down. What's more, a top night of musical entertainment lay ahead of us. The Clash, supported

A DAY TO REMEMBER

by those worthy American punk forerunners Richard Hell and the Voidoids, were appearing at the Bristol Exhibition Centre. After the debacle of The Slits gig, an event featuring two bands as musically proficient as these two proved irresistible. The Exhibition Centre was packed to overflowing with hundreds of scruffy, foul-mouthed, leather-jacketed punks, as well as one or two lapsed smoothies, one of whom still found it amazing that his musical tastes had changed so dramatically in the last year. But change they had and I was as eager as the next bloke to see and hear Joe Strummer, Mick Jones, Paul Simonon and Nicky 'Topper' Headon perform their unique, heavily reggae-influenced brand of punk, which owed as much to Delroy Wilson's sweet sounds and King Tubby's dub offerings as it did to the very band who supported them, and who were among the forerunners of the punk movement – something the majority of the audience were blissfully unaware of.

However, thanks to complimentary, if somewhat fawning reviews by the more enlightened rock critics, many punks were to eventually latch on to roots reggae and in particular the *Two Sevens Clash* album by Culture, which somehow contrived to make the album a best-seller in 1977 and to persuade many shock-haired punks to grow dreadlocks and to long for redemption in Ethiopia.

The Clash, who at the time were managed by the charismatic Bernie Rhodes who was every bit as ambitious and ruthless as Malcolm McLaren, had their roots in the pub-rock movement of the mid-Seventies. However, they now found themselves drawn to the emerging dub and roots sounds from Jamaica, due in no small part to Mick Jones. supposedly hailing from Brixton. At times, though, it seemed the band tried just a bit too hard to prove their political awareness and of their sympathy for the underclass, in particular the black community of Britain. Strummer (real name John Graham Mellor) especially came in

BOOTED AND SUITED

for flak. It was felt by some that he came from too privileged a background (he was educated at a public school) to be genuinely angry and revolutionary. To prove his credibility Strummer was rarely seen without his Red Army Faction or Red Brigade (both European terrorist organisations) T-shirts, although their credibility with their devoted fans was never in doubt, due largely to their insistence on producing incredibly inexpensive albums and to keeping admission to their gigs at an affordable price.

The gathered mass was not to be disappointed. Richard Myers, alias Richard Hell, set the scene with a fervent and musically proficient performance that included his band's superb albeit minor hit 'Blank Generation' and the orgasmic, but very short, 'Love Comes in Spurts'.

Joe Strummer, resplendent in compulsory RAF T-shirt and obligatory Anti-Nazi League badge, multi-pocketed US army jungle greens and his (and my) favourite Tiger boots, turned in a magnificent, typically throaty performance and the frenetic, speed-fuelled, pogoing punks responded by vehemently spitting at the band, as was the customary sign of approval. The mixed-up, mashed-up political variants that made up the audience put their differences aside and the fighting, when it came, was not the result of people's football or political allegiances but because of hysterical, youthful exuberance ignited by alcohol, amphetamines and raw, delirious music.

The Clash's cracking double A-sided single 'Complete Control'/'City Of The Dead' was in the charts and their superb debut album, which I had bought the previous week, predictably featured all of the tracks performed that night. The frenzy-inducing 'White Riot' – the crowd's favourite – the prophetic 'London Calling' and Junior Murvin's reggae belter 'Police And Thieves' all combined to make The Clash the best live band of that period and their debut eponymous LP, completed in just

A DAY TO REMEMBER

three weekends, was the best album of that momentous year. The album, which was produced before Nicky Headon joined the band and featured Terry Chimes, or 'Tory Crimes' as the cover gloriously dubbed him, beat off other magnificent debut offerings by other punk luminaries including the Damned's *The Damned*, The Stranglers' *Rattus Norvegicus*, The Jam's *In The City* and even The Sex Pistols' over-hyped but essential *Never Mind The Bollocks, Here's The Sex Pistols*, which despite the retail world's reluctance to display the provocative title, became the first punk album to top the best-sellers charts. The history books for 1977, however, will show that the best-selling albums were by Slim Whitman, Johnny Mathis, Elvis Presley, Cliff Richard, Pink Floyd and, inevitably, Abba and that the top-selling singles were by David Soul, Baccara, Leo Sayer and... Abba. The best-selling single of the year was the abysmal 'Mull Of Kintyre' by Paul McCartney's Wings. Something about statistics and damned lies springs to mind.

The assault on our senses over, we filed out into the cold night air. Our bodies were drenched in sweat and ached from the constant pummelling of the heaving crowd, while our ears still reverberated from the chaotic discord that passed for music. We hardly had time to catch our breath before we became aware of a host of familiar faces lined up in a mass rank across the road. Churchill, true to his word, had turned up with the rest of his boys. What's more, they weren't about to ask for a critical appraisal of that night's musical entertainment. The lines were clearly drawn and the divide was as wide as ever; Rovers and City fans locked horns and clashed not for the first time and definitely not for the last. The majority of the assembled punks were oblivious to the turf war that was raging on the streets of Bristol and watched with a mix of incredulity and indifference as the fighting spilled over from the dockside cobbled street at the back of the Exhibition Centre to the brighter lights of the city centre.

BOOTED AND SUITED

As more and more onlookers entered the fray and more drinkers in the local pubs joined in, the brawl erupted into a full-blown riot. Many of the punks were now embroiled in the fighting and for good measure the Millwall fans, who had stayed in Bristol after the game, pitched in to add to the chaos. The pavement outside the Hippodrome was a mass of fighting, snarling youths. That initial skirmish between the hard core of Rovers and City fans had escalated into a major disturbance, which the hard-pressed law were having great difficulty in controlling.

Our individual battles raged among the horrified theatre-goers and chip-munching bystanders and continued as we dodged and side-stepped the onrushing buses and cars, laden with wide-eyed occupants. The battle had now moved on to the central paved area in front of that most unsavoury meeting spot for Bristol courting couples, the antiquated, foul-smelling public toilet. I had seen off my own personal combatant, a ferret-like individual who, though initially game and owner of a devastating right hand that left me with a throbbing lip, had now skulked away once a few right-handers of my own had hit home. I looked around for my next prey and caught sight of a furious knot of arms and legs that was oblivious to the muddy puddle it was swilling around in. The limbs belonged to Hampshire and Churchill, who were continuing their perennial tussle like two pit bulls in a back alley.

No words emanated from their bloodied mouths, only animal-like grunts and incoherent expletives. It was an ugly and brutal encounter from two streetwise pugilists who had more in common with each other than they would both dare admit. I could see, however, that Churchill was getting the upper hand and had managed to pin the hapless Hamps to the ground. Churchill's right fist was giving Hamps a merciless pounding. I couldn't stand back and let it happen – I rushed towards them

A DAY TO REMEMBER

and landed a perfect kick to Churchill's temple sending him sprawling to the ground and off Hampshire's battered body.

The strength of the forearm that wrapped itself around my neck like a python caught me unawares. It was an unmistakable grip that I had felt before and which, when accompanied by the customary agonising twisting of the right arm, confirmed that I was about to help the constabulary with their enquiries. I tried to scream out in pain, but my vocal cords had been crushed to such an extent that no sound materialised and my blood-shot eyes bulged out of their vacant sockets. Relief eventually came when I was bundled into the back of an awaiting panda car, but the subsiding pain was quickly overtaken by the nausea that accompanied the realisation of my predicament.

'Fuck it.' They were the first words that I managed to utter. 'I didn't do... any... thing... it wasn't me... it wasn't my fa...'

I tailed off from the pitiful mantra as I realised I was talking to no one. The cop car was unoccupied. I put my head between my legs and spewed up, my polished Monkey boots taking the brunt of my expelled stomach contents.

'Browner! Leg it!'

I looked up from my misery. The door had been wrenched open by Stuart Sutton and Pat Shanahan, two punk accomplices of Mick and Maff. Behind them two coppers were being physically restrained by a horde of punks.

'Come on, fucking move it. What you waiting for?'

They didn't need to ask again. I vaulted out of the car and dashed across the Centre, words of encouragement ringing in my ears. My legs threatened to give way, but with the law in furious pursuit I was determined to stay upright. I careered through the onrushing traffic leaving a mêlée of blaring horns and squealing tyres in my wake. Then I skidded across the wet tarmac, straight down Baldwin Street, right down Marsh Street, left down Telephone Avenue. I had no idea where my legs were taking me, or where I would end up; I just ran and ran, my heart thumping and my breathing hammering like an asthmatic. The adrenalin once again came to my aid, giving me vital energy born of fear. My only hindrance was my leaden sheepskin coat – it threatened to drag me down and dump me at the feet of my pursuers. I darted into an office doorway and struggled to control my breathing. The urge to vomit arose again, but I knew that my retching would only betray my hiding place. I stood as motionless as I could in the darkened doorway, the sound of my own heartbeat and the rushing in my ears now drowning out the sound of the subsiding riot.

The doorway was my refuge for five numbingly long minutes. I had shaken off the law, who were now busy mopping up and pulling in as many bodies as they could. The night air was still full of the sounds of disorder, and ambulance sirens now vied with those of the Old Bill for attention. To add to the turmoil, frenzied burglar alarms rang frantically in response to a multitude of broken windows. I decided to make a move, removed my conspicuous sheepskin casually flipped it over my shoulder and headed back on to Baldwin Street, away from the Centre. I was still wary and nervous. If the law didn't manage to nick me there was still the threat of a very angry and pissed-off Churchill and his mates roaming the streets. I headed towards Bristol Bridge, but a car screeched to a halt besides me. My heart missed a beat as I threw it a glance. The door flew open, revealing a familiar occupant.

'Browner, get in!' It was Clarkey in his pride and joy, his pristine 1600E. 'You lucky fucking jammer!'

'Ace, Clarkey, get me fucking out of 'ere!'

Clarkey drove off into the night, away from the chaos of the Centre towards the comparative safety of the Black Horse. I kept my head down and my thoughts to myself. The fireworks for Guy Fawkes night exploded in the ink-black sky, The Jam's latest and

A DAY TO REMEMBER

best record to date, the blistering '(This Is) The Modern World' blasted out from Clarkey's in-car cassette player. I had visited Paul Weller's vision of the modern world that day. I had been somewhere and achieved something of which, to my peers at any rate, I could be proud of...

> *Don't have to explain myself to you,*
> *Don't give two fucks about your review.*

31
No Let-up

In 1977, there was a rash of new wave bands appearing locally including, among others, Bristol's own favourites, The Cortinas. With an average age of just 16, they could justifiably have been tagged as one of Britain's first 'boy bands'. The grammar school kiddies from the affluent districts of Sneyd Park and Stoke Bishop had named themselves after the Ford classic 'coz it sounded cheap and nasty'. The band tasted minor chart success with Fascist Dictator/Television Families and in June of 1977 appeared at the Colston Hall supporting Television and Blondie. The adoring locals were impressed, Tony Parsons writing in the *NME* less so, perhaps not just with the band but with Bristol itself (maybe it was his forthcoming nuptials to Bristolian Julie Burchill that was prejudicing his views), the word 'patronising' could have been invented for the Billericay bigmouth: 'Bristol girls think you want a hand with your washing when you ask them if they would like to do a line. Ask them for a mirror and they think you want to powder your nose,' he wrote with his cutting wit, before going on to describe Bristol as 'Redneck county'. Surprisingly, it takes him five paragraphs

NO LET-UP

before he uses the word 'yokel'. In fairness, he's a tad more complimentary to Jeremy Valentine, The Cortinas' lead singer: 'He's built with the puppy-fat beefy physique of the school-yard bully, and wears a Ford building-site jacket so convincingly that one would never guess he's studying for his A-levels. Intelligent eyes, slick-back barnet and double chin: he looks like a junior version of Garry Glitter. But with a brain.'

Jeremy himself states in the same article: 'I like living in Bristol. It's dull, it's boring, there's nothing to do and I like it!'

Just when you think Parsons is warming to the boys, 'the standard of playing is consistently high', he plummets back into his working-class inverted snobbery: 'The Cortinas... have got so much to learn that their snot-nosed, naive belligerence is not so much offensive as it is pathetic.' And when Daniel Swann, The Cortinas' drummer, commented that 'the Clash complained that the plush hotel they were staying in down here wasn't good enough for them', Parsons's indignation screams from the page: 'Maybe they did that because they live in slums in London and want to screw all they can out of the record company.' Or maybe, Mr Parsons, because John 'Joe Strummer' Mellor with his privileged boarding-school educated background really did want to stay somewhere where the showers were hot, the towels were fluffy and the beds were turned down to reveal a little chocolate on the duck-feather-filled pillow.

As well as The Cortinas' appearance at The Colston Hall, the summer of 1977 also saw the bizarre American transsexual Wayne/Jayne County perform at a gig at the Barton Hill Youth Club which erupted in violence due once again to the presence of the Rovers' National Front punks, while Richard 'Kid' Strange, fronting up the influential protopunk band Doctors of Madness at the Polytechnic, did well to avoid the beer glasses that were regularly being chucked at him – the bouncers, including our old mate Neil Emery, certainly earned their pay that night.

BOOTED AND SUITED

Woking's finest, The Jam, performed a stunning set at The Studio in which Weller and co. delighted the right-wing members of us in the audience by performing in front of an immense Union Jack backdrop which, wrongly as it turned out, convinced us even more of their political leanings. The Jam's overt use of the Union Jack, as a stage prop and as an item of clothing in the vein of The Who's Pete Townshend back in the Sixties, caused much consternation among their more left-wing contemporaries. In truth, the band, perhaps naively, never saw the flag as a symbol of political extremity, although at that time in Britain the Union Jack had been virtually hijacked by right-wing movements and the National Front in particular.

Eventually, The Jam saw the error of their ways, and, although they still believed that it was possible to be a patriot without being a fascist, they reluctantly reconsidered their position and stopped using the Union Jack. From then on The Jam expressed their patriotism through their music, most notably in their *Setting Sons* album of the following year, but it was a sad day for British music when a band allowed a group of odious right-wing bully boys to dictate to them. Moreover, it made it a little bit harder for us all to be proud of our nationality. Perhaps if Paul Weller had stood his ground and kept the flag as a symbol of pride in his country and its people, at the same time denouncing the far right, things would have been different. As it was, although The Jam probably never realised it, their reluctance to neither confirm nor deny their political affiliations merely reinforced my belief that to be a patriot you had to be a fascist. Regrettably it would be a while before I was to see the error of my ways.

Another band to visit Bristol at that time was the much-hyped and severely overrated pseudo-punk combo The Tubes, who hailed from San Francisco. Something of a show band in the vein of Alice Cooper, The Tubes did their utmost to horrify the good citizens of Britain with an act that was billed by the rabid tabloid

NO LET-UP

press as bordering on the obscene and as degrading to women. Fee Waybill, the Tubes' depraved lead singer, came in for criticism for allegedly exposing himself on stage and for simulating sex acts with scantily clad young nubiles — inevitably the tour was a sell-out.

We trooped along to the Colston Hall, as much to see the female members of the audience as the band. The punkettes, on a showy evening like this at any rate, delighted in shocking all and sundry by dressing in nothing more than skimpy binliners and fishnet stockings which brought the line 'if that's punk I want in' from a drooling Grant Davy.

Waybill was nothing more than a high-camp, third-rate showman who played more with himself than with his guitar. Much of his act consisted of thrashing around on stage with his trademark chainsaw (sorry, Eminem, it's all been done before), leading eventually to the destruction of the set, its huge dummy speakers crashing down rather unconvincingly on Waybill's head. The musical content of the evening was abysmal, with 'Don't Touch Me There' and 'White Punks On Dope' (The Tubes' one and only British chart hit) the only offerings to draw any kind of reaction from the bemused crowd. We were not impressed; this was not what punk music was all about. If I'd wanted this kind of entertainment I would have gone to see Richard O'Brien's *Rocky Horror Show* wearing my own fishnets.

The charts were now awash with punk. Elvis Costello's first hit, the quirky and funky 'Watching The Detectives', The Sex Pistols' 'Holidays In The Sun' and The Boomtown Rats' 'Mary Of The Fourth Form' all featured in the Top 30 in November of 1977 and made a welcome diversion from those Swedish superstars who were at number 1 once again with the stupefyingly inane 'Name Of The Game'. Not that every punk outfit was a resounding success. For every Clash or Jam there were a hundred nonentities in the mould of the Snivelling Shits, who, not surprisingly, failed to make an impression on the charts – not because of their outlandish and offensive name, but because they were fucking crap.

November was a memorable month. The name of our game was still having a crack. The fact that violence inevitably accompanied that crack was neither here nor there. Whether it went off on the terrace or on the dancefloor was of little relevance.

Just two weeks after the white riot on the Centre the crack went off big time again as 20 or so of us gathered in the Hofbrauhaus to celebrate Roy Cash's 21st birthday. Roy, a quiet and unassuming character, was unfortunately unable to attend his own bash as he was spending some time in one of Her Majesty's hotels, after a disagreement with a workmate left the luckless colleague in hospital. We were therefore forced to toast Roy in absence. The Hofbrauhaus, scene of many riotous disturbances since its opening some four years earlier, was a cavernous Bavarian-style bierkeller that served full-strength lager and featured its own lederhosen-clad oompah band. Inevitably it was a honey-pot for stag and hen nights and, for some unfathomable reason, the bladders from across the Severn Bridge.

The combination of lager and the non-too-convincing Germanic surroundings fuelled our neo-fascist mentalities, and it wasn't long before the bierkeller was echoing to the sounds of 'Sieg Heil!' and 'Rule Britannia'. Although the former attracted howls of shock and derision, the latter drew a more appreciative reaction and eventually hundreds of young Englishmen and women lustily joined in – much to the disgust of the visiting Taffies, who promptly responded with a rousing rendition of 'Land Of My Fathers'. And that was when it kicked off. Who threw the first punch or launched the first glass was of little consequence. A succession of lips, noses and heads were split, bloodied and cracked in the latest round of wanton thuggery that routinely followed us on our weekend pursuits and inevitably finished with a visit to the casualty department of the BRI.

Our appetite for violence was insatiable and knew no bounds. The following week we even renewed our acquaintance with our old sparring partners from Plymouth, who since our promotion some three years earlier had no longer been the thorn in our sides that they once were. The occasion was the second round of the FA Cup. Our non-league neighbours Bath City had drawn Argyle at home and with Rovers still down on their luck in the League and playing 200 or so miles away in Sheffield, a large contingent of Tote Enders decided on an excursion to the quaint Roman city as a distraction from the more earthy charms of Bristol or South Yorkshire. I had been to Bath's ground once before, in the early Seventies when bovver boots and braces reigned supreme and the local coppers had been caught unawares by the barbaric invasion from the north-west. The pre-season 'friendly' turned into an orgy of vandalism involving smashed shop windows and overturned cars; the ancient city momentarily returned to the Dark Ages.

The numerous Argyle fans, who thought they were in for a pleasant day out, were as surprised to see us pile off the train as were the local coppers. The first blows were traded with a distinct look of bewilderment on their part as we proudly announced, 'Hello, hello, Rovers are back! Rovers are back!' The Home Park boys, however, were never ones to duck a fight and they soon shook off their confusion and entered the fray with their customary relish. It got to the point where they even had us on the run, causing our fans, with their customary lack of organisation, to fragment and split into various ragged factions before making their way to Bath's decrepit ground. One such ragged faction sauntered down the Lower Bristol Road, a road that was as long as it was grubby and completely at odds with the rest of the city of Bath. The disparate crew consisted of, among others, myself, a punked-up Steff Collier, Clarkey and Hampshire, who was still nursing the wounds inflicted some two weeks earlier by Churchill.

We had just passed the Seven Stars, a pub that matched the road for its grubbiness and which, unfortunately for us, was packed to the gunnels with raucous, intoxicated Argyle fans who wasted no time in introducing themselves. A combination of 'Argyle, la la la, Argyle la la la' and 'Who the fucking, who the fucking, who the fucking hell are you?' rang in our ears; the pub was emptying quicker than an incontinent's bladder as the green-and-white-clad arse-bandits tumbled out and fell in step some 20 yards behind us.

Our pace instinctively quickened. We shot glances at each other. A dozen or so of us, in unfamiliar surroundings with a howling pack behind us. The gut feeling was to run, but none of us wanted to be the first.

'What d'you reckon?' I looked at Hamps for reassurance. Hamps was doing the same to me.

'Dunno, how many of 'em?'

'Enough.'

'Steff? You up to it?'

'Eh? What? Dunno. There's too many for us, Browner, just keep walking.'

It was unlike Steff to back down, but even he knew when we were outnumbered. My heart was thumping and my balls headed north for the umpteenth time. I looked over my shoulder. They were making a run for us now, it was either stand and become a hero and take an inevitable kicking, or leg it and preserve your bodily organs. Someone made the decision for me.

'They're coming, leg it!'

For the second time in a fortnight I was running for my life, only this time I would have actually welcomed the presence of the Old Bill. We had the edge and after a hundred or so yards

NO LET-UP

our pursuers had dwindled in number to a hardcore of mental terrorists who were determined to draw blood. We had made a left turn for no logical reason and found ourselves running up a hill that grew steeper with each leaden step. The younger, fitter members of our crew were now in front of me; only the wheezing, groaning, overweight figure of Steff lagged behind. I glanced back over my shoulder again. They were down in number to about 20, still outnumbering us but we now had the advantage of the higher ground. My sheepskin was once again proving a burden and a crippling stitch slowed me down toa trot. 'Hampshire, Clarkey, stop... stop, come on we can 'ave 'em!'

I discarded my cumbersome sheepskin and fired back down the road. Steff, with a look of relief on his flushed face, joined me. The others realised the situation and quickly rallied round. I launched at one Argyle fan with a flying kick that sent him tumbling over a garden wall and followed up with a flurry of punches that struck home and brought howls of anguish from my muddy victim. Clarkey and Hamps were now among the fray, fighting in their familiar way, arms flailing at blinding speed. Steff slugged it out with his pursuer who was offensively berating his fleeing colleagues. The younger lads from Kingswood, including Rog Mitchum and Rich Nunn (who clearly hadn't learned anything from his spell in DC and who now frequented the Black Horse with us), were busily tidying up our attackers.

The tables had turned swiftly but, as is often the case, the tide of battle could quickly turn back. Street-fighting was often a game of bluff and deceit and, careful not to find ourselves on the receiving end of another counter-attack, we finished our work then melted away into the side streets, full of self-satisfied smirks and congratulations, relieved and exhilarated that once again we had grabbed victory from the jaws of defeat.

BOOTED AND SUITED

This year had undoubtedly belonged to the punks. In 1977, the great unwashed had broken away from their art colleges and Sunday-night pub gigs and barged and battled their way into the mainstream of the British charts through sheer arrogance, self-belief and, of course, talent. Funk had burrowed further underground and become even more marginalised. Idris Muhammad's 'Turn This Mutha Out' and Garnet Mimms' 'What It Is' proved that raw, classy funk was still around. But, unless you were a bona fide soul boy, your connection with dance music was restricted to the slicker and more successful commercial sounds of Britain's own Heatwave who had chart successes with 'Boogie Nights' and 'Too Hot To Handle', Maurice White's Earth, Wind & Fire with 'Getaway' and 'Saturday Nite', and Chic with 'Dance'.

Chic, probably more than any other band of that period, filled the void in the market that The Fatback Band had come close to tapping into several years earlier. They performed eminently danceable music that bridged rock, disco and, more importantly, the black and white divide. The band were headed up by guitarist and vocalist Nile Rodgers and the immensely talented, and much-copied bassist Bernard Edwards. Their first chart hit, 'Dance (Yowsah, Yowsah, Yowsah)', sold a million copies in its first month and went to number 6 in Britain. It was a guaranteed dancefloor filler, whether spun on the decks in New York's notoriously hedonistic Studio 54, London's trendy and exclusive Tramp or Bristol's 'newest and most sophisticated' nightclub, Romeo and Juliets (the latest revamp of the old Top Rank dancehall). 'Dance' was the precursor of a further five Top 20 hits over the following two years, including 'Le Freak' and the much used and abused 'Good Times'.

'Le Freak', in fact, was originally titled 'Fuck Off', and came about as a furious reaction by Rodgers to his being refused entrance to Studio 54 by its owner, Steve Rubell. Rubell, who

NO LET-UP

employed bisexual bar staff that wore little more than tight pairs of shorts and a smile, delighted in heightening the club's exclusive reputation by barring celebrities on a regular basis. The throbbing, energetic music vied with sex, heroin and cocaine as Studio 54's main attraction and the club was patronised by the likes of Andy Warhol, Calvin Klein, Liza Minnelli and Mick Jagger, who mingled with models, drag queens and roller-skating black transvestites – but not, as it turned out, Nile Rodgers. With its baroque fittings, immense dancefloor, myriad lighting effects, neon wheels and strobes, Studio 54 became the most famous and talked-about disco in the world and, apart from the sex in the toilets, had as much in common with an average British disco as I had with Steve Rubell.

Rodgers eventually saw the folly of his tongue-in-cheek title and released it as 'Le Freak'. What's more, its original title might have been confused with the punk single 'If You Don't Fuck, Fuck Off', which for some reason wasn't receiving much airplay on Radio One. Le Freak went on to sell six million copies worldwide and became Atlantic's best-selling record of all time – and all through Nile Rodgers being refused entry to a nightclub.

Chic's next single, 'Good Times', was everything a great pop record should be and featured Bernie Edwards performing a near-perfect bass line. That bass line was to resurface in the ground-breaking first rap hit 'Rapper's Delight' by The Sugarhill Gang, which reached number 3 in the charts in 1979, and appeared again in 'Another One Bites The Dust' by Queen. Chic developed into the most musically qualified disco band of the era and should rightly be remembered as one of the most successful. Regrettably, however, the crown of disco kings rests on the golden-maned head of Barry Gibb and his follicly challenged brothers, due largely to their part in the astounding success of a certain film soundtrack.

BOOTED AND SUITED

The proliferation of new wave groups in the charts was at odds with the mushrooming disco scene. Although the destroy and chaos theory ruled with Britain's more dysfunctional and disillusioned youth, many less radical youngsters opted to escape from the country's ills in a less confrontational and more traditional way – dancing the night away under the ubiquitous mirror ball.

In Bristol, Reeves, Lautrecs, The Stage Door, The Princess Court, Curves, Shades, Le Mans and the coolest of them all, Platform One, all vied with the old favourites of Tiffany's, the Mayfair Suite, the Mandrake, Maxims, Vadims and Scamps to cash in on the disco boom. Even Rovers' sad old Eastville Stadium opened up its own disco – The Doghouse – which, intentionally or not, certainly lived up to its name with regard to its female clientele. I'm glad to say that I would never have met my latest girlfriend there.

I had known Carole for some years, she was an old friend of Jill Vickery's – an original Tote End Boot Girl – and we had first got together on one of our numerous excursions to Weymouth during the summer of '77. Our initial courting was as infrequent as Rovers' goalscoring opportunities that season, but it made a welcome change from the usual stifling relationships I had experienced in the past. Carole was level-headed, trusting and without prejudice – the complete opposite of yours truly, in fact. One day she would make someone a good wife. I didn't realise it at the time, but that someone was going to be me.

The disco boom that had been gathering momentum in the last 12 months resulted in payback time for the US, for while groups like the aforementioned Chic, The Trammps and Tavares were leading the disco invasion of Britain, the Sex Pistols were embarking on their ill-fated and disastrous tour of the States. The tour saw Sid Vicious becoming so reliant on heroin, thanks in no small part to his girlfriend Nancy Spungen, that he even appeared

NO LET-UP

on stage in Dallas with 'Gimme a fix' scrawled on his bare chest. Vicious was clearly no longer capable of looking after his own health — who in their right mind would tell an audience of redneck cowboys in San Antonio that they 'were all a bunch of fucking faggots'? Irreparable cracks had appeared in the Pistols' armour. Steve Jones refused to travel on the tour bus any more and, together with Paul Cook, took to flying by plane to the various gigs. Johnny Rotten, as was his wont, hated everybody, especially Malcolm McLaren. And Sid was barely making it from one city to another before getting serious withdrawal symptoms.

By the time the Pistols arrived in San Francisco for the end of the tour, Malcolm McLaren, ever aware of the publicity value of outrage, was suggesting a jaunt to Rio de Janeiro to hook up with the Great Train Robber, Ronnie Biggs. Rotten wasn't at all impressed and Sid had gone past caring, but the Jones-Cook axis, for whatever reason, agreed to the idea. With the words 'Ever get the feeling you've been cheated?' Johnny Rotten ended the Pistols' last gig in America at San Francisco's Winterland Ballroom. As it turned out, it was also to be their last live appearance for nearly 20 years. Rotten skulked back to his hotel alone and the whole sordid party that was the Sex Pistols entered its final, darkest hour. I had just about given up hope of ever seeing the Pistols live, although I still kept the dog-eared ticket for 'The Spots' (Sex Pistols On Tour) one-and-only appearance in Bristol's Bamboo Club in my wallet. Unfortunately the gig was cancelled, as the Bamboo Club, that stronghold of Jamaican music that had once seen the likes of Prince Buster and Desmond Dekker, burned down just two days before the Pistols were due to appear there. Sadly, it was never to reopen.

It was during the Sex Pistols' eventful tour of the US that Robert Stigwood's hugely successful film *Saturday Night Fever* first saw the light of day. The story focused largely on the blossoming disco culture. It has gone down in history as having painted a convincing cinematic portrait of frustrated Seventies' working-class youth and of the escape that the spinning, multi-coloured lights and compelling, pulsating rhythms of the disco world offered. Did it fuck. It had as much in common with the trials and tribulations of British working-class youth as Sid Vicious did with the Dallas Cattleman's Ball. Even so, the film was entertaining stuff. Aside from its musical content, it contained a fair share of gang-related aggro and sexual violence which, surprisingly, was enough to earn it an X-certificate in Britain. The film starred John Travolta as Tony Manero, a lithesome Latin who wooed the Brooklyn girls with his skills both on and off the dancefloor. His finger-pointing, hip-thrusting gyrations and penchant for open-necked black shirts, white suits and gold medallions left a legacy for a thousand middle-aged lotharios to make right pricks of themselves at weddings in the years to come.

The soundtrack of the film, which featured 'More Than A Woman' by Tavares and The Trammps' seminal 'Disco Inferno' among many other bona fide disco classics, had registered in the charts before the film was even released. It stayed at number 1 in the album charts for 18 consecutive weeks, eventually going on to sell 27 million copies worldwide and resurrecting the career of The Bee Gees, whose songs 'Stayin' Alive' and 'Night Fever' also went on to become best-sellers in the singles charts. As far as myself and my compadres were concerned though, the idea that The Bee Gees, along with Abba, were credible dance music innovators held no water. The only people I knew who bought their music were mums and kid sisters – and those middle-aged pricks in the dodgy white suits.

By the end of 1977, my musical tastes, like thousands of others in Britain, had taken a seismic change in direction. I couldn't quite put my finger on why that was the case; I loved

NO LET-UP

funk with a passion, I loved punk like I loved a pint of Courage Best (too much of it and it made me want to throw up). The fashion, however, was a different story, so for an insight on the funk/punk evolution from someone who was much more involved in it than I was it's over to Mr Williams again. This time, Tim writes in his own inimitable style of how the sophisticated soul boys traded in their pegs for bondage trousers and how he and his mates got labelled 'The Chaps' and found themselves acting as minders for The Cortinas, the young Bristol punk band who had got right up Tony Parsons's nose...

> How exactly did a group of cutting-edge American urban funk aficionados throw it all away for the three-chord thrashings of Hoxton, Brixton and Ladbroke Grove? It had something to do with music but a lot more to do with clothes.
>
> Why break up the Guildhall brother and sisterhood to ape the tabloid-tracked burgeoning punk scene like every city with a cathedral, an underpass and a Sunday market? The Guildhall was something special, wasn't it?
>
> Without doubt. Loose tribes had stumbled around the Bristol club scene, indistinguishable from one and other but fiercely loyal to their team or postcode. The big halls like the Top Rank offered room for everyone and we all crowded in, a mass of crushed velvet and the great smell of Eau Sauvage. 'Hey Girl Don't Bother Me' sang The Tams until one of them side-shuffled off the stage, denting only his pride — unlike poor Neil Winstone who bounced down most of the stairs because bouncers bounced in those days. But the Top Rank was too inclusive and too spacious and people huddled with their homies in their favoured corner or with their racial group. And the other above-ground clubs were too interchangeable. If it's Tuesday, it's The Blue Lagoon. Or is it The Top Cat? Either way, Seymour or Superfly or

BOOTED AND SUITED

someone will be there playing James Brown or Rufus Thomas and a few slow ones at the end. Time to blag of.

People ventured out of Bristol whenever a bank holiday came along, seeking the crack and the next big thing. Newquay was good but Bournemouth was better. Equal distance between Bristol and London we encountered temporary escapees from the smoke in all their finery. Mohair, plastic sunglasses, upside-down trousers and the old Puerto-Rican fence climbers. We skulked in the shadows, ashamed of our cap-sleeve T-shirts and wedge cuts. That was Bank Holiday Monday and, by Tuesday, we were desperately trying to find pants that narrowed at the bottom. In those days, the world wore flares. Your dad, your history teacher, Prince Philip, Bob Monkhouse and The Pope. Lionel Blair wore flares. London already had Acme Attractions and Johnson & Johnson. We had Millets and a second-hand clothes shop in Park Row that smelled bad.

Eventually, we found our way to SW whatever and got kitted out and returned home where we sat upstairs at the back of the bus into town and The Guildhall. It was our own private world below a spiral staircase beneath which you could watch the plastic sandals and winkle pickers come into view descending daintily before the bulk of Bobby Iles or Wendy Clutterbuck. We had our pegs and our latest imports listed from 1 to 50 on a photocopied ASA sheet. Are you ready? Do the bus stop and get off at the one near Bristol Bridge and walk through St. Nicholas market.

You knew everyone there, but occasionally a stranger put in an appearance. Mark Stewart came once or twice in pink pegs and wraparound sunglasses. He punk smirked above the older/smaller dancers. He couldn't/wouldn't dance. Did he know something we didn't? Trousers have a lot to answer for, pink or otherwise. The pegs went from cotton to something shiny and then further out to plastic, borderline fetish.

Alan Jones, ex-sax player with South Wales pop soul combo The Amen Corner managed Clobber on Park Street and also in

NO LET-UP

The Haymarket for another Welsh guy called Gerald, until he bought the branch beneath the bus station and called it Paradise Garage after the legendary New York nightclub. He had his contacts and soon some of the clothes we had to go to inter city 125 for started appearing on some very appealing pinch faced mannequins on loan from Lloyd Johnson in the Kensington Market. Alan also had a part share in a club in Newport called Rudies and the invite went out to the Guildhall faithful to pay it a visit. It was said to be worth the bridge fee.

Vernon Jozefowicz piled half a dozen of us into his Pontiac, longer than the other vehicles used that night but slower and smokier too. Ten years minimum without an air filter. A mirror reflection of the Guildhall, Rudies was upstairs and that first visit was akin to hitting the Chelsea Village in Bournemouth a couple of summers before. Our kit was wicked, their kit was... well, wicked plus. With knobs on and knobs out. Their trousers had already passed through plastic and landed on tightened up leather. Even (whisper it) rubber.

We had met Steve Harrington a few years before at Wigan Casino but the beret and the adidas bag were gone and the Blackwood accent was soon to follow as he morphed into Steve Strange. Mark Taylor was there and Chris Sullivan, later to front up Blue Rondo a la Turk before running the Wag Club in Wardour Street with Rusty Egan. But the limelight belonged to a guy called Colin Fisher, as did the chain that danced on his cheek linking his earlobe to his nostril. My God, they were, they were... well, there was no name for what they were except valley boys who had got a march on the Bristol brethren. We had been below our spiral staircase for too long. Something was afoot and it had shed its plastic sandal.

I sniffed the air. I smelled cult. Too young to be a mod, too weak to be a skinhead, I was open to suggestion. But why were they dancing to Donna Summer?

BOOTED AND SUITED

As the leaves started to turn brown, the tabloids began to see red. Punk was a New York magazine as well as a ripped-up look personified by Richard Hell, bass player with art rock CBGB dwelling, guitar duelling combo Television. Malcolm McLaren, ex Ted co-owner of Sex, way down in World's End was no stranger to this scene. He had been part of it stylising the New York Dolls through their death throes. Not only could he import the look, he could sell the clothes and so punk got wheeled into the West End in a wardrobe on casters, direct from the garment district.

As the red tops cranked up the indignation, the photographs that appeared alongside the rant featured a London face or two but Fisher, Sullivan and Harrington were at the fore. And, surprise surprise, there was a soundtrack to this scene after all. Punks did not do the hustle, the bump or the bus stop (or dance to Donna Summer). They went to see bands. White, British bands who dressed like them. The Sex Pistols were one, The Psycle Sluts another. The former swore their way to notoriety, the latter disappeared somewhere between rumour and myth.

The Guildhall was still stretchin' out and hangin' loose in a rubber band with Bootsy but who wants a rubber band when Sex are selling rubber tee shirts for £15? All of a summer sudden, the scene below Broad Street seemed tired, repetitive and as conservative as Breezin' by George Benson, the last album I bought before the debut LP by four Brooklyn would be brothers, The Ramones. You could get punk of the US variety but it was the chill of winter 76 before the UK's sound was captured on vinyl.

How many of the Guildhall faithful cashed in their funk chips for Soho nights at the Roxy? Hard to say but the vanguard barely looked back once it realised that Bristol, yes Bristol, had a punk band of its own.

The Cortinas had played the Ashton Court Festival before the nights started drawing in. They were kids from north of the river

NO LET-UP

and fee-paying schools. The drummer was 14. But with shades, skinny ties and part-time attitude, they ripped it up for the bikers, hippies and more bikers who enjoyed a free festival almost as much as a run down to Cheddar for an ice cream and a punnet of strawberries.

The road to punk was a much more direct one for the band and their followers than it was for those of us who could glare a DJ down for having the audacity to play a funk tune that you could actually buy easily in the UK. They were already listening to white British bands like The Kursaal Flyers, Kilburn and the High Roads, Eddie and the Hot Rods. Pub Rock took a step back and a line of speed, a sideways glance at Patti Smith and the rest of New York loft life and the die was cast.

The Cortinas welcomed the patronage of the former funksters with open arms. Though we had not learned to play guitar like them through terms of private tuition, we were streetwise and more than willing to scare off the beastly boys from school who had taken it upon themselves to quell the birth of punk, as they saw it, in Sneyd Park. We promoted gigs, started record labels and wrote fanzines, while our new guitar-toting friends flashed for a good while and almost made it. If nothing else they paved the way for a bigger post-punk push, led by the ironically named The Pop Group, school friends of The Cortinas but better dressed: grey shirts done up to the neck one week, cricket whites the next. Where was this sartorial elegance coming from? Singer Mark Stewart? For the real lowdown you would have to ask their first up manager, Paradise Garage owner Alan Jones. He was our Malcolm McLaren, but without the cynicism and with a much prettier wife.

In 2008, Mark Stewart was booked to play the prestigious Meltdown Festival on London's Southbank with his band, Maffia. His many fans from across the new Europe would go to any lengths for a ticket. And if they got the chance to talk with him after the

BOOTED AND SUITED

gig and ask how it all got started his response would be the same as it always is: 'Well, there was this basement pub in Broad Street, Bristol called The Guildhall. It was the wildest scene, the clothes, the dancing. Kit kids. Full on.'

32

Saints and Sinners

As all football fans know, nothing sums up the love-hate relationship that supporters have with their chosen club as much as their team's involvement in the FA Cup. Only in that magical cup tournament that has been tarnished so much in recent years can anguish turn to joy and dreams turn to nightmares, quicker than a City fan can leg it off the Tote End. For Rovers, the cup competition of the 1977/78 season made a welcome respite from the drudgery of the league. By the time Rovers played Sunderland in the third round of the cup in early January, they had recorded only six wins all season. Apart from Bobby Gould's hat-trick back in October the only thing that the Tote Enders had to cheer about that dull season was the emergence of a 19-year-old Scally from Liverpool named Paul Randall, whose speed and ball control managed to fill the void that the departure of our beloved Warboys and Bannister had created some years earlier.

Amazingly, and rather fortuitously, Rovers managed to win away at Roker Park, courtesy of a solitary goal by Bobby Gould.

BOOTED AND SUITED

The win resulted in a fourth-round tie at home to the recent cup winners from the south coast, Southampton.

The hard-core denizens of the Tote End gathered in the Black Horse on a numbingly cold Saturday lunchtime bedecked in more sheepskin coats than could be found at a second-hand car dealers' convention and touting more rightwing regalia than the walls of Hitler's bunker. The bar itself was decorated with an assorted mixture of Rovers flags, scarves and NF posters proclaiming '90 per cent of all muggers are black' and 'Smash the IRA'. The jukebox was blasting out our favourite frenetic tracks by The Jam and the Pistols, adding to the already threatening atmosphere. The rhetoric, like the alcohol, was flowing freely...

'An' that's anuvver thing, they're teaching our kids fucking Paki history... I'll tell you... it's a fucking laugh.'

'Yeah, an' they murdering IRA bastards all ought to be fucking lined up against a fucking wall an' shot.'

'Yeah, right, an' I'll tell you this – fucking country's going down the bastarding toilet, Hitler had the right idea...'

I can look back on it now and see that it was all as repetitive and tiresome as it was contemptible, but to my eternal shame I was part of it. Fuelled by alcohol and a herd mentality, it was easy to spout ignorant and uneducated claptrap. But in my more reflective moments, I was starting to wonder about my own involvement in this mess and the allegiances I'd made for myself. After all, my passion for reggae and soul music was diametrically opposed to my politics and my attitude to black people. I tried not to trouble myself about the contradiction, but deep down I felt a raging guilt, the guilt of the gullible and the naive. The National Front unashamedly exploited the genuine fears of a mass of working-class white people. The country was going down the toilet, that was for sure; the IRA were waging, and apparently winning, a bloody battle with the British people and bombs were now exploding on

SAINTS AND SINNERS

mainland Britain as often as they were in the troubled province. Immigration undeniably was causing problems on Britain's streets – and ultimately it was irrelevant whether that was because of ignorance or intolerance. Enoch Powell's warnings of 'rivers of blood' a decade earlier were beginning to ring true.

The beleaguered Labour Party couldn't even rely on their traditional support from the trade unions, who were striking with alarming frequency and attempting to hold the country to ransom. My own union, the NGA, were in constant conflict, especially with the Fleet Street bosses; inflated wages for the print workers gave a wrong and totally false impression of an overpaid and belligerent work force. For me, in a dead end job in the dead end area of Avonmouth, the only prospect of bettering myself seemed to lie elsewhere. The lure of the Yankee dollar appealed to me and Hampshire and, together with the Chelsea triumvirate of Clarkey, Egghead and China, we decided to try our luck in the States. However, we were not due to leave for the sunny delights of the New World until mid-summer. Until then we had to make the most of depressing Britain and its sole saving graces – music and football. Which brings us back to the cup tie against Southampton.

The game against the Saints promised much and delivered even more. We even managed a ruck with some Saints fans on the elevated section of the M32 that overlooked Eastville, en route to the game. A minor shunt between Clarkey's Cortina and a Capri packed with south-coast scummers quickly escalated into a bout of fisticuffs and air-kicking. Nothing much to write home about but, as it turned out, a tasty appetiser for the main course that was to follow. In fact, it turned out to be a veritable feast, with the darling of the Tote, Paul Randall, keeping his feet on the treacherous surface, scoring twice and generally causing havoc among the heavy-footed Saints defenders. The packed inhabitants

BOOTED AND SUITED

of the Tote End and North Stands were delirious. The 8,000 or so Saints fans, massed on the open Muller Road End, were not, and with less than ten minutes of the game remaining, and their departure from the FA Cup imminent, they decided on a course of action common to Seventies football matches — a full-blown pitch invasion.

We watched from our lofty vantage point at the back of the Tote with a mixture of anxiety and anticipation. As with most pitch invasions it started with a trickle, just a few brave-hearted and ardent protagonists. But the trickle increased steadily: from ten their numbers rose to fifty, then a hundred or so. The trickle became a flood, a flood of denim- and leather-clad hooligans wearing red-and-white scarves, now threateningly milling around on the brick-red dog track that encircled the frost-covered pitch. The first punches and missiles were thrown as they moved menacingly around the track, clashing with an angry knot of Dave Ashley's North Stand boys to our left. Dave and his mates, as ever, performed admirably, but, with more and more Saints fans joining the fray, we knew it was time for us to take action. As one, the Tote End tumbled down the terrace towards the pitch. 'Hello, hello, Tote End Aggro, Tote End Aggro!' bellowed a thousand voices. 'On the pitch! On the pitch! On the pitch!' As if anybody needed to ask where we were heading.

The final whistle was greeted with a huge sound from the 26,000 crowd, a roar of ecstatic approval from the home crowd mixed with a threatening roar from the Saints fans, who were making their own intentions equally plain. No sooner had the players hurriedly exited the pitch than the Saints fans replaced them and, en masse, headed towards the halfway line. Their semi-reluctant trot had now accelerated to a run and, encouraged by a lack of resistance from the law and the home supporters, they hurtled towards the Tote End hell-bent on registering their disapproval with the result. The Tote Enders did not need any further invitation. Some were already over the fence, anxiously waiting for their cohorts to follow. They danced around, arms aloft, feet entangled in the mass of toilet rolls that festooned the edge of the pitch, beckoning for others to follow. They were joined from the North and South enclosures, but the majority of the Tote End held firm.

'Come on, come on, what are you waiting for, let's get the bastards!' This from Ricky Lee, eager as ever to get on with the action.

'No, no, Ricky, hold it, get back – wait until they get closer, wait until they're here, otherwise they'll just leg it!' Hampshire was calling the shots.

Others joined in, some even pulling back their impatient colleagues.

'Wait, everybody wait, just hold it, fucking hold it!'

I could now see the sense of the plan. We were massed against the low fence, one foot up, ready to go, waiting for the signal, like a scene from a First World War battlefield. I was waiting for someone to shout, 'Don't shoot until you see the whites of their eyes.' Peripheral skirmishes were now going off, but the main battle was still to begin. The Saints fans were now on the penalty spot which, because of the curvature of the Tote End terrace, meant they were virtually surrounded. They slowed, sudden realisation hitting them right between their eyes.

'Now, come on, get the bastards!'

'Charge, fucking 'ave 'em!'

A mighty shout rang out from the Tote End, a guttural, animal-like roar emerging from a thousand or more throats. We tumbled on to the pitch, brushing aside the outnumbered stewards and coppers and piling straight in to the visiting mob. They were no match for us – we had the advantage of numbers and reinforcements were joining us all the time. I kicked one, then another; they were in disarray, the only fight in them was born of self-preservation. Now their only concern was in getting back to the comparative safety of their own terrace, a journey fraught with even more danger as the North Stand boys once more joined in the fray. I looked to my left. Russ Furnell had grabbed a corner flag and was using it to devastating effect, pole-axing one unfortunate who crumpled on to the muddy pitch where his misery was compounded by a dozen well-placed kicks.

All the Black Horse boys were there, including Tony 'Bone' White, younger brother of Jim, who, since his jailing for the Luton incident four years earlier, had become a rare sight on the terraces. Bone had carried on where big brother Jim had left off and was busying himself with a Saints fan who was putting up only token resistance. The battle turned into a rout as the infiltrators retreated, muddied and bloodied, back to their own terrace. After mopping up a few beleaguered stragglers we stood triumphant in front of them. Our mob had taken up the challenge and won; territory and honour were both intact. Deliriously happy, we raised our scarves aloft with a proud cry: 'You'll never take the Tote End! You'll never take the Tote End!'

Once again we had made nationwide TV. Football-wise our team had done the business — Brian Moore almost came in his pants as he compared Randall's finishing with that of Johann Cruyff's. Randall had now became a household name; the Tote had enhanced their reputation — eighty-nine fans were ejected, nine arrested and six police officers injured. The magic of the FA Cup.

Rovers' reward for beating Saints was a home tie against Ipswich Town, played on an Arctic-like day in February when the freezing temperature gnawed at your bones and monkeys looking for spot welders were a common sight along Stapleton Road. It made the cold of the Southampton game seem like a pleasant spring day. Snow covered the furrowed Eastville pitch and the assembled crowd was again adorned in a shabby mix of sheepskin, leather and Millets' fur-trimmed parkas.

The game itself went off with few incidents of note. Ipswich, although they were now enjoying First Division status, were in the minor league when it came to having anything approaching a respectable crew and, like the Southampton game, there was no infiltration of the Tote. Indeed, the taking of 'ends' was fast becoming a thing of the past. Crowd segregation and heavy police presence was now the norm; any violence was generally confined to the pubs, streets and car parks surrounding the grounds or, as in the Southampton game, as a consequence of pitch invasions by disgruntled fans. This time, however, the tables were turned. It was our turn to be disgruntled as a perfectly good goal was ruled out for offside – had it been allowed, it would have put Rovers 3–1 up. Ipswich grabbed a late goal to make it 2–2 and denied the gallant Rovers team what would have been their first appearance in the quarter-finals of the FA Cup.

We trooped out of the ground, cold and dejected, and headed instinctively for the Muller Road car park where the Ipswich fans' coaches stood. The law, mindful of the violence that had taken place only three weeks earlier, had other ideas and threw up a protective cordon that wouldn't have looked out of place on the streets of Belfast. The boys in blue had us sussed; not a punch or brick had been thrown. However, we were persistent bastards and were in no mood to give up so easily.

'Come on, let's leg it down the station and get their special.' We strode off with a distinct spring in our step and headed for Stapleton Road station.

'Fuck it, the law's here,' I exclaimed in genuine disappointment.

'I've never seen so many coppers at a game. It's only Ipswich fucking Town, for Christ's sake. Where to now?' Hamps asked.

'Lawrence Hill, quick.'

Lawrence Hill was the next station along the line, a mile

away through the mean streets of Easton. We trotted along, 20 or so in total, determined and focused, full of hate and anger. We took up position a hundred yards away from Lawrence Hill station on a grubby piece of wasteland which stood between the grimy Victorian houses lining the railway track. Scrabbling around in the dark we gathered up the bricks and bottles that conveniently littered the area. We didn't speak; we went about our business purposefully and methodically.

'Quick, it's the fucking train, let the bastards 'ave it!'

Lit up like a Christmas tree, the train rounded the corner at a snail's pace. Its jubilant occupants hung out of the windows bedecked in scarves and flags. Oblivious to the imminent danger, they sang joyfully: 'Wember-lee, Wember-lee, we're the famous Ipswich Town an' we're going to Wem...' The barrage of bricks, bottles, milk crates and other debris hit them without warning. The dull, sickening thuds mixed with the smashing of glass – screams and cries of anguish rang out above the roar of the diesel. We could pick our targets; it was like a duck-shoot. I felt no remorse or regret and the consequences of our actions were of little relevance. We had exacted revenge and, what's more, we had the chance to do it all again at the replay.

Ten days later a fleet of coaches ferried 3,000 plus Rovers fans to Suffolk. With the exception of Stevie Bould, whose old man originally hailed from Ipswich, it was a new experience for most of us. Stevie had assured us that Ipswich were 'a real family club' although I had doubts, remembering the visit of a coachload of them to Ashton Gate two years back when they gave the City fans a bit of a lesson. As it turned out Stevie was absolutely right. Ipswich and their fans were a credit to football – an island of sanity in a sea of hate and madness, and even though we were positioned beside them and shared the same

SAINTS AND SINNERS

terrace – admittedly segregated by ten-foot fences and rows of surly, uncompromising coppers – they resisted all attempts by us less civilised followers of the beautiful game to goad them into action.

That winter had seen the Tote End become a bastion of right-wing politics. Rigid arm salutes were a common sight and NF, British Movement and Column 88 badges were *de rigueur*. The black kids who had followed Rovers in the early Seventies had, understandably, disappeared from the terraces and the dissenters, of which there weren't many, either kept a low profile and kept their mouths shut or stayed away entirely.

Our hatred filled the cold night air and the black kids who followed Ipswich became the objects of our shameful hostility, 'White youths unite and fight, join the National Front!', 'There ain't no black in the Union Jack, send the bastards back!' rang out from the assembled Tote Enders. The nods of approval from the local constabulary and their obvious reluctance to arrest any Rovers fans for the racist chants merely confirmed our belief that the extreme right was becoming a force to be reckoned with in Britain. The Ipswich fans, however, remained unruffled and as well as vociferously supporting their talented team, who were in the process of tearing Rovers apart, responded with a telling retort that was rammed down our ignorant racist throats. 'Ipswich lives in racial harmony! Ipswich lives in racial harmony!' they chanted as one. I was at a loss for words. I thought all football fans were like us. Ipswich's near neighbours and arch-rivals Norwich City certainly were. The enlightened Ipswich fans continued with their telling ripostes: 'Black, white, unite and fight, smash the National Front!' vied with 'Paul Mariner walks on water!' as the Ipswich fans' favourite chant.

Rovers crashed to a 3–0 defeat. We were taught a lesson that

BOOTED AND SUITED

night in sleepy Suffolk. A lesson in football by Bobby Robson's team who, appropriately, went on to win the FA Cup, and a lesson in life by decent and tolerant fans. We shambled dejectedly back to Bristol, back to our prejudices and our second-rate football.

Rovers' exit from the FA Cup effectively finished our season. With the exception of Randall's goals there was little to shout about; attendances dropped alarmingly and an air of despondency and depression enveloped Eastville, much as the clouds of vaporised gas had veiled it some years earlier. The visits of Tottenham Hotspur in March and Sheffield United in April brought the only action of note off the pitch and resulted in a few brawls and arrests, one of which involved our very own Iggy Smithers. He had been nicked for his involvement in a mass stone fight in the car park with the disgruntled Yorkshiremen who had seen their team defeated 4–1. Perhaps they never had forgiven us for winning the Watney Cup.

The away game against Millwall on 1 April drew a paltry attendance of just over 3,000. This was due in no small part to it being played at Portsmouth, owing to The Den being closed after crowd trouble during their recent game with, of all clubs, Ipswich. The game itself was of little importance but saw continual fighting breaking out among the three sets of fans and, for good measure, a considerable group of Anti-Nazi League followers. The last home game of the season against Stoke City registered a similar low attendance of just 3,182 and proved just how far the fortunes of Rovers and football in general had declined in a few short years. The hooligans, with their right-wing politics, their sinister gang names and their sometimes bizarre and threatening dress code (Ku Klux Klan masks had even made appearances on the terraces) were growing more notorious by the week. Grounds around the

SAINTS AND SINNERS

country were subject to racist graffiti and stabbings and there was even the occasional death on a match day. The beautiful game had turned into a crying game — it was on its knees and, what's more, I was one of the guilty people who had put it there.

33
A Battering at the Bell

As much as we enjoyed the testosterone-induced camaraderie of the Black Horse, the sudden change in temperature brought about by a mild spring evening tempted us to shed our sheepskins, spread our wings and sample pastures new. Myself, Hampshire, Moggy Moran, Stuart Clarke and Pete Egghead Daniels entered The Bell in Redcliffe drawn by Hampshire's promise of it having a cracking disco and 'being full of fanny'. As it turned out, the only cunts in there that night were us.

'Recognise anyone in here, Hamps?'

'Nope, you?'

'Not fucking one of 'em,' I replied warily.

It was unusual, if not downright amazing, for us to enter a pub and not know anybody. Hampshire with his mouth and his manner was better known in East Bristol than the Prime Minister. Apart from the Black Horse, which was virtually our second home, we could be sure of at least a nod of recognition or a welcoming handshake in pubs as diverse as the Maypole in Hanham where fellow Tote Ender Tony Skinner and his mates

A BATTERING AT THE BELL

took up residence, or the Kensington in Redland where the likes of Mick Warbutton, Maff Simmonds and Ibby Collingwood held court. There was, however, one small detail that set The Bell apart from the aforementioned pubs. The Bell was south of the river; as the Vietnam war veterans would have put it, we were in Cong country.

Undeterred, we ordered our pints, took our first sip of the bitter brown liquid, grimaced in the fashion of Jack Regan in *The Sweeney* and studied the assembled crowd. A gaggle of over-made-up, shaggy-permed women, all failing desperately to look like Farrah Fawcett-Majors mixed with an assortment of young men casually bedecked in striped capped-sleeved T-shirts and jeans or open-necked checked shirts and smart strides.

Walter Murphy's instrumental hit from *Saturday Night Fever*, 'A Fifth Of Beethoven', boomed out from the sound system, bringing squeals of delight from the Charlie's Angels girls. Meanwhile, their boyfriends were returning our stares without a blink. A few faces looked familiar – familiar, but not friendly. I recognised one tall, rangy character as the ferret-faced tosser I had brawled with on the Centre after The Clash concert. His name, it turned out, was Chrissy Robinson, a confederate of Silvester and Churchill, who, mercifully, weren't in the pub. Robinson was in animated conversation with a short, stumpy meathead who, again, looked familiar but whose ugly features I could not place. Their steady stares unnerved me. I turned to Hampshire.

'Are you thinking what I'm thinking?'

'What? Like how to get the fuck out of here?'

'Yeah, summat like that.'

I looked over towards the door. The only exit for us was rapidly becoming barred by ever-increasing numbers. As ever, Moggy was oblivious to it all and, with a cheery smile on his face, turned to me and asked, 'Are you going to bother going down the Rovers next season?'

BOOTED AND SUITED

I looked at him incredulously. 'Moggy, shut the fuck up,' I replied, between gritted teeth.

'Why? Wh...?'

Before I had the chance to explain, Hampshire interrupted. 'Grab summat, it's gonna go off!'

'C'mon, Hampshire, you bastard!' The ugly meathead lurched forward and landed a flurry of punches about Hampshire's unprotected head.

With Hampshire's reputation it was inevitable he would be the main target, but meathead's onslaught was only the prelude to a much larger offensive. The full pandemonium of a pub fight now filled the air. Glasses broke, furniture shattered and women screamed hysterically. Incredibly, the DJ at the far end of the long, narrow pub remained unaware of the bedlam that was erupting. 'Let's All Chant' by The Michael Zager Band rang out. I could hear the irritating chorus of 'Ooh! Ooh!' as a ferocious punch embedded my teeth in my lower lip. My mouth filled with sickly warm blood.

Our assailants were now backing off; their punches and kicks had been replaced by a murderous volley of beer glasses. I raised my arms to protect my head and a glass shattered into my chest, thrown, inevitably, by Robinson. An ugly crimson stain quickly spread across my shirt.

'Remember me?' he screamed. 'Remember me, you Rovers bastard?'

How could I forget? I never forget a face, but in this ugly fucker's case I was willing to make an exception. Next to me Moggy slumped to the floor as his head took the full force of a heavy mug. A brave barmaid tried but failed to stem the flow of gushing blood with a bar towel and herself came under a cowardly attack. Moggy had finally stopped smiling.

Egghead and Clarkey cowered beside me. Glass after glass, the relentless assault continued unabated. I could see Hampshire was

A BATTERING AT THE BELL

still on his feet, miraculously still fighting back, I grabbed a glass to join him. Picking out my target – the obvious ringleader, Chrissy Robinson – I smashed the mug across his forehead. His howl of pain was matched by mine as the glass fragmented and embedded itself into my own hand. Although heavily outnumbered and severely bloodied, we were dishing out as good as we were getting. Moggy was out cold but Egghead and Clarkey were now fighting back. Unexpectedly, we were now joined by an older geezer who fought with the experience and guile of a real pro. His quick-fire punches struck home and brought cries of protests from his victims.

'C'mon, get the fuck out of here!' He signalled for us to move for the door; we didn't need telling twice. Moggy was coming round and the lull in the fighting enabled us to get outside. It was the first hiding I had had in a while and the pain was not something I was accustomed to. My lip had ballooned to twice its size and my nose, chest and hand were bleeding profusely, Moggy was in a right state, his whole face was a mass of blood. Egghead and Clarkey had a profusion of cuts and bruises while Hampshire, inevitably, was barely marked.

'You lot had better get to hospital,' our heroic ally advised, rather unnecessarily. 'An' anyway, what the fuck was that all about?'

'Bunch of City bastards just fucking started it', answered Hampshire.

'Whoah, whoah, whoah, wait a minute – who the fuck are you then, not Rovers?'

'Yeah, too fucking right,'

'I don't believe it, don't tell me I've just helped out a bunch of Rovers bastards?'

'Yeah, why? Who the fuck are you then?'

'Never you fucking mind, not a word, all right?'

He wandered off, shaking his head. A wry smile crossed his face.

BOOTED AND SUITED

'Cheers, Mike,' said Pete, who up to then had been conspicuously quiet. Being older than us and coming from Knowle, Pete knew a lot of old faces from around town.

'Who was that then, Egghead?'

'Mike Bush,' answered Pete, 'an' I've told you before – don't call me Egghead.'

'Not *the* Mike Bush, Egghead,' I replied, astonished, 'one of the old Never boys?'

'The very same,' said Pete 'We were saved by a fucking City fan.'

The irony was not lost on any of us, Mike Bush had been a well-known and well-respected face in the city for a number of years, one of the original skins from way back who used to gather in the Never on Sunday café in their immaculate Sta-Prest and Ben Shermans, their ace Vespas and Lambrettas lined up on parade outside. Mike was a genuine legend – that night he probably saved our lives.

The sounds of the sirens ebbing and flowing in the distance mingled with the rushing and reverberation in our ears as we piled into Clarkey's Cortina dripping blood and snot on to his leatherette upholstery, much to his dismay. We headed for the casualty department of Frenchay Hospital, where the doctors and nurses performed their routine weekend heroics. The turf war had erupted again. Unbeknown to us, the next round was to be held at the Black Horse the following Saturday.

Our involvement in the National Front was in the main restricted to match-day activities. Apart from regular visits to the Black Horse by the regional organiser Ray Dawkins and a one-off appearance by party Chairman John Tyndall and Chairman of the Young National Front Joe Pearce, our activities were mostly limited to sticking up racist posters and

A BATTERING AT THE BELL

selling *Bulldog* and *NF News* on a Saturday afternoon. Admittedly, Hampshire had attended the notorious Lewisham march, when thousands of racists had taken to the streets of South-east London in an attempt to provoke the local immigrants, but by and large we were content to display our badges and abuse Asian shopkeepers. For all our bravado we were far too cowardly to visit St Pauls and stir up any real trouble.

Members of the Anti-Nazi League, who were mostly white, middle-class students living in Clifton and Redland bedsits, proved a much more viable option than battling with the streetwise brothers in their own backyard. Indeed, most football fans involved in right-wing activities were probably at a loss to explain their real motives. Our involvement with the NF, just like our adoption of *Clockwork Orange* accessories several years earlier, was done purely to achieve maximum shock value. The political side of things was a secondary issue; the ability to dismay or even horrify our detractors was our main objective. If that meant saluting the air and paying lip-service to all things Nazi, then so be it.

The very real beliefs and ideologies as expressed by market trader (that's Eastville market, not the Stockmarket) Ray Dawkins and veteran right-winger John Tyndall, however, was an entirely different matter. Their calls for enforced repatriation and sterilisation of mixed-race adults and their fervent denials that the Holocaust ever happened fell largely on deaf ears. And in the case of many of our contemporaries, such as Egghead, Moggy and even dye-in-the-wool patriot Iggy, their theories met with contempt and utter disdain.

Although I was ill at ease with my own beliefs and could never really justify my own bigotry as far as the colour of a person's skin was concerned, my complete disgust with the NF and all they stood for came about as a direct result of my own prejudices — though not, as it turned out, because of those connected with race. My reluctance to attend the confrontational marches that the NF regularly organised was largely based on my cowardice and a selfish desire to preserve my liberty, especially with my visit to the USA beckoning. However, I did somewhat reluctantly agree to participate in a five-a-side football tournament arranged by the YNF to be held at a large sports centre in Stoke Newington, North London. It was a week after our ding-dong in The Bell and myself and Hampshire, together with Mick Warbutton, Maff Simmonds, Dave McDunn, Rich Nunn and a motley assortment of acne- and angst-ridden delinquents, boarded a minibus for a day out in the big city.

The young 'patriots' gathered from all over the country. Birmingham, Leicester and Norwich were all well represented but by far the largest number came from the capital itself and in particular the East End of London. Amazingly, the old murderous terrace rivalries were put to one side and fans of West Ham, Tottenham, Chelsea and Millwall all mingled, joked and swapped addresses as though they were attending some jolly school reunion. The temporary alliance of West Ham and Millwall in particular raised more than a few eyebrows — only 18 months earlier a Millwall fan had died following a clash between the two giants of aggro at New Cross Station, an event that caused so much uproar at the time the Police Federation asked the government to suspend the football season for a year.

Apart from the obvious linguistic differences between the Cockney geezers and their provincial cousins, there was one other notable feature that distinguished us from them — they were virtually all skinheads. At the start of the decade the skinhead movement had been my first love, the triumvirate of smart clothes, reggae music and the football terrace proved

A BATTERING AT THE BELL

to be an irresistible attraction for myself and thousands of other white, working-class kids. But now, nearly a decade after the original cropheads had first appeared, the re-emergence of the skinhead movement seemed strangely anachronistic. Punks, although no longer the headline-makers of the previous year, were still very much in evidence and remained a dominant force on the streets of Britain. Punk rock and new wave continued to make significant in-roads into the national charts, defying the dreadful disco boom that was engulfing the rest of the world.

I had seen one or two shaved heads and Doc Martens back in Bristol, even our own Maff Simmonds sported a sharp number one, but generally such haircuts were worn by those punks who were still determined to shock and had tired of the preening middle-class imitators who had now virtually taken over the punk movement. These London boys were cut from an entirely different cloth – the clothes still matched the standard garb I had worn many years back, but it was worn in a more overt style. Levi's jackets worn over Union Jack T-shirts were teamed up with levi's jeans that were much, much shorter than the original skins would ever have dared to wear and finished, as if manufactured that way, right at the very top of immaculately polished, cherry-red, calf-high 14-hole DMs. There were few variations of style or colour and definitely no Monkey boots. To top it all, these boys' heads were shaved and polished until they positively squeaked – not a hair in sight, something that was virtually unknown among the original skins. Indeed, anyone with hair cut under an inch in 1970 was regarded as a skinhead. This new look was not something that appealed to me. It was far too uniform and bordered on the militaristic. The rich variety, diversity and colour of the original skins was missing and the accent was now very much on an aggressive appearance. As if that wasn't bad enough, the tattoos that shouted from their shaven skulls — 'Made in London', 'White Power' and India-inked Swastika symbols — sent shivers down my spine. I was beginning to realise that I had been very much playing at this political lark, my pride and patriotism had been overtaken by my ignorance. The doubts welled up again; I was not in the same league as these boys and, what's more, I never wanted to be.

The tournament itself passed off uneventfully. The lads from Norwich deservedly won the trophy — they were a decent bunch of kiddies who were all Canaries and who had much more in common with us than the Cockney geezers. They laughed out loud when we told them of our exploits against their deadly rivals Ipswich Town and their victory inevitably left the London skins muttering profanities about carrot-crunching and sheep-shagging — at least for once they were not aimed at us Bristolians. However, the day was not yet over and we made our way to a disco and a get-together that had been arranged for us at a pub somewhere south of the river, bordering on Brixton.

We pulled up in our minibus, not quite sure what to expect. The pub was a typical London boozer, and reflected its clientele: big, bold and brassy, it would take no shit from anyone. It stood alone in an area that looked as though the Luftwaffe had just passed by. Bedecked with Union Jacks and bearing pictures of the Queen and Winston Churchill that glared down from behind its impressive, highly polished bar, this was a patriot's pub and it didn't give a monkey's what the rest of the country thought. It should have been called 'The Fuck Off Arms'. After a few pints the rhetoric started up again. Sad to say, my misgivings about the Hitler Youth earlier in the day began to dissipate with each pint. I was among other like-minded patriots and my misgivings were vanishing with each passing minute.

A BATTERING AT THE BELL

Aside from token offerings by The Jam and the obligatory 'White Riot' by The Clash, the disco was churning out ancient hits from British rock luminaries. 'My Generation' by The Who seemed as relevant in 1978 as it did back in the Sixties, but 'Satisfaction' by the Stones and 'Waterloo Sunset' by The Kinks, even though I knew they ranked as all-time classics, still could not touch my soul as numbers by Al Green and Marvin Gaye could. I longed to ask for something mean and funky, but I'm sure 'Say It Loud, I'm Black And I'm Proud' by James Brown would have been as welcome as a fart in a spacesuit.

'Denis' by Blondie, which had reached number 2 back in February, blasted out. I closed my eyes and imagined sex-goddess Debbie's luscious full red lips enveloping my...

'Having fun?'

A large, fleshy arm rested itself on my shoulder. Debbie was fading fast. The arm was owned by an even larger, fleshier individual, whom I recognised instantly as a leading figure in the NF, someone whose picture regularly appeared in the national tabloid press, usually accompanied by captions containing the words 'odious' and 'obnoxious'.

'Um, yeah, great really,' I answered. Debbie by now was a distant memory.

'Good, good. And where are you from?'

'Bristol.'

'Ah, come up with Ray, have you?'

'Yeah, an' a few others, like.'

'Good, good.'

As is often the case with someone overweight, he was sweating profusely. He was also salivating. I felt distinctly uneasy; his body odour overwhelmed me. I couldn't look him in the eye. I found myself studying the floor; he wore brown Hush Puppies. 'Never trust a man who wears brown Hush Puppies' and 'never wipe your ass with a broken bottle' were the only pearls of wisdom my old man had ever handed down to me. I didn't trust my old man on a lot of things, but he was spot on with this one. And, of course, the one about the broken bottle.

'And what's your name?'

'Ch-Chris.'

'I'm...'

'Yeah, yeah I know who you are.'

'Good, good. Tell me, Chris, would you like to go on somewhere after all this?' He was looking me in the eye and his eyebrow made a distinct twitch.

'No, no, um, I've got to go back with the others, tonight, like, on the bus.'

I knew where this was leading. I had experienced a similar approach many years before at school, with my physics teacher. He wore brown Hush Puppies as well. Call them what you want, I preferred to call them queers at the time and I fucking hated queers.

'That's all right, I'm sure I could arrange something for you. We would have a wonderful time'.

My patience had worn out. 'Go fuck yourself!' I snapped, storming off. I felt nauseous. It was another nail in the coffin of my fling with fascism, a fling that, thankfully, was coming to an end.

'Come on, Hamps, let's get out of here, I feel like throwing up.'

'Eh what? Music's brilliant, all Kinks an' that and 'e says 'e's gonna play some more Stones in a minute.' Hamps, in the music department at any rate, was beyond redemption.

We headed back to Bristol on the minibus. Unlike the others, I was not buoyed up by the day's events. I was ill at ease with myself and, again, wondered what I was doing by associating with such half-wits as the NF. I dozed off into a comforting slumber; Debbie's mouth went to work again.

A BATTERING AT THE BELL

While we were away enjoying the delights of the Smoke, somebody else had also gone to work. In revenge for our visit to the Bell, which had clearly been interpreted as a planned raid, the City boys had launched a revenge attack on a virtually empty Black Horse. Reggie Collett and the handful of locals who had borne the brunt of the assault were not amused. Reg's immediate reaction, apart from boarding up the broken windows, was to remove the Rovers flags that proudly hung behind his bar. His more long-term reaction was to look for another pub.

The following week, inexplicably, the Bell had its windows smashed, allegedly by a group of youths wearing Ku Klux Klan masks. The only people who were profiting from the tit-for-tat attacks were the glaziers of Bristol and they were loving every minute of it.

As the summer of 1978 approached, both Hampshire and I started thinking of America again. We both saw going there as an opportunity to escape from our mundane jobs and, perhaps, the start of a new, less wearisome life. The anger and violence that had dogged us throughout the Seventies, although admittedly of our own making, was now something we both wanted to put behind us. While the opportunity was still there we were only too glad to take it.

I was now approaching 23 and, against all the odds, I was still seeing Carole. Our meetings were as irregular as ever, due mainly to Carole's dislike of my drinking habits, my right-wing views and my general demeanour, which in later years was to become known as 'laddishness'. As I packed my bags for my impending departure, we both sensed that our relationship was becoming more intense. Whether it would continue after several months apart, or indeed if I would ever return, remained to be seen.

As we boarded the VC-10 at Heathrow for our big adventure,

BOOTED AND SUITED

I remembered Eddie and the Hot Rods' classic lyrics from 'Do Anything You Wanna Do':

Gonna break out of this city, leave the people here behind.
Searching for adventure is the type of life to find.
Tired of doing day jobs with no thanks for what I do.
I'm sure I must be someone, now I'm gonna find out who.

Unfortunately, I didn't.

34
Notes from a Big Country

Apart from the first few days, when the incessant rain turned downtown Manhattan into a claustrophobic, steaming version of Manchester, the sun roared and temperatures soared, bringing back memories of Britain's own heatwave some two years earlier.

The summer had been a veritable feast as far as my musical tastes had been concerned. Now, here I was in the land of soul and funk legends James Brown, Curtis Mayfield and Marvin Gaye, listening to... John Denver, ELO, The Eagles and, most disconcerting of all, The Beatles. In fact I got more pissed off than a pubic hair in a urinal telling Yanks, 'No, I don't come from Liverpool' and 'No, I've never met John Lennon.' The Americans, at least the ones I met, were living in the musical dark ages and every radio station that we tuned to dished out an insipid diet of AOR – 'Any Old Rubbish' – that made me long for the delights of Mike Read and the Radio One roadshow, '...live from sunny Bognor!'

As if hearing Jackson Brown's 'Stay A Little Bit Longer' at least once every hour wasn't bad enough, we had to put up with the

BOOTED AND SUITED

incessant adolescent wailings from the soundtrack of John Travolta's latest film, *Grease*. Not content with starring in *Saturday Night Fever*, a film that was ultimately to signal the death of disco, Travolta once again ponced around as the leader of a teenage gang, this time as the ultimate high-school cool dude, Danny.

Back in Britain, meanwhile, the sights and sounds of the sometime spike-haired punks who had menacingly filled the city streets had now come to be taken for granted by many of its inhabitants. The shock of the new, those foul-mouthed peacocks who had strutted along Chelsea's King Road, was already old hat. Company secretaries routinely dyed their hair bright green now, while pubescent schoolboys wantonly ripped their T-shirts, much to their mums' annoyance. Earrings were no longer the preserve of the punk, or the gay community for that matter, and gold-plated razor blades on chains worn round necks became that summer's ultimate fashion accessory.

Likewise, the punk music explosion from the previous year had now mellowed to the more acceptable and chart-friendly sounds of the new wave, which was now producing some of its finest offerings. 'Breaking Glass' by Nick Lowe, 'Ever Fallen In Love' by The Buzzcocks, 'White Man In Hammersmith Palais' by The Clash, 'I Don't Wanna Go To Chelsea' and 'Pump It Up' by Elvis Costello and The Jam's reworking of The Kinks' minor Sixties hit 'David Watts' had all featured in the charts by the summer of 1978, although one of the finest offerings of the genre, 'Another Girl, Another Planet' by The Only Ones, amazingly didn't register on the charts. The single featured on the group's debut album *The Only Ones*, which told tales of sleazy loving and living in urban Britain – Squeeze were to mine a similar vein a year or two later, with far greater commercial success. The album reached the lower 50s of the UK charts but remains one of the finest examples of British rock music of that era.

NOTES FROM A BIG COUNTRY

The new wave was even showing early signs of humour. 'Jilted John' by Jilted John stormed to number 4. Like The Lurkers with 'Shadow' the previous year, the song told a tale of unrequited love, only this time the school playground name-calling of 'she's a slag, she's a slut' and 'Gordon is a moron' replaced the threat of a shooting in the legs.

The biggest-selling single of 1978, and one of the biggest of the decade, was a bland and weak cover version of one of the archetypal skinhead records from way back in 1969. 'Rivers Of Babylon', originally by The Melodians but now reworked by the Anglo-German disco outfit Boney M, went to number 1 in April and stayed in the charts for a staggering 40 weeks. However, the reinvented skinheads of 1978 were probably quite unaware of the earlier heart-rending ballad, a tale of slavery and Rastafarianism. Oddly enough, the track found favour with the original and less prejudiced skins, but met only with derision and abuse from their more ignorant imitators. Many of the new skins were not inspired by reggae as their older brothers had been and those with neo-fascist views in particular had looked for, and found, a voice in some of the punk acts who were still peddling what they classed as true street music. Bands such as Cock Sparrer and Slaughter and the Dogs appealed to the new skins, and none more so than a bunch of football ruffians going by the name of Sham 69.

The band, headed up by stereotypical Cockney cheeky chappie Jimmy Pursey, were allegedly named after some graffiti seen on a wall. The graffiti had originally read 'Walton & Hersham 1969', but had faded to read only 'sham 69' after copious dousings in urine over the years. Pursey always remained nonplussed, and at times downright enraged, by the band's association with the right wing, even appearing at a Rock Against Racism gig at the Central London Poly and various Anti-Nazi League rallies throughout 1978. Admittedly, his short hair and penchant for boots found favour with the skins, but, apart from his obvious pride in his genuine, albeit suburban, South London roots, there were never any racist messages or overtly violent lyrics in his songs. That said, recordings such as 'Borstal Breakout', 'Hey Little Rich Boy', 'Angels With Dirty Faces' and the anthemic 'If The Kids Are United' underlined and promoted the band's allegiance to the downtrodden working-class kids of Britain, an area of society that the reinvented skins now claimed to represent, displacing the middle-class poseurs who pertained to be punks.

Although the USA could possibly claim to be the true birthplace of punk rock, punks, not to mention skinheads, were as rare a sight as rocking-horse shit during our travels across the States. Even Blondie, who by the summer of 1978 were taking Britain by storm with their brand of infectious punk-pop, were virtually unknown in their native country. References to the USA's very own godfather of punk, Iggy Pop, who had tasted only minor success with punk classics 'The Passenger' and 'Lust For Life' in Britain, were met with raised eyebrows.

'Iggy Pop? What kinda name's that fer a singer?' asked Joe, an ignorant Philadelphian, who was to be our driver for the next couple of months. 'An' who the fuck's Siouxsie and the Banshees, a goddamn Red Indian band?' he continued. It was to be one long, frustrating summer.

Siouxsie Sioux, Britain's punk princess and one-time member of the Pistols' Bromley Contingent, had at last made her debut in the charts back in Britain with 'Hong Kong Garden', a song that was written as a protest at the skinheads' targeting of Britain's immigrant community. The song derived its title from a Chinese restaurant in Chislehurst, the owners of which regularly attracted racist abuse, to Sioux's disgust. Even a seemingly inoffensive record like this carried a hidden political message.

I had long dreamed of hitting that legendary stretch of tarmac

NOTES FROM A BIG COUNTRY

known as 'Route 66' with a classic rock track blasting out – if not Steppenwolf's 'Born To Be Wild', from the ultimate road movie *Easy Rider*, then at least some mean soul such as 'Mustang Sally' by Wilson Pickett. But no, neither of these all-time greats featured on Joe's playlist. Instead, we were treated to John Denver's 'Grandma's Feather Bed'. Somehow John Denver's trebly warble did not have the same effect as Pickett's throaty offerings; my dream vision of America was lost for ever.

In fact, Americans as a race were lost on me. Their fashion was as bad as their mainstream music: shaggy perms, fly-away collars and flares, which were rapidly disappearing in Britain, were in full effect Stateside. Every bar and club was filled with Tony Manero lookalikes, flashing their chest hair and gold medallions, strutting their stuff and worshipping at the altar of disco to such anthems as Dan Hartman's 'Instant Replay', John Paul Young's 'Love Is In The Air' and the unforgettable 'Boogie Oogie Oogie' by A Taste of Honey. Even back in Britain, where the new wave was soon to be crowned king, the disco boom enjoyed massive chart success. Home-grown bands such as Hi Tension and Heatwave were making a big noise with 'British Hustle' and 'Mind Blowing Decisions'.

I couldn't even come to terms with 'fast food' – a trip to McDonald's (which in 1978 had not yet exerted a stranglehold on the high streets of Britain) filled us all with trepidation. Up until then, our experiences of ordering burgers were based on a cosy high street Wimpy snack bar, where your toughest decision was whether to put red or brown sauce on your chips. At home, we orderly English would patiently queue for a bag of greasy chips and religiously recite 'yes please' or 'no thanks' in response to 'do you want salt and vinegar?' The daunting question 'How do want your eggs?' brought out the stumbling buffoon in us. 'Fried?' was not the correct answer. Any nation that can possess three ways of frying an egg was not for me.

BOOTED AND SUITED

'Sunny side up? Over easy? Or half-an-half?' The waitress looked at me quizzically. I stood my ground.

'Fried', I replied, 'and don't give me any of that grits crap.'

'Pardon me?'

'Nothing'.

'Sorry, sir, I thought I heard you say something. My mistake'.

And that was another thing. I couldn't stand their ingratiating pleasantness. One more 'Have a nice day' and I was going to vomit. Not only was I longing for the Radio One roadshow, Marmite and a pint of warm beer, I was now longing for good old British surliness. I was one homesick Brit.

After eight weeks of scrawling 'Bristol Rovers F.C.' and 'The Jam' on numerous viewing decks of skyscrapers such as The Empire State Building in New York, the Trans America Tower in San Francisco and the Sears Tower in Chicago and having numerous rows with mouthy Yanks who were convinced that John Wayne had single-handedly bailed out us Limeys in both world wars and that they had made an honourable retreat from Vietnam, I was ready to come home. The others felt the same. Hampshire was not one for mixing with our colonial cousins, apart, that is, from screwing the fattest, ugliest Australian tart you could imagine, but like me he also left his mark on the USA – in the absence of a shoe-box and a wardrobe, he had a shit in the Grand Canyon.

35
Working-class Heroes

During our last week in the United States, the football season kicked off back in Britain. Rovers' first games of the new campaign were the home and away ties against Fourth Division Hereford United in the League Cup. While we were bidding our farewells to the land of the Big Mac and the even bigger arses, our mates were causing mayhem in the quaint market town of Hereford following a 0–4 defeat. Five hundred fans took part in the riot and fifty were arrested during and after the match as they attempted numerous pitch invasions and acts of hooliganism that bordered on the barbaric. Two innocent citizens of Hereford who hadn't even attended the game were assaulted and then urinated on and, for good measure, a moped was stolen, eventually to turn up on the roof of a car parked on a garage forecourt. The train carrying the fans back to Bristol fared just as badly, with barely a lightbulb or window left intact and once again someone ended up being urinated on, this time the unfortunate guard. British Rail dubbed the train as a 'riot special' and demanded payment for damages from Bristol Rovers Football Club. The club, understandably, didn't offer a penny in recompense, but vowed never to run a football special again.

The following week the chairman of the bench of the local magistrates described the fans as 'going berserk' and said that it had been an evening when 'God-fearing people were afraid to walk the streets'. The majority of those arrested were merely fined, including our old mates Roy Cash, Jimmy White and Tim Bass who received a £150 fine for insulting behaviour. Less fortunate was our very own Iggy, who was caught red-handed causing mayhem. On this occasion his cries of innocence and pleas for leniency fell on deaf ears. He was sentenced to six months' imprisonment for assault, the severity of the term due largely to the fact that he already had a suspended sentence hanging over him for his arrest at Eastville following the Sheffield United disturbance and an attack on a Manchester United fan at a game in Blackpool back in January. Even in the Seventies we all hated Man U.

Roger Mitchum visited Iggy in the cells as he was about to be sentenced.

'How does it look, Iggy?' queried Rog sympathetically.

'Not keen, Rog, not keen,' he answered matter-of-factly. To Iggy and hundreds, if not thousands of others like him, a prison sentence was an unfortunate occupational hazard.

Iggy missing from the scene was a major disappointment. Life was always somewhat quieter, if not downright dull, when the ginger-haired warrior wasn't around. But there was a sense of inevitability about the fact that his short-fuse of a temper, which had led to numerous altercations over the years, had finally caught up with him.

The violence on the streets showed no signs of abating. Indeed, with the mounting threat of the National Front and the more militaristic British Movement and Column 88 and their entourage of resurgent skinheads goose-stepping through the streets, peacetime Britain was heading for one of its darkest periods.

Not that the violence was confined to Britain. Back in America Sid Vicious was living out the trashy dregs of his punk dream. The ex-Pistol, now firmly entrenched in the twilight subculture of New York, was sharing his girlfriend's Nancy Spungen's drug-obsessed lifestyle and revelling in his role as punk's biggest anti-hero. His virtuoso rendition of Frank Sinatra's 'My Way' had been a huge hit back in the summer and was to become the undisputed highlight of Malcolm McLaren's cinematic fantasy *The Great Rock 'n' Roll Swindle*.

On 12 October 1978, Sid stabbed Nancy Spungen to death in what, according to him, was a bungled suicide pact. Within 24 hours he was charged with murder and incarcerated in New York's Rikers Island prison until McLaren and Richard Branson raised the $50,000 bail money. No sooner had Sid been released than he attempted suicide, first by mutilating his right arm and then by threatening to jump out of a hotel window, only to be talked out of it by McLaren, who promised the deranged Sid a Sex Pistols reunion. Some hope. Back in Britain Johnny Rotten had formed Public Image Limited and had reached number 9 in the charts with 'Public Image'. No future for the Pistols, it would seem.

McLaren meanwhile, never one to miss out on a marketing opportunity, wasted no time in producing T-shirts featuring a cartoon of a rose-shrouded Sid Vicious with the words 'I'm alive. She's dead. I'm yours' shamelessly emblazoned across it. The shirts sold for £6.50 from the Kings Road boutique that he co-owned with Vivienne Westwood, which had now been renamed 'Seditionaires' — sedition, meaning conduct or speech inciting to rebellion or treason. I'm sure any irony was lost on Sid who, at a party in New York's West Village to celebrate his parole some four months after

Nancy's death, died of a fatal heroin overdose. He was just 21 years old.

Iggy's imprisonment had had a sobering effect on all of us; the appeal of the terrace was on the wane, for me at any rate. I was now seeing Carole on a much more regular basis and my visits to the city-centre pubs, although often met with murderous stares from City fans who had now begun to claim the central pubs as their own, were becoming somewhat safer, as I had a female on my arm. Not that everyone from the blue half of the city was as fortunate as me. Steve Rodd, or 'Roddy' as everyone called him, one of Rich Nunn's and Roger Mitchum's mates from Kingswood, was viciously stabbed by marauding City fans as he waited at the bus stop with his girlfriend.

The hold that Rovers, and more specifically the Tote End, had exerted over me for the last ten years was beginning to weaken. Although I had attended the first few home games, it was not until 28 October that we ventured on our first away trip of the season, as much to celebrate Hampshire's 23rd birthday as to watch Rovers play.

We trundled up the M5 to Leicester in a hired transit van. Minibuses and vans were now becoming the favoured mode of transport for football hooligans since the decline and withdrawal of the specials by British Rail and the reluctance of coach companies to hire their transport to unauthorised fans. Transits had their drawbacks, but there was a distinct advantage to being able to arrive in an unwelcome town relatively unnoticed. Unless, of course, you hired one with 'Gullivers of Bristol' emblazoned across the side. As we did.

Leicester City were known to have a decent mob and although their infamous 'Baby Squad' were still attending antenatal class, they were rumoured to be up for it and, more importantly, well organised. That was something that could

WORKING-CLASS HEROES

hardly be said of Rovers' disparate set of hooligans, who were mostly a ragbag mix of skins, punks and ageing smoothies. There were, however, a couple of distinct items of terrace clothing that crossed all style and cult divides towards the tail-end of 1978, and not just in Bristol. As with most fashion trends, this one started in London and, more specifically, on the bleak and unwelcoming terraces of Cold Blow Lane, SE17, home of Millwall FC.

The Donkey jacket had for years been worn by generations of British working men and, for that matter, a handful of skinheads back in 1970 who couldn't afford a genuine crombie or sheepskin coat. It was no surprise, therefore, that this humble but durable and peculiarly British item of clothing should make a comeback in 1978, when it was worn as much as a badge to prove your working-class credentials as it was to keep out the vagaries of a British winter. This inverted snobbery was something that I had always been guilty of. And as if wearing the Donkey jacket in the style of a bona-fide Port of Bristol Authority docker, Geordie shipbuilder or Irish navvy wasn't enough, the ultimate proof of your working-class roots was deemed to be the donning of a cloth flat cap as worn by the subjects of a gloomy Lowry painting many years before. The fashion shops were aghast at this latest trend, while workwear outlets Stuckeys and gent's outfitters Dunn & Co could barely believe their luck.

We bundled out of our transit resembling a mob of 'flying pickets' — that unruly bunch of trade unionists who were bedevilling Jim Callaghan's beleaguered Labour government at the time. Once again the dustmen were on strike, as were the bakers, hospital workers and gravediggers, all of whom were protesting at the government's pay-restraint policy. The infamous winter of discontent, which was ultimately to bring down the government and unleash Thatcherism, was about to erupt. Britain was not a happy place to be.

BOOTED AND SUITED

Leicester typified the mood of the country, a mean and harsh city with a population to match. It was also a fiercely proud city, whose inhabitants didn't take kindly to intruders. Especially those who were determined to cause trouble.

Although I had abandoned the National Front and everything it stood for, I was able to sink back in to the gutter when the dangerous duo of the tribe and the alcohol combined. 'Leicester's full of Pakis, Leicester's full of Pakis, la, la, la, la!' I roared with the rest of the mob. There were even nods of agreement from the opposition fans packed by the side of us on their Spion Kop. Whether we were enticed by Leicester's reputation as top men or the promise of Hampshire buying a round to celebrate his birthday was open to conjecture, but either way we had a good turn out that caught the local constabulary off-guard. Rovers fans were capable of turning out in large numbers when it was least expected; on other occasions we could barely scrape enough support together for a meeting in a phone box.

Leicester was one of those rare grounds where the two sets of fans were positioned next to each other, albeit separated by steel fences and a 20-foot sterile area which, patrolled by thuggish coppers and oafish stewards, meant there was little chance of a bundle. That said, the home fans routinely dropped steaming cups of tea and flicked lighted cigarettes from the stand above, doing their level best to provoke and antagonise their visitors.

The action kicked off at the final whistle after the two teams had done their utmost to pacify the baying fans by producing a soporific 0–0 draw. We left the powder-keg terrace at the same time as the Leicester fans who, like us, were eagerly awaiting the ruck that was surely to come. We were now within striking distance of the very same kiddies who not five minutes earlier had been threatening us with fingers drawn across throats and of promises to remove our heads and shove them up our own arses.

The two mobs were now separated from each other by only a handful of 'couldn't care less' coppers and a line of ineffectual temporary steel barriers. The clash was brief but bloody. The barriers that had been intended to keep the peace were now seized upon by the Rovers fans and thrown through the air, to devastating effect. A throaty roar of attack accompanied the onslaught, announcing that we were to be no pushovers. The coppers' looks of dismay and surprise were matched only by the looks of anger and indignation from the Leicester boys, whom we all knew weren't about to roll over and die.

After a few token arrests the coppers tried in vain to herd us on to the supporters' club coaches where the scarf-wearing, bobble-hatted incumbents were already tucking into their cheese sandwiches and dispensing tea from their thermos flasks.

'Get on the fucking coaches, you lot.'

We were insulted. I hadn't travelled on a supporters' club coach since my brush with death at Swansea and I wasn't about to start again now.

'We're not on the coaches, we're parked up in town.'

'Well, fuck off into town then before I nick you,' came the helpful reply.

The majority of our comrades had travelled by train and were now smugly being escorted back to the station by a phalanx of coppers. Their job had been done. With a police cordon around them they could now relax, terrify the Saturday shoppers and bellow out their boastful, though somewhat inaccurate chants – 'Leicester run, Leicester run, Leicester run from everyone, la, la, la, la, la, la, la, la-lah.'

The irate Leicester boys were still milling around. We had no luxury of a police escort and sauntered off in the opposite direction, keeping our heads down and our mouths shut, the collars of our Donkey jackets upturned. Within five short minutes we had lost the upper hand and we were now feeling distinctly exposed. Across the road a bunch of lads made a move and stepped in line some 20 yards behind us.

Once again the mix of fear and euphoria rushed through my brain, and my shrinking bollocks. Few words were spoken. We were all fully aware of the situation and of the danger that we were facing. There were 15 of us in total, myself and Hampshire being the oldest. The others were made up of familiar and trustworthy faces from the Black Horse, including Mick Warbutton, now aged 21 and as fit as a butcher's dog. Mick was a natural leader — sly, wily and educated. His apprentice years long behind him, he was even prepared to upstage Hampshire, something that others had been unwilling to do in the past.

'Everyone just keep walking. How many of them are there?' queried Mick, weighing up the situation.

'Fucking more than us, that's for sure,' Hamps replied.

There were over 20 of them, biding their time, waiting for an opportune moment to strike. We were now in the town centre. The streets were devoid of shoppers and staff, it was that dull limbo period between the shops closing and the pubs opening. Mick's brain was working overtime. He was about to turn the tables.

'Right, we'll turn the next corner, get into some doorways. Grab anything, right? We'll just do it, OK?'

'How about if…' Rog Mitchum attempted to qualify Mick's plans.

'Look, we'll just fucking do it, right?'

'Right.' We answered in unison.

We rounded the corner. Unbelievably, standing there before us was a pile of rubble, left courtesy of Midlands Gas, not to mention paraffin lamps, bollards and assorted bits of street

WORKING-CLASS HEROES

debris. We grabbed what we could and scurried into nearby shop doorways. I was teamed up with Russ Furnell. Russ had made his name earlier in the year after his performance on the pitch with the corner flag against Southampton. He was about to perform again, only this time with a very different weapon.

I could hear the Leicester boys rounding the corner, anticipation of a ruck speeding up their steps. In the fading evening light they hurried down the near-empty street. Opposite me, anxiously lying in wait, I could see Mick and Hampshire. Others were positioned further on down the road. We emerged from the shadows as one. 'Come on then, you bastards!' the cry went up as we mercilessly fired in.

Our makeshift weapons proved the decisive factor as our attack caught them unawares. The ones who stood and fought quickly regretted it; lumps of tarmac, boards and lamps mercilessly rained down on our erstwhile pursuers. I ruthlessly clouted one with a road sign, sending a deep resonant 'thwack' through the street and a pulsating shockwave up my right arm, before kicking and punching him. All around were cries of anguish and pain as our missiles and fists hit home – it had been a stunning victory with virtually no injuries of our own, which was more than could be said for the luckless Leicester boys, who vanished into the evening licking their wounds. All except one unfortunate wretch, who found himself lying in the mud and debris of a six-foot-deep trench, courtesy of an untimely collision with a paraffin lamp wielded by a certain Mr Furnell.

We were full of self-congratulation as we boarded the minibus; the day's violence sparked memories of past glories. The reminiscing was as much part of the ritual of violence as any punch or kick ever was; we revelled in our behaviour and delighted each other with our acts of heroism. For that is what they were to us. To each other, if not to outsiders, we were heroes, including the poor bastard that we had left beaten, battered and snivelling in that mud-filled trench somewhere in Leicester. Fucking heroes.

36
Bridewell Blues

I'm not sure that I ever totally agreed with John Peel's weeping statement that The Undertones' excellent debut hit of October 1978, 'Teenage Kicks', was 'the perfect pop song of all time'. Not when you consider that in the same month The Jam had their sixth chart hit with their grim but magnificent tale of street thuggery, 'Down In The Tube Station At Midnight', and that only seven years earlier Marvin Gaye had released the wonderful 'What's Going On'. Indeed, if Feargal Sharkey and John O'Neill had retained their original lyrics, 'Teenage Kicks' might not have received any airplay at all, let alone have reached the lower echelons of the Top 40, and John Peel may never even have had the opportunity to form an opinion. At first the song contained the lyrics 'I wanna hold it, wanna hold it tight, get teenage kicks right through the night' – the simple word 'it' referring to the one-eyed, purple-headed womb ferret. Plainly put, the song in its original form was a paean to the delights of teenage masturbation. As Feargal Sharkey later candidly admitted, there was little else to do in Derry on a Saturday night when you looked like him. The Undertones were genuine, if unlikely, teenage heroes. Sharkey was hardly a heart-throb and their choice of clothing reflected everything that was bad about Seventies fashion: polo-neck sweaters, fake fur-trimmed Parkas and brown flares hovering way above dubious footwear. It was not a deliberate choice or even a fashion statement. The Undertones' garb consisted of real items of clothing that they wore every day – the kind of stuff your mum bought you from town. Punk fashion, which was now readily available in most high streets on the mainland, was yet to make an appearance in their troubled city.

In the troubled city of Bristol, the Black Horse and other similar watering-holes of north and east Bristol were still our favoured destination on a Friday night, when lads traditionally met their mates, drank and swore too much, listened to punk rock and habitually made a nuisance of themselves. But on a Saturday evening, when it was customary to tart yourself up, put your tapered-leg peg strides on and spend your time in the more refined company of the fairer sex, the brighter lights and sophisticated sounds of the city centre beckoned. That said, trying to find appropriate entertainment for an ageing soul boy and his partner was proving to be something of a lost cause. Steve and Adryan's Avon Soul Army had long been demobbed, leaving only a few hardy individuals to carry on fighting a guerrilla war against the relentless onslaught of disco.

The Guildhall Tavern no longer echoed to the sounds of Juggy Jones and Donald Byrd, but to less edifying offerings by Boney M and Rod Stewart. The clubs likewise sold out lock, stock and barrel to disco in the wake of *Saturday Night Fever* and, although Manu Dubango had made a welcome return with 'Big Blow', and Funkadelic's mighty 'One Nation Under A Groove' raised my hopes by rising to number 9 in December and reminded me that dance music could still be as funky as

BRIDEWELL BLUES

the devil intended, the majority of clubs gave in and dished up fare such as Rod Stewart's embarrassing 'D'Ya Think I'm Sexy' as their nightly dancefloor fillers. What's more, the City fans who were still mixing it with the big boys of the First Division had now infiltrated and overwhelmed the centre pubs and clubs in a way that only a few years earlier they could only have dreamed about. As a result, the few Rovers fans who dared venture into those venues had to keep a low profile and a tight rein on their emotions. Unfortunately that wasn't always simple to do.

My old man, apart from offering helpful homilies on brown Hush Puppies and broken bottles, always claimed that it took a man to walk away from a fight. I know his commendable theory was honourable, but, in practice, when surrounded and egged on by your mates it never quite worked out. So, from the age of 14, when I first donned my hobnails and hitched up my Levi's, I had chosen to ignore his noble theory. On a Friday afternoon two days before Christmas 1978, it was severely put to the test.

On my somewhat premature return from the United States, I reluctantly trudged back to the printing factory where I had served my apprenticeship and begged for my job back. Unfortunately they gave it to me, although, at Christmas time, with a wad of cash in my back pocket due to a seasonal bonus, I must admit it seemed worth having.

The morose blast from the hooter at 12.30 lifted my spirits and signalled the start of an extended leave from the Avonmouth hell-hole. I headed into the city centre for the customary pre-Christmas piss-up with Johnny Taylor, one of my few workmates who, though not an avid Rovers fan, shared both my beliefs and my cynical view of the outside world and a healthy dislike for Bristol fucking City. John still possessed the faintest of Lancashire accents from his native Oldham, and still carried a torch for his beloved Manchester City. But when push came to shove he sided with the blue team from Bristol as, in his own words, 'I can't watch a team who play in fucking red.'

Three hours and many pints later we staggered out of the Wheatsheaf, which like every other pub in the city centre was full of mouthy City fans, drunkenly singing along to Ian Dury's future number 1 'Hit Me With Your Rhythm Stick'. Dury, a genuine rocker who had been on the music scene for more years than he cared to remember, had tasted chart success earlier in the year with 'What A Waste', an amusing though unhappy account of his own life story. Sadly, it also reflected the lives of many young British males, who recognised some kinship with this somewhat vulnerable-looking character, who was often wont to sport a Donkey jacket and cloth cap, just like them.

The freezing cold hit us like a hammer as we exited the red-hot atmosphere of the pub, where the odd threatening glance ensured I kept a tight hold on my beer glass and an even tighter one on my emotions. Mind you, I found it nigh on impossible not to add on 'Shoot the bastard! Shoot the bastard!' after the City fans had sung their 'When the red, red, robin goes bob, bob, bobbin along' anthem.

'Fucking mouthy cunts,' I muttered to John, who nodded.

'Yeah, don't I know it – think they own the fucking place.'

'Too right, couple of years ago you wouldn't have heard a fucking word, but now...'

'Yeah, well those days 'ave gone, Browner, and it's about time you got used to it.'

'Yeah but...'

'Just fucking leave it, will you, you ain't 18 any more.'

John was right. It was a sad but undeniable fact: Rovers and their fans had lost their position of top dogs in Bristol. The City slickers had the upper hand, and those starry-eyed days of toe-to-toe scrapping when aggro was spontaneous and the taking and defending of ends was seen by many as a point of honour, even a righteous past-time, had long gone. Football hooliganism had changed. My era was coming to an end and I didn't like it, not one little bit.

We lurched our way through the miserable Christmas shoppers, who busily ushered their snotty-nosed, bawling kids away from us as if we were suffering from a dose of bubonic plague. It's a wonder that we weren't, what with the rubbish from the dustmen's strikes piling up on the streets and the dead bodies going unburied due to the continuing strikes.

Out of the corner of my eye I clocked them. Two City fans who could have passed for twins, a couple of right bladderheads, denim jackets and jeans, red-and-white scarves knotted cravat-like round their scrawny necks.

'Oi, wankers, want some?' It was a pathetic threat, but it was the best I could muster. 'Yeah you, you City cunts, come on!'

'Leave it, Browner, it's not worth it.' John was trying, unsuccessfully, to calm me down. I was wound up and raring to go – the tossers from the Wheatsheaf had seen to that.

'Go fuck yourself.'

'You fucking what?' I stepped a pace forward, fists raised boxer-like, a pissed-up pugilist.

'You're pissed, just fuck off, will you.'

My mind was made up. I was oblivious to the hundreds of shoppers and potential witnesses. I swung a lazy, drunken windmiller of a punch. It made contact but did little damage. The recipient of my blow took it easily and landed a double of his own on me before I could muster any follow-up.

'Just fuck off and leave it out, we don't want any trouble.' He meant it. Clutching an M&S bag in his other hand, he was as sober as a judge and I was as pissed as the proverbial fart. If he had wanted to he could have buried me; I was wasted.

'Yeah? Tough!' I lunged at him again, barely hearing John's shout.

BOOTED AND SUITED

'Chris, leave it! It's the law!'

Starting trouble in the middle of Broadmead, not one hundred yards from Bridewell nick, was not a good idea. I quickly came to my senses and began to leg it. If I had been sober I might have made it, but with a gallon mixture of Trophy and Courage best bitter on board, I was a slow, lumbering waste of space.

The result of my alcohol-induced scrap was that I had my collar felt for the first time in a number of years. I had been cautioned and chucked out of numerous grounds in the past more times than I cared to remember, but the last time I had been nicked, embarrassingly, was for thieving a delivery of Sunday papers from outside a newsagents on my way home from a blindingly drunken Saturday night. A £50 fine, a slap on the wrists and guffaws of derision from my mates was enough punishment on that occasion. The previous time had been the infamous 'Battle of the Yobs' back in 1973 when I was just 17 and a *Clockwork Orange* clone. I was now 23 and on the verge of getting engaged – I should have known better.

A night in the cells of Bridewell is not recommended at the best of times, but when it's the Christmas weekend and you've been told you're staying in over the holiday period, it conjured up thoughts of the Turkish prison Billy Hayes encountered in *Midnight Express*. I prayed to God that I would not meet a similar fate, for I had no wish to be buggered too. I was convinced I was going to Horfield nick and consequently spent a sleepless night pacing the foul-smelling cell worrying myself sick, vomiting in the disgusting toilet pan and listening to the echoing sounds of heavy footsteps, jangling keys and drunken wasters forlornly protesting their innocence.

As it turned out there had been so many arrests that Friday that the magistrates decided to sit on a Saturday morning to free up some of the cells and clear the backlog. I was led up into the courtroom where a tearful Carole and my loyal brother Mike sat

BRIDEWELL BLUES

clutching some hurriedly put-together personal belongings in preparation for my six-month stretch. I got a £150 fine, a three months' suspended sentence for violent and abusive behaviour and a cheery 'Merry Christmas' from the magistrate. I paid the fine in one go from my Christmas bonus, and breathed a sigh of relief. I felt like an overstuffed turkey that had escaped from the clutches of Bernard Matthews.

37

The Melting Pot Boils Over

The last year had promised so much, yet had delivered so little. And predictably, the events over Christmas 1978 had been the final boil on the backside of that disappointing year. My great love affair with the USA had proved to be a major mismatch, and although the continuing Winter of Discontent was doing its utmost to test my loyalties, deep down I knew even a ragged and battered Britannia was still my one and only true love.

The early months of 1979 proved that the reinvented skins were not to disappear as rapidly as the original version had back in the early Seventies. And when Joe Hawkins's favourite team, West Ham, visited Eastville on 20 January, you could have been forgiven for thinking that you had returned to the days when Levi's cost three quid and Desmond Dekker was murdering the Queen's English with 'Israelites'. My little run-in with the law, though not in the same league as any of Joe's fictitious escapades, ensured I gave his young brothers a wide berth. And that applied particularly to the contingent of black-shirted, eagle-wing-badged British Movement members who had set up camp in the

THE MELTING POT BOILS OVER

Black Swan and who busied themselves scaring the living daylights out of its elderly, domino-playing West Indian clientele.

In fact, the majority of Rovers fans gave the East End geezers a wide berth which, together with the 1–0 victory to the Hammers, ensured the day passed off with little incident. Moreover, the highly respected Cockneys influenced even more young Bristolians to join the ever-swelling ranks of the booted, racist bovver boy that day. By the spring of 1979 there were as many shaved heads on show on the terraces and Doc Martens stomping across the seafront as there had ever been, and, furthermore, they had been joined by the original Ben Sherman wearers, the mods, who had made a comeback thanks to the continuing promotion of the movement by bands such as The Jam and Secret Affair. Although there was no formal announcement of marriage between the two, the skins and the mods somehow contrived to produce an appealing, if somewhat flawed, bastard of an offspring in the form of the rude boy.

Not that the rude boys were a new cult, at least not with black kids. The original rude boys were a product of West Kingston's Trenchtown ghetto. They could be found causing havoc 'wid de ratchet in de waist' (ratchet being a fearsome German-made knife, a favoured and much-revered weapon of the rude boy) at any Saturday evening dance on Orange Street, when the boss sounds of Sir Coxsone and Duke Reid battled it out to find the best ska and rock-steady records around. Although the Sixties mods and early skins borrowed many ideas for clothing as well as a love of the music from Jamaica, few if any chose to dress and act like the genuine Caribbean rude boys. Therefore, when some of the 1979 version of the same mods and skins latched on to this little-known Jamaican teenage cult that many of them hadn't even heard of a year earlier and that had lasted no more than a few years back in its homeland, it begged the question: why rude boys? The answer can be found in, of all places, Coventry.

BOOTED AND SUITED

The Coventry Automatics were formed in the summer of 1977 in England's version of motor city and were fronted by keyboard player Gerald Dankin, aka Jerry Dammers. They proved to be a formidable live act and had toured, as the renamed The Special AKA, as a support act to The Clash back in 1978. The band tried, somewhat unsuccessfully, to turn the audience — a disparate mix of mods, skins, punks and their hybrid offspring, 'skunks' — on to their particular brand of punk/reggae, something that The Clash themselves had attempted with greater success. But whereas The Clash's fusion was distinctly punk with dub overtones, which worked surprisingly well, reggae fused with punk undertones as practised by The Special AKA didn't quite have the balls to carry it off.

But Dammers was a persistent and forceful character and would not be swayed from his idea of a new sound that would appeal to a much wider section of the public. Whether it was also a much-needed PR exercise and a cosmetic makeover for the heavily criticised and largely misunderstood skinhead movement was open to conjecture, but either way Dammers's decision to replace the jaded reggae beat with the more rhythmic and syncopated sounds of Sixties ska and rock steady was nothing short of inspirational.

The branding of the infectious 'new' sound was not the end of the story — far from it. In an effort to promote both their name and their music, the band went about reinventing themselves and their image. At a time when any high street in Britain could boast a melting pot of indigenous cults sporting a healthy mix of Doc Martens, brothel creepers, safety pins and fish-tail parkas, a new movement surely needed something 'special' to stand out from the crowd. The ingredients were already there and, what's more, they had been in the cupboard for years. A pinch of urbanity from a 1965 Carnaby Street mod,

THE MELTING POT BOILS OVER

a twist of Top Rank skins from 1969, a dash of terrace terror suedehead savvy from 1971. Wrap it up in an Orange Street rude boy from 1967 and let it bake on the streets of England for a month while the rest of the world stewed in its own festering juices of disco dross, and, voila, the perfectly baked British cult. And one which, in another few months or so, would contain a rather tasty, 'nutty' filling.

The final piece in Dammers's jigsaw was the creation of the band's very own 2-Tone label, with its walkin', talkin', skankin' logo Walt Jabsco, resplendent in snug-fitting black suit, wraparound shades, pork pie hat and all-important white socks. The logo was the very embodiment of the band and epitomised everything they stood for. Ditto the label's name: 2-Tone referred as much to the racial mix of the band members as to their suedehead origins and penchant for two-tone Tonik strides.

The timing of the release of The Special AKA's debut single, 'Gangsters', was impeccable. Punk had long lost its ability to shock and, like funk, had burrowed deep underground, leaving only a minority of genuine street bands such as The Angelic Upstarts and The Cockney Rejects to hold aloft the tattered punk flag. These were to eventually spawn the much-maligned Oi! movement, but in the wake of the first wave of punk the charts mostly featured mainstream new wave and squeaky-clean disco offerings.

Britain had already suffered from three terrifying number-1 disco hits when 'Gangsters' first saw the light of day in March 1979 – the frighteningly camp Village People with the so-called 'classic Seventies record' 'Y.M.C.A.', the aptly titled 'Tragedy' by The Bee Gees and the divorcees' favourite (and subsequent gay anthem) 'I Will Survive' by Gloria Gaynor. Was it any wonder that the 'Disco Sucks' movement was gathering momentum like a runaway juggernaut in the States, a movement that was to culminate in the explosive destruction of thousands of disco records in a New York football stadium and very real death threats against Grace Jones?

Personally, I was not as enamoured with 2-Tone as one might expect. It was all too contrived and too much of a rehash of old values and styles for my liking. Indeed, 'Gangsters' itself was nothing more than a reworking of Prince Buster's timeless masterpiece from 1965 'Al Capone', complete with 'Don't call me scarface' lyric as mouthed by Neville Staples, something which had already been done to death by Dennis Alcapone back in 1972. I never thought the 2-Tone stable, and in particular The Specials (as they became known after their first hit), gave enough recognition to their mentors and their influences, although everyone's favourite band Madness (and lest we forget, over the years they have racked up over 20 chart hits), to their credit, virtually made a career out of idolising Prince Buster. Their very name was taken from an early Prince Buster recording and their first two singles, 'The Prince' and 'One Step Beyond', which hit numbers 16 and 7 respectively in September and November 1979, were unashamed tributes to Mr Cecil Bustamente Campbell.

For all of 2-Tone's plagiarism, 'Gangsters' spearheaded what was to be a veritable ska and rock-steady onslaught on the charts and, although the single was originally released in March on the London-based indie label Rough Trade, it wasn't until Chrysalis signed up the much sought-after band, along with its label, and rereleased the disc on 2-Tone as a subsidiary that the track reached the charts, peaking at number 6 in July 1979.

If 'Gangsters' borrowed one or two ideas from Prince Buster's original mod favourite, their follow up 'Message To You Rudy' positively kidnapped Dandy's (aka Dandy Livingstone, aka Robert Thompson) original rock-steady rendition, it matched the original word for word, note for note, beat for beat and even

THE MELTING POT BOILS OVER

featured Rico Rodrigues, the Jamaican trombonist who was to eventually become a permanent member of the band and who performed on Dandy's original recording back in 1967. Talk about taking liberties. The Specials' first number 1, a live EP that charted in February of 1980, featured a scorching, upbeat 'Too Much Too Young' that owed much to Lloyd Tyrell's 'Birth Control', which first saw the light of day more than a decade earlier.

If nothing else though, 2-Tone successfully challenged both the record-buying public's and the skinheads' very own views of their movement which up until then had rightly been perceived as a cult that leaned heavily to the right. How could skinheads as a group appear to be so predominantly racist when the bands who played the music that they so obviously enjoyed consist of black as well as white members? Perhaps it was simply an issue that many so-say racists conveniently chose to overlook, as I had myself a few years earlier. As well as The Specials, bands such as The Selecter, The Body Snatchers, The Beat and the fledgling UB40, who all achieved moderate success in 1979, did as much to force skinheads to question their own attitudes and motives as did any Rock Against Racism concert. Not that the 2-Tone movement changed anything overnight. The 2-Tone Tour that skanked across the country during the summer of 1979 still witnessed sporadic outbreaks of violence, much as the Sham 69 concerts had the previous year. Unfortunately, it was not possible to refuse entry to every racist who was hell-bent on causing trouble – especially when not all fascist skinheads had 'NF' or a swastika tattooed across the forehead, though sadly several misguided boneheads did.

Madness, in particular, attracted the kind of following that had plagued Jimmy Pursey and his band, probably due as much to the fact that they hailed from London, unlike many of their 2-Tone stablemates, as because they were an all-white male band. Either way, like Sham 69, the band publicly distanced themselves from the sieg-heiling contingent of their audience, many of whom further enhanced their militaristic appearance by universally adopting the USAF MA1 flying jacket, in obligatory olive-green, complete with natty zip pocket on the left sleeve. Combined with Lonsdale sweatshirts and T-shirts, the jacket completed the uniform of the non-politically correct skinhead. Madness emphatically denied any right-wing associations and wisely declared themselves to be totally apolitical, much to the chagrin of the zealots from the Anti-Nazi League and the Rock Against Racism movement.

Madness had first performed as The Invaders back in 1976 and even then were obsessed with ska music and its latter-day derivatives, rock steady and reggae. The band's original line-up included, among others, Mike Barson on keyboards and Lee Thompson on saxophone and vocals. However, it wasn't until Graham 'Suggs' McPherson joined them that they changed their name to Madness, making their debut on the same fateful day in May that Margaret Thatcher became Britain's first woman prime minister.

The band, unlike Thatcher and for that matter the rest of the 2-Tone movement, possessed a rare quality that had been sadly lacking in British music for many a year: humour. At times their songs were downright rib-ticklingly hilarious, at others, bitingly satirical. Madness's distinct trademark 'nutty' sound, which successfully combined wit with Barson's accomplished saloon-bar piano playing and Thompson's skyscraping sax solos, endeared them not only to shaven-headed teenagers but their mums as well. This ensured the band's continuing success, in contrast to many of the other 2-Tone outfits who were to disappear without trace once the novelty of the label had faded, unlike Thatcher, who was to hang around and leave an indelible mark on Britain.

THE MELTING POT BOILS OVER

Margaret Thatcher's Conservative government was elected with a majority of 59 and promised a complete transformation of the British industrial and economic climate. This was to include sweeping trade union reform, something the country was undeniably in need of thanks to the previous two winters' alarming scale of disruption caused by the out-of-control trade union movement. One of Thatcher's first deeds in office was to sanction huge pay rises for Britain's police forces, a deal that she was not to let them forget in future years.

The general election campaign had been a bitter and sometimes bloody battle that culminated in the death of Blair Peach, a New Zealand teacher who had been bludgeoned by a police truncheon during a demonstration against the National Front on the streets of Southall. The NF had been keen to prove to the British electorate that they were a legitimate and viable political party with aspirations of becoming Britain's third force ahead of the fading Liberals. Back in 1977, during local council elections, the NF had even managed to secure 250,000 votes but by 1979, and the Tories playing the race card themselves with quotes of 'if you want a nigger neighbour vote for Labour' once again emerging on the hustings, albeit unofficially, the NF were a spent force. Furthermore, the re-emergent skinheads, who had largely been associated with the far right, ensured that the NF was always to be associated with booted, shaven-headed bully boys.

By the mid-summer of 1979, with the momentous decade on its last lap, Thatcher embarked on her one-woman crusade to rid Britain of socialism and to abolish the working class once and for all. Meanwhile, Britain's fashion- and cult-conscious youth, driven by admirable ethics of pride and a healthy arrogance, qualities shared by Thatcher herself, could take their pick from a multifarious and ever-changing mix of street cultures.

BOOTED AND SUITED

The word 'diverse' was inadequate to describe the motley crew of teds, mods, skins, suedes, smoothies, punks, skunks, rude boys, soul boys and headbangers that filled Britain's streets, terraces and concert halls and who listened to a cacophony of music ranging from rockabilly to jazz funk by way of punk and ska. If you couldn't find something there to please you, your life wasn't worth living. And after all, you could always don your white suit and medallions and take yourself off to the disco to listen to the 'real' music of the Seventies. Shame on you if you preferred Barton Hill Youth Club over New York's Studio 54 or Camden Town's Electric Ballroom over Old Bond Street's Embassy, or your wardrobe was more Fred Perry than Fiorucci. After all, the Seventies was one big Boogie Wonderland, wasn't it?

Not that 'Boogie Wonderland' was a particularly bad record of its genre. Indeed, it was probably one of the best, and performed stylishly by a combination of Earth, Wind and Fire and The Emotions it reached number 4 in May. The track vied with 'Turn The Music Up' by Britain's own Players Association and 'Sexy Lady' by The Thomas Heights Affair as dance music's best offerings that year. It also made a mockery of the better-known dancefloor fillers 'In The Navy' and 'Go West', as performed by New York's campest, The Village People.

The new wave, which by mid-1979 had outgrown its punk origins, had now become firmly established as mainstream 'pop' music, with groups such as Blondie, The Boomtown Rats and The Police all enjoying huge chart runs and all claiming number-1 slots by the end of the year. Their success was aided in no small part by a new promotional medium, the videotape. The Police, in particular, after serving a punkish apprenticeship, had at last seen their nights of performing in second-rate venues to second-rate audiences pay off. The group came together in London from diverse musical backgrounds but had equally impressive

THE MELTING POT BOILS OVER

pedigrees, something that ensured vocalist and ex-teacher Sting (Gordon Sumner), American drummer Stewart Copeland and the hugely accomplished guitarist Andy Summers would achieve long-term success. Like The Clash, The Slits and the aforementioned Coventry Automatics, The Police experimented with reggae. Their music could hardly be compared with that of The Clash, let alone Dennis Brown who himself had enjoyed chart success with 'Money In My Pocket' in March 1979. However, the band's well-seasoned instrumental talents paid dividends — musical ability was a quality that was notably lacking in many other outfits of that era.

The Police had released their debut album, *Outlandos D'Amour*, in late 1978 and apart from featuring a couple of punk-influenced renditions, 'Born in The 50s' and the embarrassing 'Peanuts', the album was made up of easy-on-the-ear 'white reggae' offerings, including their first two hit singles 'Can't Stand Losing You' and 'Roxanne'. By the end of the year, The Police, with their bleached-blond hair and good looks, had become the darlings of the new wave. In October 1979 they released their second album, *Regatta De Blanc*, which contained their two best sellers to date, 'Message In A Bottle' and 'Walking On The Moon'. Both went to number 1, eventually becoming two of the best-selling records of 1979.

Three records aptly encapsulated the sounds of Britain 1979-style: The Members' classy February hit 'Sound Of The Suburbs', John Lydon's Public Image Ltd with 'Death Disco' and, the best of the lot, The Ruts' awesome 'Babylon's Burning'. The single, with its opening chords accompanied by the sounds of emergency sirens, was a frighteningly accurate tale of Britain's melting pot of youth cults and street violence, a melting pot that in the summer of 1979 was in danger of boiling over. The Ruts, headed up by the distinctive throaty vocals of Malcolm Owen, were yet another punk outfit who were enamoured with, and heavily influenced by, reggae. As much as an act of appreciation of the music as a political statement, the band played numerous Rock Against Racism benefits, often appearing on the same bill as London reggae artists Misty. Ironically The Ruts often attracted right-wing boot boys to their gigs, much to their obvious disgust.

Like many bands before them, the violence at The Ruts' gigs became a source of great frustration, especially for Owen whose heroin habit, which was ultimately to cause his death the following year, was also causing problems. Nevertheless, The Ruts' debut LP, *The Crack*, demonstrated that musically they were one of the most accomplished products of the punk-rock era. Numbers such as 'Something That I Said' and 'Savage Circle' were tuneful and powerful punk anthems. 'Jah War', an account of an anti-National Front riot, underlined the band's mastery of Jamaican dub rhythms, while 'Sus', a song about excessive police powers and in particular the law's treatment of young blacks on 'arrest on suspicion' offences, was testament to the band's empathy with the black community.

As if these gems weren't enough, 1979 also saw further hits for the Jam with 'Strange Town', 'When You're Young' and 'The Eton Rifles', the latter a critique of class conflict that was their best single release so far. Likewise, The Clash produced their finest single and best-selling record to date, the clarion-call to the world 'London Calling', a track taken from the album of the same name. Although the album was a double offering, the band insisted it should be sold for the cost of a single LP, something that once more endeared them to their adoring fans. The album had something for everyone and received widespread acclaim on its release. The Clash's love of reggae clearly showed on *London Calling*, with 'Guns Of Brixton' and 'Rudie Can't Fail' being stand-out tracks, while even Mick Jones's weak voice performed well on 'Lost In The Supermarket'.

THE MELTING POT BOILS OVER

Billy Idol's Generation X finally got some chart recognition with 'King Rocker' and 'Valley Of The Dolls' and The Sex Pistols, although no longer an active unit, still managed three hits with 'Something Else', 'Silly Thing' and 'C'mon Everybody'. South London's finest, Sham 69, appeared twice in the charts, with their legendary anthem 'Hersham Boys' and the heartfelt 'Better Man Than I'. The mod revival was also represented, with 'Time For Action' by Secret Affair and 'You Need Wheels' by The Merton Parkas. Mod's second coming saw a few old favourites resurface once more and, in the last month of the decade, old Stax houseband Booker T and the MGs reached number 7 with the belting instrumental 'Green Onions'. The track that had first hit the charts in the Sixties and was now featuring in the mod movie *Quadrophenia*.

The film had first been shown in 1979 and had been an adaptation of Pete Townshend's epic double album of the same name; members of The Who acted as executive producers on the project — its release ensured an even greater resurgence of the Sixties mod movement. *Quadrophenia* starred Phil Daniels as Jimmy, a teenage mod living in London in 1964, who divided his time between pill-popping, dancing and brawling with his arch-rivals, the rockers. Daniels gave a faultless performance as Jimmy, desperately searching for his identity and coming perilously close to the brink of self-destruction, a theme that clearly struck a chord with the film's largely teenage audience. Among others who appeared in *Quadrophenia* were Leslie Ash, Toyah Willcox and Sting who starred as the 'Ace face', a legendary tasty mod who, as it turned out, wasn't quite as much of a 'face' as he seemed.

Quadrophenia was one of the most accurate films about youth culture ever made. Not since the amateurish but magnificent 1970 black-and-white skinhead film *Bronco Bullfrog* had the frustrations of bright young Britons who had no future been more accurately portrayed.

Away from the fantasy celluloid world and back to the real one, and 1979 proved to be a watershed year for the Bristol music scene. Three-chord punk outfits evolved into more musically proficient bands, influenced not only by the punk movement of the previous couple of years but also the soulboy sounds of the Guildhall Tavern from the mid-Seventies. Vice Squad, The Hybrids and The Pop Group all started to make a name for themselves in 1979, due in no small part to the Radio One DJ John Peel who seemed to be on his own one-man mission to put the embryonic 'Bristol Sound' on the map. What really got the national music press salivating, however, was the release of the compilation CD album *Avon Calling, The Bristol Collection* on Heartbeat Records which John Peel described as 'The compilation by which all others should now be judged... truly superb and not a bad track on it' – praise indeed from the esteemed DJ. Vice Squad featuring Bekki Bondage in particular benefited from Peel's patronage. Bekki recalled, 'Peel took a shine to our track [on the *Avon Calling* album] and played it to death... We had two other strokes of luck in 1979, playing our debut gig as last-minute additions to a Rock Against Racism bill at the Bristol University Anson Rooms on 12 April (where Heartbeat boss Simon Edwards spotted us), then supporting The Damned and The Ruts at the Bristol Locarno. These events were a staggering contrast to the TV Brakes days [their previous garage band's incarnation], when we considered ourselves lucky to secure gigs at the local Railway Preservation Society, and even the local Borstal, and meant that we soon picked up a sizeable local following. The problem, though, was that most of our new friends verged on the psychopathic, and we were

THE MELTING POT BOILS OVER

quickly banned from playing most venues in the South West of England.'

Davey Woodward, lead singer and guitarist with The Hybrids and later The Brilliant Corners, likewise recalls those heady days when Bristol was making a big noise on Britain's post-punk scene, here's an extract from the excellent Bristol Archive Records website (www.bristolarchivesrecord.com):

When someone asks you to look into the past and tell it like it was there's always a temptation to make it sound better, to re-invent, maybe make oneself sound more important than one was. I will do none of these things.

Everyone knows about 76, Punk!! It was also the year Chris [Galvin] persuaded me to buy a guitar. Naturally I did because he was in the brainy class and he must have had a good reason for asking me to do this.

The reason for having a guitar was to turn an amp up loud and pretend you were Hendrix and, oddly enough for that time, Ted Nugent. That's when I knew I would have to learn to write songs. What also inspired me was seeing this kid called Damon from school playing in a punk group called The Pigs. With a click of the fingers this non-descript lad from 4S was transformed into a god! And I wanted some of that! Bristol bands that meant something to me then were The Media and The Cortinas. By 78 Chris and myself and a 13 year old called Jimmy were in a band called The Hybrids. We were unashamedly Jam copyists with a bit of Kinks, Clash and Stones thrown in for good measure. There was this great little pub called The Stonehouse where Bristol's handful of mod/skin/punks hung out to watch their mates' bands. We had no mates but because I would always smash my amp up people liked us. We began to play the place on a regular basis and to my surprise became quite popular. We used to play with a band called Thin Air who really were like the Jam, many years later Thin Airs singer Paul Sandrone

BOOTED AND SUITED

would play in the last line up of The Brilliant Corners. Fitting in a strange way.

Another band I remember back then was Concrete Contraption. Now they could play proper but they were crap! Interesting to note that Si John of Reprazent fame started life in this band. You could see an interesting band every other day at The Stonehouse. Today it's an office block.

I can't remember exactly when, or even if, this is totally right but Jimmy who played drums left because his mum was either fed up of taking us to gigs, me and Chris throwing up in the van (Jimmy couldn't get drunk while his mum was around) or us buying a Doctor Rhythm drum machine.

When you're sixteen and playing live every other week you develop fast. In the space of a few years The Hybrids had become two boys and a drum machine. Not too surprisingly we sounded like Echo and the Bunnymen meets Joy Division. We played places called Mistys Nite Club and the Ace of Spades where I snogged my first fan. She was very drunk and threw up in my mouth while we were wriggling tongues. We went to a gig every night. I don't know where the money came from; well I do actually, um, stolen goods. We discovered amyl nitrate, speed, dope, and sometimes sex.

When I left school I got a job as a lab technician. It was while doing this I met a lad called Dan who played in a band called The Glaxo Babies. They had a record out and had been played on John Peel. I was awe struck! Dan would bring his guitar into work and at lunchtimes he would show me things called dis-chords which totally blew me away. He also told me to check out Captain Beefheart, which I did not get at all. Around this time I saw The Pop Group play (which I did get) and Essential Bop and Art Objects and all those Fried Egg bands that people referred to as the Clifton Scene. At that time I had a real problem relating to the so-called Clifton Scene. The people in those bands made me feel dumb. Me

THE MELTING POT BOILS OVER

and Chris had working-class chips on our shoulders. I would see these people in the Dugout*but I had nothing in common with them. I never got invited to parties or happenings. This lot were educated and pretentious and boy were we jealous!

There were loads of bands hanging out at the Dugout but I think The Hybrids were the only ones that danced to soul at The Turntable Club and slid on our jackets at Romeo and Juliet's to James Brown, but that's another story.'

---

*The legendary Dugout Club on Bristol's Park Row, which in the 1980s was to become the home of Bristol's burgeoning music scene. On the heaving, sweaty dancefloor Bristol's 'Trip Hop' scene was born with members of the Wild Bunch (Robert Del Naja, Grant Marshall, Andrew Vowles, Tricky, Nellee Hooper, Miles Johnson aka DJ Milo and Claude Williams aka Willy Wee) cutting their teeth on the wheels of steel. Some of these DJs and clubbers not only caused a stir on the decks, they were just as well known on the streets of Bristol and our paths crossed many a night at the arse end of the Seventies/early Eighties. But credit to them, several went on to form the hugely influential Massive Attack, while other musical luminaries such as Smith & Mighty and Roni Size all made appearances at the famous club. For a detailed and well-documented history of the club that was at the centre of Bristol's 1980s music scene visit: www.electricpavilion.org/dugout/home.php

38
The End of an Era

For all of the classic records that emerged in 1979, one virtually ignored disc struck a chord with me more than any other: the memorable 'Saturday Night (Beneath the Plastic Palm Trees)' by The Leyton Buzzards. It was 'memorable' to me not because of its musical content, but because of its amusing and heart-rending lyrics referring to the sad demise of the Locarno ballroom and of a way of life that would never be seen again. The late Sixties' soul and ska scenes had been an era of sharp dressers and ace music, an era that the youth of 1979 were trying, but failing, to re-create. It had been a time of leaning against the plastic palm trees of the Bali Hai bar while 'listening to the sounds of The Guns of Navarone' (a reference to the definitive ska record by the legendary Skatalites).

As a dyed-in-the-wool Rovers fan and erstwhile Tote Ender, the word 'demise' had virtually become my middle name. By the end of the Seventies, it was clear that the glory days of the 'ends', and in particular those of the Tote, had long gone, and with them the tribes and mobs who had frequented such fearsome places during the last decade. With the advent of rigidly enforced crowd

THE END OF AN ERA

segregation and more sophisticated police operations, including plain-clothed officers and the use of fledgling CCTV surveillance cameras, the pitched terrace battles between the warring factions had disappeared, never to be seen again.

Not that the violence had been eradicated from the game – far from it. The terrace terrors had become as sophisticated as the police forces who attempted to put an end to their escapades and, although the reinvented skinhead was still very much the order of the day in 1979, a smarter and altogether more streetwise hooligan was waiting in the wings. This kind of hooligan made his debut in 1979 in either Liverpool or London, depending on which style bible you read, and relied more on cunning and wit to get his kicks. On first sight, he would be the last person you would expect to cause trouble. With his penchant for smart, labelled clothing as favoured by the golfing fraternity, he was eventually to be dubbed a 'casual', and would rule the aggro end of football throughout the Eighties and beyond. The casual was as far removed, in appearance at any rate, from the skinhead as could be imagined.

The casuals' physical appearance was not the only thing that set them apart from their predecessors. With the demise of the 'ends', the casuals took to inhabiting the seated grandstands, a move that would not only remove them from the gaze of the law but also enhance their reputation as lads who were a cut above the riff-raff of the terrace and who delighted in letting the world know it. The move to the stands necessitated a new title. No longer could these elite football thug sophisticates be known as run-of-the-mill Shed End Skins, North Bank Boot Boys or Argyle Aggro Merchants – not while they were wearing trainers and clothes that cost more than the Rovers front line was worth. Millwall fans had led the way several years earlier with their Bushwackers and F-Troop name tags. They were joined by such illustriously titled mobs as the ICF, Headhunters, Zulu Warriors and 6:57 crew, with every mob in the country now being known as a 'firm' and every firm possessing generals, lieutenants and foot soldiers among its ranks.

Frankly, the kind of cult that left a calling card emblazoned with the legend 'You have been visited by the 909 Inter-City Soul Crew Under-19 Central Baby Squad Element Casual Naughty Boys' to announce who you were was not the kind of cult I could readily take to. I always thought 'Take that, you City/Northern/Cockney bastard' was sufficient. And furthermore, I could not see the appeal of spending a fortune on a designer-label jacket only for it to be ripped off your back in a bloody street battle, and getting your pristine trainers muddied in a pot-holed car park. I still had distinct and bitter memories of shedding a tear when I ripped my first pair of Sta-Prest.

My only concessions to keeping up with the myriad cults that engulfed Britain in 1979 were a bleached-blond haircut in the mode of Sting, straight-legged blue-denimed Lee jeans, 'Strange Town' badge in honour of The Jam and an occasional airing for my favourite sheepskin coat and battered Monkey boots. That said, I sometimes favoured a beige FU's zip-up jacket over a two-buttoned baggy French Connection shirt, pale-blue Pods shoes or white trainers that carried no particular logo. I did not wish to miss out on the fashion stakes on a technicality.

As far as Rovers were concerned, the 1978/79 season had fizzled out miserably. Rovers failed to score in seven out of the last ten games, due in no small part to the departure of the last terrace hero of the Seventies, Paul Randall, to Stoke City. Apart from minor skirmishes at the home game against Sunderland in April and the obligatory brawl around the grim streets surrounding Ninian Park with the Grange End – the future Soul Crew – the action off the pitch was as dull and as infrequent as that on it.

Iggy's imprisonment had not helped matters. Bob Doughty,

THE END OF AN ERA

who a year earlier further enhanced his notoriety by throwing a Fulham fan off Putney Bridge, had dished out one kicking too many and had likewise found himself incarcerated in Her Majesty's prison. Not only had Rovers continued to plummet down Division Two and flirt once again with the perils of relegation, but the Black Horse, our refuge from the perils of marauding City fans, was about to undergo a change of ownership, and with it a change of character.

Reg and Shelly Collett had grown tired of their clientele. The attack by City fans the previous year and the continuing threat of further attacks had persuaded them to call it a day. We were devastated. The Black Horse had been our sanctuary for the last few years and, with a new landlord installed who cared for neither our football preferences nor our musical tastes, it was time to move on to pastures new. We had always been a disparate crew, hailing from many districts of Bristol – Henbury, Lockleaze, Lawrence Weston, Fishponds, and even, as in Egghead's case, Knowle, south of the river. We gingerly ventured back into the city centre, where a rather grim pub, the Bunch of Grapes, became our latest 'local'.

'Harry's Bar', as the Bunch of Grapes was more commonly known, was situated in St Nicholas Street, not a bottle's throw across the road from our old favourite, the Elephant, which was now universally known as a gay pub. Apart from its punk- and reggae-dominated jukebox, Harry's Bar had little to offer us, but we were in no position to be choosy. The predominance of City fans around the city-centre pubs and clubs ensured we kept our heads down and our mouths shut, which in the case of Hampshire was an anatomical impossibility. It wasn't as if man for man the City boys were superior to us, but with three seasons in the First Division behind them, weekly battles with top geezers from the likes of Arsenal and Leeds and their head-count growing all the time, they were tactically and numerically streets ahead.

BOOTED AND SUITED

We lost count of the number of times we had run-ins with the City boys during the summer of 1979. There was the time when a mob of more than 50 of them surrounded Egghead and myself as we exited Dunlops on the Centre, which necessitated an embarrassing police escort off the premises. On another occasion, we entered the Naval Volunteer on Kings Street, only to be forced to make a hasty retreat and to find ourselves being chased ragged through the very same streets that we had dominated only a few years earlier.

On the rare occasions when numbers were more or less equal, we were still able to give a good account of ourselves. One occasion springs to mind. An enjoyable evening spent in the cosmopolitan wine bars and pubs of trendy Clifton was winding down with a final pint in the White Hart on Park Row, a pub that generally attracted a more peaceable clientele, namely students and the down-at-heel. The pub's position half a mile from the trials and tribulations of the Centre lured us into a false sense of security. We exited the White Hart, revelling in the atmosphere of a rare trouble-free evening and buoyed by an excess of alcohol. However, the atmosphere was soon to change. Across the road stood our well-known adversaries. They spilled out of the nearby Princes Court at the same time that we left the White Hart and we swiftly made eye contact. For once we had a good crew, headed up by myself and Hampshire. Wary bruiser Rich Nunn was also present, as was Roddy, who was still nursing the stab wound that he had suffered the previous year.

Hopping and jumping, we exchanged insults and picked out likely opponents, goading each other into making the first move. We weighed each other up and a quick mental count by both sides confirmed our observations – even numbers, 20 or so fit young men from either side of the divide. We clashed, brutally, fighting in the street between parked cars, passing traffic and bemused students. Punches and kicks connected viciously. I

THE END OF AN ERA

fought toe-to-toe with a lad called Clay who, ironically, I was to thank the following year for saving me from a big kicking from his mates in an incident in Harry's Bar. But that was 12 months away, and right now he was offering me no such charity. The City boys, without their usual numerical advantage, fought half-heartedly and sustained their first beating for some time. Finally, with one eye on an honourable exit, they fled along Park Row, our insults and abuses ringing in their ears. We weren't kidding anyone. We knew they would be back. Unfortunately, they were back sooner rather than later.

'Fucking showed them bastards!' I snarled between bloodied lips.

'Yeah, 'bout time too, had it their own way for too fucking long,' added a delighted Roddy. At last he had delivered some form of retribution for his injury.

'Wass reckon, Hamps?'

'Yeah, we did all right, but we'd better leg it, the bastards are sure to be back.'

We filed warily down Park Street, past the garish neon lights of Curves and Maxims, the boom-boom of the disco dross reverberating around the once-elegant street. As we entered the Centre, the familiar sights of gangs of unknown youths greeted us. We crossed the Centre heading for the bus stops of Baldwin Street and our escape routes home.

It was impossible to miss them. Across the road, a swelling number of youths watched our every move.

'Spotted 'em?' I asked no one in particular nervously.

'Too fucking right,' answered Ralph, a mate of Roddy's from Kingswood.

'Fuck's sake, there's hundreds of the bastards,' chipped in Rich. He was not exaggerating.

'Don't look round, just keep walking,' Hamps cautioned us.

I glanced over my shoulder. Baldwin Street was a mass of

shadowy characters, both sides of the road now, spilling from the pavement into the road.

'Where the fuck have that lot come from?'

'Dunno, wass reckon?'

'Come on! Come on! What we gonna do?'

The panic was beginning to show in our voices. We all waited for two simple words. They eventually came from Hampshire.

'LEG IT!'

We took off, quickly. The huge mob behind us let out an almighty bellow. I was at the back with Roddy and Ralph. For some unfathomable reason, the three of us, feeling separated from Hampshire and the rest, made a beeline for the safe haven of an Italian restaurant. We crashed through the flimsy doors and sought refuge among the astonished clientele and the unsympathetic staff.

'Get outta my restaurant! I don't wanna no trouble!'

'Get the law, quick!'

'No, get...'

'Just get the fucking law – NOW!'

'No, I...'

They crashed through the doors behind us, hell-bent on exacting their revenge. Plates, ashtrays and wineglasses crashed down on us.

'Come on, you Rovers bastards, have summa diss!'

We huddled in a heap against the far wall, trying to make ourselves small and less of a target, our arms wrapped around our heads, fending off the missiles.

'Get out! Get out! I've phoned the police!'

The mob exited the restaurant as quickly as they had entered, leaving behind them a pile of broken glasses, smashed plates and ruined pasta. Our injuries, surprisingly, were minor, and our egos vied with our bodies for the most bruises.

Hampshire and the others also escaped unscathed, although

THE END OF AN ERA

the chase through Castle Park to Old Market had been a tad too close for comfort. Truth be told, it had been an evening packed with the kind of excitement we hadn't particularly enjoyed. And unfortunately, the night's events were not to be an isolated incident. Over the following years, the City fans continued to enjoy both numerical and territorial advantage and, although we offered belligerent resistance and inflicted one or two results of our own, deep down we knew our time as top dogs was long gone.

Those halcyon days were now a dim and distant memory. The times when I lived only for the weekly buzz of performing on the terraces, which were my stage, were over. Fashion was no longer an ever-evolving process that changed almost weekly. It had become merely a regurgitated, recycled mishmash of styles that had long passed their sell-by date. The same was true of the music. The only 'new' sounds on the horizon were hip hop's tiresomely repetitive beats, rap, which had been brewing on the streets of US ghettos for the last few years, and new romanticism, which preferred the medium of video by way of MTV to the sweaty rigours of the stage. For Grandmaster Flash's rap read U-Roy's version and for Duran Duran read Bryan Ferry's Roxy Music – same horse, different jockey.

Nearly a decade earlier, my first away game of the Seventies had been an eventful visit to genteel Torquay; I had donned my Sta-Prest and bovver boots and had been in awe of my elders. Coincidentally, my last away game of the same decade was to the very same seaside town, for an uneventful League Cup tie. This time, instead of being accompanied by my mates, whose approval and plaudits I craved, I took Carole, who had now become my fiancée. My own wardrobe had changed somewhat in the intervening ten years, but all around me stood 1970 clones participating in Seventies aggro. Predictably, a pub known as The Bristolian was the choice of watering-hole for visitors from our

BOOTED AND SUITED

fair city. By now, I was trying to distance myself from the antisocial behaviour that I had once thrived on, although the attack on Carole by a fearsome police Alsatian and its foul-mouthed handler as we left the pub severely tried my patience.

Hampshire and Iggy, as well as many of the others with whom I had shared the roller-coaster ride of the Seventies, were also there, and, while many of them were still pursuing the crack, I was endeavouring to put it behind me. Ahead of me, in the early Eighties, lay a new, more sedate adventure. Nevertheless, it was an adventure that held just as many terrors, in the form of house-buying, unemployment, marriage and fatherhood in Thatcher's Britain.

Iggy got married in 1981, at a time when England's inner cities were erupting in flames of racial conflict, sparked off, incidentally, by a riot in the St Pauls district of Bristol in April 1980. Both Hampshire and I tied the knot in 1982, though not to each other, I hasten to add. Marriage and fatherhood changed our outlook on life drastically, and, although rucks on the dancefloor and on the terrace still occasionally flared up – the following February, Chelsea's North Stand lads, headed up by Egghead's idol, the legendary 'Eccles', battled with us on the streets of Eastville – they were mostly events that I no longer dared, or even cared, to participate in.

As for Rovers, the Eighties brought about not only flirtations with relegation but also the very real threat of bankruptcy. The same was true for City who, in 1982, went perilously close to going out of business themselves; they languished in the lower reaches of the Fourth Division, their heady days in the First Division long forgotten. In 1987, Rovers board failed to secure a satisfactory new lease from their landlords and the club found itself staring extinction in the face. The decision to move out of Bristol and ground-share with non-league Bath City was understandable, but it brought cries of dismay and anguish from

THE END OF AN ERA

long-suffering Rovers fans, who couldn't bear to leave their beloved, though much-neglected stadium.

The move brought about a premature end to the Tote. The atmosphere and ambience of that foreboding terrace had disappeared forever and the Tote End itself was demolished in the Nineties. Sadly, a monstrous IKEA store now stands in its place. Where once tribes of youths performed their 'rites of passage' and bodily fluids flowed in the name of love, hate and pride, Justin and Kate now bicker over which wood-flooring they should choose — it fucking kills me. The Tote and its inhabitants may have long gone but it, and they, will never be forgotten.

Football and its associated baggage continued to evolve. The hooligans, no longer content with terrorising just the domestic scene, found pastures new. They exported the 'English disease' and the 'In-ger-land' factor to Europe — not only for club encounters, but for international matches as well. Club crews joined forces, forming wary allegiances with previous foes to do battle with their European counterparts.

The disasters of Heysel, Bradford and Hillsborough and the ensuing Taylor Report drastically changed both the appearance of the stadiums and how we were to view the beautiful game. TV money, sponsorship, corporate involvement and an influx of foreign players ensured that football was no longer a simple, working-class spectator sport played by simple, working-class men with names like Alf, Stan and Tom. Likewise, the intimidating but genuinely atmospheric terraces of many famous old grounds have now disappeared forever. With their demise came the disappearance of the terrace terror. Like many of the stadiums, which themselves have been transformed from ugly ducklings into beautiful swans, the thugs who first appeared as crop-headed boot boys back in the Sixties finally metamorphosed into label-obsessed casuals.

By the Nineties, the casual had turned his appearance and his

BOOTED AND SUITED

outlook into an art form. The Stone Island label replaced the bovver boot as the item of clothing most synonymous with the football hooligan, and the mobile phone and the Internet became his most treasured weapons. It was not a style I could readily take to. I was, after all, cut from a different cloth.

What comes around goes around. In December 1979, the last month of *my* decade, The Specials released a live EP. Among its two-minute bursts of frenetic ska and reggae lay Symarip's 'Skinhead Moonstomp', sounding not too dissimilar to a certain record by Derrick Morgan, one week at number 49, January 1970...

My era had ended. An era that had seen both the best and the worst of British youth culture, and its trappings, was over. Regrettably, today it's a time that is remembered for nothing much more than disco music, Abba and flares. But perhaps, just perhaps, next time someone invites you to a Seventies party, instead of the loons and Afro wig you'll don a pair of Doc Martens or Monkey boots matched up with a check Ben Sherman; maybe even a baggy bowling shirt and a pair of plastic sandals. Or maybe you'll sport a pair of bondage trousers and a ripped T-shirt held together with safety pins. You just might take along a scratched LP by The Maytals, The Ohio Players or The Only Ones. But whatever you do, watch yourself, because some bastard just might come up to you, kick you in the bollocks and say, 'Welcome to the *real* Seventies.'

Goodnight Irene.

The publishers are grateful to the following for permission to reprint certain material:

John Weller for permission to print from 'Modern World' and 'All Around the World' by The Jam.

Guinness World Records for permission to print from the *Guinness Book of British Hit Singles*.

THE END OF AN ERA

Western Daily Express.

Bristol *Evening Post.*

Lyrics from 'Do Anything You Wanna Do' (Hollis/Douglas) ©1977 by kind permission of Universal Music Publishing Ltd.

The Rough Guide to Reggae, published by Rough Guides Ltd in 1997. Authors Steve Barrow & Peter Dalton.

The Rough Guide to Rock, 2nd edition, published by Rough Guides Ltd in October 1999. Edited by Jonathan Buckley, Orla Duane, Mark Ellingham and Al Spicer (online).

www.modculture.co.uk
www.bristolmod.co.uk
www.punk77.co.uk
www.bristolarchives.com